Dangers, Tests
and Miracles

Dangers, Tests and Miracles

The Remarkable Life Story of
Chief Rabbi Rosen of Romania
as told to
Joseph Finklestone

WEIDENFELD AND NICOLSON
LONDON

To my beloved Amalia, in testimony of deep gratitude

First published in Great Britain by
George Weidenfeld & Nicolson Limited
91 Clapham High Street, London SW4 73TA

ISBN 0 297 81067 7

Photoset by Deltatype Ltd, Ellesmere Port, Cheshire

Printed and bound in Great Britain by
Butler & Tanner Ltd, Frome and London

Contents

Illustrations

anniversary as Chief Rabbi, 19 June 1988

Being greeted as Chief Rabbi by Vice-President Emil Bodnăraş, 1948

With President Groza

Charles Jordan in Bucharest just before going to Prague, where he was murdered, 1967

With Nahum Goldmann, 1970

Amalia, my wife, accompanying Golda Meir in Bucharest, 1972

With Menachem Begin in the Choral Temple, 1977

With Lord Jakobovits, Chief Rabbi of Great Britain, in Bucharest

Shlomo Goren, Chief Rabbi Emeritus of Israel, speaking at the Choral Temple on the occasion of my thirtieth anniversary as Chief Rabbi, 1978

Amalia

(All the photographs come from the author's private collection.)

Foreword by Lord Jakobovits

Chief Rabbi of Britain and the Commonwealth;
President, Conference of European Rabbis
Written on the occasion of Chief Rabbi Rosen's
fortieth anniversary as Chief Rabbi of
Romania, June 1988

*D*uring the eventful epoch following the Holocaust and its after-math of desolation and regeneration, several rabbinical personalities have risen to make an indelible mark on the contemporary history of our people – some for their outstanding scholarship, some as leaders of world stature, some as builders of famous institutions, and some as inspired writers enriching Jewish thought and literature.

Chief Rabbi Rosen has uniquely combined all these roles, excelling in every sphere of rabbinic endeavour and statesmanlike leadership. Under conditions that would have daunted lesser mortals, he mani-fested supreme courage, superb vision and profound wisdom in rallying the broken remnants of Romanian Jewry, helping the bulk of them to reach Israel in the highest *aliyah* success rate of any sizeable community, and presiding over the spiritual and communal fortunes of the rest by maintaining a vibrant fabric of organized Jewish life and social services, often under exceedingly difficult conditions.

In addition, his irrepressible personality soon asserted itself on the international stage, where he is now known and respected throughout the Jewish world, from Israel to the four corners of the earth, as an outstanding spokesman for his people, forcefully expressing his opinions and championing the lofty beliefs to which he is committed with passion and conviction.

His colleagues of the Conference of European Rabbis are particu-larly proud of his creative association with them, having most actively participated as an invaluable member of the Executive and a leading contributor to Conference deliberations for well over two decades. We treasure his partnership and with intense pride hail his significant role in enhancing the respect for the rabbinical fraternity and strengthening its influence as the principal custodian of the Jewish heritage.

We greet him as a legend in his own lifetime, assured of an immortal place in the annals of our people. He has earned the gratitude and admiration of countless contemporaries, rabbinical as well as lay, all joining in warmest felicitations and affectionate wishes for the future to him and his equally remarkable life's partner.

Preface by Joseph Finklestone

*R*abbi Moses Rosen, Chief Rabbi of Romania for over forty years, is undoubtedly one of the most remarkable Jewish spiritual leaders in the world today. Once the object of bitter controversy, he is now acknowledged as having achieved the near impossible. He persuaded the strictly Leninist–Marxist Communist regime of Romania to allow the Jewish community, reduced by the Holocaust from 800,000 to about 400,000 people, not merely to practise its religion and to maintain its synagogues and the system of *shechita* (ritual slaughter of animals), but to allow the opening of Talmud Torahs (Jewish religious schools) to teach young Jews the faith of their forefathers.

While in the Soviet Union and other Communist states, Judaism waned and, in some areas, almost disappeared entirely, in Romania it flourished. Not only did Chief Rabbi Rosen ensure that the existing synagogues and Talmud Torahs continued to function where there were still Jewish communities who needed them, but he increased Jewish religious tuition when he thought that essential. Thus, Bucharest, which had only one Talmud Torah, despite a large Jewish population, was provided with a further eighteen. The result of his educational work was that, during his Chief Rabbinate, tens of thousands of children and youngsters received a Jewish education despite the Communists who opposed this activity. We can conclude that a whole generation of Romanian Jews was saved from disappearance.

While the rest of the Communist world barred the activities of the American Joint Distribution Committee, a giant charitable organization, and vilified it as a tool of American imperialism, Romania welcomed it back. For many years Chief Rabbi Rosen worked patiently and with infinite skill to persuade the Romanian Government to arrive at an agreement with the Joint, as this organization is

3

popularly known. He did this because he knew that the Joint could save the lives of thousands of people suffering from near-starvation. It is a common saying among Jews: 'It is hard to be a Jew.' But in Romania, as a result of the social aid of the Joint, in a humanitarian programme devised by Chief Rabbi Rosen and his devoted and highly intelligent wife, Amalia, it could be said: 'It is better to be a Jew.' When Rabbi Rosen proclaims with pride, under the present circumstances, 'There is not one hungry Jew in Romania,' he is telling the truth.

Chief Rabbi Rosen's crowning achievement was to persuade the Romanian Government to permit the vast majority of Romanian Jews to leave for Israel. These Romanian *olim* (immigrants to Israel) have become an important segment of Israeli society. Endangering his life many times in the period of Stalinist terror, fighting for years with the *Jewsectzia*, he was able to change radically the atmosphere surrounding *aliyah* (emigration) and Zionism. A Jew who wants to go to Israel is no longer a 'traitor' or a 'spy'; his right to 'go home' is recognized. That is how forty years of Rosen's leadership have reduced the number of Romanian Jews from about 420–430,000 to 22–23,000, i.e. by ninety-seven per cent.

Romanian Jews fitted in perfectly into Israeli national life because they arrived with a knowledge and a love of their religious heritage. Most Romanian Jews who left the country went to Israel and remained there. Any other course was inconceivable for them. In contrast, the vast majority of Russian Jews who leave the country have chosen to settle in the United States rather than in Israel. Chief Rabbi Rosen sees this contrast as a sad vindication of his beliefs. Jewish leaders, he says, have concentrated their efforts on a 'Let My People Go' policy towards the Soviet Union, using protests and demonstrations to force the Soviet hand, but have neglected to ensure that the departing Jews are knowledgeable and dedicated Jews, willing and able to face the problems of living in Israel. He can understand why such Jews should choose an easier life in the United States, with its promises of wealth and comfort. And he sees no valid reason why the Soviet Union should be antagonized and great efforts expended in order to enable certain Jews to live in Philadelphia rather than in Odessa. In his view, a total rethinking of the world-wide campaign for Soviet Jewry should take place.

At one stage of his remarkable life, Chief Rabbi Rosen was opposed by powerful forces – the Romanian Jewish Communists, eager to see an end to a religious Jewish community, and, paradoxically, by certain influential Israeli circles. Emerging victorious from the struggle, he achieved this not by confrontation – though he did stand up against the Jewish Communists – but by argument and by a policy of 'give and take'. His methods were, at first, widely misunderstood in the Jewish world and even by some of his opponents in Romania.

I first met Chief Rabbi Rosen over ten years ago, when he invited me and Jewish leaders in Europe and the United States to visit the country. I was astonished by what I saw and heard. The Cold War still froze relations between the Western Powers and the Eastern bloc. I had wished to visit the Soviet Union but had been refused a visa. Jewish leaders were complaining bitterly of the Soviet Government's attitude to its Jewish population of about three million. There were no Jewish religious schools, no Jewish newspapers and only one synagogue in Moscow. Anyone found teaching Hebrew was imprisoned.

Yet a Hebrew choir of youngsters welcomed us at the magnificent Choral Temple synagogue in Bucharest. Jewish religious schools were flourishing. The children of Jewish Communists were eager to learn about their Jewish heritage and to make their home in Israel. The Chief Rabbi appeared to have extraordinary influence with the authorities. We discovered that the famous Jewish *shtetl*, so lovingly described by Sholem Aleichem and made vivid to millions by the musical *Fiddler on the Roof*, still existed in Romania, the only place in the world where one could see it. Jews, dressed in a manner straight out of Sholem Aleichem, came from their flat-roofed houses to greet us in his language, Yiddish. We were thrown into a world of the past, yet one hit by the Hitlerite massacres, the Stalinist terror and now having to deal with the special problems of living under a strictly Communist regime. I noticed their veneration for their Chief Rabbi, but it was a veneration tinged not with fear but with love, as they approached him and his beautiful wife.

What is the secret of this remarkable man? I asked myself. He exuded confidence and control, factors which have proved of immense importance in his colourful life. His face would suddenly dissolve into a smile as he relaxed, but one felt he would never be caught off guard. Though already in his late sixties, he exuded energy. In the years that have followed, there has been no diminution of his energy and powers, of his fierce commitment to the cause of Jews in general and Romanian Jews in particular.

When the opportunity was given me to write the life story of such a man, I grabbed it with excitement. Chief Rabbi Rosen is unique in his achievements and unique in his personality. His philosophy has close relevance to the efforts to establish peaceful co-existence between the Communist world and the Western democracies in the nuclear age. He has changed the attitude of governments by argument and not by protest, by proving that their interests coincide with those of Romanian Jews.

It is fortunate that, in describing the stirring events in his life, Chief Rabbi Rosen has an exceptional ability to recall in vivid detail the events of his youth – he was imprisoned when still a boy – the constant dangers which he faced and the struggles in which he was involved. Particularly striking is his ability to recall dramatic conversations and clashes with his opponents. These read like excerpts from a powerful play. He sheds new light on the methods and intentions of Communist leaders when facing religious opposition. Many vivid characters appear, none more so than the brother of Ana Pauker, the Communist Jewish 'empress' of Romania, and the saintly Rabbi Portugal. There are also villains, some in unexpected places. I was gripped by the story of one man standing up against such overwhelming forces – and triumphing.

I First Encounters with Anti-Semitism

A shot rang out in the middle of the day, in the Romanian city of Cernăuţi, in 1926: a Christian student, Nicolae Totu, had killed a Jewish fellow student, David Falik. The murderer was tried by the court in Cîmpulung in Bucovina, but the trial was farcical and ended with Totu being set free. The judgement was a signal for huge demonstrations by anti-Semites and Fascists, with the young criminal being acclaimed a national hero. This event was to have a profound effect on my life.

I was then fourteen years old, but was mature for my age. My upbringing had taught me to oppose injustice and what happened after the shooting was certainly the height of it. Far away at my school in Fălticeni, the Moldavian *shtetl*, I seethed with indignation. I told the other pupils: 'This is criminal injustice. The civilized world must not tolerate such crimes.'

Dan Protopopescu, an anti-Semitic teacher, heard about my remark. As he was always looking for opportunities to punish me, he thought that he now had a chance. Not having any legal possibility of punishing me for my opinion of Romanian justice, he invented another 'crime'. He proclaimed that I had insulted King Ferdinand and Queen Maria of Romania by casting doubts on Romanian justice, whose guardians they supposedly were. Next day, a 'conference' of teachers at Nicu Gane, my high school, accepted his proposal that I should be expelled from all state schools.

On 19 April 1927, in the middle of the festival of Passover, I was summoned to appear at the State Prosecutor's office. Throughout the day the prosecutor tried to convince me that I was guilty and should confess. I refused, arguing that I was utterly innocent of any crime. The official told me that he would arrest me if I did not confess. I still refused, whereupon a group of men entered the room, got hold of me and dragged me off to prison.

News of my imprisonment caused consternation and astonishment among the Jews of the town. That a boy of fourteen, and the son of the respected local rabbi, should be placed in a primitive prison with violent thieves and murderers, on the say of an official, was beyond comprehension. My parents were appalled, but their appeal went unheeded.

Yet here I was in the town's prison, a dark, forbidding place. Never could I have imagined such a fate for myself. As the huge, iron doors closed on me I shuddered.

I was dragged to a cell where an evil-looking man was sitting. His mouth opened in astonishment when he learned that I was to share it with him. What could a boy of fourteen have done to deserve such a sentence? His surprise did not lessen when I told him what I was being accused of. When I, in turn, asked 'What have you done?', he replied, 'I cut up a man.' Apparently, in a drunken rage, he had murdered a man with a knife.

Throughout the night, I trembled for my life and could not sleep. I feared that at any moment the murderer would pounce on me and try either to strangle me or to kill me with a hidden weapon.

I appealed to the prison governor, who decided to move the man to a different cell. When the governor asked me if I was not afraid to be alone, I quickly replied, 'No. Don't keep me in the same cell as the killer!' I also won another little victory. As it was Passover, I refused to eat any prison food, and the governor agreed that my parents could bring me food parcels.

I did not allow the frightening atmosphere of the prison to overwhelm me or to depress me too much. Despite my age, I was filled with a spirit of confidence and revolt. It was the injustice done to me as a Jew which I could not accept. I even sat down and wrote a long memorandum consisting of twenty-eight points, which was taken by my mother to Constantin Toma, a lawyer in Iaşi, the capital of Moldavia, where a higher court was to hear my case. Toma, a former mayor of the city, took up my defence and kindly remarked to my mother that the memorandum helped him to obtain my release on 3 May. My parents were overjoyed. My feelings were of immense relief.

However, the authorities had not ended their fight with me and another court decided that I should be expelled from all schools. I was even denied the right to have examinations conducted in private.

My case was taken up by two leaders of the Bucharest Jewish

community – Dr Willy Filderman and Dr Mayer Ebner, a member of the Romanian Parliament. That an innocent boy of fourteen should be persecuted in this utterly callous manner by the authorities did, indeed, seem uncivilized and brutal. They started a protest campaign and succeeded in partially reversing the court decision. I was given the right to take examinations at the Aron Pumnul high school in Czernowitz. But, in the meantime, I had lost a year's formal schooling.

From that time, I carried for many years the stigma of being a Bolshevik. Despite the fact that I had proved my innocence, I was seen by the anti-Semites in the town as a symbol of Jewish disloyalty to the state, the rabbi's son who had insulted the King and Queen. The authorities resumed the campaign against me and, on 15 June 1928, a new court decision was announced. I was sentenced to one month's imprisonment. I was again arrested, taken to prison and put in a cell. Again I mixed with thieves and murderers. Again I felt the horror of the evil prison atmosphere. The authorities seemed unaware of the wrong they were doing.

For the second time, Dr Filderman, Dr Ebner and many other Jewish leaders protested strongly. These protests reached the highest authorities in the land and caused some concern. King Ferdinand had died in June 1927 and a Regency Council was acting on behalf of his grandson, King Mihai. The Council nullified the court decision and rendered void all charges against me. That the Regency itself acted so firmly in a matter of *lèse-majesté* was the best proof that the anti-Semitic trial was a fake. The whole 'affair' had to be cancelled.

Returning to school, I had to face Dan Protopopescu again. Despite all the suffering he had inflicted on me and my parents, he was still not satisfied. Now he demanded that I should take part in written exams on the Sabbath, well knowing that I would never desecrate the holiness of the day. My parents appealed to the Minister of Education, Costăchescu, in Bucharest and the order was given that I should not have to take exams on the Sabbath. However, my stay in the high school was sheer torture. The teachers appeared to take a vicious delight in persecuting me and making my life a misery. I felt a sense of deep oppression, which was not lifted until I passed my final examination, under very special and difficult circumstances, in Dorohoi, and I was the only Jewish boy from a Fălticeni high school to achieve it. My pride and that of my parents was cut short when, for some unknown reason, my final certificate was declared invalid. Again my parents appealed to the Minister of Education and the certificate was restored to me. But by the time all the battles were over, I had lost another year of schooling.

In fact, this was not my first encounter with injustice and anti-Semitism. I had been taught a lesson before I was nine years old, when I had *payot* (sidelocks), which were small but still prominent. *Payot* were and still are symbols of strict Jewish orthodoxy. While in the street one day, I was approached by a Romanian Christian boy, Dumitru Contici, who was much older than me. He snatched at my *payot*, smacked me a number of times in the face and shouted at me: 'Dirty Jew, *Tartan* [rump, an insulting term for a Jew]. I don't want to see you again with these *payot*!' I ran away, filled with a sense of burning outrage. How was it possible for such an injustice to happen in our town? My eyes were still filled with bitter tears when I returned home. In great indignation, I told my parents what had happened and I expected justice from them. To my amazement, I heard my mother say to my father: 'We must cut off the *payot* this morning.' She was obviously wanting to protect me from Contici. Hearing these words, I burst into loud sobs. I did not want my *payot* cut off, nor did I want to satisfy the vicious Contici. But my *payot* were cut off, and when Contici saw me next day without them, he burst out laughing. He had triumphed over me. I felt a sense of deep humiliation. To this day, the memory of Contici laughing at me shorn of my *payot* fills me with anger and shame.

I believe that my imprisonment on false charges, the suffering and persecution which I underwent, the hatred which I encountered, the humiliations to which I was subjected in these incidents at an age when I should have been enjoying my schooldays, transformed me from a child into a young adult. I knew I was innocent, yet all the time evidence was being fabricated against me. I knew then that I would encounter prejudice and hatred all my life. My experiences in prison, instead of breaking me, made me determined to fight injustice at whatever cost. My humiliation over the *payot* made me determined to fight for human rights and dignity. I knew I had to fight with utter determination to achieve justice and to oppose mindless tyranny. This became the story of my life.

2   *Rabbinical Background*

I was born in Moineşti, in Moldavia, in 1912. My father was the rabbi of the local community. Though small, this community became famous in the history of the rebuilding of modern Israel, because it was from Moineşti that the first Romanian Jewish settlers left for Palestine in 1882. Members of the famous movement, *Hovevei Zion* ('The Lovers of Zion'), they were among those who built Zichron Yaacov and Rosh Pina, two of the most important settlements in the country. The slogan was coined: 'Through Moineşti to Eretz Israel'.

Yet Moineşti was a typical Jewish *shtetl* of Eastern Europe, so graphically described in the stories of Sholem Aleichem – narrow little streets, some cobbled and some no more than dirt tracks, and small houses with flat roofs. Some of them still exist today in the small towns of Moldavia, the last remnants of a totally vanished world.

These little houses presented terrifying fire risks because they backed on to each other, owing to the dire shortage of land and possibly also for self-protection, as the Jews always had to fear violent anti-Semitism. If a fire broke out in one house, the whole street would go up in flames in one tragic disaster. Jews marked periods of time by saying, 'It happened before the third or fifth fire.'

Most of the Jewish inhabitants lived in abject, grinding poverty. The tradesmen tried to sell clothing and trinkets to the equally poor peasants who arrived with their produce. The water-carriers, shoe-makers, tailors, milkmen and all the other bewildering array of artisans that made up the *shtetl* sought desperately to find customers. Many went hungry. Yet what for many made life bearable was the comradeship which the *shtetl* created, the close friendships, the help they gave each other – and their love for traditional Judaism. Many simple artisans would spend numerous hours after their exhausting and ill-paid work studying the Torah (the five Books of Moses) and the Talmud (the commentary on the laws of Judaism). Daily, in the early morning and in the late evening, they sat in the synagogues and continued to learn, since 'that was their life'.

Those Jews in the area who lived in the small houses could consider themselves fortunate. When, in 1916, my father became a rabbi in Fălticeni, a larger town than Moineşti, with thirty-four synagogues, including the famous 'painted synagogue' with views of the Land of Israel by artists who had never visited it, I went with him every day to the street of the hand-workers on our way to our synagogue. These tinkers, roof-repairers, water-carriers and carriers of wood from the forests lived in underground caves with their wives and children. I looked in amazement at the sight. Their condition was hardly better than that of beasts in the forest. Yet, despite their desperate poverty and their inhuman living conditions, they remained cheerful and never lost heart. They wanted to hear words from the Torah and to recite psalms in Hebrew, whose meaning they did not understand.

I loved to study the Torah and the Talmud. My father was my teacher and I learned quickly. Every year from the age of six, on my birthday, which coincided with the festive day in the Hebrew month of Av 15, I was invited to deliver an hour-long address to the congregation at my father's synagogue, Habad. Perched on a small stool in front of the Ark, so that I could be seen by the congregants, I spoke about biblical teachings and the comments in the Talmud. My parents watched with delight and pride.

I mention this fact not to prove that I was in any way a genius. I was precocious, certainly, and had an avid desire to study, even when a child. But in those days it was not unique for a child of my age from a rabbinical home to give such a discourse in synagogue. However, it was rare enough to give my parents special pleasure.

I was born into a renowned rabbinical family, on both my father's and my mother's side. My father, who was born in Galicia, was considered one of the greatest Talmudical scholars of his time. He was the author of numerous works and his book, *Shaalot V'Tshuvot* (*Questions and Answers*), became particularly well known. A few years ago, the first volume of his *Halachic* work, *Eitan Arie*, was printed by the Harav Kook religious printing house in Jerusalem.

My father had a truly fanatical love of study. I cannot recall ever seeing him asleep, except when he was an old man. In the quiet of the night, while everyone in our house was soundly asleep, he would sit in his room and write his commentaries and responsa. I don't know when he slept. When I got up in the morning he was already at his prayers. As he prepared tea or coffee for himself and for us, he would sing a psalm. The melody, the old and emotional Jewish 'psalm-melody', I will not forget till the last second of my life. His attitude was that every second is golden and must not be wasted. His books and manuscripts were the belongings most precious to him. One day, a fire broke out in our *shtetl* and there was a danger of the whole street being enveloped in one huge flame. The fire had already taken a grip on our house, when my father suddenly disappeared. A few minutes later, he reappeared from the burning house with books and manuscripts in his hands. His beard had begun to burn and we feared for his life, but we managed to quench the fire and he escaped serious injury. He was relieved that he had saved his precious possessions. This image, of the man with his books in his arms, amidst the flames, has also sunk deep in my memory.

My character was formed by listening to his words and trying to follow his example. Once he believed that some action was necessary for the good of the community, he insisted on taking it. He stubbornly stuck to his principles and beliefs, even when they were against his own personal interests. Consequently, he encountered many problems and suffered a great deal.

Most sons come into conflict with their fathers at some time in their lives. I can honestly say that I never had any such problems. I worshipped my father, he was my ideal. Even today, when I have a specially difficult problem to tackle, I try to imagine how he would have dealt with it. I never questioned or resented any demands he made on me.

He used to wake me at three or four o'clock in the morning to go to the *mikvah* (ritual bath) at a considerable distance from our house. I would leave a warm bed to trundle through the streets with him in the cold and dark. The sharp cold bit into me, but I did not complain. I could see the shadowy figures of Jews already going to synagogue to pray, and I could hear knocking at the doors of congregants to wake them up for prayer.

I remember, too, how my father used to put me – his David Moshele, as he called me – under his *tallith* (prayer shawl), place his hand on my head and bless me as the Cohanim (descendants of the ancient priests) recited their blessings in the synagogue, their hands outstretched as in biblical times.

My mother was, of course, strictly Orthodox in her religious beliefs, but she was anxious to give her children a modern education and imbue them with a modern spirit. She insisted that her children should have an opportunity to study secular as well as religious subjects, and attend high school and university. By the age of five, I already had a teacher for French and German. I went to high school, university and also became a rabbi. My elder sister, Bracha, was also given an opportunity to study and she completed her doctorate in philosophy. She married the Viennese rabbi, Wolf Gottlieb, who, after fleeing from Austria, was head of the *Beth Din* (rabbinical court) in Glasgow, Scotland, for more than twenty years. My elder brother, Elias, also became a rabbi and served the Jewish community of Auschwitz, called Oswiecim, before the area became the notorious Nazi death camp. He, his wife and two children were transported by the Nazis to Benzin in Poland, where they were murdered. Another sister, Clara Bombach, together with her husband and children, was murdered by the Germans in Lwow. My elder sister, Leah, married an architect, Yitzhak Koch. She survived the war and died in Vienna at the age of eighty-eight.

My parents had to make severe sacrifices to enable us to study as my father had a very small salary. We lived in poverty like the rest of the Jewish population, but we never allowed it to grind us down. Lack of comforts or luxuries never affected us or our parents. Our home in the *shtetl* became a centre for young people, the friends of my sister Bracha and myself. It was also a centre for Jewish culture, combining both Jewish tradition and European learning. Even in the *shtetl* there was already a tendency among some Jewish youth to seek assimilation into the general Romanian population. This assimilation was different from that sought, for example, by the Reform Jews of the United States, who also seek full participation in Jewish life. In Romania, assimilation, a result of ignorance, was intended to lead to the disappearance of Jewish life and a merging with the Romanian people. In our little *shtetl* we tried in our small way to fight this trend.

My genealogical 'tree' goes back, generation after generation, to distinguished and famous *gaonim* (rabbinical leaders). My grandfather's grandfather was Rabbi Leibish Auerbach in Stanislawow, Galicia, and my ancestors include Rabbi Moshe Iserless of Krakow, the Noda Biyehuda (Rabbi Yeheskel Landau) of Prague, the Great Rabbi Loew (Maharal) in Prague and Rabbi Naftule Frankfurter, whose son was the first Hacham-Basha of Moldavia in the eighteenth century. Generation after generation the *Ichus* of my father leads to

Rashi (Rabbi Shlomo Itzhaki). My mother's grandfather was Rabbi Simcha Yoel Laksner, the rabbi of Tirgu-Neamt-Romania and the author of *Chalat Lechem*, *Mei Hashiloach* and other important rabbinical studies. My name, David Moshe, was given to me by my father in memory of Rabbi David Moshe, rabbi of Tchortkow, the eldest son of the Rijiner Rebbe.

Whether I have lived up to this 'golden chain' of illustrious stars of the Torah is a question I often ask myself. The answer may be found in this autobiography.

3   *A Multi-Coloured People*

*R*omania was a country with over 800,000 Jews, who were affected by striking differences in appearance, culture and outlook, as well as religious observance and practice. The provinces which made up Romania had different historical developments, some being part of Eastern Europe and some looking to Central Europe. The Jews, likewise, displayed these differences. Only their religion and the fear of anti-Semitism, always rampant, united them.

Our province of Moldavia was a centre of Chassidism, the passionate, extrovert display of religious fervour. Singing and dancing – by men only, of course – in synagogues and small places of worship, known as *shtiblech*, on festive occasions, was an elemental part of Chassidism. Central to it also was the system of Rebbes, each of whom had thousands of followers and was a kind of Jewish prince. Many Jews travelled long distances to spend a festival at the 'court' of the Rebbe, as has been described by Isaac Bashevis Singer. Famous dynasties were established by the Rebbes: on his death, the Rebbe was succeeded by his son or, if that was not possible, by a close relative, as in a royal family.

In our philosophy there are two ways of reaching the Almighty. One is that of thinking, studying, learning, the way of *tefilin shel rosh*, of the brain, of knowledge, of questions and answers. This is the way of the aristocracy of *Talmidei–Chachamim*, the men who dedicate their lives to entering the *Pardes*, the marvellous garden of the Torah.

And the other? What is the way to God of the masses of simple working people, obliged to toil day and night for a piece of bread for their wives and children, with no time to study?

It is the way of the soul, the way of *tefilin shel yad*, of the heart, of belief, of enthusiasm, of singing and dancing, of 'feeling' the Father in Heaven. The Chassidic movement has given these masses the sentiments of pride and consciousness, so that their lack of learning is compensated by their warm souls and by the fervour of their prayer.

Chassidism gave a special role and importance to the simple, unschooled trader and artisan. Joining in the passionate singing and dancing and listening with fervour to the words of their Rebbe made them feel close to Heaven. They forgot their suffering and poverty. Receiving a piece of *challah* (the white bread eaten by Jews on the Sabbath) from the hands of the Rebbe was more precious to them than a feast.

And so there developed in Moldavia the famous rabbinical courts of the 'dynasty' of Rabbi Israel of Rigin; the courts of the Pashcaner Rebbe, of the Buhusher Rebbe, of the Stefanester Rebbe (whose mortal remains I had the privilege of taking to Israel) and of the Adjuder Rebbe. The moral power of these Rebbes also influenced the non-Jewish population in the little towns and villages.

There was an entirely different atmosphere in Transylvania, on the other side of the Carpathian Mountains. There the influence of the Habsburg Empire was clear. The area had a Central European climate. The synagogues were larger and the people more sophisticated, but not as 'warm' as in Moldavia. This greater sophistication could be felt also in religious matters. While in our area of Moldavia there was only one Jewish religious tendency, the Orthodox, in Transylvania there were at least three: Orthodox, Neologues (Reform) and Status Quo, which was in-between the first two. Among the Orthodox were the Chassidim of Satmar, who today have strong bases in Bnei Braq, in Israel, and in Williamsburg, New York. The Satmar were anti-Zionist, because they claimed that the Zionist movement was not based on the Torah. The Orthodox were strict in their observance of traditional Judaism and the community created hundreds of *yeshivoth* (schools for the study of the Torah and the Talmud). There was a pulsating Jewish life in the towns and villages of Transylvania.

In the area of Satu-Mare and Sighet in Maramureş there were Jewish peasants who cultivated considerable tracts of land. The Tharaud brothers, well-known writers of the time, described these interesting people. In contrast to the anti-Zionist Satmar, a very strong Zionist movement existed in Bessarabia. It created and supported a network of Jewish schools, called *tarbut*, which produced many thousands of Hebrew-speaking Jews who also possessed a modern Jewish culture.

Bessarabia also generated strong and proud Jewish personalities. Rabbi Yehuda Leib Zirelson, Rabbi of Kishinev and a former member of the Duma (the lower house of the Russian Tsarist parliament), was a member of the Romanian Senate after the First World War, when Bessarabia became part of Romania. He protested in the Senate against the excesses of the anti-Semites. However, on the proposal of the poet Octavian Goga, who became Prime Minister for a month and a half in 1938, the Senate voted unanimously not to include the speech in its official record.

Disgusted, Rabbi Zirelson left the building in tears and resigned his membership of the Senate. He was one of the greatest Talmudical scholars of his time, one of the founders and leaders of *Agudat Israel*, a strictly Orthodox movement. He died during the Kishinev pogrom in 1941, when the German and Romanian Fascist armies occupied Bessarabia.

Bucovina again was different: it was Viennese in atmosphere and German in influence. The capital, Cernăuţi, was a lively town with nearly 70,000 Jewish inhabitants who spoke German. This did not help them when the Nazis arrived. My cousin, Rabbi Dr Abraham Jacob Mark, was killed by the Germans in 1941. He was brought to the synagogue by the Nazis, who burnt it down and then murdered him and 110 other Jewish notables on the River Prut.

There was a strong Jewish cultural life in Cernăuţi. Yiddish writers and poets, such as Yaacov Steinberg and Yitzik Manger, from Iaşi, were active there, and the first world congress of the Yiddish language was held in the town. Cernăuţi was also a centre of Zionism and Jewish socialism.

Wallachia, which includes the capital city of Bucharest, was, surprisingly, not the great centre of Jewish tradition and culture that one might have expected. On the contrary, the Jews of Bucharest were less knowledgeable in Judaism than in other areas. They had assimilated more into general Romanian culture. This is well illustrated by the fact that, in a city where there were 150,000 Jews, there existed only one Talmud Torah and even that had a small number of pupils.

Bucharest Jews have still not lived down a shameful episode in Jewish history. One of the greatest Jewish scholars of all time, Meir Leibish Malbim, settled in Bucharest in 1858 and became its rabbi. There he wrote his famous commentary on the third book of Moses (1860) and printed his comments on the Song of Songs, *Shirei Hanefesh*. Malbim encountered bitter opposition from the rich and assimilated leaders of the community, who denounced him to the Government as a foreign agitator. At their request, he was expelled from the country in 1864. As a result, Romania lost an outstanding scholar.

Thus a group of ignorant people decided the destiny of the Bucharest community for many years to come. Bucharest Jews tended not to follow Reform Judaism but wanted to become assimilated with the general Romanian population. This continued until after the Holocaust.

Despite lacking some of the sophistication of other provinces, Moldavia could claim an important achievement. It was in Iaşi that Abraham Goldfaden established the first Yiddish theatre in the world. Yiddish flourished in the province and with it great writers like Yitzik Manger, Yaacov Gropper and Dr Shlomo Bickel. *Licht*, a literary magazine, also had a powerful influence on the development of Yiddish literature.

Moldavia also produced some outstanding Jewish personalities. Among them were Dr Ghelerter, the Socialist leader, who devoted his life to helping Jews in need, and Dr Lippe, who presided at the first Zionist Congress in Basle. Both Chassidism and Zionism established strong roots. The congress of the *Hovevei Zion* in Focşani could even be claimed as the first modern Zionist gathering.

A personality of high cultural stature was Dr Jacob Itzhak Niemirower, who was a rabbi in Iaşi, became the rabbi of the Sephardic community in Bucharest and, in 1921, was elected Chief Rabbi of Romania.

Despite the differences between the provinces, despite the fact that different organizational bodies governed Transylvania, Bessarabia and Bucovina, it was necessary to find a form of unity for the purpose of fighting against the common danger of anti-Semitism and promoting common Jewish interests. Chief Rabbi Niemirower was the 'right man in the right place'. Blessed be his memory!

4   *To Be a Jewish Student and Soldier*

*I*n 1931, at the age of nineteen, I entered the faculty of Law at Bucharest University, where I encountered virulent anti-Semitism. Hitler came to power in Germany in 1933, but the Romanian authorities did not wait for him to enact anti-Jewish measures. Gangs of Christian students regularly beat up Jewish students, leaving them bleeding badly on the ground, but the police did not interfere. Any Jewish student who entered a class at the university faced a constant danger to his life.

It was also in 1931 that I went for the first time to Vienna, to complete my rabbinical studies at a seminary there which had a very good reputation. Up to then I had been studying the Torah, the Talmud and all the various commentators for many hours every day with my father, who was such an inspired teacher. In spite of my fervent wish, I could not remain long in Vienna because I lacked the necessary funds. After returning to Bucharest and again studying with my father, I obtained, in 1938, my *semicha* (rabbinical diploma) from some of the greatest scholars of the time: Rabbi Chaim Rabinovitch, the *Av Beth Din* (president of the rabbinical court) of Bucharest, Rabbi Baruch Glantz and Rabbi Moshe Berger (members of the same rabbinical court), Chief Rabbi Dr Niemirower and Chief Rabbi Dr Mark of Bucovina.

On finishing my university studies in 1935 and receiving my law diploma, I was called up to the army in Fălticeni. What followed was a nightmare. One officer in particular, whose name was Toma, seemed to be intent on killing me. He was violently anti-Semitic and a Fascist, and I was everything he hated. I was the son of a rabbi and I was considered to be a Bolshevik. My trial and conviction for having defamed the monarchy was still remembered, as it had been a minor Dreyfus Affair, which had divided the public – Jews and democrats on one side, pro-Fascist forces on the other. I was the prototype of a 'Judeo–Communist'.

During the autumn manoeuvres we were forced to march in the rain from Fălticeni to Dorohoi, a distance of 100 kilometres. During stops I rested on bare earth and suddenly discovered that I was in a feverish condition and could hardly move. Nevertheless, I forced myself to continue marching in the rain until we arrived at Vîrful Cîmpului, not far from Dorohoi. By then I had a high temperature, but the officer refused to take me to a hospital. I did not insist in my confused state, apparently even wanting to prove that I did not need hospital treatment. However, at midnight I fell down and lost consciousness. The officer and the other soldiers left me at the side of the road, where I lay unconscious with the rain still pouring down on me. Some hours later I regained consciousness and discovered that I was lying in a pool of water. My head and body ached. Despite the wetness and cold, I appeared to be burning because of my extremely high temperature. I felt certain that I was going to die.

I tried to rise, but could not. I then tried to lift myself up with the use of my rifle, but failed. Suddenly I saw a light at a house nearby and a peasant leaving it. He came closer to me and shone a lamp on me. Noticing that I was a soldier, he asked, 'What has happened?'

I told him, 'I am ill. I cannot stand up.'

'I will help you,' he replied.

As he grabbed me and put his shoulder underneath me to lift me up, I cried out in pain, 'Oi, Oi.' The man stared at me sharply, having suddenly realized that I was a Jew. He dropped me to the ground, exclaiming, 'You are a Jew! So burn like a match!' He gave me a push as he walked away angrily.

I was now more certain than ever that I was about to die. However, I was to be rescued unexpectedly. Two Jewish soldiers of my company (I remember their names, to bless them: Adolf Strul and Arthur Heinic), who had marched away with the others leaving me on the ground, clearly felt conscience-stricken and decided to return and find me. They took me to a small hospital in the village of Suharau. The hospital consisted of one large building, but all the twenty-two beds were in one room. On my arrival, every bed was occupied.

Among the patients was a peasant woman who was suffering from anthrax, a highly infectious and dangerous disease. A soldier came into the ward and injected her with some medicine. Without cleaning the needle or disinfecting it, he continued to use it on other patients. When he came up and said that he was going to inject me, I told him, and a doctor who accompanied him, 'You must first disinfect the needle.'

'No, you are a soldier and must do what you are told. If you are not injected you will die,' said the doctor.

'So let me die. I will not be injected with this dirty needle.'

Now very angry, the doctor threatened that he would send me to a military court if I did not obey him. I was desperate. I was convinced that if I was injected with this particular needle, I would be infected with anthrax. I could not immediately see a way out. But as I was arguing with the doctor, I heard another Jewish patient, in the bed next to mine, whisper that in the village there was a Jew, Yitzik Hangiu, who would help me.

I rose from the bed, grabbed my clothing and began to leave. The doctor shouted at me, 'You are a soldier and must stay here.' I ignored him, rushed out and went to the village. There I found Yitzik and told him my story. He kissed me and said that he would look after me. He fully carried out his promise. One of his most effective methods was to put me on top of a warm oven in his room. I slowly recovered and regained my strength. Yitzik had saved my life.

Understandably I finished my army service in 1937 with a feeling of great relief. I decided to return to Vienna and continue my rabbinical studies. I was twenty-five and very eager to resume work at the seminary I had attended briefly in 1931. But for the second time my plans were disrupted: Hitler arrived. The *Anschluss* changed my life again.

I saw with my own eyes the fickle nature of a population. In March 1938, the Austrian Chancellor, Kurt von Schuschnigg, went to see Hitler in Berchtesgaden. On his return, he announced a referendum, so that he could obtain a vote of confidence from the Austrian people to enable him to stand up to Hitler. Oliver Cromwell is said to have remarked when the populace applauded him: 'The same people will applaud when I am being beheaded.' I noticed a similar phenomenon in the period of the *Anschluss*. A million people reportedly took part in an anti-Nazi demonstration in the Viennese Ring on a Friday before the Jewish festival of Purim, which commemorates the deliverance of the Jewish people in the ancient Persian Empire from their arch-enemy, Haman, who sought to destroy them all.

'We don't want to be a German colony,' the Viennese demonstrators shouted.

A few hours later, at 6 p.m., Seyss-Inquart became Chancellor and broadcast a proclamation welcoming the Nazis. After Friday night Sabbath prayers, I went back to the Ring. The same million people were demonstrating for the Nazis. There were swastikas everywhere. The people had gone over to Hitler in a couple of hours.

I was young and eager to see what had happened. I did not have a beard then and thought I would not be recognized as a Jew. The next day I walked through the streets and was appalled and astonished to see buildings almost wrapped in Nazi flags. A million Nazi flags must have been unfurled that day. Only days later, on 12 March, Hitler entered Vienna to a tumultuous welcome. Not quite appreciating the full significance of the event and the dangers that a Jew now faced in Vienna, and still driven by a sense of curiosity and, perhaps, adventure, I decided to walk through the centre of Vienna once more. As a somewhat inadequate safeguard, I attached a tiny Romanian flag to my coat.

When I entered the Schwarzenberplatz, a man came up to me and asked politely if I were a Jew. I told him 'Yes'. He then asked me in a concerned tone, 'What are you doing here? Come with me. I will show you the quickest way to your place.' I agreed to go with him. On the way, he said, 'God has brought me to you. I am a Christian and I have a job as a secretary in the city tax office. When I was preparing my documents for my "Aryan book", I discovered that one of my grandmothers was Jewish. This means that I will lose my job. I am desperate. I don't even know a single Jew. You Jews have your synagogues, your communities, you are together. What will happen to me, alone? Neither Christians nor Jews will help me. Please advise me what to do.' The peculiar tragedy of this man affected me deeply. The memory of his anguish haunted me for a long time.

On the following days, Jews began to disappear. My uncle, Rabbi Marcus Rosen, was taken from his home in Springergasse by the SS. A few weeks later a letter arrived from the Dachau concentration camp asking his family to send a certain amount of money – to receive his ashes.

My eagerness for walks in central Vienna had been dampened by now, but I had to go to the Romanian consulate to obtain a visa to return home. When I reached Heinestrasse – an appropriate enough name in the circumstances – I noticed two young boys, no more than ten or eleven years old, wearing swastikas, who were making fun of a well-dressed old lady who appeared to be a member of the aristocracy. The boys were egged on by some hooligans standing nearby.

As I watched this horrible scene, somebody realized that I was a Jew and shouted at his pals to attack me. I was thrown to the ground, to whoops of joy from the hooligans. I was given a brush and a pail of water and, kicked and pummelled, I was forced to erase the slogans that had been printed before the *Anschluss*: '*Wir wollen keine Kolonie sein*' ('We don't want to be a colony').

More people, some old, some young, many well dressed, joined the hooligans in spitting at me, deriding me and kicking me. How long this terrible ordeal continued, I cannot now say. Perhaps it lasted an hour, perhaps more. Eventually I was allowed to crawl away, bruised in body and spirit. The venomous hatred on the faces of these people has remained a horribly vivid memory to this day.

On my way home, I closed my eyes and saw 'my poor *payot*', my 'good' teacher sending an innocent child to prison and the peasant who had told me 'to burn like a match'. I saw all this and cried.

> *Heute gehört uns Deutschland*
> *Morgen die ganze Welt*
> (Today Germany is ours
> Tomorrow the whole world)

was the song that filled the streets, the answer to my tears and my question: what was going to happen to us?

5 *The Russians Are Coming*

I was happy to be able to return to my home in Romania in May 1938. I studied with renewed vigour with my father. Inspired by him and driven by my own desire to learn, I spent every possible moment day and night on my Judaic studies. I obtained a further *semicha* from Rabbi Chaim Rabinovitch, Rabbi Moshe Berger and Rabbi Baruch Glantz, and also passed an official state examination. The special rabbinical board of the Ministry of Cults was presided over by Dr Jacob Niemirower, and one of its most distinguished members was the late President of the Orthodox Rabbis of Transylvania, Rabbi Joseph Adler from Turda. I was greatly elated when I learned that I had fulfilled all the requirements of this examination. I was now a rabbi recognized by both the Jewish and non-Jewish communities, as the board was an official body authorized by the Romanian Ministry of Cults.

That is how my rabbinical career began at the age of twenty-six. It started very modestly indeed. My first post was at the comparatively small synagogue, Mahala, in Fălticeni. At the end of 1939, I was invited to be a candidate for a rabbinical post at Suceava, a town in Bucovina some twenty kilometres away. I was gratified by this offer because the incumbent of the post, Rabbi Meshulam Rat, was a renowned scholar, who had left for Cernăuți to take over the important position of *Av Beth Din*. I delivered my first sermon at the Suceava synagogue on 10 May 1940. On the same day, the president of that community offered me the position of rabbi, starting in two months' time. But another event occurred that day: the German army entered Belgium and Holland. One month later, France was also occupied. At the end of June, the Russian army entered Bessarabia and northern Bucovina (both being Romanian provinces) and, therefore, in July 1940, instead of returning to Suceava, I found myself in a concentration camp. *'L'homme propose et Dieu dispose'* – this French proverb of Latin origin, reminding us that 'man proposes and God disposes', was again confirmed in my life.

The Second World War was no longer a 'theoretical' topic for me. It entered my life and radically changed all my projects.

As a result of their agreement with the Germans, the Russians were able to march into Bessarabia and Bucovina on 28 June 1940. The Romanian anti-Semites, unable to vent their anger on the powerful Russians, sought an easy scapegoat: the Jews. Pogroms broke out in various parts of the country. Anti-Semites in Dorohoi, in Moldavia, accused Jews of having welcomed the news of the Russian occupation of the two provinces. A Jewish army officer was killed by an anti-Semite and the Jewish community was ordered to bury him at the Jewish cemetery. A large number of local Jews went to the funeral service to honour the dead man. A unit of the Romanian army also arrived, ostensibly to honour the officer, but during the religious service, the soldiers began shooting at the Jewish mourners. When the shooting stopped, eighty men and women lay dead on the ground. The Dorohoi pogrom was accompanied by many others in small towns and villages during the retreat of the Romanian army from Bessarabia and Bucovina. The rumour spread that the Jews were Bolsheviks, that they were happy the Red Army was coming and so they had to be killed.

Being seen as a Bolshevik and with a file already assembled against me at the Fălticeni police station after my arrest for 'insulting the King', I began to fear that, in the prevailing atmosphere, the anti-Semites in the police and army would take some action against me. And so it happened.

On the night of 3 July 1940, I was sitting with my parents at home when an army officer entered the house, walked up to me and bellowed: 'Hands up! You are the chief of the Communists in the city!'

My parents and I were dumbfounded. It was a dangerous accusation which could cost me my life. It made no difference that it was a total lie: somebody was clearly determined to imprison or to kill me.

My father extended his hand to the officer in a conciliatory gesture. Ignoring him, the officer placed a revolver at my temple. I felt the cold steel.

'Give me the list of the Communists in the town immediately. Otherwise I will kill you like a duck!'

I replied truthfully that I did not have any list, nor was I the chief of any party.

The officer looked at me searchingly and removed the revolver. He feverishly began to rummage through all my parents' belongings, looking for incriminating evidence. My father had a huge library of thousands of books. The officer and his soldiers began throwing them about the room and tearing out leaves.

He discovered a postcard sent by my grandfather from Potok-Zloty, a little town in Galicia, a province of Poland which had been occupied by the Russians in September 1939 after the Ribbentrop–Molotov pact. My mother had been born in Potok-Zloty and her father, sisters and brother still lived there. Now, a postcard coming from this Communist town became a criminal document and was 'evidence' of my guilt! 'Bolshevik,' the officer shouted at me. He also grabbed a book by Count Gobineau, a racist and anti-Semite who had written *Théorie des races*. In his ignorance, the officer believed that he had uncovered further evidence of my Bolshevism.

I have always had a sardonic sense of humour. Seeing the officer holding a Fascist book as evidence of Communism, I momentarily forgot the danger I was in and could only think how ridiculously he was behaving. I said to him, 'Yes, confiscate this book, but please give me a receipt!' He stared at me with surprise, but duly gave me a receipt!' I then said to him sarcastically, 'This author is a good Fascist.'

The search lasted four or five hours, till three o'clock in the morning. All the rooms had been thrown into chaos and the officer knew that there was nothing to be found, but by now he was in a frenzy of frustration and violence. My mother began to weep.

The officer then told me that he was taking me away. My parents, shocked and pale, looked at me in anguish, fearing the worst. As the soldiers grabbed me, I heard the officer tell them, 'Don't harm him. We are not like the Jews who killed Romanian soldiers in Bessarabia.' One hour later, I understood what his order meant.

I was taken to the courtyard of my old school and placed against the wall. It was dark and cold. The officer then said to me, 'Say your last prayers because we are going to shoot you.' I heard him give an order to the soldiers to load their rifles. Expecting to be shot at any moment, I prayed silently and repeated the magnificent declaration that Jewish martyrs proclaim when facing death: '*Shema Israel*'. No shot came. After what seemed hours, but which must have been only a few seconds or minutes, the officer said, 'We won't shoot you now. We have something else to do to you first.'

I was taken to a classroom, where a number of soldiers were sleeping. Even in the dark I recognized the room as one I had studied in. The officer forced me to get under his bed while he jumped on top

27

of it. He then took off one of his shoes, grabbed me and began hitting me frenziedly with it. Luckily for me, a soldier came in with a message and the officer stopped beating me and left. But shortly afterwards, the soldiers also started beating me up. They tore at my hair and stamped on me. They tried to force me to cross myself and to polish their shoes, but I refused. I don't know how many people beat me. Ten? Twenty? In a few minutes I was covered with blood and was in great pain, but despite the torture, I resisted. It was a matter of human dignity.

When it grew light, I rushed to the window, broke the glass with my fists – covering my hands with blood – and started shouting, 'Help! Help! They are killing me.' As the high school building was in a busy street, I hoped that people would be able to hear what was happening to me. However, as a result of my outburst, the soldiers began beating me again.

Another officer, who had heard my shouts, came into the room and asked what was going on. When I told him that I was constantly being beaten up by the soldiers, he ordered them to stop and left the room.

After a while, the officer who had arrested me returned to the room and said to me, 'You are a Communist and your grandfather is a Communist. But we are a civilized people and have nothing against you personally. Today you will cross the border into Russia, but first you must sign a paper saying that you wish to go. Your parents will then also be able to join you.' (In those weeks of July 1940, when the Russians occupied Bessarabia and Bucovina, the borders were open and many youngsters, afraid of the situation in Romania, fled to Russia without any passports.) The officer spoke in a strange, wheedling tone, as if he were trying to persuade me that he was doing me a great favour. I realized immediately that he was offering me a death sentence. He wanted me to sign the piece of paper so that he could kill me, bury me and then tell my parents and other inquirers that I had crossed the border into Russia.

I, therefore, flatly refused to sign the piece of paper. Seeing that his ruse had failed, the officer hissed at me, 'You will go! If you don't go voluntarily, we'll kill your parents while you watch and then we'll kill you.' When I still refused to sign, he summoned a sergeant and ordered him to go and shoot my parents. Praying that he was bluffing, I once again told him that I did not intend to sign any paper.

'You can save the lives of your parents,' he said. 'If you don't sign, you will be responsible for their deaths. What terrible thing am I asking you to do? I am giving you the chance to join your family in Russia. Is that so bad?'

For one hour he tried to force me to sign the paper. When I continued to refuse, he turned to the soldiers and asked, 'Has anyone harmed this man?'

'No,' they dutifully replied.

'Now we'll deal with you,' he told me, his face white with fury.

I again ran to the window shouting for help, but this time none came. The officer grabbed me by the arms and made me face the wall. For the third time a gun was pointed at my head, but this time from behind me.

I said to the officer, 'If you are going to shoot me, shoot me face to face.'

He did not reply, but I felt the gun being removed from my head. I turned round and saw him leaving the room. A few minutes later he returned, alone, and put a piece of paper and a pencil on the table. He carefully placed a revolver next to them and looked at me searchingly. 'This is my final offer to you. You have five minutes to sign the statement that you wish to leave for Russia. Otherwise I will definitely shoot you. There will be no more delays.' Then he got up to leave the room again.

But why was he leaving the revolver in the room? It made no sense. Realizing that he hoped that I would shoot myself, or else try to shoot him so that he could charge me with attempted murder, I said to him, 'You have forgotten your gun. Take it. You will never make me sign anything.'

The officer stared at me for a long time. Then, quite unexpectedly, he walked up to me, took my hand and said, 'My name is Dionisie Fotescu and I am a doctor of philosophy, with degrees from Rome and Berlin. You have passed all the tests. I congratulate you. You can leave!'

I looked at him in amazement, trying to fathom his strange words, but I did not stare for long. I was eager to leave this torturer and his brutal men. Bruised and aching in every part of my body I somehow managed to walk home. When my parents saw me, they wept with relief and concern. But, alas, their joy was short-lived. Two days later, some men from the Romanian secret service arrived at our house and took me to a concentration camp for political offenders.

6 *Kosher Food in a Fascist Concentration Camp*

*M*iercurea Ciuc – the first concentration camp in Romania – had been opened a year previously for the Fascist Iron Guard members who had murdered Prime Minister Armand Călinescu. Many Iron Guard men were then shot by the authorities. A large grave containing their bodies was in the centre of the camp. In my cell I noticed these words cut out with a knife: 'The night of 21–22 September 1939'. Next were two crosses and then the words 'The following comrades were killed . . .', followed by a long list of names.

On this list was the name of Nicolae Totu, the Iron Guard man who had killed David Falik in 1926, the tragic event which had so affected my life. The words of Hillel, the sage, from the *Pirkei Avot* came to my mind: 'He once saw a skull floating on the water and he said: "Because you had drowned a man, you were drowned and the end of him who drowned you will also be drowning." ' Despite all, there is justice in this world.

Now it was the Iron Guards' bitter enemies, the Communists, who were being sent to the camp. Some Jews were also there. Hitler's victories had persuaded the King that he had to change his foreign policy and publicly to flatter the German dictator. A right-wing government was established, headed by a man called Gigurtu, which was influenced, though not entirely dominated, by the Iron Guard. It organized pogroms and tolerated attacks on Jews. It was in this period that the terrible pogrom of Dorohoi occurred.

After the First World War, Romania's royal family had experienced incredible changes. Prince Carol, the son of King Ferdinand and Queen Maria, had become involved with Zizi Lambrino, who was considered unsuitable in royal circles; as a result, he had renounced his right to the succession in 1918. Later, he made peace with the royal family and married Princess Helena, sister of King George of Greece. They had a child, Prince Mihai.

However, Carol then fell in love with the wife of an officer at the Palace, Madame Lupescu, the daughter of a Jewish tailor. On 4 January 1927, he again renounced his right to the succession. Mihai was proclaimed Crown Prince and succeeded to the throne when King Ferdinand died the same year. As Mihai was only a child, a regency was established. This situation continued until 8 June 1930, when Carol returned to Romania from abroad and successfully claimed the throne; Mihai reverted to being Crown Prince. Although Carol was supposed to be formally reconciled with Princess Helena, who had become Queen, he continued his liaison with Madame Lupescu and it was she who wielded the real power behind the throne by greatly influencing the King's policies. She tried to deny her Jewish roots and her inner circle of friends included members of extreme right-wing parties which were both Fascist and viciously anti-Semitic.

Carol's foreign policy, like that of the traditional National Liberal and National Peasant parties which ruled Romania until the Second World War, was to look to Britain and France for support. It was these powers which, through the Treaty of Versailles, had ratified Romania's important territorial gains, notably of Bessarabia, Transylvania and Bucovina. Germany and Russia were seen as dangerous enemies. However, with the fall of France and Britain's desperate plight, the corrupt King's position became untenable. Bowing to the inevitable, on 28 June 1940 Romania accepted the occupation of Bessarabia and half of Bucovina by the Russians and, in August 1940, the Vienna *Diktat*, by which Hitler and Mussolini handed over the northern half of Transylvania to Hungary. In September 1940, Carol abdicated in favour of his son, Mihai.

When Mihai ascended the throne for the second time, he was nineteen years old and had little influence and less power. Ion Antonescu, a tough army general, became the most powerful man in the country. He assumed the title of Conducător (leader). His strength lay in the fact that he represented the armed forces, which were desperate to ensure that the mighty German forces would not occupy Romania. Antonescu brought members of the Iron Guard into his Government, so as to placate the Germans, but his relations with the Iron Guard were always uneasy and eventually exploded into a full-scale struggle for supremacy.

Antonescu did not, like Hitler, set out to kill Jews. In fact, in the early days of his administration, he tried to stop the Iron Guard killing them. However, later, wishing to please Hitler, he transported over 100,000 Jews from Bucovina to Transnistria in the Ukraine, where nearly 80,000 died. The pogrom in Iaşi (29 and 30 June and 1 July 1941), in which nearly 12,000 Jews were murdered, was carried out with Antonescu's knowledge and approval. Terrible pogroms took place in other towns, either at the hands, or on the orders, of the Romanian army. Altogether 300,000 Jews died under Antonescu's rule. Later, when the tide of war changed, Antonescu did offer asylum to a number of Jews escaping from Adolf Eichmann's and Nikolaus Horthy's death camps in the Hungarian-occupied part of Transylvania, but this in no way absolves him from his huge war crimes against the Romanian Jewish people.

The changes in the monarchy and the government affected the lives of the Romanian Jews, including mine. The camp in Miercurea Ciuc was more like a detention centre and life was not too harsh. It could not be compared with the conditions of the German death camps. I shared a room, not a cell, with a young Russian, Nikolai. The Communists had to live in more crowded conditions, but I benefited from the fact that they objected to sharing a room with a rabbi, a religious man, whom they did not trust.

Taking advantage of the presence of a *shochet* in the camp – an old, deeply religious man called Coler, who had been taken there in lieu of his son, a notorious Communist who had fought in Spain against Franco and was now in hiding – I managed, after much effort, to start a kosher kitchen. Staging a hunger strike, I soon forced the camp authorities to give in to my demands for kosher food. They also agreed to my organizing a kind of synagogue with regular services. Every Friday evening, I delivered a sermon. Among those who came to listen – perhaps out of a sense of curiosity or as a means of breaking the monotony of camp life – were leaders of the Communist Party like Athanase Joja, Baruch Berea and Gheorghe Apostol, who later became vice-premier. One of them was a man called Lucreţiu Pătrăşcanu, who was appointed Minister of Justice in the first government after the Communists came to power on 23 August 1944, but who was later arrested, charged with various crimes and executed in 1954, on the orders of Gheorghe Gheorghiu-Dej, the 'boss' of the Communist Party.

Despite the comparative leniency of camp life, a cloud always hung over us. An officer had told us, 'It was just as quiet when the Iron Guard were held here. But one day a command came to kill them on the night of 21–22 September, so we did', and we realized that this could happen to us, too.

The stories told me by Nikolai about life in the Soviet Union came as a total shock to me. He described the great famine in the early 1930s, when millions of peasants died as a result of Stalin's collectivization plan and destruction of the so-called *kulaks* (rich peasants). While the famine raged, Stalin exported large quantities of food to the well-fed West. Nikolai, then still a student, had remarked to one of his friends that the Government was selling their bread for nothing while they were dying from hunger. His friend had denounced him to the authorities and he was arrested and jailed for six years at a prison near the Romanian border. He had managed to escape and cross into Romania. However, the Romanians arrested him and held him on suspicion of being a Russian spy. Unable to find any evidence against him, they jailed him for illegally crossing the border and then sent him to the camp for Communists. As the Communists considered him a traitor, he was placed in a room with me.

Intelligent and talkative, Nikolai fascinated me with his stories of Russian life. He described the problems of buying a suit. To obtain one, a person needed points and had to stay in line for days and nights.

When I mentioned the writings of Ilya Ehrenburg, the famous Soviet author, whom I considered representative of Communist writers and who gave a favourable impression of conditions in the Soviet Union, Nikolai laughed. 'His books are not meant for Russians. They are forbidden in Russia. They are meant as propaganda for Western countries,' he said. Nikolai added sombrely, 'Remember my advice. They will arrive here. If you want to survive under their rule, you have to realize that you cannot even afford to think against the authorities. If you do, you are lost.'

Though fascinating, Nikolai's words caused me deep concern and great disappointment. Even as a student, I was never a Communist and did not remotely have any Communist sympathies – my deep religious faith would have made that impossible – but, like many other students, Jewish and non-Jewish, I saw the Soviet Union as the one great power which could hold back the evil march of Fascism and Nazism, and which would save the Jewish people from Hitler. We did not believe the propaganda of right-wing Romanian governments against the Soviet Union as we knew nothing of the excesses that Stalin was committing.

In the meantime, my parents, who were unable to learn any details about what was happening to me, became desperate about my plight. They had heard that inmates were being killed daily in the camp and feared that such a fate would befall me. Ill though he and my mother were – she could walk only with the use of crutches – they decided to appeal directly and personally to the Minister of the Interior, General David Popescu. They went to his home in Bucharest and stood all day at the entrance waiting for his arrival.

General Popescu knew my father and had agreed to his request in March 1940 that I should be made a chaplain in the Romanian forces and not have to serve as an ordinary soldier. This came about because I had been called up in 1939 to serve on the Russian border and was in grave danger from a certain Major Carp, who wanted to kill me. (When the Romanian army retreated from Bukovina, Major Carp personally murdered many Jews, and as he went from place to place, he was heard to shout, 'Where is the soldier Rosen?') My father, who was naturally concerned that I should not be subjected again to the sadistic cruelties which I had previously experienced, managed to obtain a letter from Rabbi Mark of Cernăuţi to General Florea Tenescu, the then army Chief of Staff, who nominated me as a chaplain.

When the General saw my aged parents – my father so impressive with his long, white beard and my mother so obviously in pain – he showed immediate concern and asked what they wanted from him. They explained that, without any cause, I had been sent to a concentration camp and they feared for my life. The General asked for my police file. He studied the so-called evidence against me and reached the conclusion that I was innocent: it was clear to him that the charges against me were ridiculous. He ordered that I should be released immediately from the camp.

This was the last document General Popescu signed as a minister on the night of 6 September 1940. The next day Gigurtu's Government, in which Popescu was one of the very few decent men, fell. General Antonescu took over power, bringing in the Iron Guard. While the changeover was taking place, I left the camp. Had I remained there only a few more days, I doubt that I would have survived. The Iron Guard would either have instigated my death or I would have been sent to Transnistria, where conditions were so appalling that many thousands of Jews were either killed or died from hunger or illness.

7 Evading the Iron Guard

*F*rom the camp I travelled in haste to Bucharest to meet my parents, who had remained there after petitioning General Popescu. I had to decide urgently what to do next. I was without the necessary identity card and would be arrested if suddenly stopped by a policeman. When I told a friend that I did not possess an identity card, he warned me, 'The Iron Guard will kill you.'

We were approaching Rosh Hashanah, the Jewish New Year, and my parents naturally wished to return home. They wanted me to go with them. After long and anxious discussions, I told them that I would not return to Fălticeni, but would remain in Bucharest. This decision probably saved my life. The police and Iron Guard in Fălticeni knew me well and would have been delighted to grab me and deport me to another camp. In a big city like Bucharest, it was much easier to avoid the clutches of the police and the Fascists.

My parents wept when I saw them off and bade them farewell. I, too, had tears in my eyes. In the chaotic conditions which prevailed in the country, we might never see one another again. As I sadly walked away alone from the station, I realized that I had other immediate problems: I had no job, no home and no income, and the little money I had was quickly running out. My prospects did not appear very bright.

However, two days before Rosh Hashanah, Moritz Glickman, the president of a small synagogue, Reshit Daat, came to see me at the house of Rabbi Dr Heinrich Alperin, who had organized this 'meeting' between us. He had somehow heard of my presence in Bucharest. He said to me, 'I understand that you are a rabbi. We have no money to pay for a rabbi the whole year round as our members are poor, but we would be able to pay a small amount if you agree to conduct the services on Rosh Hashanah and Yom Kippur [the Day of Atonement].' I accepted the unexpected offer with eagerness. When I arrived at the synagogue on the eve of Rosh Hashanah, I had to reveal with considerable embarrassment that I did not possess any rabbinical clothes for ritual service. But the same Rabbi Dr Alperin offered to lend me his robe, which I accepted gratefully.

I have delivered thousands of sermons in my long rabbinical life, but I do not think I have ever spoken with more passion and with more feeling than when I gave my sermon at this service. My heart was heavy. I shared with the congregants the fears that engulfed Romanian Jewry. Pogroms had started and many Jews had already been brutally killed. The power of the Iron Guard, whose hatred of Jews had no bounds, was growing. It seemed to us as if the very walls of the synagogue were weeping. I finished the sermon and was reciting the prayers for the blowing of the *shofar*, the ram's horn (traditionally sounded at synagogue services on Rosh Hashanah and Yom Kippur), when I was approached by Leonte Karmitz, a very rich man who was said to be the owner of many pharmacies in the country. The man was crying like a child. He said to me, 'You must remain our rabbi. I will personally pay your salary.' I was astonished at this interruption and did not want to speak to anyone during this particularly solemn part of the service, so I signalled to him to remain silent.

Shortly afterwards, Mr Karmitz spoke to the cantor of the synagogue and asked him to pronounce a *misheberach* (blessing) for his well-being and that of his family. He then announced that he was donating 36,000 lei annually to the synagogue to be used to pay the salary of the new rabbi. It was certainly an adequate amount. My astonishment was shared by the congregation. This gesture was to prove of immense importance to me. It made it possible for me to remain in Bucharest and encouraged me to extend my activities. Within a few weeks, I added to my duties by becoming the rabbi of another synagogue, Beit Keil in Emigratului Street, which was close to Reshit Daat. I also began to teach Hebrew and religion in a number of Jewish schools. I was very busy, but I greatly enjoyed my work. After a few days, the leadership of the Bucharest Jewish community and Chief Rabbi Alexandru Safran ratified these nominations.

I decided to bring my parents to Bucharest. My father was seventy-one and frail, and I felt that he would not be able to deal with the new problems that the war had brought. The anti-Semites were on the rampage. Attacks on Jews were common and in a little town like Fălticeni an elderly rabbi would be a particularly tempting target. I hoped that in Bucharest I would be able to look after him – as long as I was free. My mother was ill and in constant pain. I worried about her and I wanted to be near them. There was also another, more selfish reason. I felt that if they remained in Fălticeni, they would be a constant reminder to the local police that I existed. They would want to arrest me, charge me with being a Bolshevik and either put me in prison or deport me.

It was with deep relief and gratitude that I welcomed my parents in Bucharest. Though I was working hard at the synagogues and schools, I was still earning comparatively little and could afford to rent only one room for myself and my parents. But I had a far more urgent problem: I heard that the Fălticeni police, on hearing that I had left for the capital, had asked the Bucharest police to arrest me.

From then on, I lived in a state of tension. At any moment day or night I expected to be seized by the police. As a rabbi and teacher, I had to live under my own name in a city bristling with police and Iron Guard men. I could not go into hiding because this would have precluded me from earning money to feed my parents, who totally relied on me. I was in constant fear that the leaders of the community would learn that the police wanted to arrest me and would dismiss me instantly, so as not to bring retribution on the community for employing a wanted man.

When my parents were still in Fălticeni I told them to write to me at a certain address in Bucharest, which was not where I lived. I feared that if I gave the correct address, the police would arrest me. I visited this second house regularly to pick up my mail. One day, when I came to collect my letters, an elderly rabbi, who lived at the house, told me, 'The police have been here looking for you.' Alarmed, I ran to the house where I lived. I intended to hide there for a while, hoping, perhaps naively, that the police would discontinue the search after not finding me at the other address. Alas, the rabbi, who had possibly become confused by the police questioning, had given them my correct address. I realized this immediately when I entered the house. Some sixth sense told me not to go directly to my room, but to enter the kitchen through a side entrance. As I did so, the maid told me, 'Two gentlemen are waiting for you in your room.' It needed no great intelligence to know that these two 'gentlemen' were policemen.

I ran out of the house into the street, but the two men, who were looking out of the window, caught sight of me and, realizing who I was, began to chase me. By then I knew the area well and I hid in a courtyard. They came close to finding me, but after a while they disappeared. I heard afterwards that they stopped people in the street and inquired if they had seen a man with a beard. When people asked who I was, they replied, 'He's a man from the NKVD [Stalinist secret police].'

Though I had escaped arrest, I was in a very desperate situation. I could not return to my room, as the house was certainly being watched by the police, nor could I get my few belongings. These, I later learned, had in any case been taken away in two suitcases by the two 'gentlemen'. I wandered the streets and stayed out at night in the open. I led a tramp's life for a while, but this could not continue.

I went to see Dr Filderman, the president of the Federation of Jewish Communities, and asked for his help. 'Yes, I can try to help you, but you must first go to the police,' he said. 'I cannot intervene on behalf of somebody who is hiding. I can provide you with a lawyer. He is actually an Iron Guard man, but we employ him. He does not mind taking money from us Jews. He will accompany you to the police station, but you must pay him a large amount.'

'The Lord preserveth the simple' (Psalm 116:6). I agreed to go to the police station with Musat, the unscrupulous lawyer, who took from me most of the money I possessed. Any logical person could have told me that I had almost no chance of leaving the police station a free man. Moreover, Pădure, the police officer who wanted to question me, was a vicious and cruel man. Only a few days before, he had killed a fifteen-year-old Jewish boy, Lucien Rosen, by throwing him out of a fifth-floor window.

When I entered the main room of the police station, I saw that it was full of tough-looking Iron Guard men. They stared at me, but with curiosity rather than hostility. How could they possibly imagine that a rabbi, of all people, would dare or be so unwise as to enter such a place? They apparently assumed that I was a priest of some Christian cult. Seeing these men, who would kill a Jew without giving the matter much thought and with a sense of satisfaction, I felt like Daniel in the lions' cage. I had walked into a murderers' den – voluntarily! All the men were armed and there was a perceptible air of tension in the room. Pădure beckoned to me and asked me who I was. When I told him, he reacted with obvious surprise. He said to me, 'You've been running away from us. You've been in hiding.'

I explained that I was living in fear of being tortured because I had already experienced it. 'Who tortured you?' he asked indignantly. 'Whoever did it could not have been an Iron Guard man.'

This was not the time to argue about the behaviour of the Iron Guard, whose barbaric cruelty was already well known among Romanian Jews. I noticed that Pădure appeared very preoccupied and tense. He kept glancing around the room and talking to other men. After a while, he said to me, 'I have no time for you now. You must come back here in a week's time. If you try to hide again, we'll find you and kill you.'

He told me to take my belongings, which were in two battered suitcases on the table. Noticing that they were very light, I quickly opened one and then the other and saw that they were empty. Pădure looked at me furiously and, when I pointed at the empty suitcases, he exploded, 'What's wrong? You *Yid* [Jew], are you insulting us by saying that we are thieves?'

Now thoroughly alarmed, I replied in a conciliatory tone, 'No sir, everything is all right.'

Pădure was not satisfied with my reply and glared at me. I looked at Musat for support. Pădure called his men and told them to seize me and take me to a cell. There was a moment of tension and then Musat motioned to me to leave the room. I started to walk out and Pădure allowed me to do so. Then Musat asked if I had any more money. I gave him all I had and he went back to talk to Pădure for a few minutes. Then Pădure told me, 'Take your suitcases and we will have an inquiry next week.'

And so I did. At any second I expected to hear Pădure's vicious voice ordering his men to seize me, but no command came. I walked out of the room and then into the street, my feet trembling. When I felt the fresh air on my face and realized I was still a free man, I felt wonderfully elated. I recited several psalms in thanksgiving.

The date of my visit to the Iron Guard police station was 17 January 1941. Four days later (21 January), I fully understood the reason for the tension among the Iron Guard men and Pădure's remark that he had no time to deal with me. The Iron Guard were putting the final touches to their plan to eject Antonescu and seize total power in the country. As part of this plan, a pogrom was to be carried out. Killing and maiming Jews, and confiscating or destroying their possessions, would be to the liking of the Romanian population and would facilitate the seizure of power. Hitler had used similar tactics. On 21 January 1941 – a date which will always remain in the memory of Romanian Jews – the Bucharest pogrom started. As a preliminary measure, the Iron Guard killed all those held in the cells at the police station I had visited. Had I been there, I would inevitably have been one of the victims.

Aided enthusiastically by hooligans, the Iron Guard looted Jewish homes, burned Jewish shops, and burned or desecrated synagogues.

Jews were seized and taken to the forests near Bucharest and shot. The elderly rabbi, Hersh Guttman, was taken, together with his two sons, Iancu and Iosef, to the Jilava woods. The Iron Guard shot the two sons, who died in their father's arms. They shot at him, too, but somehow he survived. Amazed that he was still alive despite the volley of bullets which miraculously – so it seemed – missed him, the Iron Guard became confused. Suddenly convinced that they were dealing with an indestructible holy man, they beat a hasty retreat.

Other Jews were taken to the municipal slaughterhouse. Their throats were cut and their bodies hung on hooks, with the sign 'kosher meat' around their necks. When the Iron Guard desecrated the Great Synagogue, they took out the Scrolls of the Law from the Ark and shot at them. One of the Scrolls became entangled high in a chandelier. In the Choral Temple, they entered during the evening prayer. In the middle of the service, they took the cantor, Osias Kopstück, and other congregants and killed them after cruelly torturing them.

One of the men who organized and kept the flames of the pogrom alight was a young priest called Valerian Trifa, the commander of an Iron Guard student group. In the centre of the city, I saw a poster signed by him, calling for the death of Jews. His men, armed with guns and carrying torches, were looking for Jews to seize and kill. I hid in doorways and courtyards and managed to avoid them, but the sight was etched in my mind. It was still vivid many years later, when I fought to have Trifa expelled from the United States.

When I became convinced that the Iron Guard were about to start a pogrom, I decided not to sleep at home that night. I went to my friend, Heinrich Sternbaum, who lived outside the Jewish area of the city, in Str Traian 146. When I told him of my fears, he laughed and tried to calm me down. I described the tension in the Jewish district, and the arrogant and brutal behaviour of the Iron Guard who were roaming the streets. Although unconvinced, he prepared a bed for me.

Still certain that a catastrophe was about to befall us, I could not sleep. I got up and stood nervously at the window. Suddenly shots rang out. I stared into the street, but could not see anyone. I alerted Sternbaum and his family. They laughed no more and trembled in panic.

A car stopped outside the building at two o'clock in the morning. Straining our eyes, we saw six men get out of the car. We heard them knocking at the outside door of the building and, after a short while, being let in by the Christian servants. It appeared that the men were expected. The plan was clearly to kill the Jews in the building and to loot their flats. We huddled together, expecting the raiders to enter our first-floor flat and attack us, but they decided to start with the fourth floor. Finding no one in, they began to throw into the street everything they could grab – clothing, shoes and bedding. In their fury, they even threw out porcelain, which smashed on the ground. Having cleared out the place, they went to the third floor and hammered on the door of the flat occupied by a Jew called Taubman. Fearing that the Nazis would enter Bucharest and deport all the Jews, he had bought himself a South American passport. On hearing the knocking and realizing who the assailants were, he went out onto the balcony and began to scream, 'I am a South American citizen.' The streets were empty, everybody was hiding at home and machine-guns were firing, but this poor, naive Jew was shouting for help in the hope that his 'South American' citizenship would save his life.

The men kept on hammering, disregarding his protests, and began to break the door open. When he saw that they were about to enter the flat, Taubman rushed to the window and jumped out, impaling himself on the iron gates below. He was terribly disfigured, but did not die. He remained an invalid for the rest of his life.

Going to the second-floor flat, the Iron Guard men ransacked it thoroughly. There was no one there. They took all the clothing and furnishings, piled them outside and then pushed them into the car. It was now our turn to be visited by the robbers, to be seized or killed on the spot. But, to our astonished relief, we saw the men leave the building, crowd with difficulty into the large car, now packed with stolen possessions, and drive away. I guessed that they were going to their homes to disgorge their plunder and intended to return for further looting. I told my friends, 'They will return. We must run from here.'

I suggested that we should go to the house of a neighbour called Ziegelbaum, whom I knew well because I had taught his children for many years. He trembled with fear when we knocked at his door. He was a poor man and I thought it unlikely that the Iron Guard would bother to loot his house when they had much richer pickings elsewhere. On recognizing me, he motioned us to enter. I allowed my friends to go in first and was about to follow them when a car suddenly appeared with a number of men inside. I realized that they had seen me and decided not to enter the house, but to walk away and pretend that I was taking a stroll – at three o'clock in the morning! I suspected that they were Iron Guard men, possibly the same ones who had ransacked the building we had just left. I feared that, if I entered the house, they would follow me and kill everyone there.

I continued walking, hoping desperately that my ruse would succeed. But the car stopped next to me, a gun was pointed at me and a voice shouted, 'Get into the car!' I had no alternative but to do so. Then the same voice demanded, 'Show me your identity card.' I was now absolutely certain that I would be shot immediately, as the identity card revealed that I was a rabbi. A man shone a torchlight on the card and studied it carefully. Then, to my utter astonishment, he barked at me, 'Get out!' I clambered out quickly and found myself again on the pavement. Why had they let me go? I felt bewildered, but very relieved.

I carried on walking. Snow was falling lightly and creating a white blanket. Never before had I considered light to be a danger to life. Now, the first condition for my survival was not to be seen, but the white snow and the strong electric lamps made me visible to everybody. I was certain that I could be seen for miles around. I decided I must quickly find a dark place to hide until morning. I saw a building in darkness in Plantelor Street, an ideal hiding-place. As I approached, I heard voices. Somebody in the street was trying to wake up a person inside. After a while, a figure came to the window of one of the flats. Almost at the same time, the man outside saw me, rushed up to me and pointed a gun at me. 'If you move I'll kill you!' he hissed.

He took out a pocket lamp and shone it in my face. He seemed very surprised. 'Aren't you the man we spoke to, a while back, in the car?' he asked. 'Yes,' I replied. 'What are you doing here, you a rabbi, on such a night?' he demanded. 'Go home!' Noting my total confusion, he quickly explained that he and his friends were General Antonescu's men and were looking for Iron Guard insurgents. When they had first seen me, they suspected that I might be one of them. Realizing that I was a rabbi, they freed me. This particular man was a colonel's driver and was simply waking up another driver. I now realized that I must go to Ziegelbaum's house, where my friends welcomed me warmly. They feared that I had been snatched by the Iron Guard. I heard a tale of horror. The Fascists had returned to the building, as I had suspected they would, and had burst into my friend's flat. Not finding anyone in, they grabbed all his belongings. Any Jew that they saw in the building was taken away, tortured and killed.

The Iron Guard failed to topple Antonescu because he had an unexpected ally – Hitler. The Nazis were already planning to attack the Soviet Union in a few months' time and needed the support of the Romanian forces; they certainly did not want them as an enemy. And so, when Antonescu appealed to him, Hitler quickly abandoned the

Fascist Iron Guard. Left on their own, the Iron Guard were no match for the Romanian army and were soon crushed. Their leaders ran to the German Embassy in Bucharest but, instead of getting aid, they were provided with an aeroplane and taken to Germany, where they remained for the rest of the war. A grateful Antonescu promised Hitler that the Romanian army would join Germany in fighting the Soviet Union. When the Germans crossed the Soviet borders six months later, on 22 June 1941, Romanian troops were at their side.

It was then that the particularly brutal massacre of the Jews in Iaşi took place, a unique incident even in the unparalleled tragedy of the Holocaust. The killing was done by Romanian soldiers and policemen, together with some German officers, led by Antonescu, who was looking for ways to please Hitler. When Russian planes bombed Iaşi, which is near the Soviet border, Romanian soldiers alleged that the local Jews had signalled to the Soviet pilots. A terrible scheme was then concocted by the Romanian army, police and other authorities. On Sunday, 29 June 1941, the unsuspecting Iaşi Jews were ordered to go to the police station, which was in the centre of the town. They were told that their identity cards had to be changed. In order to enter the police station, they had to pass two lines of armed soldiers and policemen. When over 6,000 Jews, among them mothers with babies in their arms, had assembled, they were suddenly set upon by the soldiers and policemen and beaten to death in the most horrifying manner, the soldiers using the butts of their rifles to smash open the skulls of men, women and children. Huge piles of bodies filled the large courtyard of the police station, and a river of blood ran into the street, as every one of the Jews was butchered. This happened in the morning, in the centre of a European town, with the Christian population looking on. And Romanian army generals, who could have stopped the massacre with a single command, were seen to be giving orders on how best the mass killing should proceed. A local council worker, who came three days later to clean up the courtyard and the street outside, walked in pools of blood several centimetres deep.

Other Jews, who, for one reason or another, had not come to the police station and been murdered, were seized and packed into horse waggons attached to trains. In a waggon made for three horses, they put 150–160 people. So crowded were they that there was no room to sit down and barely even to stand. The heat inside in the hot July weather quickly became unbearable. To add to the agony of this tragic human cargo, the authorities covered up the ventilation holes. The trains were then taken out of Iaşi for short distances, for days and nights on end. In their agony, the Jews clawed at their own flesh and drank their own urine, because nobody gave them a drop of water. Their suffering was unimaginable. At each railway station, the doors of the waggons were opened and the bodies tumbled out. Only a very small number of Jews survived this sadistic torture.

That is how the Romanian anti-Semites destroyed the famous 500-year-old famous Jewish community of Iaşi. Jews had been among the founders of the town and there was a tombstone in the old Jewish cemetery, Ciurchi, dating back to 1467. But on the day of the massacre, which Romanian Jews refer to as 'Yenner Suntig' ('That Sunday'), the murderers forgot all this. In their hearts was only vicious hatred.

With Antonescu's Romania an ally of Hitler's Germany in the war against the Western democracies and the Soviet Union, the Nazis did not occupy Romania. This saved the lives of 400,000 of the 800,000 Jews who had lived in the unmutilated country before the war. But no Jew could feel safe. At any moment he could be seized by Antonescu's police and taken for slave labour or deported to Transnistria. For a Jew and a rabbi like me whom, for totally unwarranted reasons, the Bucharest police were seeking at the request of the Fälticeni police, the situation was particularly dangerous. I could not give up being a rabbi and a teacher, because that would have meant starvation for me and my parents. How is it then conceivable that I survived the four years of Romania's war a free man? Even today I find it hard to believe that I was not arrested again and deported. I gave sermons in the synagogue, I conducted many weddings and I taught at Jewish schools. I can only attribute my survival to God's miracles and to the stupidity of the police. They never seemed to ask the obvious question: what is Rabbi Rosen doing? It would have been easy enough to go to the community where I was officially registered and remunerated (as the rabbi of Beit Keil synagogue and as a religion teacher) to find out the places where I was present daily. Had they done so, they would inevitably have found me. Nevertheless, there were many occasions when bribery saved me.

I remember a particular escape on the eve of Yom Kippur 1942. My synagogue could not hold any services, as members of the German military mission had commandeered the building. Members of the congregation, therefore, decided to join me in praying at my father's synagogue, which was in a room next to the one we lived in. A man arrived at the synagogue and asked to see Rabbi Rosen. My mother, who saw the man, asked him whether he sought Rabbi Rosen senior or junior. He replied that he wanted to see the young Rabbi Rosen.

Suspicious of his dour appearance and convinced that he was not a Jew, she told him, 'He is not here. He won't be coming today.' When the man went away, my mother hobbled into the street and asked Jewish people there to warn me not to enter the room which I shared with my parents. I went to a neighbour's house and had something to eat, as the twenty-five-hour Yom Kippur fast was about to start. I wrestled feverishly with the problem: how could I avoid going to the synagogue and delivering a sermon on Kol Nidrei night, the holiest night of the year for the Jewish people? The leaders of my community and the whole congregation expected this of me, but going to the synagogue laid me open to instant arrest. The police had clearly found out where I was.

However, I decided that I must go to the synagogue and give the sermon, even if it were my last one. As I did so, I kept looking at the door, expecting the mysterious man to walk in, perhaps with other policemen, and arrest me. But he did not appear. That night I did not sleep at home. Next day, Yom Kippur, I spoke at a number of synagogues to congregations seeking solace in their suffering. Many members had lost relatives and were themselves under threat of deportation, and I felt I had a duty to give them hope and comfort from the Torah. I knew that some of my friends were coming to my father's synagogue to hear my sermon after the *Izkor* (memorial) prayer and, not wanting to disappoint them, I took a foolish, suicidal decision: I walked back to my father's synagogue.

At the gate I saw a man waiting and immediately realized who he was. Even if I had not been warned, I would have guessed that he was a plain-clothes policeman. Taking a chance that he did not know what I looked like, I went up to him and asked, 'Are you waiting for somebody?' 'Yes, for young Rabbi Rosen,' he replied. 'He should be here, I'll go in and send him out to you,' I responded.

Entering my parents' room, I was at first tempted to go to the back of the house and escape, but I feared that the man had stationed his agents there. I knew that my only chance lay in taking another risk, a display of *chutzpa*. I went up to the man and said to him, 'Young Rabbi Rosen was here some time ago. He has already left, but he is coming back. Please wait.' Not suspecting a trick, the man nodded and I went on my way. He waited patiently for another hour. Afterwards, he started stopping everyone who went in and checking their identity. By then, I was already far away.

For some time, I did not sleep in my parents' room, lest the man should return. But for some unexplained reason, he suddenly stopped his vigil and I decided to go back. However, a senior police officer, called Miron Ionescu, began to visit my parents' home. In the room there were two beds and a settee. When he asked for me, my mother told him that I was not living there. He looked hard at the settee, which I used as a bed, and realized the truth. He said to my mother, 'Tell your son to hide himself because there is an order to have him sent to Transnistria. I am risking my life in telling you this. All the same, don't place your confidence in policemen.'

Having studied my police file, Ionescu appeared to know a great deal about me. One day he surprised my mother by saying, 'Your son is an interesting person. It is a pity he will be a dead man if the police find him.'

My fears about him diminished somewhat, but I did not trust him altogether. Neither did my mother. There was a secret passage leading from our room to a cave-like room at the bottom of the building. Whenever I heard his distinctive knock at the door, I immediately disappeared into my hiding-place.

After chatting amiably with my parents for a few weeks, Ionescu suddenly said to my mother, 'Madam, I feel your son is here in the building. You know very well that I am protecting him. I am curious to meet him.'

My mother replied, probably with a wry smile, 'Do you remember advising me not to have confidence in policemen? Well, I must take your advice.' He looked at her for a long time but remained silent.

Ionescu refused to take any money that mother offered him. We came to believe that he was an honest and courageous man, who did not seek my destruction but wanted to help me. However, after a while he ceased coming to see my parents. His place was taken by another officer whose presence frightened them. They considered him a monster. He arrived regularly, every month, and demanded a considerable sum of money, which my parents found very hard to obtain. He was not interested in my fate, but only in money. Thus I escaped arrest twice, once because of an honest man and once thanks to a bribe-taker.

Looking back on all those days and nights of fear and of hiding, whilst at the same time leading a public life by giving sermons and teaching and yet not being 'discovered' by the police, I believe that there is but one explanation: the miracles of the Almighty.

8   *Elected Chief Rabbi of a Devastated Community*

When the Russian troops entered Bucharest on 23 August 1944, I and the remainder of Romanian Jews were overjoyed. It was a day of liberation for us all. We felt that we had been saved from Hitler's death camps. True, Antonescu had begun to change his policy towards the Jews after the German and Romanian disaster at Stalingrad, and had become less willing to meet Hitler's demands or to win his favours by taking callous action against the Jews. Had Hitler occupied Romania, Romanian Jews would have faced total annihilation. The magazine of the German Embassy in Bucharest had predicted with glee that by the end of 1944 Romania would be *Judenrein* – free of Jews. Trains had already been prepared to send us all to the Belzec extermination camp in Poland. However, seeing the tide turn, Antonescu and the Romanian army changed sides. The Germans bombed Bucharest, but to no avail. Manfred von Killinger, the German Ambassador in Bucharest, committed suicide and the rest of his staff surrendered. But after the Russians entered Romania, which he had tried desperately to prevent, Antonescu was overthrown: he was invited by King Mihai to the palace and arrested. The Romanian Communist Party then joined a government coalition. They were to become increasingly powerful and eventually to force the King's abdication, but at the beginning they were content to share power and bide their time.

Romanian Jews felt an immense gratitude to the Soviet Union, a feeling which I shared. This was not because of any sympathy for Soviet Communism, but from the belief that the Soviet Union had saved our lives. However, there were many individual Jews who did become staunch Communists, some by conviction, others through opportunism, and who became members of the party leadership. As in the Government, Communists joined a coalition in the leadership of the Jewish communities, working harmoniously with the six other parties, including the Zionists, the Jewish Party, the Liberals and the Union of Romanian Jews.

At the end of 1946 I assumed three main responsibilities in the religious life of Bucharest: chairman of the Committee for Cult Affairs, member of the Rabbinical Council of Bucharest – I had been co-opted onto the Council on the written approval of Chief Rabbi Safran – and rabbi of the Great Synagogue. In these positions, especially as chairman of the Committee for Cult Affairs, I found myself confronted by an unbearable situation: chaos and irresponsibility reigned over religious matters. Every synagogue conducted its religious services in accordance with the wishes of local personalities. Elementary rules were ignored. *Matzah*, the ritual unleavened bread eaten at Passover, was baked in awful conditions, both from the religious and the hygienic points of view. *Kashrut*, the dietary laws and ritual slaughter of animals, was almost non-existent. And, most important of all, the meaning of our teaching as *Toraht Hayim*, a Book of Life, was distorted. The prayers of *Kaddish* and *Izkor*, both connected with the dead, remained the sole vestiges of our religious faith. There was public indifference to the higher rabbinical authority. I set myself to work.

Looking back on those years of uncertainty, one must feel a little embarrassed. The social and political frameworks of Romania were radically changing and we were trying to restore Jewish life in the country, but we often clashed over matters of minor relevance to the huge tasks which had to be tackled. The old leadership did not fully understand the omens of the changed conditions. They seemed to care less for the fate of their communities than for their own positions and safety. There was a lack of guidance and authority.

I took over my work with energy and perseverance. No wonder that I became quite popular. There was, first of all, a need to put everything on a legal basis. It might seem strange but I had the full support of a Communist, Leon Stern, the chairman of the Administrative Council and later president of the Bucharest Jewish community. He and Dr Jean Aberman, a devoted Jewish activist and Zionist leader, helped me to ensure the proper baking of *matzah* and the provision of kosher meat to Orthodox Jews.

Then I dealt with the Sabbath problem and put an end to the incredible situation that had lasted for so long in Jewish schools, where pupils and teachers had neglected the Sabbath altogether. I opened a *mikvah* and a house for sick and elderly Jews, who had returned from the camps and needed good care from the community. I was also amazed by the negligence in regard to religious marriages and divorces, which had led to a number of doubtful marriages taking place. I considered this a matter of cardinal importance and, therefore, required a proper investigation of the religious and civil backgrounds of couples wishing to marry. Thus I began to put an end to the improprieties which were disfiguring Jewish life.

Above all, I initiated guidelines for regulating religious services. A real *tohu va-vohu* (chaos) reigned over synagogue services and practices. Anybody keen to do so could officiate in a synagogue, without any control. At a heavy price I established a rabbinical authority over these matters. Those interested in financial gain only, in profiting from religious services, protested loudly, claiming that they were championing democracy and the independence of synagogues, whereas they were, in fact, the enemies of Jewish unity and the Jewish faith. They attacked me bitterly, but to no avail because I had the support of the Jewish masses.

The political situation of the survivors of the Jewish population was also full of anomalies. Four hundred thousand Jews had disappeared in the crematoria and mass graves, and each surviving family was torn by mourning and suffering. I shall never forget my first visit to Oradea in 1945. There I found a community without old people and children. The survivors had escaped death only because they were doing hard labour for the Nazis. The liberation had come just as they were about to be thrown into the gas chambers. They pointed at photographs on the walls: 'Here you can see my wife, here my parents, here my brothers and sisters.' Pictures, shadows, memories. They were ill; they had almost been driven mad while experiencing the torments of hell here on earth, and they all felt terribly lonely. For many of them, the only way to make a new start in life was to take the road to the Land of Israel. They no longer trusted anyone – and with reason. If they were to go on living, they had to become masters of their own fate and that of their children, to live normal and independent lives. Ships were sailing for Palestine crammed with these desperate Jews. The Jewish masses eagerly awaited these ships and Jewish youth craved for the unique opportunity of being reborn to a life worth living: *aliyah* to the Land of Israel.

However, the Jewish Communists, true to their beliefs which were opposed to emigration, did their utmost to stop or reduce the wave of departures to Palestine. The Jewish Democratic Committee (CDE), dominated by the Communists but also including left-wing Zionists and the Union of Romanian Jews, had actually assumed control of the communities. Its leaders included many people who not only did not want to restore the synagogues, Talmud Torahs, *mikvaoth* and other institutions, but pursued a policy of liquidating Jewish communal life.

On the other hand, the nationalist and religious Jews, most of whom intended to leave the country, did not care about the future of the communities. There was, in fact, a tacit, undeclared agreement between the Communists and the Zionists to do away with the Jewish communities. Each group had its own motive, but the saying that '*les extrêmes se touchent*' was once more confirmed. The truth of the matter was – and the following decades proved it – that both camps were short-sighted and did not see things in their true perspective. By destroying the institutions concerned with the religion, culture and welfare of the Jewish people, the Communists actually accelerated the emigration process. Even Jews who did not have a strong Jewish orientation, but who wanted to remain Jewish, could see the daily erosion of the possibility of continuing to live in the Jewish spirit in this part of the world. If they hesitated, the CDE dispelled their doubts by the atmosphere it created.

To maintain the spirit of an *aliyah* worthy of the name, the Zionists needed a community with a solid foundation, kept firm by Jewish education and unity. Instead of appreciating this, the Zionists favoured chaos and disorganization within the community. They did not understand that to have a constant flow of *olim*, the Jews had to be educated in a religious and national spirit, otherwise emigrants would choose to go to the United States instead of Israel. Most of the rabbis who could provide this education, including those who were on the staff of the communities, had already packed their bags to leave and were not interested in consolidating Jewish life.

At the end of 1947 an unexpected situation emerged, which continued until the middle of 1948. One day a rumour spread widely that Chief Rabbi Safran had left the country. Nobody could have foreseen such a development. The Chief Rabbi's position was strong. The Communists, who sought to build up their prestige and to consolidate their hold on Jewish life, and the Zionists, who wanted the religious leader to support *aliyah*, did everything possible to gain his favour. In fact, he attended the meetings of both sides with equal magnanimity.

I was a member of the Rabbinical Council and chairman of the Religious Affairs Council and yet I knew nothing about the Chief Rabbi's sudden departure. The day before he left, I had visited his residence and discussed with him the agenda of forthcoming religious events. He did not mention to me any plans for travelling abroad. We had known each other for many years – our families respected each other – and we felt quite close. Nobody knew that during his many trips abroad in 1946–7 the Chief Rabbi of a community of 450,000 people, the largest in Eastern Europe, outside the Soviet Union, with the heaviest responsibilities on his shoulders, was seeking another place of quiet and rest. (He eventually became Chief Rabbi of Geneva.)

So a vacuum was created at the top of the religious community. In the following months, I was approached by Israel Bacal, a Communist and a prominent CDE member, with the proposal that I should become a candidate for the Chief Rabbinate. It appeared that I qualified for the post more than any other member of the Rabbinical Council. The other rabbis were either without a general academic background, though they were well-versed in religious matters, or they were too old to assume such a strenuous task. I was young and energetic: my candidacy was acceptable to all sides. For the Communists I seemed to be a true democrat, who had shared the hardships of their leaders in the camps, and was close to the masses of the deprived, the majority of the Jewish people. Moreover, I had become affiliated to the Social Democrats, a party of liberal European tradition. The Orthodox community saw me as the true offspring of the Fălticeni Ruv, my revered father, a sage in Israel, a great *Halachic* authority and a guarantor of my fidelity to the Law. For all I represented a man of the times, a rabbi with a modern approach to the new exigencies of the Chief Rabbinate office.

Despite all this and my desire for enhanced Jewish activity, I declined Bacal's offer. I insisted that there should first be a clear and public statement about the Chief Rabbinate vacancy, with a specific recognition of the need for free elections. When the vacancy was eventually declared, I agreed to become a candidate on one condition. I told Bacal, 'Now you are in love with Zionism, but things might change and you might bitterly oppose it. Don't ever ask me to attack Zionism from my chair.' Bacal replied, 'We might attack Zionists in the future, but we will never attack Zionism as such.' Bacal later acknowledged the condition I had made, but by then things had indeed changed for the worse.

On 16 June 1948, an assembly of rabbis and representatives of all the Jewish communities and groups elected me Chief Rabbi of Romania. It was a most prestigious gathering. Among those present were Rabbi Yitzhak Friedman of Bohuşi, Rabbi Joseph Adler of Turda, the *Gaon* David Sperber of Braşov, Dr Drechsler of Timişoara, Moshe

Benvenisti (president of the Zionist Executive), Profeta (president of the Sephardic community), and many Orthodox and Neolog (reform) rabbis, Zionist leaders, Communists, Social Democrats and members of the Union of Romanian Jews. My opponent had been Rabbi David Safran, a nephew of the former Chief Rabbi. After careful examination of the candidacies, I was elected by an overwhelming majority. In a secret ballot, an absolutely free election, I received hundreds of votes while my opponent got only fourteen. Suddenly I found myself on top of a religious pyramid without any experience for such a responsibility.

On 20 June 1948, I took the seat of the Chief Rabbi of Romania in the Choral Temple, the main synagogue of Bucharest. The Vice-President, Stefan Voitec, the Minister of Cults (religious denominations), Professor Stanciu Stoian, and other high-ranking officials attended the ceremony. My father put his hands on my head and uttered the moving words: 'May the Lord bless you and guard your way. . . .'

I listened in awe and was deeply shaken. How many dangers would I have to face in the future and how many enemies would I be confronted with? I felt a heavy burden on my shoulders.

Listening to my father's blessing I could not but recollect the feelings of the hero in Sholem Ash's *Der Tillim Yid*. Crowds of Jews had assembled outside the doors of his house, each with his needs and his sufferings. All this Jewish torment was put in a bag and the Tillim Yid felt it his duty to carry it on his shoulders to the top of the mountain. The bag grew heavier and heavier, a rainstorm beat against his cheeks, becoming ever more violent, and his feet were torn by the boulders on his way. But the Tillim Yid had to fulfil his mission and could not turn back.

These were my feelings on that memorable day; this was why tears flowed from my eyes. And this is the way I became Chief Rabbi.

9 *Montreux 1948: The World Jewish Congress*

*S*hortly after becoming Chief Rabbi, I left for Montreux, together with a fourteen-strong community delegation, including Zionists and Communists, to attend a meeting of the World Jewish Congress. I wore a crimson *yarmulka* (head covering) after taking off my hat. Wearing a *yarmulka* is a long-established custom among Orthodox Jews, but what was unusual was the colour of mine. As I was the only Chief Rabbi from a Communist country, the colour of my *yarmulka* was given – ridiculously, of course – a special significance, and some people began to refer to me as the 'Red Rabbi'. I was more amused than angered by this appellation. Occasionally, critics of my policies in Romania have also used this description, but I have never attached any importance to it. Now I know of no one who even remembers it.

I was greatly moved by this visit to Montreux. It was my first opportunity to see world Jewish leaders after the Holocaust and the death of six million Jews. Polish Jewry, which had numbered three and a half million, had been reduced to a few thousand. Every other major Jewish community in Europe had suffered grievously. Some had ghost communities. Europe was a huge cemetery for the Jewish people – except that millions did not even have graves.

It was at Montreux that I first met Nahum Goldmann, a founder and president of the World Jewish Congress. A man of high intelligence, wit and consummate diplomatic skills, a superb public speaker, a man of courage who was ready to clash even with such formidable personalities as David Ben-Gurion and Golda Meir, the Israeli leaders, he made a profound impression on me. I discovered that we agreed on nearly all important topics.

It was also at Montreux that I met for the first time Dr Stephen Wise, the American Reform rabbi, communal leader and Zionist. He was an impressive-looking man with a high reputation. He shared with

Goldmann the chairing of the conference, which he did with skill – as he had to do if it were to succeed. This was the first time that Jews from Communist countries met Jews from the West, and problems inevitably arose.

It had previously been decided that each Jewish community had the right to send one delegate for 50,000 Jews and each delegate could speak for five minutes. The Romanian delegation, which represented 400,000 Jews, was therefore given the right to speak for forty minutes. We divided the time allotted to us in the following way: the Communists were given twenty minutes, the Zionists ten and I ten. Leibovici Şerban, general secretary of the Federation of Jewish Communities, was a Communist and was asked by his fellow-Communist delegates to speak on their behalf. But he had a problem: the East European delegates were speaking in Yiddish, but he had not mastered the language and could not speak enough to be able to deliver a speech. It had been agreed between us that the Communists would take the floor first and it would have been embarrassing to change the order. Şerban was expected to speak on the first day, but he kept silent. The delegates were surprised and then mystified. I am sure that a few of them attributed his silence to some profound matter of state. Their mystification grew when he remained silent on the second day. We, the Romanian delegates, representing the largest Jewish community in Europe outside the Soviet Union, were chagrined by his silence. We had to take emergency action. It was decided that the Zionist, Esselsohn, should help Şerban prepare his speech in Yiddish: the ideas would come from Şerban and most of the words from Esselsohn.

When Şerban finally took the floor on the third day, most of the delegates, including Esselsohn, would have been happier if he had remained silent. He spoke as a dedicated Stalinist and pointed an accusing finger at 'Jewish reactionary forces' which were allegedly trying to undermine the Soviet Union. He was angrily interrupted several times and was unable to finish his vitriolic speech.

Goldmann, who was presiding, was very strict in the allocation of time to the speakers. Anyone who spoke longer was cut off abruptly in the middle of his oratory. However, my address lasted almost twice the allotted time.

As I sat down, Goldmann said to the delegates, 'Please forgive me. I am well aware that Chief Rabbi Rosen was on his feet for a total of seventeen minutes though his speech was limited to ten minutes. But my watch showed that the applause with which he was interrupted several times lasted a total of seven minutes.'

I mention this remark not to suggest that I overwhelmed the delegates with my oratory. Frankly, I do not consider myself an effective public speaker in any language except Romanian. What the delegates applauded was not rhetoric, but the facts I was able to relate. I spoke of the synagogues which were full of devout worshippers, of Talmud Torah classes, where children were learning daily about their Jewish faith and Jewish history, and I gave figures of thousands of such Jewish children being educated in a Jewish spirit. I also spoke of the freedom which Romanian Jews had to practise their religion. The delegates were amazed to learn that all this was happening in a country which was coming under increasingly strict Communist rule. They had feared that Romanian Jewry would suffer the same fate as Russian Jewry.

It was clear to them that my words were not propaganda and that my purpose was to do everything to safeguard Romanian Jews. Their surprise and relief were reflected in their spontaneous applause.

10 *My Rabbinical Honeymoon Is Over*

When I returned to Bucharest, I was immediately thrown into my first crisis. The honeymoon period of my Chief Rabbinate had lasted a very short time indeed. The struggle into which I now entered was to last for many years and to cause me much suffering and anxiety. I constantly feared that I would be arrested and made to disappear. But it was a struggle which I could not avoid. It was for the heart and soul of the Jewish people of Romania.

The Romanian Government was now – in the second half of 1948 – firmly in control of the Communists, following pressure by the Soviet Union. This had been applied by Andrei Vishinsky, the chief prosecutor in Stalin's 'purge trials' in the 1930s, when many of the Bolshevik leaders were found guilty of the most ridiculous charges and executed. Vishinsky who had overseen the incorporation of Latvia and Lithuania into the Soviet Union, was now involved in foreign affairs – he was to become Foreign Minister a year later – and spent a great deal of his time in Bucharest.

One of the first measures taken by the Government was to nationalize all schools. Jewish Communists, always more zealous than their gentile comrades, were anxious to go one step further: they sought to destroy every Talmud Torah class in the country. The CDE was established to take over control of the Jewish communities, to install their officials and to dismantle Jewish religious life. The Communists pointed at a paragraph in one of the new laws which stated that the cults were not allowed to have their own separate educational system. Only the state, which gave every citizen freedom of conscience and freedom to be either a believer or an atheist, would be responsible for education. The CDE was similar to the notorious *Jewsectzia*, which had been established in the Soviet Union to terrorize the Russian Jews and to liquidate Jewish religious and national life.

At the same time, the most important 'mission' of the CDE was to 'convince' Jews *not* to go to Israel, to 'unmask' Zionism as a reactionary movement, a 'poisonous weapon' of Anglo–American imperialism, and to spread terror among the Jews. It forced the famous charitable organization, the American Joint Distribution Committee, to stop its noble social work, which helped tens of thousands of Jewish survivors of the Holocaust, and took over all the communities, all the synagogues and every aspect of Jewish life. It organized a network of thousands of its men, paid from the funds of the communities, with the purpose of extinguishing the last Jewish light in Romania.

When I heard of the CDE's announcement, in August 1948, that all Talmud Torah classes were being closed down, I rushed to the Minister of Cults, Stanciu Stoian, and told him that Jewish religious life could not continue without the Talmud Torah. The order attacked the very life-blood of the Jewish community. I was pale with emotion, but the Minister replied that Talmud Torah courses were a matter for the Jewish community. In any case, he had been assured that nobody wanted Talmud Torah classes. He therefore advised me to take my request to the Federation of Jewish Communities. It was not difficult to understand this tactic: it was not the state that was doing away with Talmud Torah classes, but the Jewish leaders themselves!

The CDE began to establish secular schools for Jewish children. The language of tuition was Yiddish. The children learned Romanian history and geography in Yiddish. They could have studied these subjects much more adequately in Romanian. They learned nothing of Jewish history and nothing of the Bible. Jewish parents refused to send their children to such barren schools and kept them at home. After a while, the classrooms became empty and the CDE was forced to close down the schools.

I was anxious to mobilize the Jewish communities throughout the country against the new measures, so it was essential that I should win their full confidence. I felt that there was a certain amount of suspicion against me because I had been elected Chief Rabbi with the approval of the Government and I was a man with a European culture. I sympathized with ordinary Jews who had no notion of the role I was playing. I could not yet tell them openly what the CDE was planning to do and I had to tread carefully so as not to fall into a trap set for me by its leaders. But I had to find a way to save our Talmud Torah classes from final extinction and with them avert the extinction of Jewish life in Romania.

Even before closing down the Talmud Torah courses, the CDE

tried to impose its philosophy on them. I saw a remarkable example of this in September 1948, when I went to Arad, a town which then had 10,000 Jews, some of whom were Orthodox and Chassidim. There was a thriving Chassidic Talmud Torah class with 200 children, who had *payot*, while their *melamdim* (teachers) had beards and wore the traditional Chassidic black garb. I first went to synagogue to demonstrate publicly my determination that the Talmud Torah courses should continue. I then went to attend a class. In the middle of the room was a large photograph of Stalin bedecked with red flags. Anything more incongruous could hardly be imagined. The local representatives of the CDE had forced this ludicrous display on the leaders of the Talmud Torah courses. They had also insisted that the children should learn by heart certain adulatory phrases about Stalin and the Soviet Union. They were also taught about the 'evil-Anglo–American imperialists'.

Just as I entered, I heard the *melamed* testing the children to make sure that their parrot-like answers were satisfactory. How ridiculous these phrases were I was soon to discover.

The *melamed* was asking in Yiddish, 'Children, who is our father?'

'Stalin, Stalin, Stalin,' they replied in chorus.

'And who are our enemies?'

'The Anglo–American imperialists.'

'And who are our friends?'

'The great Soviet Union.'

It was as if the children had learned a song by heart. Looking at their faces, I was certain that they had not the slightest comprehension of the words they were uttering. I did not interrupt the 'play' but, when it was over, I wanted to test their degree of Jewish knowledge.

I went up to a child of about five or six and asked him to translate a passage from the week's *Sidra* (the portion of the Torah read at the Sabbath morning service). The *Sidra* happened to be '*Ki Taitse*' ('When You Go Out to War against Your Enemies'). The child translated the passage adequately, word by word. I then asked him, 'And who are our enemies?'

Unhesitatingly, he replied, 'All the *goyim* [gentiles].' So much for the CDE's ideological inculcation!

For a young Chief Rabbi, who had no special political training and who lacked advisers, the general situation was bewildering and paradoxical. The Soviet Union, which had attacked Zionism as a dangerous, nationalist creed, had astonished the world by voting in favour of the establishment of a Jewish state in Palestine. Stalin encouraged the Czechs to sell arms to the newly emerging Jewish state, which was about to be invaded by several Arab armies. So poorly armed were the Jews that it is doubtful whether they could have held back the Arab onslaught without those weapons. Apparently, the Romanian Government was also told by Stalin to allow the emigration of Romanian Jews to the new state to bolster its army.

To this day, there are arguments about Stalin's precise motives. Some historians claim that his main objective was to undermine Britain's position in the Middle East. As Britain was opposed to the establishment of a Jewish state, Stalin could not resist the chance to join the Americans in an anti-British stand. There is another, less likely view, mentioned by Nahum Goldmann in his autobiography, that Stalin felt sympathy for the plight of the Jewish people, which had lost millions in the Holocaust, and felt it was right to vote for a Jewish state. Whatever the reasons for his support, it did not last long. He soon reverted to his bitter anti-Zionism and anti-Semitism, which threatened the very existence of the millions of Russian Jews. However, while it lasted, Stalin's support for Zionist aims had crucial effects both militarily and diplomatically. It also affected the attitude of the satellite regimes in Eastern Europe.

As I have already mentioned, Romanian Jews, who had suffered so tragically in the Holocaust, were eager to seize the opportunity to start a new life in the new State of Israel. Every week, a ship left Constanṭa for Israel, with a thousand Jews aboard. With their deep religious and Zionist traditions, the great majority of Romanian Jews chose Israel for their new homes, despite the war with the Arabs and despite the hardships they knew they would encounter. Very few, indeed, went to the United States or any other Western country, where conditions were so much easier.

The Zionist and Orthodox Jewish leaders thought only in terms of *aliyah*. They believed that the mass of Romanian Jews could be transported quickly to the Jewish state. They, therefore, did not attach great importance to the anti-religious measures which the Government was pushing forward with the aid of the CDE. The Jewish Communists who occupied high positions in the Government were unhappy about *aliyah*, but they had to accept it as part of government policy. Instead, they sought to keep the Jews in Romania by transforming them into secular Jews with no religious allegiance. These Communist Jews were dangerous for the Jewish community. They were more zealous in propagating their views than the gentiles. Often they would refuse a simple request from the Jewish community for fear of being branded as Jewish nationalists.

Although I, too, was a fervent Zionist and naturally thought of *aliyah*, I felt that as the newly elected Chief Rabbi I had a special, inescapable responsibility for the Romanian Jewish communities. I realized instinctively that many years would elapse before most of the Romanian Jews would be able to leave for Israel. There was always the possibility that *aliyah* would be interrupted, which indeed happened. How could these communities survive if their children ceased to attend Talmud Torah classes, to learn how to pray in their ancient Hebrew language and to learn about their faith? We are still suffering today from the tragedy of these secular schools. Elderly men and women, who were pupils there, come to our synagogues and are unable to pray.

My position at this time was rather paradoxical. The Jewish Communists wanted the Jews to remain in the country, but to become totally assimilated. Therefore, even if they agreed to maintain communities, their final purpose was completely opposed to mine. On the other hand, the Zionists, my natural allies in my struggle for strong communities, saw in this struggle a danger of 'stabilization', a danger for *aliyah*. Every improvement, every concession I obtained was, for them, an impediment to emigration.

In other words, the good Jews were not at all interested in maintaining Jewish institutions. On the contrary, they thought that 'worse means better' (worse in the Diaspora offered better chances for *aliyah* to Israel). My work, they thought, was against their interests.

The truth is that both were wrong. My work over the past forty years has demonstrated that *aliyah* does not mean the destruction of the Diaspora, and that Zionism and Socialism can co-operate with good results for both.

In my loneliness, with very few rabbis willing to give me advice, I also instinctively evolved a method of fighting the CDE. I knew I was opposed by clever men, who would stop at nothing to discredit me, in order to carry out their plan for destroying the religious and cultural life of the Jewish communities. The most powerful man in the CDE, and formally Bacal's superior, was Bercu Feldman, the son of a tailor and a veteran Communist. He was almost illiterate, but he had an innate intelligence. He was always polite to me and frequently smiled, but I quickly realized that he was a dangerous enemy. Bacal, too, pretended to be friendly and to understand my predicament, until there came an open split between us. Later I was able to see documents which revealed how he tried to destroy me. Another important official was Leibovici Şerban, also a lawyer, who had formerly been a left-wing Zionist, but was now a convinced Communist. In the climate of *aliyah* that followed the UN vote in favour of a Jewish state, thousands of Jews held a rally in the main synagogue in Bucharest. Şerban addressed the rally and told everyone to put away their suitcases ('*geamandan*' in Romanian); after that speech, he was known among Romanian Jews as Şerban Geamandan.

How was I to nullify the intricate plans of these men? Feldman was influential in the highest circles of the Communist Party and commanded thousands of agents. The CDE had become supreme in communities throughout the country. It was they who paid the salaries of the rabbis and the *shochetim*, and the Talmud Torah classes were under their control. A direct clash with them would inevitably lead to my defeat. I realized that I had to outwit them, to use effective arguments and to speak directly to the Government.

I went to see the Minister of Cults and told him that I intended to resign from my position as Chief Rabbi in protest against the measures taken against the Talmud Torah courses. The Minister, who was not keen to see a crisis, advised me not to take any precipitate action and invited me to come back shortly afterwards. He then said to me, 'Chief Rabbi, I know that you are a logical man. The Christian Orthodox Church is more powerful than your Judaic cult. Millions of children belong to the Church, yet the Orthodox Church has no religious schools. How can I give you schools which I do not grant to the Church? How can you even consider resigning in such circumstances?'

He looked at me as if he were convinced that he had put forward an unanswerable argument. Indeed, the argument did seem logical. However, I replied, 'Sir, there is a vital difference between a Romanian Jew and a Romanian Christian. A Romanian Christian youth, who has never attended a religious school, can go to church at the age of eighteen, pick up a prayer book, written in his own language, and proceed to pray. He can ask a priest to pray for him. This youth can decide whether he wants to practise his Christian faith or not. Your Government has given him freedom of conscience – to be religious or not. He can make use of this choice. But a Jewish youth, who has not been given the opportunity to attend a Talmud Torah course, has no such choice. If such a youth comes to synagogue at the age of eighteen and opens a Jewish prayer book, he will be completely at a loss. He will not be able to read the words because they are in Hebrew, of which he is totally ignorant. Our rabbis do not undertake to pray for the congregants. Therefore, the youth will not be able to ask a rabbi to recite prayers on his behalf. Such a youth will not be able to practise his Jewish religion. Thus, if you deprive the Jewish community of

Talmud Torah classes, you also deprive the Jews of freedom of conscience.'

The Minister appeared to be impressed by this argument. I considered that while the Talmud Torah courses might be formally forbidden because they contradicted the law against religious schools, the authorities would turn a blind eye to the existing ones. I even took the huge gamble of opening new Talmud Torah classes – dozens of them immediately and hundreds in the years that followed. The CDE, having been outwitted, was furious but impotent, because the Government wanted to avoid a major religious quarrel with the Chief Rabbi at that time. My conflict with the CDE was known to very few people; the communities assumed that I had government permission to maintain the existing Talmud Torah courses and to set up new ones. The CDE, which controlled the communities, refused to grant me money for the new Talmud Torah classes. I, therefore, called meetings of leading members of the communities and asked for donations, which were willingly given. Nobody had the slightest idea that the Chief Rabbi was taking action against the will of the Government.

Astonishingly, Bucharest, with its 150,000 Jews, had only one small Talmud Torah class with ten or fifteen pupils. This fact is symbolic of the degree of assimilation which had befallen the Bucharest Jewish community. However, I was now able to establish no fewer than eighteen more Talmud Torah courses in Bucharest alone, which educated thousands of children. Yet formally these and other Talmud Torah classes were illegal. That was the most incredible paradox of Jewish life in Romania. However, other paradoxes abounded, which I had to deal with.

11

The CDE
Declares War –
Amalia Helps Me

*T*he turning-point for Zionism came in September 1948, with the appearance of a letter by Ilya Ehrenburg, which was published by the Soviet newspaper, *Pravda*. It reopened the campaign against Zionists in the Soviet Union. Inevitably, Romania had to follow suit. Gangs from the CDE went to the offices of the Zionist organizations, smashed windows and carted away their archives. Zionists were accused of being spies and traitors. It was a signal that Stalin was reversing his Middle East policies: Israel was to be designated as an imperialist puppet tied to the United States, while the Arab countries were to be courted. Stalin saw far more benefit for the Soviet Union in such a volte-face. It was a classic example of *Realpolitik*.

Yet while the Zionists were being abused and the campaign against them led by the CDE became increasingly bitter, the Romanian Government, in contrast to the Soviet authorities, still allowed Zionist aims to be fulfilled – a ship continued to leave each week for Haifa, filled with Romanian Jews. One cannot be totally certain of the reasons behind this paradoxical policy. Probably the pressure by Jews to leave for Israel was now so intense that the Government felt that it was impossible to smother it. The Jewish Communists did everything in their power to dissuade Jews from leaving for Israel. Those who had applied for *aliyah* were branded enemies of the people at special public meetings, but the Jews ignored the campaign and insisted on settling in the Jewish state.

It was in this curious atmosphere created by the virulent attacks on Zionism and continuing *aliyah* – two totally contradictory developments – that we welcomed, in January 1949, the arrival of the first Israeli Ambassador to Romania. He was Reuven Rubin, a painter who had been born in Romania and settled in Palestine before the establishment of the state. He was from my *shtetl*, Fălticeni, and we had been good friends, a friendship which we renewed when he came to Bucharest with his wife, Esther (she is now our neighbour in our Tel Aviv home). Their arrival coincided with an intensification of the anti-Zionist campaign. Two months earlier, the Central Committee of the Romanian Party had passed a resolution violently condemning Zionism, clearly at the behest of Stalin, whose agents were installed in every important Romanian government office and it was they who controlled policy. What became known as the 'Stalinist terror' began. People suddenly disappeared and were never heard of again, or only reappeared many years later. Others died in mysterious circumstances.

It thus came as a surprise when, after his arrival, Ambassador Rubin made it known that he intended to visit the Choral Temple the following Sabbath morning. It was the magnificent synagogue at which I had prayed since becoming Chief Rabbi. Posters outside the synagogue announced the Ambassador's visit. The CDE had ample notice of the event and decided to sabotage it. They sent more than 1,000 of their agents to the synagogue early on the Sabbath morning, so that by eight o'clock every seat was occupied by them. Hearing of this invasion, Ambassador Rubin cancelled his visit.

However, unaware of the Ambassador's decision, the agents remained in their seats. Seeing these proclaimed atheists sitting so silently and with such discipline in the synagogue, I could not resist taking some innocent revenge on them. I took out the Scroll of the Law as usual and walked with it down the aisles, encouraging the fake congregants to kiss it. They were startled, but as they had been told to behave like genuine believers, they felt obliged to kiss the Scroll. It was a scene which I, with my sardonic sense of humour, recall with considerable relish.

Learning from his mistake, Ambassador Rubin came to the Choral Temple on the following Sabbath, without any previous announcement. Nobody knew that he intended to be there that morning, and there were only sixty to seventy congregants present when he arrived with his wife. However, the news spread quickly that he was there, and thousands of Jews rushed out of their homes to walk to the synagogue. The streets became so crowded that the trams had to stop for a time. The Jews rushed into the synagogue and filled every seat; soon it was even difficult to find any room to stand. I noticed the excitement and joy on everyone's faces. They strained their necks to be able to catch a glimpse of the Israeli Ambassador. There was an electrifying atmosphere in the synagogue on that historic Sabbath morning.

Caught up myself in this mood of excitement and fulfilment, I called Mr Feigenbaum, the elderly choirmaster, and ordered him to tell the choir to sing the Israeli national anthem, *Hatikvah*, which speaks of the Jewish people never giving up hope, for 2,000 years, of returning to their national home, Eretz Israel. Feigenbaum stared at me in amazement and began to sob, 'Please, Chief Rabbi, don't bring a misfortune on me.' I told him, 'Don't worry. If somebody attacks you, tell him that I gave you the order.' I then went to the Ark and welcomed Ambassador Rubin in Hebrew and Romanian. As soon as I finished, I gave the signal for *Hatikvah* to be sung. Despite his fears, Feigenbaum obeyed me. The choir began singing the anthem and immediately the huge congregation joined in. It was one of the most moving occasions of my life. Many people were in tears, tears of joy. Alas, *Hatikvah* was not to be heard in the Choral Temple for another twenty-three years: it was not sung again until May 1972, when Golda Meir, then Israel's Prime Minister, visited the Choral Temple. She, too, had tears in her eyes.

Deeply moved, I asked myself, *Hatikvah*? Our hope? Where is it?

Suddenly Laurenţiu Bercovici, the secretary of the Bucharest section of the CDE, whom I knew as one of Bercu Feldman's agents, walked up to me and sharply told me that he had an order for me from Feldman to end the service immediately. I replied, 'Tell Mr Feldman that the service will not be cut short. It will continue as usual.'

Bercovici went away, but returned a few minutes later. 'Feldman wants to see you; he is waiting for you in the street,' he said.

'Please tell Feldman that he can come to see me after the prayers,' I responded.

Bercovici left the synagogue again, but returned very quickly. 'I'll tear your beard out!' he hissed at me. Ambassador Rubin, who was sitting next to me, heard this threat and became pale with indignation.

I summoned Berkowitz, the *shammes* (beadle), and told him, 'Please throw this man out of the synagogue.' In full view of the congregation, the *shammes* got hold of Bercovici and escorted him out. Bercovici looked bewildered; he had clearly not expected my reaction as his boss, Feldman, appeared to wield so much power.

After the service, Feldman came to see me and said, 'So, you want to fight us, Chief Rabbi? Don't you know what happened to Cardinal Mindszenty [head of the Catholic Church in Hungary, who was in prison; later, during the Hungarian revolution in 1956, he was granted asylum at the American Embassy in Budapest]? He has eight million people in his Church, but this has not helped him. Whom have you got that you dare to oppose us? Don't be childish. Try to be serious, Chief Rabbi.'

Thus war was declared against me and all the values I stood for. Feldman and his henchmen in the CDE sent men to synagogues all over the country, denouncing *aliyah* and Zionism. The CDE also sought to stop us from singing and dancing in the synagogues on special festive occasions. They argued that a synagogue was like a church, and who had ever heard of singing and dancing in a church? When we celebrated Chanucah, the CDE leaders ordered the congregation to finish their prayers and go home immediately. I stood up and declared, 'A synogogue is not a church. It is a house of learning, of study, of meeting, a *Beit Haknesset*. It is not merely a *Beit Hatfillah*, a house of prayers.' When we refused to leave, the CDE men called the police to eject us, but the police refused to take any action.

And what were we singing? And what were we dancing? From the bottom of our hearts we sang, 'Fear and dread shall fall upon them; by the greatness of thine arm they shall be as still as a stone; till thy people pass over, O Lord, till the people pass over, which thou hast purchased' (Exodus 15:16). On whom shall terror and dread fall? Who is to pass over? Where shall we pass over? The CDE knew the answers very well, but we were shielded by the Bible when we proclaimed, in these words, all our hope to 'pass over' to Eretz Israel.

Members of the staff of the Israeli Embassy came regularly to services at the Choral Temple, and I was happy to see them. However, the CDE told me, 'You must forbid them to come to the synagogue.' I replied indignantly, 'You ask me to forbid Jews to come to synagogue? Never!'

My position as Chief Rabbi became so intolerable, and the attacks on me were so persistent, that I told Feldman and the other leaders of the CDE that I no longer wished to remain in the post. They had usurped all the powers of a Chief Rabbi; they controlled the synagogues and the cemeteries; and they used community funds for their anti-Zionist activities. Thankfully, I was still able to maintain the Talmud Torah classes with funds which I had collected privately.

The CDE and their henchmen in the Federation of Jewish Communities refused to accept my resignation as Chief Rabbi, but they did not explain this refusal. Possibly they feared an unfavourable reaction in government circles if there were a public discussion on the resignation of the Chief Rabbi. More probably, it served their purposes better to have a Chief Rabbi shorn of all power and influence. They also took away my office. The room which I used at the Choral

Temple was now without a table and chair. When I needed to see Leibovici Şerban, I had to wait in a queue with other ordinary people, sometimes for hours.

The purpose was clearly to humiliate me, to break my spirit and to discredit me in the eyes of the Jewish community. But the CDE failed utterly in all its aims. My spirit was not broken. And, far from discrediting me, its attacks on me had the contrary effect. Until the vicious campaign against me was started by the CDE, there was still some suspicion about me because of my collaboration with the Government. There may even have been some people who referred to me as the 'Red Rabbi'. Now every religious and committed Jew realized that I was a genuine leader, prepared to suffer and fight for all the eternal Jewish values, for Zionism and for Talmud Torah courses. The majority of Romanian Jewry was ready to put its trust in me.

One event in 1949 compensated me for much of my suffering and was to give me the strength to continue with my struggles; it also provided me with the counsellor I could turn to in the darkest days. That event was my marriage.

I met my wife, Amalia, during the war, in Bucharest. She was from Suceava, a town some 400 kilometres away from the capital. By being in Bucharest, she avoided deportation to one of the camps. However, her mother and her two sisters were deported to Transnistria by the Romanian authorities. Her mother was put in a room with twenty-four other people, at Moghilev, in the Ukraine. All the Jews suffered from hunger and disease. Amalia tried desperately to help her mother by selling her coat and watch to buy medicines for her. She then had to bribe a Romanian officer to take the medicines to her, not knowing for certain whether he would honestly fulfil his promise. Other men, who had undertaken to deliver medicines and received money, had sold them for their own profit. However, Amalia had no alternative but to take the risk. She was a lawyer by profession, but was not allowed to practise because all Jewish lawyers were banned. She was, therefore, obliged to become a teacher at a Jewish school in Bucharest and received a small salary. But she still insisted on sending money to her mother and sisters, to enable them to survive. As a result, she herself often went hungry. Her efforts on behalf of her mother proved unavailing: she died of hunger and disease.

Highly cultured and of noble character, Amalia had been educated in the spirit of Judaism by her father, Mayer Ruckenstein, who built his own synagogue, Vijnitzer Klaus, in Burdujeni. She had studied at

Cernăuţi and had passed her law exams brilliantly. She had also attended the faculty of Beaux Arts under the guidance of Professor Tzigara Samurças.

When I first met Amalia it was impossible for us to get married. For four years I was pursued by the police, certainly ineptly, but I could never establish a permanent home with a wife. After the liberation, I was involved in the intense work of rebuilding the shattered communities. There was the additional question of whether I would remain in Romania. My sister, who was living in Glasgow, was angry at my remaining and urged me to leave; she even sent me an entry visa for one of the South American countries. Then came my election as Chief Rabbi and the turmoil into which I was thrown. It was only in 1949 that I was able to ask Amalia to marry me. She became more than a partner in my work: she inspired and encouraged me.

Another person might have expressed fears and even dread of danger. For years it appeared inevitable that our lives would end in catastrophe, and it was against all logic that we should escape unharmed. Had she been a different person, Amalia might have said to me, 'Please don't place me in such a dreadful situation.' But, on the contrary, she showed incredible courage and coolness in the most dangerous and tense situations. She understood from the very first moment of our life together that it was my inescapable duty to act the way I did, even if it meant imprisonment and death. She dedicated her whole life to the vital work of helping the poor, the elderly and the sick, going daily to their homes, giving them not only money but also good advice and encouragement.

If there is any merit in what I have achieved, it is as much due to Amalia as to me. With her wisdom and courage, with her wonderful will to do good to simple people in need, with her unlimited capacity for self-sacrifice, she has been my help, my inspiration and my leading adviser.

12 *Ana Pauker Defends My Father's Coffin*

The renowned Vishnitzer Rebbe, Rabbi Israel Hager, was buried in Oradea. He had thousands of Chassidic followers, who were anxious to transfer his remains to Israel. In January 1950, they approached me and I managed to obtain the approval of the authorities for the transfer. The coffin, with the remains of the Rabbi, was duly taken to Constanţa to be put on a ship bound for Israel.

A few minutes before the Sabbath, Rabbi Yitzhak Friedman of Bohuşi unexpectedly arrived at my house. He amazed me by saying that, just as the ship was about to sail, an order was given for the coffin to be removed. A charge was being made that it contained not only the remains of the Rebbe, but gold and dollars which the Jews intended to smuggle out of the country. Policemen boarded the ship and, while the Vishnitzer Chassidim looked on in consternation, they took the coffin and transported it to a cellar in a building in the port.

This was such an appalling accusation, which could affect the welfare of the whole of the Romanian Jewish community, that I felt that, even though the Sabbath had begun, I had to appeal directly to Ana Pauker, the Foreign Minister, a powerful figure in the Government. I suspected that a plot had been concocted by some secret police agents with the aim of discrediting Jews in general and me in particular. I also thought that the CDE was not innocent in this affair.

Ana Pauker was one of the most remarkable women in modern European history. Some people saw a resemblance between her and Golda Meir. Both were solidly built; both had plain, expressive faces; and neither had much or any use for cosmetics. They wore severe, practical clothing, with hair styles to match. Both were highly efficient and dedicated to their tasks. But the comparison should not be taken too far. Golda was as fierce a fighter for her beliefs as Ana, but she had the extra qualities of kindness and humour which made her a beloved

DANGERS, TESTS AND MIRACLES

figure in Israel. Though I believe that great injustice has been done in the assessments of Ana, she could never be described as a person whom the population loved; but she was respected.

Ana was the daughter of a kosher butcher, Hershel Rabinsohn, and she inherited some of his characteristics. He was a fighter for various causes. He fought against the rabbinate, but not because he was in any way irreligious. On the contrary, he accused the Bucharest rabbinate of not doing enough for Jewish religious life. Ironically, his daughter became a fervent atheist. Her early life gave no clue to her later career. Influenced by her father, she became a Hebrew teacher in a Jewish school called Zion in Bucharest. She fell in love with a young Jew, Steinberg, who later established the famous Jewish library, Hasefer. Despite his avowed love for Ana, Steinberg married another girl, the daughter of Rabbi Dr Beck. Ana's distress was so great that she decided to leave her home and country. She went to Paris, where she met and married Marcel Pauker, a Jewish Communist. She, too, became a passionate Communist.

By order of the party, she returned to Romania, secretly and illegally, and organized and ran a Communist cell. She became a well-known figure in the Comintern, the Communist International. However, in 1933, she was arrested and sentenced to several years' imprisonment. By coincidence, her husband was also arrested – but by Russian Communists. He had decided to visit the Soviet Union during the period of the Soviet 'show trials', when Stalin liquidated the old Bolshevik leaders, as well as many thousands of other innocent people. Marcel was accused of being a Western spy and saboteur. When she heard of her husband's arrest and execution, Ana did not protest. She believed that he must have been guilty of all the crimes with which he was charged. Her belief in Stalin was so great that she could not conceive of him being wrong in any action he took. In her eyes, Stalin was infallible.

When the Russians occupied Romanian Bessarabia in 1940, they arrested the local authorities in Kishinev. They told the Romanian Government that they would only release them if Ana Pauker were freed. The Government accepted the offer and Ana was set free. She immediately left for Moscow, where she was invited to the Kremlin by Stalin. They became firm friends.

After the Romanian victory over the Germans, Ana returned to Bucharest and became the most powerful figure in the Communist Party. She was not formally given the post of leader only because of the anti-Semitism which was still widely prevalent in the country. When, later, the Communists took over the Government, Ana became Foreign Minister, but this post hid her real power – hers was the most influential voice in the country. David Ben-Gurion, the Israeli leader and Prime Minister, described her as 'The Empress of Romania'.

It was thus logical that I should want to appeal to her in my despair over the terrible accusation concerning the Rabbi's coffin. But I could never have got in touch with her had it not been for her brother, Zalman Rabinsohn, of whom I will speak later. In total contrast to Ana, he was a fervent Zionist and extremely religious, yet Zalman and Ana loved and respected each other. And Zalman was eager to help his fellow Jews and the Zionist cause.

When I told him of the situation, he immediately went to see Ana. Her door was always open to him, day and night. She listened carefully and then said, 'The public has to be given an account of this matter. The coffin must be opened to see whether the charge that it contains foreign currency and gold is well-founded.'

I feared that the security agents would put dollars into the coffin while it was being opened in order to substantiate their claim. I realized that they would not be so foolish as to open it secretly and to introduce false evidence. The coffin was well-secured and it would be obvious that it had been tampered with.

With this in mind, I therefore sent the following message to Ana: 'If government agents open the coffin and claim that they have found dollars inside, no one will believe them. If nobody else is there to represent the Jewish community, people will say that the Government itself put the dollars into the coffin. I myself am prepared to travel to Constanţa and witness the opening. If dollars are found inside, I would certify a document to that effect.'

My offer was accepted by Ana. On Saturday evening I travelled to Constanţa, where I was met by a group of people, including a Jewish woman Communist who remarked, 'I would be happy if they found gold and dollars in the coffin.' Outraged, I said to her furiously, 'You would be glad, you a leader of the Jewish community, to see a disaster befall the Jews!' After this, she remained silent, but not for long.

We were met by a Romanian general, who asked me what procedure we should adopt for opening the coffin. He explained that it had now been taken to a synagogue. I proposed that we should all go there immediately, but I stipulated that only Jews should do the work as this was the coffin of a holy Jewish sage and it was right that only Jews should touch his coffin and remains; he and the other gentiles could watch, but must not touch anything. The general did not protest, but the Jewish woman Communist exclaimed indignantly, pointing her finger at me, 'This man is a racist! He is making distinctions between Jews and non-Jews. Why shouldn't non-Jews touch the coffin? Are they impure?'

I replied, 'The best proof that we are not racists is that you, too, though Jewish, will not be allowed to open the coffin. Only *Shomrei Shabbat* [observers of the Sabbath] will do so! Our "discrimination" is not between Jews and non-Jews, but between observers of our religion and non-observers.'

Thus, while the general and other gentiles, as well as non-observant Jewish Communists, stood and watched, I, the rabbi of Constanţa, Rabbi Joseph Chaim Shechter, and other observant Jews struggled to open the coffin. It took us some time to remove the lid. Inside were the holy Rabbi's remains, but there was no sign of any dollars or gold. What we and the observers saw were hundreds of notes, *kvitlach* (brief requests written on paper), addressed to the Rabbi, beseeching him to intercede in heaven on the writers' behalf: they pleaded for good health, good fortune, the chance to emigrate to Israel, etc.

Having satisfied themselves that a false accusation had been made, the general and the Jewish Communists allowed us to close the coffin. Embarrassed, they slunk away silently. With joy in our hearts, we lit candles and recited prayers. Within days, the coffin was put on a ship sailing to Haifa. There it was met by the Rabbi's son, Rabbi Chaim Meir Hager, who had been in touch with me and knew of the opening of the coffin. We all heaved an immense sigh of relief.

However, I was to undergo a similar experience eighteen months later. In October 1951, my revered father died, at the age of eighty-two, on the second day of Rosh Hashanah. He had expressed a wish that his body should be taken to Israel. His wish was known, but few people believed that, at the height of the anti-Zionist campaign and of Stalinist terror, it could be fulfilled. For the Chief Rabbi to send the body of his father to Israel would be seen as a particularly provocative action against the authorities. Surely I could not possibly dare to do such a thing because the consequences might be very serious for me and my family.

However, my reverence and love for my father was such that I yearned to fulfil his last wish. I did not consider the risks. I mentioned my desire to Philip Rothenberg, a Communist, but a good Jew, who came to see me after I had sat *shivah* (seven days of mourning). He told me that he would help me. He got in touch with the director of

Customs and Excise and informed him that he wanted to send a body to Israel. Surprisingly, the director replied, 'Why not? You can send the body as a package.'

On hearing this almost unbelievable news, I told the director that nobody must know of the plan. It must be kept a secret. He agreed to this. However, he still had to get the formal approval of the Ministry of Health and the police. To my great relief and surprise, he obtained the necessary certificates. Despite all the formal approvals (from the Ministry of Health, the Ministry of Internal Affairs and the Ministry of Foreign Trade and Customs), I knew very well that the greatest danger to this operation was from the CDE with its agents in the community. Hence the need to keep everything strictly secret so that the leaders of the CDE would be faced with a *fait accompli*. Otherwise they would not tolerate it.

Two months after my father's death, the guardian of the main cemetery was astonished to see me arriving early one morning in the company of several rabbis. His amazement increased when I told him that we intended to remove my father's coffin. He began to protest, but when I showed him the official documents, duly signed, his resistance collapsed, though not his surprise.

However, after removing the coffin from the cemetery, I still had a major obstacle to overcome. If the CDE leaders learned at the last moment that I was sending my father's body to Israel, they would do everything possible to prevent it. So far they had been kept completely in the dark about my intentions, but now it seemed almost certain that they would hear about my plan. The cemetery guardian was bound to telephone the leaders of the community and tell them about my visit. I would then be accused of trying to trick the Government. The outcry against me would be horrendous.

In desperation, I rushed to see the president of the Bucharest community, Leon Stern. I had to take the risk, as there was no other way out. I knew, of course, that he was a Communist, but I felt that, in his heart, he was still a good Jew. When I told him what I was about to do, he shook with alarm and agitation. He exclaimed that he would have to inform the CDE. I begged him to help me. I told him that I was certain he was a good Jew and would not harm his Chief Rabbi, who wanted to fulfil his father's last wish.

After my fervent appeal, the man stood silent and irresolute. I reminded him that the CDE was meeting that morning and there was a strict rule that no telephone call was to be answered until ten o'clock. I said to Stern that if the cemetery guardian rang him about the removal of the body, he was to reply that he would come immediately to see what was happening. By the time he arrived at the cemetery, carried out an investigation and telephoned the CDE, my father's body would already be on a train bound for Constanţa.

Stern, pale and distraught, agreed to my suggestions. He acted heroically. He must have realized that he was risking his position, if not his life. Afterwards the CDE suspected that he had collaborated with me, but they had no proof. When he died in 1981, I delivered a sermon in his honour and revealed his brave deed.

When the CDE leaders heard about the removal of my father's body, they accused me of having stolen it. I arranged with a reliable man to accompany the coffin to Constanţa and to inform me immediately of any problem that might arise. The coffin duly arrived in Constanţa and was put on the ship sailing for Haifa. However, the next day – the first day of Kislev 5712 (December 1951) – just as the ship was due to leave, the police boarded it and took the coffin away, claiming that there were dollars and gold inside it. My man in Constanţa rang me up to tell me what had happened. It was 5 p.m. and the ship was to leave for Israel two hours later.

When I heard the news, I felt faint and on the verge of collapse. I remembered, of course, what had happened to the coffin of the Vishnitzer Rebbe and I feared that this time the ending would be less happy as the security agents had probably learned their lesson. I was sure that the authorities would open the coffin before I could get to Constanţa. They would take advantage of the fact that I could not accompany it, as that would have attracted the attention of the CDE.

I rushed in great alarm to Zalman Rabinsohn and pleaded with him to intercede again with Ana Pauker. He immediately agreed to do so. Ana told him that she knew that the accusation was false, but that it was essential to open the coffin so that the truth of the matter should be known to all. When Zalman told me of his sister's decision, I protested strongly that the ship was due to leave for Haifa within the hour and the coffin would have to remain in the harbour for a week, when another ship sailed. Zalman ran back to Ana to give her this information. Ana thought for a few seconds and then sent an order to Constanţa for the ship's departure to be delayed while the coffin was searched. The ship remained in port overnight. The 1,000 passengers had no notion of the cause. The coffin was opened by Jews in the presence of the authorities and no dollars or gold were found. The coffin was then closed, sealed and put back on board the ship, which sailed immediately. The Chief Rabbi of Israel, Isaac Herzog, Rabbi

Chaim Meir Hager and other dignitaries were waiting in Haifa. They participated in the funeral ceremony at the Sanhedrin Cemetery in Jerusalem.

There was an intriguing sequel. Bercu Feldman knew all about the accusation concerning the alleged presence of gold and dollars in my father's coffin and that the latter had been removed from the ship, but he did not know that Ana Pauker had ordered the sailing of the ship to be delayed. He believed that the coffin was still in Constanţa.

He came to see me and, in a revoltingly hypocritical voice, said, 'Chief Rabbi, why did you make such a secret of your wish to send your father's body to Israel? If you had told me I would have helped you.'

'Thank you,' I replied, hardly able to stop myself from smiling. 'If I have a similar problem in the future, I will certainly ask for your help. I am glad to know that you don't think I did anything wrong.'

'Of course not. It was a perfectly natural thing to do. You wanted to fulfil your father's last wishes. Why not?'

Coming from the man who had led the campaign against me and accused me of theft when he heard of the removal of my father's body, this statement reached new heights of hypocrisy. He was inwardly enjoying what he thought was his moment of triumph over me. He probably assumed that, even if no gold and dollars were found in the coffin, the authorities would forbid it to be sent to Israel and I would be discredited as well as disconsolate. The CDE had, at long last, got the better of me! A few hours later, Feldman heard that the ship had been delayed and that it was now carrying my father's coffin to Israel. I did not need anyone to describe to me his shock, consternation and fury. I must admit that his reaction to the news can still make me smile today.

Strangely enough, my first meeting with Ana Pauker was also connected with a corpse and took place at a cemetery. It threw some light on Ana's character. She had a sister, who had also become a Communist and who, during the war, had fled to the Carpathian Mountains, where she had died. After I became Chief Rabbi in 1948, I was asked to go to the Jewish cemetery in Bucharest and told that Ana had ordered the remains of her sister to be brought there for burial. I saw Ana enter the cemetery and speak to David Schiffer, the president of the burial society, *Chevra Kadisha*. Schiffer then came up to me and said, 'There is to be no religious service at this funeral. That is Ana Pauker's order.'

I told him, 'If she does not want a religious service, she must take the body to the crematorium.'

He looked thoroughly startled. In a trembling voice, he replied, 'Chief Rabbi, do you realize what you are doing? I have received an order from Ana Pauker!'

Overhearing some of these words and noticing his distress, Ana approached us and asked me what was the matter. I answered bluntly, 'Madam, I don't want to upset you, but I must point out that whoever comes to this cemetery must respect our laws. To bring a body here without having observed the ritual rules is a profanation of our laws. If you are unwilling to accept them, you can take the body to a crematorium, or you can open a special cemetery for atheists. However, I am prepared to make a concession in your case. I will not give any sermon and the cantor will not wear any vestment at the burial. But *tahara* [sanctifying the body] must take place and *Kaddish* must be recited at the graveside.'

Ana Pauker, the most powerful person in the country, who could have insisted on her wishes being carried out, accepted my conditions. After the burial, she said to me, 'I did not object to my mother having a religious funeral because she was religious, but my sister was an atheist.' I again suggested to Ana that she should consider opening a cemetery for atheists. She never took my advice.

However, after Ana's acceptance of my ruling, no Jewish Communist ever dared to demand a non-religious funeral service.

Ironically, when Israel Bacal, one of the leaders of the CDE who conducted the whole anti-religious campaign, died in 1960, his body had to 'suffer' a religious funeral. I myself gave the sermon.

13   'Enemy of the People'

When we celebrated Chanucah in December 1951, I gave an address in the Choral Temple in the presence of the Israeli Ambassador. In it, I criticized the American Government for its attitude to peace during that period of the Cold War. At the time two American secret agents were reported to have been parachuted on to the mountains in Transylvania with the apparent objective of spying. They were discovered, tried, sentenced to death and executed. This incident added to the Cold War tension. However, the CDE leaders were furious because I had not criticized Israel but, on the contrary, had welcomed the Israeli Ambassador.

On the following day, Feldman telephoned me and said angrily, 'Last night you again bowed to the imperialists. You flattered the spies of the Israeli Embassy. You will meet the same fate as the American spies.'

'You are crazy,' I told him, heatedly. 'Go to hospital for treatment!' and I banged down the receiver.

Within days I realized that Feldman's threats signalled the CDE's new effort not merely to remove me from my post but to have me arrested and, possibly, executed. The Minister of Cults remarked to me, 'Chief Rabbi, you are in danger of losing your head.' The removal of my father's body had brought my conflict with the CDE into the open. Everybody in the Jewish and even non-Jewish circles commented on my gesture, interpreting it as a clear demonstration of my love of Zion. The decision to punish me, to cut off my head, was taken, but not for the sin of sending my father's coffin to Israel. They were on the look-out for another 'sin': the Chanucah sermon was what they were waiting for.

I knew that before the CDE could achieve their aim, they had to 'unmask' me. I had to be shown to be an 'enemy of the people'. This had become the normal system in Romania for destroying somebody. In my case, the unmasking had to take place in three stages: the first at a meeting of the Bucharest Jewish community, where I was the Chief Rabbi; the second at a meeting of the Presidium of the Federation of Jewish Communities throughout the country; and the third at a series of public meetings at which the 'masses' of 'honest Jews and good patriots' were to 'unmask' me, before I was sentenced to imprisonment or made to disappear for ever.

The Communist leaders of the Bucharest community first met privately to establish the precise form of the accusation against me and what each one of the members should say about my conduct. They quickly decided that I should be accused of three offences: that I was an opportunist, a flatterer and an enemy of the people. The first two charges were serious and dangerous, but comparatively innocuous. The third one was fatal; if found guilty, I would inevitably be arrested or would 'disappear'. Such a decision against the Chief Rabbi could not be made without the approval of the highest party leaders. Apparently, my fate was sealed.

Next day I was summoned to attend a meeting of the Bucharest community leaders. I looked at those fifteen fanatics and realized how much they hated me and wanted to destroy me. I was in their way. With me in prison, they could carry out their scheme to destroy all the religious and cultural life of the Jewish community. They might even be able to frighten the Jews into no longer demanding to go to Israel. At long last, they believed that they had cornered me and had the Government's full backing to charge me with being an 'enemy of the people' and, therefore, ripe for liquidation. But once again they were in for an unpleasant surprise. They had decided my 'Endlösung', my 'final solution', but God in Heaven again decided otherwise.

The meeting had all the appearance of a trial: I was the accused and the fifteen CDE leaders were the accusers, as well as the judges. One man began to speak against me, and then another. Each accused me of being an opportunist and a flatterer. I was waiting for the dreaded words 'enemy of the people' to be uttered, but they did not come. Then the vice-president of the Bucharest community, Morel Farchy, who was not known for his intelligence, rose to speak and almost immediately described me as an 'enemy'. As he did so, I noticed the look of consternation on the faces of the other leaders, particularly the president, Stern. Some crucial event had occurred, a decisive intervention, perhaps, of which I was not aware. It was a critical and dramatic moment. I was possibly misreading their attitude, but I had to test the situation immediately. I rose to my feet and said sternly, 'This man·has described me as an enemy of the people. If he does not apologize, I will not continue to take part in the discussion.'

Stern stared at Farchy with contempt. It was the look of a teacher about to castigate a particularly stupid child. He then apologized to me for the epithet. I learned later that the Government, having been informed of the meeting, had ordered at the last moment that I should not be described as an 'enemy'. (Farchy had participated the day before in the 'dress-rehearsal', when the word 'enemy' had been given as a slogan; he had forgotten that this accusation had been withdrawn and had, therefore, repeated it at the meeting.)

I realized that I had won that particular tussle with the CDE. I proceeded to reprove the leaders, while they listened sheepishly to me. I questioned their right to judge me. I pointed out that it was ludicrous to describe me as an opportunist and a flatterer. Had I been such a person, I would have hidden my true beliefs and pretended, like so many others, that a new political faith had superseded my religious convictions and I would have accepted all the demands made on me to break up the Jewish communities. I, however, was continually placing myself in great danger by refusing to accept opportunistic offers. It was they, not I, who were opportunists.

Three days later, a second attempt to 'unmask' me was made at the meeting of the Presidium of the Federation. My courage had increased in the meantime, since I felt that 'somebody' was opposing my 'decapitation'. Despite the fact that I was surrounded by secret agents and considered as a 'man liable to be liquidated', despite the hatred against me, 'somebody' seemed to think that 'it was too early' and that my exposure as an 'enemy' must wait for another political moment.

In the Presidium meeting of the Federation, I analysed the word 'opportunist'. It refers to a person who changes his mind according to changing circumstances. I gave as examples the members of the Presidium, one after the other. Tiberiu Reny, the president (from Arad), a former banker, was now a Communist; Yitzhak Friedman, once a rabbi and the son of the Bohuşi Rebbe, was now an atheist, an anti-Zionist and a Communist; Streissfeld, who had been Dr Filderman's secretary before the war, was now 'exposing' his boss; etc. In my speech, I truly 'unmasked' all these people – genuine opportunists – and I concluded by reminding them that previously, when they had held important positions, I was in prison and in a concentration camp. Therefore, who was guilty of opportunism?

Them or me? The CDE leaders were so stunned that no one answered me. The meeting ended in total confusion.

Yet I knew perfectly well that this was not the end of my struggle with the CDE. Even though the dreaded word 'enemy' had not been used against me, I knew that it had been considered and only a last-minute intervention by the Prime Minister had saved my life. I did not know why I had been reprieved. So great was the bitterness of the CDE against me that the charge might be renewed at any moment, and I could never be certain that there would be another government intercession in my favour. Moreover, anyone who had been tarred with the word 'enemy', even if the charge were withdrawn, could never be certain that he would not be arrested or made to 'disappear'.

After one of my attempted resignations, Feldman invited me to see him. 'Chief Rabbi,' he said, 'you speak about resigning. Do you really think that this is possible? Can you imagine yourself walking in the street and somebody asking, "Who is this man?", and somebody else answering, "He's the former Chief Rabbi of Romania." Such a thing is not possible in our country. Instead you will have to disappear.'

Let me now make the following remark. It was clear to the CDE and to me that my fate was virtually sealed and that my 'execution' was only a matter of time. My survival, if somebody who does not believe in miracles wants a logical explanation, is due to these successive 'postponements'.

The campaign against emigration to Israel was intensified. One day, a large poster appeared outside the door of the president of the community, which read: 'Zionism is the poisonous arm of Anglo–American imperialism, to take the Jews out of the Socialist camp and place them in the capitalist camp.' While pursuing their curious two-faced policy of allowing emigration and, at the same time, allowing campaigns against it, the Government still believed that the CDE would be able to persuade the Jews to remain.

The difficult economic and social situation in Israel appeared to provide the CDE with powerful arguments against emigration to the Jewish state. There were not enough houses for the thousands of immigrants who were arriving from Europe and the Middle East. They were put in *maabarot* (special camps of huts and tents), and suffered from heat in the summer and cold in the winter.

There was a famous joke about David Ben-Gurion arriving in Haifa port and asking old and crippled immigrants from Romania, 'Why have you come?' 'We have come to die here,' was their reply. '*Nu,*' Ben-Gurion is supposed to have responded, 'what are you waiting for?'

It is true that the Romanian authorities did send many elderly people to Israel at that time, but large numbers of middle-aged parents had also gone. They were eager for their children to join them. Children also frequently went first and anxiously awaited their parents. Thus families were divided and apprehensive. Hopes for a quick reunification were not always fulfilled. Jews were not discouraged from applying to leave for Israel despite the harsh economic situation there. Their eagerness to live in a Jewish state was such that they were prepared to endure every hardship.

The pressure for *aliyah* was increasing, despite all the difficulties. For religious reasons, for national reasons, for family reasons and for economic reasons, people remained firm in their determination to go to Israel.

Moreover, the economic situation of Romanian Jews suddenly deteriorated catastrophically. The nationalization measures taken by the Government hit all sections of the Romanian population, but the Jews, who depended largely for their living on retail trade, were particularly affected. First the authorities confiscated a large amount of money from the community. The money which Jews retained became almost valueless overnight because of devaluation. Goods were taken away from the shops, and many Jews faced destitution and starvation. The clamour for emigration to Israel increased. The attempts by the CDE to stem the tide were doomed to failure. The Government did not want to face demonstrations by thousands of desperate Jews, anxious to leave. So the ships kept sailing from Constanţa to Haifa and the prisons were filled with increasing numbers of Zionists. This was a bankrupt, illogical policy, but it would take many years yet before the Romanian Government realized it – years of struggle, danger and argument.

14   *A Saint in Our Midst*

Zalman Rabinsohn, Ana Pauker's brother, played a unique role in helping Romanian Jews in their agony. He can be considered a *Lamed Vuvnik*, one of the thirty-six righteous men on whom, according to Jewish legend, the existence of the universe depends. He had a thin, ascetic face and figure. He took no interest in his personal appearance and wore shoddy clothing, but he was a man of high culture and intelligence. In 1944, he had settled in Israel, together with his wife and children, but decided to return to Romania when he heard of the plight of Romanian Jews. He knew that his sister had become a powerful figure in the country and clearly hoped to influence her for the good of his people.

No two people could have held more different views than Zalman and Ana – he a deeply religious Jew and a staunch Zionist, she a convinced Communist and atheist. Yet they had a profound love and respect for each other. They recognized that, in their different ways, they were idealists. When Zalman first came to her house, Ana embraced and kissed him and said to him in Yiddish, 'Zalman, you have come home.' To this he replied, 'Home is Israel, not here.'

Ana provided Zalman with an apartment in the residential district in which she herself lived, and he was known in the area as 'Comrade Solomon'. But he made no concessions whatsoever to her policies, nor did he fear that he might embarrass her. The Communists were known to be against Talmud Torah courses, but Zalman, who was a considerable Hebrew scholar, became a *melamed* at the Emunah Synagogue Talmud Torah. He took children, sat down with them and began to teach them. I was the second *melamed* at this Talmud Torah. When parents heard that the Chief Rabbi and Ana Pauker's brother were teaching at a Talmud Torah, it had an electrifying effect on them. The number of pupils increased enormously. The CDE was afraid to take action against Ana Pauker's brother.

Zalman was a follower of the Bohuşi Rebbe, Rabbi Yitzhak Friedman. At first he did not come to see me as he suspected me of being close to the Communist Party. But he gradually began to show confidence in me and to visit me regularly. I could never discover what he was thinking. He would hardly say a word. He would listen silently as I told him of the tribulations of the Jewish community and write down the details in pencil. He would then get up, say 'Shalom' and leave. He never mentioned his sister's name, but more than once I noticed that some community problem had been solved after his visit.

Zalman was a man of amazing courage. When the Romanian authorities arrested the Zionist leadership on 10 July 1950, Zalman was outraged. He heard that the Romanian leaders, whom he knew well, as he had met them at his sister's house, were having a meeting with her. He burst into the room where they had assembled, holding a piece of paper. The startled leaders asked him what he wanted. 'I have a written request to make,' he replied. 'You have arrested the heads of the Zionist organizations. I am a Zionist. Please arrest me too.' The Communist leaders burst out laughing. They found his intervention highly amusing and even attempted to exchange jokes with him. They could not believe that he was being serious. They allowed him to leave the room – but, two and a half years later, they were to approve his request and send him to prison.

It was not always possible for Zalman to help us, though he tried hard. Before every Passover, I visited the Ministry of the Interior and requested *matzoth* for the Jews in the various prisons which were filled at the time with people accused of political and economic crimes, some of whom were allegedly 'black marketeers'. In reply to a request to the Minister, I was told to come to his office at eleven o'clock in the morning, which I did, punctually, but the gate was closed. I waited in the rain for an hour before an officer arrived and asked me to follow him. He led me to a small room and told me to wait. It was bare, except for a table and chair. I waited for several hours, but nobody came to call me. At five o'clock in the afternoon, a soldier appeared and told me that I was to pick up the telephone receiver in another room. As I did so, I heard the voice of the Minister's principal secretary, Colonel Dulgheru, a Jew, who said to me curtly, 'We know why you have come. You can go home.' He then hung up.

Arriving home in the evening, I found my wife greatly alarmed. She was sure that they had already arrested me.

I turned to Zalman for help. I grieved for the Jewish prisoners who suffered acutely if they were not provided with *matzoth* on Passover.

He immediately spoke to Ana, but she replied angrily, 'What does the Chief Rabbi think? Does he believe he can use you to obtain *protekzia* [unfair influence]. We have already given him an answer. Tell him not to intercede again through you. It will do him no good.'

Although that year (1950) I was unable to obtain extra *matzoth* despite Zalman's intervention, the concessions which we obtained through him were numerous. The Bohuși Rebbe said of Zalman, 'He is our telephone to the Kominform.'

He never accepted an invitation to dinner, either from me or from the Bohuși Rebbe. At Succot, when it is forbidden to eat except in a *succah* (tent), he used to come daily to the *succah* of the Yeshua Tova Synagogue in Atena Street to eat something. The president of the synagogue, Joseph Feuerstein, told me that, during the seven days of the festival, Zalman's daily meal was no more than one tin of sardines.

There was a mystery about Zalman. We never saw him put a piece of food in his mouth. He appeared to be fasting all the time. We were startled to see how thin and weak he looked. One morning there was a commotion near the Choral Temple and I was told that the security police were requesting a *tallith* and *tefillin* (phylacteries). Amazed at such a request, I contacted the police and was told that Zalman had collapsed in the street from lack of food. He had been taken to hospital where, on regaining consciousness, his first words were, 'Please give me a *tallith* and *tefillin*.'

Alas, Zalman did not receive the rewards he deserved for his heroic conduct. On the contrary, he was to suffer much both in Romania and Israel. When his sister was deposed in 1952, Zalman was shunned by those who previously sought his company. Ana had been declared an enemy of the people and it was considered dangerous to have any contacts with a person so close to her. He continued to visit my home, still saying very little, but one evening he suddenly broke down and wept. He said to me, 'I know I will be arrested. What will happen to my family? You were right to advise me not to bring them from Israel to Bucharest. Nobody wants to receive them.'

I had indeed advised Zalman not to bring his wife and daughter to Romania. I had heard that he was being urged to do so and wondered what the motive was. I was sure that the presence of members of his family would cause him problems and would lessen his independence. He had not followed my advice, but this was no time for any recrimination, even of the mildest form. I called my wife into the room and we both assured Zalman that we would do everything possible for his family. We would never abandon them.

We did not attempt to convince him that his fears of imprisonment were ill-founded. We knew only too well that he might be arrested any day. Yet when it happened, I felt shattered, as did my wife. Zalman had sacrificed himself for the Jewish people and I had promised to help him and his wife and daughter. Yet what could I and my wife actually do? I, too, faced possible arrest. And I was earning only 3,000 lei (about $300) a month. With this sum I had to keep up my ailing mother's house and my own.

I felt conscience-stricken, but my wife and I knew that we must do everything possible to help Zalman's family and to keep in touch with them. We invited his wife and daughter to our house and told them, 'Don't worry. Your husband and father is a hero. He is suffering not because he has done anything wrong, but because he has sacrificed himself for his fellow Jews. It is our duty to help you.'

We decided to give them 1,000 lei from my salary, but I warned them not to approach the Israeli Embassy for any money, for they could then be accused of spying for the Embassy. 'You will be followed by agents of the Romanian Government,' I warned Zalman's wife. 'They will check your expenditure. If they ask you what you have spent, tell them the truth. The truth is less dangerous than what they will believe.' However, she did not always follow my advice.

The daughter, a proud girl, refused to accept any money from us. 'Do you think we are beggars?' she asked. We were in a quandary about what to do, but my wife, as usual, came up with a solution. She suggested that the girl give her Hebrew lessons, for which she would be paid. The suggestion was willingly accepted and she came regularly to our house. It was indeed a gratifying solution for both my wife and the girl.

Shortly before Zalman was arrested, the Sculener Rebbe, Rabbi Zisse Portugal, Rabbi Friedman and I wrote a letter to Moshe Sharett, the Israeli Foreign Minister. We stressed that Israel's policy of alignment with the United States was putting the Jews in Romania in mortal danger and we pleaded with him to change this policy. This was undoubtedly a very naive letter – none of us was a politician – but we felt desperate. The knife appeared to be at the throats of Romanian Jews, and we felt that it was our duty to tell the Israelis in what danger they were placing us.

I gave the letter to Zalman to pass on to the Israeli Embassy for transmission to Israel. Proving fearless as usual, Zalman went to the Embassy and handed the letter over. Any other Romanian Jew would have been arrested immediately by the numerous agents who surrounded the Embassy. However, they knew Zalman by sight and they were reluctant to stop him without a specific order.

Two months after Zalman's arrest (on the night of 30 April 1953), his wife came to my house in tears. In her hands was a letter, in Hebrew, written by Zalman. She explained that a woman had come to her house, told her that she was a doctor at the prison where Zalman was being held, handed over the letter and asked for an answer. The letter, addressed to me, read, 'I must tell you that I have confessed everything about the letter to Moshe Sharett. Don't deny it, because it is too late.'

It was undeniably written by Zalman and bore his signature. I was dumbfounded. Many questions raced through my mind, including how the authorities had made Zalman confess. This was a very serious development. Linking me with the Embassy and with Ana through her brother could prove a deadly accusation. But why did somebody use this roundabout way of informing me that the letter to Sharett had been discovered? I was mystified, but after a while I came to a decision. I gave the letter back to Zalman's wife and told her, 'Do they think I am a stupid man? I know nothing. I don't accept such letters. Please go.'

She protested that Zalman wanted an answer, but I told her that I did not want to discuss the matter any further. Reluctantly, she went. Later I learned that the authorities had somehow obtained a photocopy of our letter to Sharett and had concocted a clever scheme in which Zalman would confess and, at the same time, write me a letter which would trap me into a confession.

To achieve this, they had placed one of their Jewish agents in Zalman's cell. He claimed to be a Zionist who had been condemned to twenty years' imprisonment and was now ostensibly being investigated for another crime. Every night he was taken out of the cell and apparently interrogated for several hours. When he returned, he appeared to be covered with blood and said that he was being tortured. Zalman's heart bled for him.

One evening, a woman doctor appeared in the cell to examine them both. The other man asked her if she was Jewish and she said 'Yes'. He then pleaded with her to help him. Asked what he wanted, the man said that he needed a pencil and a piece of paper to write a letter. The woman doctor replied indignantly, 'You are suggesting that I should commit treason. You are trying to get me imprisoned. No, no!' The woman left the cell. However, she turned up again on the following evening and said, 'After leaving you, I did not sleep at all last night. I want to help you.' She then gave the man a pencil and a piece of paper and he began to write. He then turned to Zalman and said, 'Here is a golden opportunity for you to write to somebody.'

When Zalman was shown a copy of the letter to Sharett he felt that he had no option but to admit that he had taken it to the Embassy. Now he felt that he had to warn me that he had confessed. The men behind this plot assumed that, on receiving this surprising letter, I would immediately panic and write a confession. How little they knew me!

Zalman was a saintly, but naive man. After leaving prison, where he remained for two and a half years, he told me that he was convinced that the woman doctor had genuinely wanted to help him and the other man. He could not be persuaded that he was the victim of a security police trick.

When Zalman returned to Haifa with his family, he did not find the appreciation which he so richly deserved, but which he never sought. Those who should have helped him ignored him. Certain people, powerful in Israel, knew very well, perhaps better than I did, how Zalman had sacrificed himself and his family by trying to assist his brethren. Nobody helped him. I protested and unsuccessfully knocked at many doors. I did all I could, but it was still not enough. In the end, we had to send him money from Romania.

In the history of the Romanian Jewish people, the *Lamed Vuvnik* Zalman Rabinsohn will not be forgotten. He died two or three years ago. He was close to eighty and had a wonderful spirit. I consider him one of the great heroes of our time, but he died, alas, an unsung hero.

15 *My Beard Is in Danger Again*

*R*ealizing that they were losing the battle over *aliyah* to Israel and knowing quite well that their jobs and privileged positions depended on persuading Jews not to leave, the CDE leaders evolved a desperate measure. They knew that the country's leaders were examining what the CDE anti-Zionist campaigns had achieved at a tremendous expenditure of effort and funds, and they were aware that they would be found wanting. They had to acknowledge their failure, but wanted to place the guilt on a scapegoat: the Chief Rabbi.

Suddenly, an unexpected meeting of the Presidium of the Federation was called at ten o'clock one evening in February 1952. Before the meeting was a proposal that the whole Presidium should resign and immediately hand in its resignation to the Minister of Cults. The reason to be given was that it had failed in its main purpose: to persuade the Jews of Romania not to emigrate to Israel. The cause of this failure, according to the initiator of the resolution, was sabotage by the Chief Rabbi.

I was totally unprepared, but I demanded to speak and face my accusers. I spoke for many hours, explaining in detail why Jews wanted to leave Romania and settle in Israel. The Romanian Government had liquidated the Jews' businesses and the *Jewsectzia* had hampered their religious life. Rabbis and *shochetim* received very poor salaries, and it was difficult to establish a Talmud Torah class. Jews were finding it hard to obtain kosher food or to cope with the problem of keeping the Sabbath. Thus it was the CDE that was driving the Jews to Israel, I exclaimed. I followed this up with a declaration that I would not support the proposal, or sign any resignation document. 'I will resign for my own reasons,' I declared.

When the CDE leaders saw that I was not prepared to fall in with their wishes, as they wanted – for the moment – to avoid a public clash, they interrupted the discussion and arranged for another meeting the following Sunday at which the entire board of the Federation would be present. On the eve of that meeting, I met Bacal and Şerban, who tried to change my mind, but without any success. I told them, 'If I were to give in to your pressure, tell the Jews not to go to Israel and attack the holy ideal of Zionism, they would have the right to cut off my beard.' I said these words passionately and in deep anger. I had made it clear on numerous occasions that I would never condemn Israel, our Jewish state which we had to cherish, nor would I do anything to hamper *aliyah*. I reminded Bacal of the condition on which I had agreed, in May 1948, to become a candidate for the position of Chief Rabbi: that I would never attack Zionism and should not be expected to do so. Bacal and Şerban's persistence, laced with implied threats, was an affront which I found intolerable. We finally agreed that, while holding to our own views, we would not attack one another personally.

I kept to the agreement when the meeting opened and did not say anything against Bacal and Şerban in my speech. However, ordinary members of the board began to attack me viciously. The leaders did not join in, giving the impression that they were abiding by the agreement, but it was clear that the other members had been instructed by them. Soon even that pretence was dropped. It was disconcerting to find support for the anti-*aliyah* policy coming from a rabbi and a *shochet*. The rabbi remarked, 'I attack Zionism, elegantly not crudely. I tell young Jewish married couples, "You are building a new home here in your homeland. Where else do you want to go? Here are the graves of your parents and grandparents." ' The *shochet* also spoke in favour of remaining in Romania. But they did not attack me personally.

The onslaught came from Bercu Feldman and Şerban, one indirectly and the other directly. Feldman remarked that there were three categories of rabbis in the Warsaw Ghetto: those who were like the rabbi who had spoken, those who were with the people, and Chief Rabbis who were traitors and enemies of their people. It was clear enough in which category he placed me.

Şerban, totally disregarding our agreement, fulminated against me and then remarked, 'A certain high rabbinical figure told me that if he attacked Zionism, the Jews would have the right to cut off his beard. My answer to him is that we will cut off his beard if he does not attack Zionism.'

I interrupted him. Pointing an accusing finger at Feldman and Şerban, I exclaimed, 'Not since the liberation of Romania have such words about cutting off rabbis' beards been uttered. Now we hear this

Fascist slogan in the speeches of the "leaders" of our community. I refuse to continue to sit at the same table as these new Fascists.'

I rushed out, banging the door behind me, and went immediately to the Minister of Cults, to whom I offered my resignation for the third time. But he again refused to accept it. I was in such a state of nervous tension that my face came out in a rash. When my wife saw me, she was astonished.

On the following day I went to see Bacal and formally handed him my resignation. 'Now you can arrest me,' I told him. 'I am not afraid of you.' Being clever and cynical, he replied, 'Chief Rabbi, you deserve to be arrested for two reasons. If you have committed an offence against the Government, it is logical that you should be arrested. If you have not committed any offence and are totally innocent yet consider that we are capable of arresting an innocent man, then you deserve to be arrested.' Despite my contempt for Bacal's attitude, I had to admit to myself that his answer had a certain perverse logic.

Though confirming his refusal to accept my resignation, the Minister of Cults realized that he had to take decisive action. He was disgusted at the words used by Şerban and felt that we had reached such a state of tension that future co-operation with him in the Federation was no longer possible; he therefore had him transferred to a minor government post. I agreed to continue, but the question remained: when would the 'danger' to my poor beard loom again?

16 Anti-Zionism Intensifies – The Slansky Trial

*A*na Pauker fell from power in June 1952 and with her downfall came a stoppage of emigration to Israel. During the period when she was the most powerful personality in the Romanian Government, no fewer than 100,000 Romanian Jews left Romania and settled in Israel. Yet she was a passionate, convinced Communist, who totally rejected the Zionist thesis of the existence of a Jewish nation whose country was Israel. She strenuously argued that Romanian Jews were Romanian nationals whose duty it was to build up their Romanian homeland together with the Romanian masses.

However, a question mark will always be attached to Ana's name. Was she influenced by her Zionist brother, Zalman, to allow Jews to leave for Israel? Though unlikely, this notion cannot be ruled out altogether. Was she influenced by the Holocaust, realizing the fate that might await those who remained in the Diaspora? What is evident is the fact that, while campaigning against Zionism, she opened the gates and more than 1,000 Jews from Romania arrived weekly in Haifa. She herself appears to have been a victim of an anti-Semitic campaign orchestrated by Stalin, once supposedly her friend.

Significantly, her downfall came four months after the arrest of Rudolf Slansky, Vice-Premier and Secretary-General of the Czechoslovak Communist Party. Like several other high officials arrested, Slansky was a Jew. The Jewishness of the defendants and the fact that they had changed their Jewish-sounding names was emphasized in the prosecution case. Moreover, they were accused of being Zionists; it was the first time that such a charge had been brought in court against anyone in the Communist world or, indeed, anywhere else. Some of the Jewish defendants committed suicide; Slansky and ten other former Communist leaders, seven of them reputedly Jewish, were executed.

A violent anti-Semitic climate was deliberately created in Eastern Europe, a development which must have had Stalin's full approval if not his blessing. Ana was accused of right-wing deviation, stripped of her membership of the Politburo and finally dismissed from her post of Foreign Minister. The charges against her had probably been concocted by Beria, head of Stalin's secret police. However, as Stalin had died in the meantime and Beria was himself executed, Ana was not put on trial, as was the custom in such cases, and did not have to go to court. She remained powerless, but comparatively free.

Vasile Luca, the influential Finance Minister, was also stripped of all power. He, too, was accused of right-wing deviation and even of being a right-wing agent. As I read the news of his sudden downfall, I recalled a conversation I had had with him in 1949. I had attended a government reception and found that my car had not arrived to take me home. Noticing this, Luca offered to give me a lift, which I accepted. Since he was then the man in the Politburo responsible for the cults in Romania, he was interested in talking to me and he took advantage of this opportunity. We had a long discussion, for more than an hour, which was remarkably frank on both sides. I said to him, 'You have overall responsibility for the cults and I admit that you grant us absolute freedom. We know, nevertheless, that this is only a tactical move. At the first opportunity, when your interests dictate such a course, you will liquidate us as religious groups.'

Luca replied, 'Chief Rabbi, I appreciate your frankness and, therefore, I will be just as frank. We are learning from the experience of the Soviet Union. The USSR has been very successful in nearly everything it has done, but in the religious field it has failed. The Soviet authorities were forced, twenty years after the revolution, to reopen churches. Why? Because a government can take everything from a man – his shop, his house, his good name. A government can use tanks to do all these things, but it cannot use a tank to take away a man's soul. So we have decided on different methods. We don't want to crush you, because we don't want to make martyrs of you. We don't hurt you on condition that you don't hurt us. As long as you remain loyal to us, you will enjoy all due rights for your existence. How will it end? I can tell you that time is on our side. You will disappear and we will continue to exist and to flourish.'

While Luca died miserably, the 400,000 Romanian Jews did not disappear. They went to Israel to rebuild their home. Time was not on his side.

The sudden stoppage of emigration to Israel came as a terrible blow to the Jews of Romania, apart, of course, from the Jewish Communists, who must have been delighted. There were heart-rending stories of children and parents being separated, of families that had disposed of their homes and belongings as they prepared to leave for Israel. There were thousands of destitute Jewish families, threatened by starvation. At the same time, the Stalinist terror campaign was intensified. Many people were arrested or just disappeared. Zionists were seen as particularly obnoxious enemies. Romanian Jews walked about in fear.

Yet the CDE could not dampen the inner religious fervour of the masses of Jews, or remove from their hearts the hope for a better future in Israel. The CDE controlled hundreds of propagandists who regularly visited the synagogues in Bucharest to deliver anti-Zionist diatribes. These speakers were at first listened to in deadly silence, but suddenly, as if somebody had given a prearranged signal, though no such a person was ever discovered, the whole congregation began to stamp the floor and to make other noises. The din was similar to the one made in synagogues every year during the reading of the Book of Esther on the occasion of the Purim festival, when the name of Haman, the Persian king's counsellor who sought to destroy all Jews, is mentioned. The speakers, though furious and making threatening gestures to the congregants, had no option but to conclude their meetings and hastily leave the synagogues.

Pogăceanu, the Minister of Cults, also tried to convince me to change my views, especially in regard to Zionism, but he used much subtler tactics. His attitude could be harsh, but also deceptive, as happened on at least one occasion.

He had invited me to speak at an ecumenical conference which was to take place in Bucharest, on 25 November 1952, and asked me to send him the text of my speech. There was nothing surprising in this request. In Stalin's empire nobody, be he the Prime Minister or a simple clerk, could make a public speech without first having it vetted by the censors. Somehow I had been able to avoid this regulation by pleading that I could not speak from a written text and by giving an assurance that, while I would keep to my firmly held opinions, I would not embarrass the Government at public gatherings when I represented the Jewish community. However, on this occasion, I agreed to send the Minister the text of my speech, because it was to be short and formal.

On receiving it, the Minister personally inserted a sentence which accused Zionism of being an inimical instrument of imperialism. The amended text was brought to me by the Minister's secretary. When I saw the insertion, I trembled with indignation. Zionists were appearing in various courts of law and being sentenced to long terms of imprisonment. Attacking Zionism at that time implied that I, the Chief Rabbi, approved of the unjust treatment they were receiving. This was against my moral feelings and impossible for me to do.

Arriving at the conference, I went up to the Minister and challenged him to justify his unwarranted insertion of the sentence condemning Zionism. Stressing that I had always refused to attack Zionism since 1948, I demanded that the Minister erase the sentence.

He looked at me angrily and said, 'Have you not seen today's newspapers? Are you going to maintain your attitude after having read them? Don't you fear sharing Slansky's fate? Please think twice before you speak today. Your words will decide your own fate.'

I had, indeed, read that morning's newspapers with horror. They referred to the 'Jew Slansky'. The majority of the other defendants in Prague were also described as Jews and their previous names were spelled out. These Communist figures had changed their names at the request of the party, but this was not mentioned. It was as if the Nazi era had returned, as if the way was being paved for nationwide pogroms.

The Minister's rebukes did not intimidate me. I was too angry at the words I had read and too indignant at his duplicity to react meekly. I said to him, 'You have argued that each national cult is duty bound to attack its own Fascists. So why isn't the Patriarch attacking the Iron Guard, and why isn't the German bishop condemning the Nazis? And why aren't the Hungarian bishops criticizing Nilosz [a notorious Hungarian Fascist]? Why should I be the only one to attack people in my community? If the Christian leaders agree to launch attacks, I will follow suit. Otherwise, I will insist on refusing.'

The Minister turned away from me without replying. He did not request the Christian clergymen to voice any criticism. I made up my mind what I was going to do. When I rose to speak, I laid aside the text which had been amended by the Minister, took out my original text and read it firmly. As I was concluding my speech, I looked at the Minister and saw that he was furious. When I walked down from the platform, he demonstratively turned his back on me. The President, Dr Petru Groza, who did not know what was happening, was chairing the conference. After my speech, he embraced me warmly. Paradoxically, on account of one and the same speech, the President of the Republic was enthusiastically congratulating me and the Minister of Cults was in a rage.

On the following day, the leading Bucharest newspaper, *Scînteia*, carried a lengthy report of the meeting. In reproducing my speech, it included the anti-Zionist sentence inserted by the Minister. Being certain that, despite my protests, I would be intimidated by his threats on account of the Slansky affair and would utter the anti-Zionist words, he had sent the amended text to the newspaper even before I had delivered my speech.

I rang him up, but got an evasive answer from his secretary; it was clear that he did not want to speak to me. I warned her that I had a very serious matter to discuss with him and, after a while, he picked up the receiver. I said to him, 'I know you are angry with me, but I have an even greater reason to feel outraged. I must tell you that, if you don't deny that I uttered the anti-Zionist words ascribed to me in today's *Scînteia*, I will use the pulpit in the synagogue tomorrow, Friday evening, to make a special declaration to our congregation — and through them to the whole country — to the effect that I did not utter those words and that what has appeared in *Scînteia* is a forgery. People will know who has committed it.'

I expected an angry reaction from the Minister, but none came. There was total silence and then I heard him put down the receiver. But he must have acted very quickly afterwards. That very evening, Bucharest radio broadcast the recording of my entire speech as I had delivered it and not as it had appeared in *Scînteia*. Anyone listening to it would have realized that I had not attacked Zionism and that the newspaper report had been falsified. The addresses delivered by the other leading speakers at the conference were broadcast in a very truncated form.

Minister Pogăceanu had hit on a skilful method for making amends. Next day, he telephoned me and asked, 'Are you satisfied? I hope that your sermon tonight will not contain any sensational denials.'

Strangely enough, our relationship improved after this clash. We agreed that we would not discuss or argue about Zionism and emigration to Israel. Each of us would stick to his opinions — for the time being.

And so, in November 1952, at the height of the Stalinist terror, a rabbi obtained a denial of an alleged anti-Zionist statement. It seems unbelievable, but the proof is to be found in the archives of the Bucharest Broadcasting Station.

17   *Hero or Madman?*

*T*he tension caused by the Stalinist terror campaign, orchestrated by the KGB officials who were in overall control of the Ministries, as well as of the security services, was at times unbearable. November 1952 saw an intensification of the campaign which had lasted for many months. Thousands of people were seized in the streets or in their offices and taken to unknown prisons. Often men and women were invited to visit a Ministry to discuss some imaginary problem and then seized. Security men arrived at people's homes in the early hours of the morning and took away the husband or the wife. I say 'seized' and not 'arrested' because the latter word implies the existence of the authority of the law. It was absent. There had been a total collapse of the law.

I began to feel desperate. What chance did I have of remaining free? The CDE was eager to see me liquidated. It would now, more than ever, find willing listeners in the security services. Why should it treat leniently a stubborn rabbi who refused to comply with its wishes? I was informed that security agents were questioning many people about me: members of our congregations, my co-workers and my acquaintances. They were looking for incriminating evidence. Cars followed me wherever I went. Men stood outside my house. I felt trapped. In desperation, I decided that I must confer with other rabbis before I was arrested because the fate of our communities was at stake. But how was I to assemble the rabbis for a private discussion? If I sent out invitations, the CDE would immediately hear of my plan and Bacal would insist on chairing any meeting. I reflected bitterly that all my sacrifices would have been in vain and that the CDE would find rabbis who would be willing to speak out against Zionism and emigration to Israel.

By a fortunate coincidence, a number of leading rabbis happened to be in Bucharest as they were attending the ecumenical conference of 25

November. I hit on the idea of inviting them to my house for a secret meeting. The Federation was kept in total ignorance of the gathering. On the evening of the 25th, H. Guttman, A. M. Beck and L. Alpert (Bucharest), S. Guttman (Iaşi), I. Sapira (Galaţi), F. Klein (Tg. Mureş), M. Spitz (Bistriţa) and S. Deutsch (Satu-Mare) arrived for a truly dramatic encounter. In reporting faithfully what occurred, I do not wish to cast aspersions on any of these fine men. Only those who have experienced life under the pressures of Stalinist terror can fully understand what happens to people overcome by fear, either for themselves, their families or their congregations. I myself do not know how I would have reacted had I been subjected to torture in some dark, cold cell.

I opened the discussion with the rabbis by informing them of the pressures I was being subjected to and of the imminent danger of my arrest. I demanded that they advise me in the spirit of the Torah and Jewish ethics. The choice before me was stark but clear: should I surrender to the authorities, abandoning all the beliefs I cherished, or continue struggling for Judaism and *aliyah*, and by doing so risk my life?

The rabbis knew as well as I did that if we approved the authorities' declaration that Zionism was the poisonous tool of the Anglo–American imperialists, it could be used to justify the sentencing of the Zionists then held in custody to long terms of imprisonment. The rabbis also realized that my arrest or disappearance would badly affect our religious and social institutions. With me out of the way, the CDE would be able to destroy all our institutions which had been established with such love and dedication. What were we to do? What course should I adopt? Should I attack Zionism, thus endangering the lives of the imprisoned Zionists but saving the community? Or should I refuse and thus jeopardize Jewish life altogether?

Most of the answers I received from the rabbis were, alas, inconclusive and disappointing. Rabbi Guttman of Iaşi stood up and said that he would have to leave immediately because he did not want to miss his train. (Several years later, when I visited Iaşi, he complained to me, 'Why did you invite me to such a dangerous meeting? You could have destroyed me.') Rabbi Alpert gave an evasive answer. Rabbi Spitz (who now lives in New York) said, 'As my answer would affect not only my fate, but that of my wife and children, I have to consult my wife before replying.' Rabbi Guttman of Bucharest remarked, 'Chief Rabbi, we know what you expect from us. You want us to display solidarity with you. We cannot do so.' Rabbi Klein referred to a Talmudic passage which, he claimed, meant that if one has to choose between shedding one's own blood and shedding that of another man, one's own life comes first.

The contribution by Rabbi Sapira of Galaţi, who was a leader of the religious–Zionist Mizrachi movement, was particularly striking. He was a man who often displayed sardonic humour and brutal frankness. He showed these qualities on this occasion as well. He said, 'Chief Rabbi, I understand you well. On the eve of your arrest – which you clearly believe to be imminent – you wish us to pledge ourselves not to do what you have been refusing to do: attack Zionism and *aliyah*. You wish us to resist the authorities' pressure on us when you are gone from our midst. Chief Rabbi, don't believe any such pledges. Whoever says to you now that he will definitely oppose the authorities is not telling you the truth. I will tell you what will happen. Not only will we give in to pressure, but we will even denounce you as an agent of Anglo–American imperialism and unmask you as an enemy of the people.'

I considered Rabbi Sapira a fine man, an outstanding Talmudic scholar and a staunch Jew. I mention his words not to criticize him, but rather to praise his honesty. He knew very well the terrible conditions we were living under and how wrong it would be to give me false hopes.

The only clear encouragement came from the elderly and frail Dr Beck. In a moving, shaky voice, he said to me, 'I attended Theodor Herzl's funeral in Vienna. As I stood at the side of the coffin, I took an oath of allegiance to Zionism, to dedicate myself to it, even at the cost of my life. Chief Rabbi, you can depend on me, on my not breaking that oath.' These wonderful words, spoken with such noble emotion by the elderly rabbi, still ring in my ears, thirty-seven years later.

The meeting ended inconclusively. I was forced to make the vital decision by myself, a decision which was going to affect the lives of hundreds of thousands of Romanian Jews. Fortunately for me, there was one other person on whom I could rely and whose judgement I valued: my wife. The decision I made was to keep on fighting.

Shortly afterwards, in December 1952, the National Congress for the Defence of Peace was held in Bucharest. I was invited to join the country's leading political, scientific and cultural personalities, as well as the heads of the various religious groups, in the Presidium of the Congress. I was also asked to make a speech.

However, a dispute about the contents of my projected speech broke out once more between me and Pogăceanu. Again I was asked to attack Zionism and *aliyah*, which I refused to do. This time the Minister did not use threats but persuasion. However, when, at the end of the second day of the Congress, I still had not spoken, while addresses had been given by all the other religious heads, Pogăceanu became very nervous and said, 'Chief Rabbi, you must make a speech. It is inconceivable that you should be the only religious head to remain silent.' The Congress was taking place in the impressive Athenaeum building and our discussion took place in one of the offices behind the stage. But I noticed that, whenever I made any proposal or put forward a new argument, Pogăceanu disappeared into another room. This happened several times and I could not help showing my surprise. Finally he exclaimed, 'I don't know what to do. Let them discuss the problem directly with you. They refuse to talk to you. But they are Jews, too. You should be able to understand one another better.'

I now learned that the people in the adjoining room were Iosif Chişinevschi and Mihai Roller. Chişinevschi was a member of the Politburo, a powerful Jew who hated everything Jewish. Mihai Roller, the son of a rabbi, was the cultural boss of the party and had stirred up anti-Semitism with his provocative 'reforms' of Romanian language and literature. They had chosen to negotiate with me but, mysteriously, through the Minister. It was a stupid idea and I am surprised that Pogăceanu even considered it in the first place. In the end, he refused to continue the discussion and there was no point in my talking to the other two men. On the last day of the Congress, I delivered a speech, but made no reference to *aliyah* or Zionism.

Watching the proceedings I saw how fear can affect even the most illustrious personalities in a state. On the platform were men who had made important contributions to literature, science and the arts. In the audience were the most outstanding personalities in the country. Yet whenever the name of Stalin was mentioned, they dutifully stood up. They applauded every reference to his 'genius' and to his overwhelming wisdom, and repeated his name with fervour. As I saw this utter degradation, this general attempt to retain honours and gain safety, I asked myself what right I had to adopt a different course. My lips moved as if in prayer, as I murmured to myself, 'You have gone mad, old man. Nobody is displaying any opposition to the Stalinist regime. These great creative figures around you are, on the contrary, cheering Stalin. What you are doing is sheer madness.'

Those great intellectual figures were behaving in a logical manner if they were to stay alive. They followed the ancient Romanian proverb which says that he who bows is not beheaded. And Jewish religious beliefs hold that it is life and not death which offers us a chance to defeat our enemies. But I have never been a logical person. The force that drove me to continue the struggle was irresistible. Was it not madness? Why such a struggle, when everybody was surrendering? Where was the boundary between courage and madness? I was trembling with fear, fear for myself.

18 *The 'Doctors' Plot'*

At the beginning of 1953, the accusations against Zionists intensified. Every day newspapers referred to the 'high treason' of Rudolf Slansky and his Jewish accomplices. An atmosphere conducive to a pogrom was created. Jews feared that, at any moment, mobs would fall on them and slaughter them. It was as if the days of the terror of the Nazis and their Fascist collaborators had returned. What made the nightmare even worse was that the CDE and its thousands of paid agents joined in the attacks on Zionism and Judaism and thus stoked up the hatred of the Jews.

Into this terrifyingly tense atmosphere a bomb was thrown: the story from Moscow which became known as the 'doctors' plot'. The official Soviet news agency, TASS, carried a report that several leading Jewish doctors had been arrested and charged with a dastardly plot to poison the Soviet leadership. Among them was Stalin's personal physician. TASS claimed that all the accused had already confessed. The Soviet newspapers printed front-page reports about the doctors' 'terrible plot'. The American Jewish Joint Distribution Committee was accused of being a partner in the plot, on behalf of American imperialism. The great Jewish actor–manager Mikhoels, who had served with distinction during the war as a member of the Jewish anti-Fascist committee and had helped to raise support for the Soviet Union in the United States, but who had been killed by Stalin's murderers, was now described as 'an infamous criminal'. International Zionism was branded as the originator of the plot.

Many Jews came to me and said they were convinced that Romanian Jews, as well as Soviet Jews, would now be deported to camps and exterminated. Such was the panic which gripped ordinary people. Indeed, such a course appeared logical. People who had been described as traitors and enemies would not be allowed to remain in their homes and enjoy a normal existence.

Though I believed the CDE to be capable of the most contemptible actions, I was still shocked to find that its newspaper, *Unirea*, backed the Nazi-like anti-Semitic campaign. Professor Benedict Menkes, of Timişoara, wrote a particularly nasty article in which he condemned the Jewish doctors as poisoners. It was similar in tone to the one written by David Sefard, a Warsaw Jew, under the revealing heading, 'Criminals in White Smocks'.

A new campaign of pressure and terror was led by the CDE with the aim of forcing distinguished Jewish personalities to publish similar infamous articles, justifying the terrible accusation against Jews.

I will never forget the unexpected arrival at my home of the Yiddish writer Yaacov Gropper. He was a good friend of mine and I used to invite him on the occasion of various Jewish festivals. This time, he suddenly knocked on our door. When I let him in, Gropper, a man who was faithful to Jewish tradition, a noble soul and a talented poet, began to weep. He had come from Bercu Feldman's office, where he had resisted all kinds of pressure. They wanted him to sign a letter similar to those published by Menkes and the other traitors to the Jewish people. He had refused and had come to ask me, 'Chief Rabbi, how can you resist? I want you to teach me how you manage. My nerves can no longer withstand further menaces and dangers.' My answer to him was that in a matter of life and death, nobody could give him any advice. He had to make the decision himself. Gropper succeeded in resisting. May his memory be blessed!

While the anti-Semitic agitation was at its height, I received a registered, confidential letter from a rabbi in Transylvania. He wrote: 'As the plot discovered in Moscow involving Jewish doctors and the Joint in the assassination attempt against the Soviet leaders once more proves how infamous Zionism is and how dangerous its actions are, is it not your duty, Chief Rabbi, to adopt a clear and unequivocal policy? Should you not convene the Supreme Rabbinical Council in order to brand Zionism and its tools as dangerous forces? That would remove a great danger that is threatening the Jewish community.'

Appalled as I was by this letter, I realized almost immediately that the rabbi was being used to trap me. I knew him well. All his previous letters to me were, naturally, written in Hebrew; this one was in Romanian. The others were always handwritten; this one was typed. Somebody had ensured that there would be a copy of the letter. I was in a dilemma. Pretending that it had not arrived would be dangerous. The police agents who had the copy would use it against me and try to prove that other rabbis rejected my arguments in favour of Zionism and *aliyah*. On the other hand, if I handed the letter to the authorities, it would be assumed that I was changing my views and weakening in my opposition to the authorities' demands.

I decided to play for time and use every possible tactic to evade the trap. I wrote to the rabbi acknowledging the receipt of his letter. I added that, as it was confidential and as the Talmud forbids the disclosure of confidential information, I would not be able to convene the meeting of the Rabbinical Council, as he recommended, because I would have to reveal the source of the recommendation. However, I did not gain much time. Within a few days, he answered, stressing that it would not be necessary for me to divulge his name as he was a man of little importance. He added, 'The Chief Rabbi, because of his exalted position, is the only person who can take action. He should not need any prompting.' In a postscript, he informed me that he had told the authorities that he no longer wished to leave the country and settle in Israel. Several days later, another letter arrived. His father, a great scholar and a Chassidic rabbi, wrote in Hebrew making the same request. Referring to the Zionists he wrote: 'I have always been disgusted with them and their ideology.'

When I read this letter I felt as if the trap had shut fast. There appeared to be no means of escape from it. Rabbis Klein and Deutsch whom I consulted were dismayed. They, too, thought that my enemies had me, at long last, in their clutches. I would have to convene the Rabbinical Council and give in to the authorities' desires. Otherwise I would be branded as a man who stood out against the wishes of the people, including his own rabbis.

As I was agonizing over the letters and trying, with increasing desperation, to find a way of escaping defeat and humiliation, a final ploy occurred to me. I went to see Feldman, who – I was certain –was deeply involved in the plot against me, and put the rabbis' letters in front of him on his desk. He read them with keen attention, pretending all the time that he was surprised by their contents. He then remarked with obvious satisfaction, 'Well, Chief Rabbi, now you too can see that the rabbis are democrats. You have only to give the signal and they will follow and support you.'

'I am willing to comply with your proposal to convene the Supreme Rabbinical Council,' I replied. He looked at me with a gratified smile. I could see the triumph in his eyes. But the smile quickly disappeared from his face as I added, 'The problem of the doctors' plot did not appear in Romania, but in the Soviet Union. I therefore consider it necessary to organize a meeting in Moscow of the Chief Rabbis of all the Socialist countries – Romania, Poland, Hungary, Czechoslovakia, Yugoslavia, Bulgaria, East Germany and the Soviet Union – so that a joint attitude can be adopted.'

I had chosen my words very carefully and was certain that the Romanian authorities would never accept my suggestion. Since becoming Chief Rabbi, I had not succeeded even once in exchanging letters with any Chief Rabbi of these countries. The Iron Curtain existed not only between East and West, but also between the member countries of the Communist bloc. I calculated that some time would elapse while the authorities considered, or pretended to consider, my proposal and I would have a respite from their pressure. Possibly they might even drop the demand to convene the Rabbinical Council.

As I was speaking, I saw Feldman's face cloud over and his eyes stare at me angrily. He was no fool. He realized what the proposal aimed to achieve. I was in his clutches, but now I was trying to escape once again. However, he had no option but to pass on the proposal to the higher authorities. My strategy worked, more than I had really expected. I received no reply to the proposal, but neither did the authorities press me to convene the Rabbinical Council.

My escape further infuriated the CDE. I heard that Ladislaw Meister, a secret police officer who was head of personnel in the Federation, described me as a traitor. At meetings of the Federation he more than once remarked, looking significantly at me, 'The party crushes all those who stand in its way.' Madame Frankel, one of the officials of the Bucharest community council, frequently entered my office, forced open drawers and rummaged among my papers, looking for incriminating evidence against me. Anti-Zionist slogans and cartoons appeared on the walls of the Choral Temple. I considered this a sacrilege and tore them down. Wardens of the Malbim and Atena synagogues were threatened with imprisonment if they did not spy on me. A network of spies was created throughout the community.

Day and night, police agents watched my home. My every step was followed. Again, the danger was drawing nearer and nearer. With David, the bard of the Psalms, I began asking myself, 'Wherefrom will my salvation come?'

But I knew the answer very well: 'My salvation will come from Him, from the Almighty.' This time, too, He helped me.

With Passover approaching, I had to prepare a message to the Jewish community. Twice a year, for Rosh Hashanah and for Passover, it had become my custom to praise the Romanian Government for the religious liberties granted to the Jewish population. I occasionally criticized Anglo–American imperialism and briefly castigated the Ben-Gurion Government for aligning itself with it. I did genuinely believe that the Israeli Government was making mistakes in its foreign policy and was not taking sufficiently into account the existence of millions of Jews in the Communist world. It was in any case important that I should show my independence, as this would improve my credibility with the Romanian authorities. As I still vehemently refused to attack Israel as a Jewish state, Zionism and *aliyah*, the CDE remained bitterly hostile. But now a new demand was to be made on me.

After I had handed my proposed message to Bacal, I was summoned to the new Minister of Cults, Professor Petre Constantinescu-Iaşi. He had taken over from Pogăceanu, who was apparently glad to leave a post which had caused him so many headaches. With hardly a greeting or a preliminary discussion, the Minister told me that I must include in the message a sentence branding the 'criminals, the poisoners, the treacherous doctors' who had been lackeys of the Joint and tried to kill the Soviet leaders. He spoke in a harsh, bullying voice, as if giving an order to a junior official. I was astonished at his attitude. We were old friends. We had been together in the Miercurea Ciuc concentration camp. He was a very good professor of history, a democrat, a friend of the Jews and a man who had fought against anti-Semitism and the Iron Guard; suddenly, he was quite different, harsh, cruel, hostile and menacing.

On such occasions I believe in taking the initiative. I felt I had to be blunt and straightforward in my reply. I said to the Minister, 'You are a professor of history and, therefore, it is not necessary to remind you of the fountain poisoners [during the Middle Ages a false rumour had been spread about the Jews poisoning water fountains and wells; another rumour claimed that Christian children were being killed in order that their blood could be used for baking Passover *matzoth*; as a result, thousands of Jews had been killed]. Mark my words: the allegation against the Jewish doctors in Moscow will be shown to be as wicked a concoction as the story of the fountain poisoners. Nothing will force me to aid a conspiracy against the Jewish people.'

The Minister exclaimed angrily, 'How dare you insult Soviet justice! How can you have doubts about it?' His voice rose in fury and he banged his fist on the table. Refusing to be intimidated by him, I said calmly, 'I am not referrring to Soviet justice. So far the Soviet law courts have not become involved in the matter. There has only been a police statement and the police often make mistakes. I am convinced that the time will come when this statement will make you feel ashamed.'

It was not a reply that the Minister expected. He clenched his fists and began to threaten me. 'How long do you think we are going to tolerate your attitude?' he asked, wagging an accusing finger at me.

'I am a rabbi,' I said, 'and I must never do or say anything that will cause me shame and reproach. What I sign today I must be able to sign in twenty years' time as well.'

Bacal fully supported the Minister, but he realized that I would not be browbeaten into changing my stand. Apparently hoping to pacify him, he remarked, 'We at the Federation will issue a statement that will contain all the words that the Chief Rabbi is refusing to utter.'

Far from mollifying the Minister, Bacal's intervention threw him into a frenzy. I have never seen a member of government behave with such a total lack of dignity. He had now completely lost control of himself and was shouting at me. I quietly said that, in view of the discussion, I would withdraw my message altogether and would not address the community during Passover. With these words, I rose and slowly began to leave the room. The Minister stared at me silently, making no effort to delay my departure.

The Federation ignored my wish to withdraw the message. It was read in the synagogues on the first night of Passover. It did not attack Zionism and made no reference to the doctors. But the Federation's message, which had to be read at the end of Passover, before the *Izkor* prayer, in all synagogues throughout the country, included a vicious attack on Zionism and on the 'Jewish poisoner doctors'.

Passover arrived and with it tension and fears. So intense were the fears that some people actually expected another ritual murder allegation. The verses of the *Haggadah* (the collection of prayers and stories read during the Passover *Seder* meals) appeared terrifyingly up to date; we recited with trepidation the words, 'Not one only has risen against us, to exterminate us, but in every generation they rise against us, to exterminate us, and the Almighty saves us from their hands.' Would He save us again?

As I sat down to the *Seder* meal and, following ancient tradition, opened the street door so that the Prophet Eliahu should be able to enter, I looked down the deserted street. I imagined I saw a man crouching, with a bundle on his back. A terrible vision arose in my mind. The man was carrying the body of a Christian child which he was about to throw into my house, to accuse me of committing a ritual murder. I shook my head violently to rid myself of the vision. I knew that the man was carrying cheap propaganda material, sent out by the CDE, accusing the Zionists and the Joint of various ridiculous crimes.

On the Sabbath *Hol Hamoed*, the Saturday in the middle of Passover, I arrived as usual at the Choral Temple at nine o'clock in the morning. In the courtyard I noticed a man whom I had seen before in the synagogue, but whom I did not know personally. I later learned that his name was Adalbert Blau and that he was a watchmaker and jeweller. As the man approached me, I saw his eyes were shining with excitement. He clearly wanted to tell me something very important. 'Chief Rabbi, I have been waiting for you,' he burst out. 'I wanted to be the first person to give you the good news. The BBC has broadcast a communiqué issued in Moscow, which says that the allegation against the Jewish doctors is a fabrication. They have been set free and those doctors who gave evidence against them have themselves been arrested.'

This development seemed like a modern version of the biblical Book of Esther, in which Haman, who had wanted to destroy all the Jews in the Persian Empire, was himself arrested and hanged. 'This is too good to be true, in such a world as ours,' I murmured to myself. I looked sharply at the man, suddenly suspecting that he had invented the story in order to trick me. When I looked into his eyes and questioned him, I became convinced that he was telling the truth.

When I entered the synagogue, I immediately asked a number of close friends to interrupt their prayers and check if the report could be confirmed. I could not rid myself of doubts. They returned shortly afterwards and assured me that Moscow Radio had indeed broadcast the sensational news. Only Bucharest Radio had not referred to the denial and was apparently waiting for further instructions. On hearing this news, joy filled my heart. As the news spread, people in the synagogue began to smile. An immense burden had been lifted from our shoulders.

Although it is forbidden in Judaism to use the telephone on the Sabbath, I decided that it was essential for me to break the injunction on that day. I telephoned Yitzhak Friedman, the general secretary of the Federation who had succeeded Şerban. Friedman's extremism sometimes offended even Feldman and Bacal. Ordinary Jews hated him because of his having abandoned the teaching of his great and worthy father. As was usual with him, he was profaning the Sabbath and working in the office of the Federation.

I said to him, 'Mr Friedman, you have sent a message to all the communities, which is to be read in all synagogues on the last day of Passover. Part of the message deals with the vile anti-Semitic fabrication against some innocent Jewish doctors in Moscow. This fabrication has now been denounced as a total fake. I demand that you send a telegram to the communities cancelling the message and apologizing for it.'

Friedman later told me that he believed I had gone mad. For a sane Chief Rabbi to telephone on the Sabbath was incredible. The words I used seemed to him absolutely crazy. As he listened only to Bucharest Radio, he had not heard the news from Moscow. Moreover, for the Chief Rabbi to speak so frankly, well knowing that the telephone was bugged, suggested some form of insanity. He thought that I had cracked under the tension I was experiencing. It took me a long time to convince Friedman that I was sane and that the report I gave him was correct. A few hours later, Bucharest Radio confirmed my words. Friedman and the CDE leadership were stunned. They had no alternative but to send a message to the communities cancelling their message. It was not a happy day for the CDE.

Again a miracle had occurred at the last moment. Again we had survived.

The miracle happened in April, a month and a half after Stalin's death on 5 March 1953. The least I can say is that he died at the right time. For if he had not died then, who knows if we might have survived?

Stalin died on Purim day. The 'doctors' plot' was discredited during Passover. Who can say that history does not repeat itself?

19 *Terror and Happiness*

*L*iving under the Stalinist regime, people spoke of three kinds of happiness. The first consisted in waking up in the morning and finding oneself in one's own bed, because most of the arrests took place at night. The second was achieved by arriving at one's place of work and not finding a letter of dismissal; and the third by coming home and finding one's furniture still there. It was customary for the authorities to seize a man's furniture and other belongings while he was at work, and then to evict the whole family from the house.

As I was expecting to be arrested without warning at any moment, I kept near my bed a parcel containing woollen socks, a vest and other necessities. If I were arrested in the summer, I had to be prepared for the bitter winter months in prison. However, the security authorities were to surprise me more than once.

I realized that, in prison, it would be very easy to forget the Jewish calendar – in many cells, it was impossible to tell day from night, because they were never penetrated by sunshine – so, in order to be able to keep the High Holy Days, I learned by heart the *Keviot*, the calendar calculations, for twenty years.

One morning a letter arrived from a Jewish woman in a Moldavian provincial town. She informed me that she was sixty-two and married to a widower, whose children were opposed to the marriage, and now he wished to leave her. She asked me to bless her, so that her husband would remain with her. She sent seven lei for me and three lei for the warden of the synagogue. I was surprised to notice that the woman had enclosed the receipt for the postal order, which should have remained at the post office, but I attached no importance to the fact. I sent her back the receipt and the postal order, giving her my blessing 'free of charge'. The poor woman was obviously accustomed to the old-style 'rebbes' ('wonder rebbes' who were supposed to perform miracles) and did not know that I never took money from anybody. The letter amused my wife and myself and we quickly forgot about it.

A few weeks later, a man came to my home and invited me to go with him to the post office. I was convinced that the moment of my arrest had arrived. The police frequently arrested people in government offices, after finding some pretence for getting them there. I gathered my little parcel and said good-bye to my wife. We both wept. I silently recited a few Psalms as I walked to the main post office, the man at my side.

On arriving there, I was taken to a room and asked to sit down. I sat there for two hours, but nobody came. Then two men walked in and immediately began to question me. Did I know the woman? I had no idea what woman they meant? They explained that she had sent me money. To what purpose? What had I done with the receipt which should have remained at the post office? How had a state document (the receipt for ten lei, which at the time represented the cost of half a kilo of meat) come into private hands?

I now fully remembered the letter I had received. Still bewildered by the importance the police were attaching to it, I told them that I had noticed a receipt and been surprised to see it, and had therefore returned it to the woman. I also explained why she had sent the money to me. The two policemen told me that the woman had been questioned about the receipt and her explanation had not been believed. That was why I had been summoned to the post office. It seemed incredible that so much importance should have been attached to such a minor matter, but I did not delve overlong into the mystery. The men told me that I could leave and I quickly went home. When my wife saw me, she burst into tears of happiness. It reminded me of an old Jewish popular saying: 'When is a poor man happy? When he loses something and then finds the lost object.'

A few months later, my wife entered the room where I was resting and gave me a piece of paper, without saying a word. On it were the following words: 'Matter of security. You are invited to come to our office at 6 p.m. today.' My wife gave me the little parcel, we embraced and wept. Now there seemed to be no doubt that I was to be arrested. When I instructed my driver to take me to the security office, he looked at me in panic and consternation, as if I had told him to drive me to hell.

It was late autumn. A cold rain pelted the streets. When we arrived at the security office in Rahova Street, I noticed several armed soldiers guarding it. I presented my written 'invitation' and was taken inside and shown into a room. Then black spectacles were placed on my nose. It was as if I had been blindfolded: I could see nothing around me. Then I felt somebody grip my arms and lead me up one staircase and then another. Afterwards I was forced to go down a flight of stairs. Up and down we went, seemingly for hours. Apparently I was being subjected to a security police method meant to demoralize suspects. Eventually I was propelled into a room, a chair was placed near me and I was made to sit down. Two men began to interrogate me. Their questions surprised me as they wanted to know all the details of my youth, starting from my childhood in Fălticeni. I waited for them to inquire about my more recent activities as Chief Rabbi, and then to put forward allegations and accusations, but, to my immense relief, they did not. I began to notice that I was not the target of their questioning. A certain Jewish lawyer, Yaacov Bacal (no relative of the CDE leader), had been arrested, though innocent of any crimes. He had been born in Fălticeni and had a good reputation there. Wishing to confirm his standing in the community, he naturally thought of the Chief Rabbi. That was the reason for the 'invitation' by the security services. It was symbolic of those times that the Chief Rabbi could be treated so harshly, with such a lack of respect. My wife, though appalled at the treatment I had received, saw me return with much happiness, made all the sweeter by its unexpectedness.

A close friend of mine, Riki Theiler, was less fortunate. He was walking in the street in the centre of Bucharest when a car stopped near him. Three men rushed out of the car, grabbed hold of him and bundled him into it. People in the street saw the incident, but nobody dreamed of intervening: this had become a normal occurrence. The men took Theiler to a cellar and asked him if he knew where he was. He had no idea. 'You are in the building of the Ministry of the Interior,' they told him. 'Thank heaven it is the Ministry,' my friend exclaimed. 'I thought this place belonged to gangsters.'

However, he had nothing to be thankful for. He was kept in prison for two and a half years. Nobody ever came to question him. When he asked what his offences were, nobody answered him. He never came before a judge and was never formally sentenced. One day, a man entered his cell and told him harshly, 'Get out!' Theiler rushed out, in the pitiful garb he was wearing. To this day he has no notion why he was seized and held in prison.

In its effort to control the community, the CDE appointed its own security officials to various posts. One man, who was ostensibly the head of personnel at the Federation, started files, similar to those used by the secret police, on every member. He certainly had a thick file on me. Even worse was Madame Frankel, a woman in her sixties, whose son was a colonel in the Romanian security service. That was, indeed, a high position. Wanting his family to have an additional salary, the colonel appointed his mother head of personnel of the Bucharest Jewish community. The personnel office was actually a section of the security police.

Madame Frankel was an illiterate and stupid woman, but she wielded immense power. Many people were rightly terrified of her. Her word was enough to cause the downfall of a respectable member of the community, and even to send him to prison. Her extremism in her efforts to please her masters even surprised leaders of the CDE. Thus, on May Day and on 7 November, the anniversary of the Russian Revolution, she ordered all Jewish institutions to be decorated in red. Not only had red flags to be flown, but the walls had to be covered with red material. As the latter did not exist in sufficient quantities, she took the white shrouds from the cemeteries (which, according to Jewish ritual prescription, were meant for *Tachrichim*, for clothing the dead), had them painted red and turned into flags. No wonder she gave the impression that she had gone mad. If so, it was a dangerous madness. She told the authorities that Jews put gold and dollars into the graves of their relatives, and she regularly went to the Jewish cemetery to watch the funerals and look for proof. Jews ran away from the cemetery when they saw her arriving.

After visiting the Soviet Union, she gave lectures to the community. At one of her thoroughly boring talks, in which she praised the 'glorious Stalin' and the wonders of life in the Soviet Union, she remarked, 'And now I will describe to you the most exciting moment of my life. It was when I sat under a tree in Moscow, where Comrade Stalin had sat! To mark this great occasion, I took several leaves from the trees and brought them here.' She then produced some leaves from a basket and distributed them to the bemused audience, which simulated great interest in and happiness on seeing 'Stalin's leaves'. What made her action even more ridiculous was the fact that the leaves were not from Moscow, but from a tree in Bucharest.

Madame Frankel had an assistant, a man called Shraga, whose title was general secretary of the Jewish Bucharest community but whose real job was to spy on his fellow Jews. He came to synagogue not to pray but to keep an eye upon the congregation. I was, of course, the main object of his activity. He was particularly keen to observe if I talked to members of the Israeli Embassy who came to our services. In one of his written reports, which later fell into my hands, he informed the CDE and, through them, the security police that 'The Chief Rabbi did not exchange any words with the Embassy officials, but their eyes exchanged such looks! It was terrible!'

Anyone wishing to obtain a job in the community institutions had first to visit the office of the head of personnel. The applicant had to write down a detailed account of his life, starting from his childhood. There were hundreds of questions to be answered. Shraga once explained to me the reason for this: 'When a man writes his autobiography, he denounces himself. The best agent to uncover a man's guilt is the man himself. He believes that he can get away with not telling the truth, but he is wrong. I can, in fact, hit two birds with one stone. If I summon a friend mentioned in the autobiographical account, there is always a slight contradiction between what the man has written and what his friend remembers about him. Thus the friend also falls into our hands. Even if he is his best friend, he will usually provide new information about our man in order to escape from our clutches. I then go back to the first man and tell him what the other one has said about him. He is naturally upset and begins to blurt out information about the two of them.'

This was the situation in which we had to live. This was the depth of degradation to which the CDE had reduced life in our community.

When Chaim Weizmann, the President of Israel, died in 1952, the Israeli Embassy asked for a memorial service to be held at the Choral Temple thirty days after his funeral, as is traditional in Jewish life. But Bacal and the other leaders of the Federation would not allow the Choral Temple to be used for the service and offered a small synagogue instead, which was totally unsuitable. I therefore had to reject the offer and no Weizmann commemoration took place.

On Simchath Torah (Celebration of the Law), a truly joyful festival, when congregants sing and dance holding the Siphrei Torah (Scrolls of the Law), a specific order was given by the CDE that no member of the Israeli Embassy, who came to join in the celebration, should be presented with a Scroll. I countermanded this order by giving the *gabbai* (warden) of the Temple a quite different one. The whole day before Simchath Torah, the poor *gabbai*, whose name was Filip Stopler, ran from one place to another. On the one hand, he had been threatened by Bacal, who had ordered him not to hold out the Scroll to the Israelis; on the other, he had been firmly told by me to disobey the order. At the last moment, when the doors of the Ark opened, Stopler implored me, 'Chief Rabbi, you are destroying me. I must obey them.'

Fifteen hundred people were in the Choral Temple when I took out the first Sepher Torah from the Ark. I then pronounced in a solemn voice that the *Hakafot* (the procession and rejoicing with the Scrolls) would not proceed unless I gave a Scroll to a member of the Israeli Embassy. I heard a murmur of approval from the huge congregation and presented a Scroll to Mr Drory, a senior Israeli diplomat. As I did so, a man sitting next to Drory heard him remark to another Israeli, in Hebrew, 'The Chief Rabbi is *meshuga* [mad]. He is committing suicide.' The CDE leaders present stared at me venomously, but they knew that they could not bring such a service to an end. They might well have been manhandled by a furious congregation. So the joyful celebrations continued. I knew, of course, that the CDE was planning to make me pay dearly for my disobedience.

20 *A Dramatic Sabbath in Bucharest*

*N*ews of Stalin's death in March 1953 brought great relief to Romanian Jews, but hopes that this would bring an end to the anti-Semitic, Stalinist terror quickly disappeared. This was, indeed, puzzling. We heard that Beria, Stalin's murderous head of the security services, who had helped the tyrant to send millions of people to their deaths, had been dismissed and executed by Stalin's successors. Radical changes in the Soviet Government were announced, and the public was given to understand that the Soviet Union could look forward to a new, freer era.

However, in Romania, the Stalinist grip did not slacken. In fact, some deeds which were not perpetrated when Stalin was alive were now carried out after his death. Pătrăşcanu, one of the most notable Communist leaders, who had been seen as a dangerous rival by President Gheorghiu-Dej and therefore imprisoned, was now tried, accused of all kind of crimes, sentenced to death and executed. This was because Gheorghiu-Dej feared that the probable liberalization would bring about Pătrăşcanu's release. Of course, a Jew had to be involved in the Pătrăşcanu plot and, thus, engineer Calmanovici, a veteran Communist fighter, was also executed.

Gheorghiu-Dej became the most powerful figure in the country. It was he who first evolved the revolutionary idea that Romania should loosen the Kremlin's grip and that the country should be independent, while remaining strictly Marxist–Leninist and a loyal member of the Communist bloc. This notion was to have a dramatic effect on the fate of Romanian Jews.

As slowly, too slowly, the effect of Stalin's death began to be felt even in Romania, I was puzzled by the Government's policy towards the Jewish community. The ban on emigration to Israel was strictly observed. More Zionists were arrested, to add to those who had disappeared in 1950.

In April 1954, the arrested Zionists were brought to trial. Their cases were rapidly heard behind closed doors and more than 200 of their leaders (among them Moshe Benvenisti, the president of the Romanian Zionist organization, and the author A. L. Zissu) were sentenced to life imprisonment, or to twenty or fifteen years in prison.

The atmosphere became almost unbearable. The secret police dominated every synagogue. In May 1954, a dozen young Zionists were arrested. Among them were Rabbi Ephraim Guttman, my secretary; Dr Aron Kahane, the son of Rabbi Saul Kahane; Rabbi David Safran, a nephew of the former Chief Rabbi; and others. I approached everyone who might help to save the lives of these young people. I called on Patriarch Justinian and pleaded with him to intervene. I sent a letter to the Minister of Internal Affairs, Alexandru Drăghici, pleading particularly for Rabbi Guttman and Dr Kahane. I pointed out that Dr Kahane was the son of the *shochet* who had survived the Iaşi death-train ordeal, and that Rabbi Guttman's two brothers had been shot dead in the arms of their father during the Bucharest pogrom. They had both been victims of Fascism and racism. I asked that they should be freed, as they were not guilty of any crime, but I received no reply.

However, a little later, on 12 June 1954 – this date has assumed historic importance for me and my communities – I was 'invited' to appear on the following morning at eight o'clock at the Ministry of Cults to discuss a matter of 'extreme importance'. The timing of the invitation amazed me. The authorities knew very well that I always refused to attend meetings on the Sabbath, yet I was intrigued by the invitation. I became convinced that there had been an important development and that it was essential that I should know about it. I decided to break my rule and to attend the eight o'clock meeting. As the synagogue service did not begin until nine, I hoped to be there in time.

When I arrived, Minister Constantinescu-Iaşi was waiting for me in his room. With him was Bacal. Both looked very serious. The Minister immediately launched into a tirade: 'President Eisenhower and the reactionary Western press have unleashed attacks against Romania in regard to the trials of the Zionists. You must help us to nullify this campaign by issuing a statement denouncing the calumnies against Romania. You must point out the guilt of these spies and traitors. You must fully dissociate yourself from these Zionist criminals and must protest against the attacks by our enemies abroad.'

Trying to play the innocent, I replied, 'I don't know what trials you are referring to, Minister. No newspaper has mentioned any trial.'

Visibly startled, he responded, 'The BBC refers to them every evening.'

'I don't listen to the BBC,' I said. 'I have only just learnt from you that many Jews have been tried behind closed doors and have been sentenced to long terms of imprisonment, yet you want me to say that I approve of the sentences and that they deserve the punishment. Minister, never will my hands be smeared with the blood of these innocent people.' I was shaking with emotion as I pronounced these words. What he was asking me to do was even worse than a theoretical denunciation of Zionism. He was demanding that I should take part in the destruction of brave and dedicated Jews, and that I should condone horrible injustice.

He retorted angrily, 'How dare you cast doubts on our Socialist justice?'

'Minister, this is precisely the way you talked to me fifteen months ago, when you tried to force me to attack the "Jewish poisoner doctors" in Moscow. You became indignant because you felt I was insulting Soviet justice. Now you say I am insulting Romanian justice. I told you then that the "doctors' plot" was an invention, and that the day would come when you would be ashamed of it. That day came sooner than I expected. I am telling you exactly the same thing today. Therefore, it is totally impossible for me to do what you have asked.'

His anger rising, the Minister hissed, 'So you make common cause with the Zionist traitors.'

'Minister, don't try to intimidate me,' I replied. 'Others have tried to do so and failed.'

'The Politburo is waiting for an answer from you, but you even refuse to discuss the question,' he said. Then, turning to Bacal, he exclaimed, 'Comrade Bacal, is this the way you have done your work at the Federation? How can you expect us to deal with such a Chief Rabbi? You must all resign. I intend to resign, too. Our country needs our support and we are not giving it.'

'Minister, neither you nor Mr Bacal needs to resign,' I said quietly. 'I shall resign. I alone am to blame.'

Bacal remained silent. He appeared stunned by the vehemence of our discussion. The Minister impatiently brushed aside my offer as being inadequate and impractical. We kept on talking for several hours, during which he dropped his extreme demands. He would, he said, accept a statement from me confirming that the Jewish communities enjoyed religious freedom and had synagogues, kosher meat, *matzoth* and all the prerequisites for a full religious life.

117

As all this was true, the Minister had no doubt that I would agree to such a statement. When I replied that I would not, he stared at me in amazement.

'How can you refuse?' he exclaimed. 'You yourself have spoken many times of this freedom.'

'True,' I said. 'And I will repeat my words, but not now. If I help you now, I will be an accomplice in the destruction of innocent people.' As I said this, I thought of the Zionists who were suffering appalling conditions in Romanian prisons and were facing long terms of imprisonment which would destroy them. I had to make one supreme effort to save their lives.

Hearing these unexpected words, the Minister totally lost control of himself. He stamped about the room in a fury. I already knew, of course, about his uncontrollable temper, but only later did I learn the real reason for his frustration. The top Romanian leadership, which was holding a meeting that very day, was already toying with the idea of winning Western support for a new policy to bring Romania nearer to the Western powers so as to enable it to be more independent of the Soviet Union. President Eisenhower's accusations had come as an unpleasant shock. Western opinion would be influenced by his statement and the planned new Romanian approach would be jeopardized. It was vitally important for Gheorghiu-Dej and the rest of the Politburo that Eisenhower's accusations should be refuted. There could be no more suitable person to accomplish this than the Chief Rabbi. Hence the intense pressure on me.

In desperation, the Minister calmed down slightly and began to bargain with me. Could I declare that there was no anti-Semitism in Romania? 'No,' I said. However, beginning to sense that I might yet obtain important concessions in regard to the imprisoned young Zionists, and noting that the Minister was no longer threatening me, I said to him, 'I am prepared to meet the Government half-way in regard to the existence of religious institutions, but I alone cannot sign such a statement under the present circumstances. I am willing to convene a meeting of all the rabbis in the country, to talk to them and to persuade them to join me in signing a declaration that there exists religious freedom for Romanian Jews. However, can you imagine, Minister, that Rabbi Hersh Guttman, whose son was recently arrested, could sign such a statement? I must tell you frankly that, if the young Zionists arrested last month are still in prison when the rabbis meet, I will not be able to obtain such a declaration. I, therefore, suggest to the Government that it should immediately free the young Zionists. As soon as this is confirmed, I will convene a rabbis' meeting. It could take place on Monday.'

The Minister quickly reverted to his aggressive stance. Again he became angry and said heatedly, 'How dare you impose conditions on the Government. I absolutely refuse to talk to you any more.'

I rose from the chair and walked out of the room. The Minister remained seated and silent. I could see him clenching his fists. Bacal also remained seated. He looked as if he had been shot.

I walked home in a state of near exhaustion. I felt hot and ill. I recited the Sabbath prayers and was about to sit down to a meal when a government messenger arrived. I was 'invited' to go immediately to the Council of Ministers building in Victory Square. I set out once more on a long walk, fearing that I might collapse at any moment.

When I arrived, I was surprised to find Rabbi Hersh Guttman there. He, too, had been summoned. We were escorted into a large chamber, where we were welcomed by the Deputy Prime Minister, Petre Borilă, who was sitting at the top of the table. With him were Minister of the Interior, Alexandru Drăghici, Constantinescu-Iaşi, another man, who remained silent throughout, and a secretary who took notes.

Borilă received us very politely. He was calm and tried to give the impression that there was no conflict between us. It was as if he wanted to wipe away the memory of the accusations I had been subjected to that very morning by the Minister of Cults. Speaking gravely and quietly, as if he were pronouncing a legal judgement, Borilă said, 'Chief Rabbi, you have sent us a statement about the arrest of two young Zionists, Guttman and Kahane. I believe you know that they are being investigated in regard to political crimes. I am also sure that you appreciate that such a file containing details of the inquiry has to remain secret while the questioning of the accused is still proceeding. Nevertheless, we have decided to make an exception in this instance. Although the investigation has not been completed, we will show you the file because we want you to realize whom you are defending and what kind of scandal you are meddling in.' Then, with a theatrical gesture to impress me the more, Borilă handed me the file.

I carefully read several statements, allegedly made by Rabbi Ephraim Guttman. They were written and signed by him. All were in identical style: 'On such and such a day I met so and so in my father's synagogue and we had a counter-revolutionary discussion', 'I admit that I prepared counter-revolutionary actions', etc. The words 'counter-revolutionary' also appeared frequently in all the statements made by Kahane. They were confusing and contained no precise details.

When I had finished reading the statements, Constantinescu-Iaşi said to me, 'Chief Rabbi, you have declared that you are prepared to stake your head on the innocence of these men. Well, you ought to put your head on the table. You can see that they admit their guilt.'

Drăghici followed this up by sternly remarking, 'From now on you must be more careful about your intercessions. This is not the first time that you have defended our enemies.' It was as if I had suddenly become one of the accused.

Thanking Borilă for allowing me to see the file, I said to them, 'Please excuse me if I am blunt, but it is my duty to reveal all my thoughts about this matter. I cannot understand any of the statements made by Guttman. He does not mention a single criminal offence that he and others have committed. He must provide a full account of his actions so that the judges can determine if they are indeed counter-revolutionary or not.'

Drăghici responded angrily, 'So, Chief Rabbi, you don't believe us in this matter either. We decide to be helpful to you and show you the secret file, but you reply by insulting us!'

'It is not my intention to insult you,' I said, 'but I must understand what offences these two young men have committed. This file does not reveal a single criminal offence committed by either of them.'

'You are always ready to defend the Zionists, who are worse than the Iron Guard,' declared Drăghici. Then he added, wagging his finger at me, 'You have also accused us of being Fascists.'

I was amazed by this claim. When was I supposed to have done this? Drăghici handed me the letter I had written requesting that Guttman and Kahane be freed. The handwritten letter (I could not trust anyone at the Federation to type it for me) described the sufferings of their fathers. Drăghici pointed to the words on the second page, where I had referred to these elderly men as having been the victims of Fascism and had asked that their sons be freed, and said that I had insulted the Communist Government by describing it as Fascist.

Now thoroughly roused, I said, 'If you, the Minister of the Interior, in the presence of the Deputy Prime Minister and the Minister of Cults, can mention the second page of my letter without referring to the first page, which clearly explains to whom I was referring when I wrote about Fascists – the organizers of the Bucharest and Iaşi pogroms – then I can imagine what is happening to those being interrogated by your agents in the prisons. You say that the Zionists are worse than the Fascists, but I should like to ask you if you have caught a single Zionist who wants to overthrow the Government and kill you, as the Fascists do. The Zionists want to go to Israel. They are not plotting against any Communist regime.'

Noticing that I had not been interrupted I decided to continue speaking: 'You accuse me of not educating the rabbis to be patriotic. Three rabbis have been arrested during the six years of my Chief Rabbinate – Rabbi Grosz of Carei, Rabbi Eliezer Portugal and Rabbi Dr N. Schönfeld of Arad – all of whom were set free after their innocence was established by the highest authorities. It was not I and my search for truth that had harmed the country, but your agents who had arrested innocent men. Now a fourth young rabbi has been seized.'

I mentioned that hundreds of Christian priests had been arrested and accused of Fascist plots against the Government, among whom were former members of the Iron Guard. The Government met with little opposition from the Orthodox Church, to which the great majority of the population belonged, but Roman Catholics, with their continued allegiance to the Pope in Rome, created a major problem. I argued that by arresting only four rabbis, the Government itself was admitting that the rabbis of Romania were not disloyal.

At this moment, Rabbi Guttman, who had remained silent, intervened. With tears in his eyes, he begged for his son's freedom.

I now decided on a new tactic: to challenge the Communist leaders in their own stronghold. I had noticed that the Ministers were listening to me with attention. Could they be made to understand Zionism and thus lessen their unreasonable hostility towards it? It was worth trying.

I, therefore, said to the Ministers, 'You Communists say that no phenomenon can be dealt with unless its origins are analysed. I have never yet succeeded in analysing the phenomenon of Zionism in front of you. Have you got time to listen to me?'

'We have all the time that is necessary and we are willing to listen to you, Chief Rabbi,' Borilă replied.

Thus encouraged, I launched into a prolonged analysis of Zionism and how it had been treated in the Soviet Union and Romania. In Russia, the Jews had been told from the very beginning, from the first day after the 1917 revolution, that they could not leave for Palestine because Russia was their motherland. But in Romania, the Communist Party had organized the departure of tens of thousands of Jews to Israel. It had participated in Zionist meetings and co-operated with the Zionists in every aspect of Jewish life. Suddenly, in November 1948, Zionism was denounced as a crime and Zionists as criminals. Yet, while the Zionist offices were closed down, the weekly voyages of ss *Transylvania* to Israel continued, with thousands of Jews aboard. The ordinary Jew was bewildered by this paradox. What added to his bewilderment was that families were haphazardly split up: parents were allowed to leave for Israel, but not their children, or vice versa. And now emigration had totally stopped. No one had given a credible explanation for these decisions.

I described the ideals of Zionism, the wish to establish a home for a people which had suffered more than any other nation in history, and asked, 'How can it be claimed that Zionism is an enemy of the Romanian Communist Party and people?' I gave examples of how Jews who were friends of Romania and of the regime had been maltreated while the real enemies had escaped justice. My wife's sister, Jenny Ruckenstein, who had survived deportation to Transnistria, had taken a government job in Bucharest and had been so conscientious and hard-working that she had been given as an example for others to follow; but the moment she had applied to go to Israel, she had been dismissed from her post. A colleague of hers called Tomaziu, a member of a Moldavian land-owning family whose fortune had been confiscated and a bitter enemy of the Communist regime, had been ordered by the personnel officer not to have any contacts with my sister-in-law. Shaking with laughter, Tomaziu had said to Jenny, 'You are their enemy and I am their friend. What stupidity!'

I complained that only Jews were subjected to special tests. A mere accusation of Zionism could destroy them, while the Romanians, Germans and Hungarians could proclaim their devotion to the regime and be believed despite any charges of disloyalty. Jews had been sacked when applying to go to Israel and been stranded when refused permission to leave. At the same time, their children were thrown out of schools and universities. I spoke with deep emotion, as if I were making my last will and testament. I did not expect to leave the room a free man. I spoke for nearly four hours. The Communist leaders listened attentively to the end. Not once was I interrupted. The only sound heard in the room, apart from my voice, was that of the pencil used by the secretary to take notes.

When I finished, Borilă thanked me and told me that the Government would take into consideration what I had said. They would analyse the problem afresh. 'We have never heard such a point of view,' he remarked.

Assuming again the tone of a judge, Borilă said, 'Chief Rabbi, we are willing to comply with your request to set free the young Zionists who are under arrest, but there have to be conditions. They took money from the Israeli Embassy. Rabbi Ephraim Guttman, who acted as your secretary, received money frequently. Do you agree to put in writing that you will re-educate him, so that he should not do anything of the kind in future? Do you promise that, if he commits another offence, you will denounce him to the authorities?'

Before I could answer, Drǎghici interrupted to say, 'You will not obtain this promise from the Chief Rabbi. He trains his people not to be *moosers* [informers].'

'Indeed,' I said, 'I teach my staff to behave morally. Informing on others is an immoral action. Your people should do their jobs, and mine should do theirs. But I am prepared to sign a declaration that I shall be responsible in future for their not repeating the mistake of taking money from the Israeli Embassy.'

Borilǎ suggested that they should draft the declaration, but once again Drǎghici interrupted, saying, 'The Chief Rabbi will not sign any declaration now. It is the Sabbath and he will not sign anything before three stars are visible in the sky, proclaiming the end of the Sabbath.' Clearly Drǎghici had learned some details of Jewish customs. I confirmed the accuracy of his words, but we nevertheless went ahead with the preparation of the statement.

We agreed that in the evening I would go to the Council of Ministers and sign the declaration. Immediately after the signing, the Zionist prisoners would be set free. On Monday morning, a meeting of the rabbis would take place. They, too, would sign the statement confirming that Romanian Jews had synagogues, kosher food, Talmud Torahs, *mikvaoth* and all other requisites for a full religious life.

After they promised to release the group of young Zionists, I raised the problem of David Safran, who was also in jail. For some unknown reason, he frequently slandered me, although I was unaware of ever having done him any harm. On the contrary, I had helped him in a number of ways. He had also slandered his uncle, the former Chief Rabbi. When I mentioned Safran's name to Drǎghici, he gasped, 'Don't you know that he keeps making statements accusing you of all kinds of crimes?'

'That's why I am asking you to set him free,' I replied. 'This man is totally irresponsible.' Drǎghici made a note and promised to free Safran.

I left the Council of Ministers totally exhausted. Rabbi Guttman, who was with me, feared that I would collapse. My legs were shaking and I reached home with great difficulty. My wife was anxiously awaiting me. She had not eaten anything, fearing that I had been arrested. Rabbi Guttman gave her a full account of my confrontation with the Ministers and the release of the Zionists. I could see the happiness that she felt.

In the evening a car arrived from the Council of Ministers, which took me, Rabbi Guttman and Rabbi Saul Kahane to Victory Square. We all three signed the declaration, watched by Constantinescu-Iaşi.

The whole group of young Zionists were set free before midnight. On the following morning, I sent telegrams to all the rabbis throughout the country, inviting them to the meeting on Monday. The decision taken by the Ministers on that Saturday was to have a crucial effect on the destiny of Romanian Jews.

From that day on, the leadership of Romania began to view the Jewish problem, Zionism and Israel in a different way. We were no longer 'spies' and 'traitors'. A certain comprehension concerning our fate, our way of thinking, and our hopes and ideals came to be felt in my relations with the Government.

The Sabbath was a 'great Sabbath' in the history of Romanian Jewry. Just as Sabbath Haggadol prepared the way for Passover, the day of freedom, this Sabbath of ours prepared the opening of the gates for our journey to the Land of Israel.

2 1   *President Groza: A Remarkable Human Being*

Although we did have religious freedom, I was always conscious of the fact that we had to be prepared to defend every part of it, and not merely the synagogues. Thus, one day in April 1954, we were surprised to see our kosher butchers turned away from the slaughter-houses. An order had been given forbidding them to perform their duties. I discovered that this prohibition applied not only to Bucharest, but to every kosher slaughterhouse in the country. Without any warning whatsoever, the Romanian Jewish community, 300,000 strong, was deprived of a basic food: kosher meat.

When I urgently sought information from the meat departments in the various ministries – Cults, Food and Internal Trade – I realized that the ban was not due to any technical problem or to a temporary shortage of cattle. It was due to a hostile political decision. Such a decision could have been taken only at the highest level of the Government.

I was given various explanations for the ban. One was the old argument that Jewish ritual slaughter was a barbaric method and caused more suffering to the cattle than the more modern method used by the rest of the population. Another argument against the Jewish method, *shechita*, was that Jews were allowed by their religion to eat only the front part of the animal, which was of superior quality, leaving the inferior back part to the gentiles. I collected a mass of expert scientific veterinary material to disprove the first claim as absurd. As for the second one, I analysed the prices established by the Govern-ment, which clearly demonstrated that the back part was more expensive than the front part and was, in fact, of superior quality. However, I made no progress and Jews were without meat for several months.

Feeling that I would never succeed in having this decision reversed if

I kept on appealing to the Ministries, I decided to approach no less a person than President Groza, with whom I was on very good terms and whom I considered a friend of the Jews.

He immediately espoused our cause and promised to do his utmost to put an end to the situation. However, at our next audience, I found him very much distressed. He told me in a sad voice, 'I raised the problem of the meat at the end of a meeting of the Political Bureau [Politburo], but met with harsh, stubborn opposition – in fact, with a flat refusal. I was very upset and could hardly sleep last night.'

I sent a well-documented statement on *shechita* to Gheorghiu-Dej, but received no reply. There now appeared little chance that the anti-*shechita* decision would be reversed. Very powerful forces were obviously against it. I now supposed that the Russian authorities had suggested such a ban, for reasons best known to themselves.

On 7 December 1954, I led a delegation of rabbis to congratulate President Groza on his seventieth birthday. As usual, the President received us kindly and with much respect. I was also invited to a dinner given by the Government and the Communist Party at the Grand National Assembly in honour of the President. I told my wife that I was feeling relaxed because I would not have to make a speech. On such formal occasions only representatives of the Government, the party, the armed forces, the peasants, science, literature and the trade unions made speeches. If it was thought necessary that the Cults should have a speaker, the choice inevitably fell on the Orthodox Patriarch, who would speak on our behalf.

When I went to take my seat, I noticed an unusual seating arrangement, which could not have come about by pure chance. Patriarch Justinian was sitting in the sixth or seventh seat after Gheorghiu-Dej and Groza. In terms of places, I was farther away from these two leaders, but my seat was opposite theirs. Formally it could not be said that I had been given precedence over the Orthodox Patriarch, with his many millions of followers, but the fact remained that my seat was nearer the leaders. In Communist countries such facts have special significance.

Following a number of speeches, the Patriarch rose to speak and took out a piece of paper from his pocket. As he did so, I noticed the President whisper something into Gheorghiu-Dej's ear. When the Patriarch finished speaking, Gheorghiu-Dej rose and, to the amazement of all present, walked round the table, came up to me and asked me to address the assembly. Very surprised, I murmured, 'But, sir, the Patriarch has already spoken.' At that very moment, a technician came up and placed a microphone in front of me. Gheorghiu-Dej told him, 'Take the microphone away. The Chief Rabbi is not ready yet. He will speak a little later.' I interrupted him, saying, 'As the microphone is already here, I will speak now.' Gheorghiu-Dej went back to his seat, satisfied. My spontaneous words were well received. It so happened that the microphone in front of Groza and Gheorghiu-Dej had not been switched off and every word they uttered was heard by the assembled guests, although they were unaware of this. As I spoke, the guests heard them make complimentary comments. It was an extraordinary experience for all present – and for me.

As the food was being served, Groza once again began to speak to Gheorghiu-Dej, who nodded, stood up, came up to me and asked, 'What can we offer you?'

'Thank you very much,' I replied, 'but I suppose you know that we Jews have become vegetarians as we are prohibited from eating kosher meat.' Gheorghiu-Dej started laughing and said, 'I know the situation, but you have scored a hit.' He then turned to Borilă, who was responsible for trade, and said, 'I want to speak to the comrades who are dealing with meat problems.' Shortly afterwards, Pascu Ştefănescu, Minister for Meat, and Podoleanu, Minister for the Food Industry, both of them Jews, made their appearance. Gheorghiu-Dej told them, 'Tomorrow, the Jews will once again have kosher meat!'

It was a happy moment for me. Groza seemed to be equally delighted. After the dinner, as we were walking to the cloakroom, the President came up to me, kissed me on both cheeks and said, 'Chief Rabbi, I would like you to have a meal, including meat, at my residence.'

'Sir, you know very well that this is not possible,' I said. 'I am very honoured by your invitation, but meat is forbidden. I will have coffee or tea with you with great pleasure.'

Smiling, he remarked, 'Not only you, Chief Rabbi, but also other Orthodox rabbis, whom you will select, will have a full meal, including meat, at my house.'

I looked at him in surprise. What was in his mind? He went on to assure me that I could not possibly object. What he intended to do would meet all my *kashruth* requirements!

Indeed, that is precisely what happened. The kitchen of the President of Communist Romania was stripped of all utensils. New utensils were brought in – and what utensils! The President had just received as a birthday gift 700 pieces of a splendid dinner service from Pieck, the President of East Germany. The service had still not been unwrapped. Groza ordered that the plates should be used for our dinner. Saul Kahane, who was supervising the *kashruth* requirements of the dinner, told the President that the plates would have to be ritually immersed in the *mikvah*. 'Please, do so,' the President told him. He also visited the kitchen to ensure that all Rabbi Kahane's *kashruth* instructions were followed by the staff. The dinner, which took place on Tuesday, 1 February 1955, was very festive, with a full meat course. Several leading Orthodox and Chassidic rabbis joined me. It was a kosher meal that they would never forget.

For four hours, special synagogal and Jewish folk music accompanied our meal. A photograph was taken of the whole group with the President and his wife.

The dinner was excellent, but – more important – thousands upon thousands of other lunches and dinners in all the kosher homes in Romania were the result of the friendship and the humanitarian feelings of a great man and statesman: Dr Petru Groza.

Groza was to play a unique role in my life. Although the President of an atheistic state, he continued to show me warm personal friendship. He was forever smiling and he enjoyed a joke. He actually wielded very little political power, because the real power was in the hands of Gheorghiu-Dej. But Groza had some influence, as he showed in the mysterious affair of the decision to ban and then to allow kosher meat. I still don't fully understand today why Gheorghiu-Dej behaved in such a friendly fashion at the dinner. He was probably in a particularly good mood and happy to enjoy a temporary truce with a Chief Rabbi with whom he was in such basic conflict. Or perhaps this was his birthday gift to Groza.

Groza was the son of a priest and he was brought up in an unusual spirit of tolerance and respect for other religious views. He used to describe how he had attended a *cheder* (a Jewish religious school) when a child, because there was no Christian school near his house. He recalled with relish certain Jewish traditional dishes, especially *cholent* or *sholet*, which were popular on the Sabbath. At our dinner, Groza insisted on having *cholent* on the menu, despite the fact that it took place on a Tuesday and not on the Sabbath.

Despite his background, Groza became a successful financier and landowner. He went on to form a peasants' party, calling it the Ploughmen's Front, and made an alliance with the Romanian Communists when they were being persecuted. When they took over the Government, Groza was invited to join it, probably because he was

...t high school in Fălticeni, 1927. Back row, second from left is Dumitru Contici, with whom I had my ...rst encounter with anti-Semitism; I am at extreme right.

...y mother, Rabbanit Taube Rosen

My father, Gaon Avraham Arie Rosen

Standing with my family, 1938. Seated left to right: my brother-in-law Rabbi Dr Wolf Gottlieb, my parents and my sister Bracha.

My wedding

Bar-Mitzvah ceremony in 1948

My brother Elias, who was killed in Auschwitz

Rabbi Zisse Portugal

With Chief Rabbi Wilhelm of Sweden, 1956

With members of the delegation of the Rabbinical Council of America in Bucharest and Professor Dogaru (extreme left), CDE leader Israel Bacal (third from left), and Minister of Cults Constantinescu-Iaşi (fourth from left)

During an audience with President Petru Groza and CDE leaders Bercu Feldman and Leibovici Şerban

resident Ceauşescu and members of his Government receiving the heads of cults, 1965

Left: Distributing 3,500 scrolls in
Israel, Jerusalem 1966

Right: Talking to children
during a *Seder* in Bucharest

bove: European rabbis dancing in Dorohoi

ancing with the scrolls on Simchat Torah in Bucharest

Speaking on the anniversary of the Iași pogrom

The first delegation of rabbis to the Soviet Union at a meeting with the Secretary of the Supreme Soviet of the USSR, 1989

popular with the public. He accompanied Gheorghiu-Dej and Stefan Voitec on a mission to the Kremlin after the Russians' victory. Describing the scene to me, Groza said, 'As we were walking up the Kremlin stairs I noticed that Gheorghiu-Dej was as excited as a schoolboy going to see his headmaster and Voitec's beard was shaking. I felt composed and proud, having decided what I was going to do. From the very first moment of our meeting, Stalin and I became friends. The atmosphere of the discussion was very relaxed. Between drinks, I was able to save Romania from a great misfortune – Soviet occupation.'

Before the Communist take-over, Groza was for a time Prime Minister of a very divided, acrimonious government. Right-wing and left-wing members were always squabbling. During one particularly stormy meeting, when ministers almost came to blows, Groza banged the table and said, 'Gentlemen, I am adjourning the meeting for two hours. In the meantime, will you please accompany me to another place.' The surprised ministers put their coats on and followed him outside. When they entered their cars, he ordered his driver to take him to the astronomical observatory. All the other cars followed in a long procession. Inviting the ministers to enter the building, he asked them to watch carefully the harmonious movement of the planets. They did so, while thinking all the time that he had lost his reason. 'Well,' he said to them, 'what have you got to say now? Look how small our planet is, compared with others. What is the point of our quarrelling? Would it not be better if, like the stars, we lived in harmony?' According to Groza, the ministers calmed down and even began to exchange jokes with one another. They then returned to the Cabinet chamber and resumed their discussions in a more friendly frame of mind.

Once, Groza invited me to visit his cellar. There I saw a very beautiful statue of him, by one of the best sculptors in the country. With his normal sense of humour, Groza explained, 'You know, a day will come when it [the statue] will be put up and I will be put down [in the grave]. But as long as I am up and about, I want to keep it down here.' Every time I pass through the street where the statue stands, I think of Groza's joke.

The President astonished me one day by telling me that he had stipulated in his will that I should be one of the officiants at his funeral. With a broad smile, he told me, 'I wish to make certain of winning the game. One can never tell what is up there. Perhaps you, Chief Rabbi, are the one who is right.'

129

I thought he was joking and forgot his remarks. On 5 November 1957, my wife and I were invited by the President and Madame Groza to visit them. He had had an operation and looked pale, but he was as high-spirited as ever. It was a lovely morning and we took a walk in the park. Suddenly, Groza said to me, 'I hope you have not forgotten that I want you at my funeral.'

I protested and said, 'You have tremendous vitality, Mr President. You have recovered well, and it seems to me that you will carry on with your duties and will accomplish your mission. You still have a long time ahead.' The President answered with a parable: 'You might know, Chief Rabbi, that men are like candles. Some candles bend at the end of their burning and others burn straight to the last inch of their thread, keeping their posture. I am like the latter. I'll keep standing as long as I live, like a candle burning to the very end.'

Two months later, on 7 January 1958, I was visiting a Jewish cemetery at Piatra Neamţ, when I was called to the telephone. A government official informed me that the President had died. His will contained a request that I should be an officiant at the burial service. I returned immediately to Bucharest and, on the following day, wearing full rabbinical canonicals with a Magen David (a Shield of David emblem), I stood at the side of the coffin in which the dead President lay. Near me were the Prime Minister and other government ministers. The burial service began with the Patriarch of the Christian Orthodox Church reciting Christian prayers. Then I was invited to conduct a traditional Jewish funeral service in Hebrew. The Romanian public, watching the funeral on television or listening on the radio, must have been deeply impressed.

My friendship with Groza would have had little effect on the problems of our community if it had not been for his barber, Max Friedman, a very loyal and devoted Jew. In times of crisis, no one could approach the President so decisively as Max. No minister or official could be so persuasive. What we told Max at midnight would reach the President's ears at six o'clock next morning, when he was being shaved.

Many Jewish lives were saved through Max's interventions. Zionists should erect a statue in his honour. For example, when we heard that Moshe Benvenisti, the former president of the Zionist Organization of Romania, was dangerously ill in prison, I immediately contacted Max. The information I had been given was that Benvenisti would die if he were not released and given special treatment. It was even said that he had already gone into a coma. Max gave the message to the President on the next morning. Benvenisti was released and his life was saved.

My wife and I regularly invited Max and his wife to our house for meals. We also visited them at their home. Though very poor, Max would never accept any money from me. He would say to me, 'Chief Rabbi, I am not well off and the money would be useful, but I cannot take it. If you asked me to help you in arranging an appointment which would benefit you personally, I would have no hesitation in taking money from you. But what you are doing, Chief Rabbi, is for the sake of our community. Don't I have the right to a small share in your good deeds?'

It would be pleasant to say that Max eventually received due reward for his goodness of heart and sterling character. Alas, this did not happen. He and his wife decided to leave for Israel and sold their few belongings. He had hoped to continue working as a barber but, for one reason or another, he found that impossible. Officials in Israel did not prove very helpful to him. He was given a job picking oranges, which was not very congenial. He became ill, but remained cheerful. He never complained. When we heard of his plight, I sent him small sums of money. However, his health deteriorated and he died, still a comparatively young man. His wife died a few months later. My wife and I arranged for their gravestones. We were profoundly shocked as we owed Max so much and gave him so little.

22 *The Story of a Magen David*

*I*t was on Yom Kippur, October 1940, that I first wore on my chest a large Magen David. Having just returned from the concentration camp at Miercurea Ciuc, I was invited to preach at the Reshit Dat synagogue in Bucharest. As I have already mentioned, I had no rabbinical vestments and had to borrow some from Rabbi Alperin. Leonte Karmitz, the rich man who had arranged for a tailor to make my new rabbinical vestments, also asked me what else I needed. I told him that I would like a Magen David, as it was a symbol of Jewish solidarity and hope. At that dark period of Jewish history, this symbol had taken on additional significance. Karmitz ordered the Magen David to be made of gilt, and my mother gave me the gold chain she used to wear on festive occasions.

Then came the years of the Yellow Star, which the Nazis forced Jews to wear. What the Nazis used to try to shame us, I turned into a source of pride. In my sermons I emphasized that the Magen David, the Star of David, which our enemies wanted to represent as ignoble, was in fact an emblem of our glorious national history, of a time when we had our own country and our own capital, the City of David.

After our liberation from Nazism, which I saw also as the liberation of the Magen David, I displayed it everywhere. I explained to my congregations the Magen David's special significance and the hope that it provided for me and for the Jewish people. However, I began to notice that the CDE men were looking askance at the Magen David as they saw it as the equivalent of the Zionist flag. At the beginning they hesitated to complain, but when they started to raid synagogues and erase the painted Magens David from the walls, they tried to persuade me to stop wearing it. Feldman, Şerban, Bacal and Friedman continually raised the question and argued that I was wearing a Zionist symbol, but I stolidly refused to accept their demands. In their secret denunciations to the authorities, they frequently mentioned my wearing of the Magen David as proof of disloyalty to the regime and of championing the cause of Zionism.

On a Saturday morning in July 1953, while I was attending the service at the Choral Temple, a special messenger delivered an invitation to me from Gheorghiu-Dej. I was asked to be present at luncheon in the Palace of the Council of Ministers in honour of the heads of delegation to the Youth Festival, a major event of that time. Wearing my rabbinical vestments, I walked over to Victory Square, where the Palace was situated. As no kosher food was available, I only ate some fruit.

As I prepared to leave, Gheorghiu-Dej walked up to me and invited me to watch a football match between Romania and Hungary, which was part of the festival and was also meant to inaugurate the new stadium. Despite the fact that this invitation was very strange, I could not refuse it. I am sure that he did not realize that, being a Sabbath, I would have to walk a long way to the stadium. Having to wear my rabbinical vestments was an additional burden, especially as it was a hot midsummer day. I was utterly exhausted by the time I reached the stadium.

I was surprised and gratified to find that I had been allocated a place in the grandstand, where Gheorghiu-Dej and the rest of the Politburo were sitting – the only Cult head to be so honoured. Another, even more gratifying surprise awaited me. At the opening ceremony the foreign delegations entered the stadium in alphabetical order. My heart filled with pride when I saw a group of young Israelis marching. In front of them, two young men were holding aloft the blue-and-white flag of Israel with its prominent Magen David.

Sitting there also was Iosif Chişinevschi, a member of the Politburo. Though a Jew, he was extremely hostile to all things Jewish. He was a powerful politician, who, for a time, headed the propaganda machine and was held responsible for the Stalinist terror. Anti-Semites were spreading hatred against us by pointing at Chişinevschi as the 'evil Jew' who was the source of all the troubles that had befallen them.

When the Israeli delegation entered the stadium with their flag, Chişinevschi rose from his seat and said icily to Gheorghiu-Dej in my presence, 'Comrade Dej, now you can see with your own eyes that I was right. The Chief Rabbi wears the Israeli flag on his breast.'

Hearing this remark, I felt stunned. Gheorghiu-Dej, noticing the expression on my face, laughed and, in a friendly and even sympathetic voice, told me not to worry. At the end of the performances,

Gheorghiu-Dej came up to me, shook my hand and thanked me for accepting his invitation. He had been informed that I had walked all the way to the stadium and he remarked with a smile, 'Chief Rabbi, you have taken a lot of exercise today!' When I tried to explain to him that the Magen David was the symbol of the Jewish religion of ancient times, he laughed again and said, 'There is no need for any explanations.' It was clear that he did not attach any importance to the complaints against me on this score.

In the following year, Bulganin, Khrushchev and Mikoyan, the three new rulers of the Soviet Union after Stalin's death, paid a visit to Bucharest. A reception was given by the Romanian leaders in their honour. I was one of around 200 guests at the Council of Ministers when the Russian visitors walked in. They walked between two rows, bowing their heads in acknowledgement of the greetings but not shaking hands. As Khrushchev was about to pass me, he saw the Magen David on my chest. He stopped, shook my hand and began to speak to me in Russian. Noticing that I did not understand the language, he summoned the translator who accompanied him and began to ask me questions. He wanted to know how many Jews there were in Romania, how they were being treated and how many rabbis remained in the country. The conversation lasted several minutes. Bulganin, who had preceded Khrushchev, noticed that he had stopped and walked back to join us.

The Politburo leaders and the other guests looked on this scene with amazement. Khrushchev's unusual behaviour at international gatherings became well known in later years when he rose to be the sole Soviet leader, but at that time it was still a total novelty. That Soviet leaders visiting a fellow Communist state, and arriving at an official reception, should make a point of having a long conversation with the Chief Rabbi, while ignoring the country's leaders and dignitaries, was beyond all belief.

It was a tremendous sensation. I was totally at a loss to understand Khrushchev's aim in singling me out in such a public manner. His gesture could be taken as an open demonstration of sympathy with the Jews. Coming so soon after the death of Beria, the visit to Romania may have given Khrushchev a chance to distance himself from the previous regime. Whatever the explanation, Khrushchev's gesture became the great talking-point in Bucharest. When I met Professor Constantinescu-Iași, the then Minister of Cults, on the following day, he shook my hand and said smilingly, 'Your hand, Chief Rabbi, shook Khrushchev's hand. You have no idea how people envied you!'

When I participated in the ecumenical peace congress in East Berlin, in 1960, I addressed the 2,000 Germans who had gathered in the hall: 'Look at my chest. On it is a sign that the Nazis meant to be a stigma of infamy on us Jews. May God be praised for granting me this moment when I can proudly wear, here in Berlin, before your eyes, this emblem of Jewish pride.' In his speech, the Minister of Cults of Communist Germany said, 'David's star on your chest, Chief Rabbi, is the symbol of hope and justice for you, the remnants of the Jewish people.'

Before President Richard Nixon paid a visit to Bucharest, he had been asked by some of my American friends to make a gesture of friendship to me. When he pointed out that he did not know me personally and might not recognize me, he was told that I wore a distinctive Magen David on my chest. My wife and I were among the guests who awaited the President at the reception arranged in his honour; as he walked in, Nixon searched the hall, with his eyes darting from one person to another. Eventually, he looked at me and saw the Magen David on my chest. He smiled at me and winked.

When the orchestra stopped playing the national anthems of the two countries, Nixon walked straight through the rows of ministers and other important personalities without saying a word. While everyone gaped in astonishment, he came up to me and embraced me warmly. 'What a pleasure to meet you here, my friend,' he said. Mrs Nixon, who followed her husband, embraced my wife. We had, of course, never met before and so this was a highly political gesture. Again, David's star was meant to be a shield for me.

We were joined by President and Madame Ceauşescu, while the Romanian Politburo leaders looked on with astonishment. And so, in times of sorrow and in times of joy, the Magen David has played its role as my protector.

I cannot finish this story without relating an episode of misapprehension. In 1968, twenty years after my election as Chief Rabbi, there was an impressive celebration in our community. Many leaders from Israel and the Jewish Diaspora, East and West, participated in the festivities in Bucharest. The Israeli Sephardi Chief Rabbi, Rabbi Yitzhak Nissim, arrived, too, and I received him with all the consideration that his personality deserved.

Several months later, when I visited Israel, Chief Rabbi Nissim and his wife held a reception in honour of my wife and myself at their Jerusalem residence. During the evening, the Chief Rabbi took me aside, apologized in advance for what he was about to say and assured me that he was acting out of sheer friendship.

'Please don't be angry with me, my dear colleague,' he said. 'It's the Magen David which you are wearing and which no other rabbi in the world exhibits. It is an imitation of a non-Jewish rite. Your Magen David looks like the cross on the breast of Christian clergymen. Don't wear it any more, my beloved friend. Please take it off. It looks like a cross.'

I burst out laughing. Chief Rabbi Nissim, who had expected a totally different response, looked at me in astonishment. He could hardly say a word and waited for an explanation of my reaction.

'Do you know why I am laughing?' I asked. He shook his head in puzzlement. 'Let me explain,' I said. 'If anybody had told me during my long and dangerous struggles in Romania, when in order to wear the Magen David and to show my love for Zion I had to face denunciations and to risk my life, that there would come a time when the Chief Rabbi of Israel would tell me in Jerusalem that wearing the Magen David was not Jewish, I would have thought the very idea totally fantastic.

'Thank God I have been wearing it up to now. I shall go on wearing it, for it is a holy sign. If I wore this sign during all those evil days, why should I not do so now? For almost twenty-eight years this golden Shield of David has defended me in time of danger. I keep it not only on my breast but deep in my heart. It speaks to me of past hardships and of hopes for the future. We have become one because we have survived together.

'No, dear Chief Rabbi Nissim, no, with all respect to you, I will never take it off. I will always say to the Shield of David the words of the Prophet: "Make us glad according to the days wherein thou hast afflicted us, and the years wherein we have seen evil" [Psalm 90:15].'

23 *A Landmark: The Helsinki Peace Congress*

By 1955, the effects of Stalin's death and Beria's execution were being felt in Romania to a more marked degree, but it was still a very slow thaw. Thousands of 'little Berias' still existed in the country, clinging tenaciously to power – and to their jobs. Fear had still not been eradicated. Nevertheless, fewer people were disappearing. A series of trials began and people about whom nothing had been heard for years suddenly reappeared. Now at least when people were jailed, the courts of law seemed to be active again. There also appeared to be cracks in the wall that had been erected around Romania during the Stalinist years. From time to time, a foreign delegation arrived and was welcomed. Anyone shaking hands with a foreigner was not inevitably seen as a possible spy who deserved immediate arrest and prolonged interrogation. Only the Zionists were being treated in the same hostile manner. Their leaders were still in prison and there was no sign that they would be released soon.

Yet I felt that the time was ripe to test the authorities' attitude towards me. The opportunity came with the announcement that a major Romanian delegation would participate in the World Peace Assembly that was to take place in Helsinki at the end of June 1955. The Romanian delegation was to be representative of the nation, including the various religious groups. Apart from being Chief Rabbi, I had been active in the National Committee for the Defence of Peace, of which I was a founding member. I was, therefore, fully entitled to be considered for inclusion in the delegation, but would I be allowed to travel abroad? The security police still had doubts about my loyalty to the regime, and some agents, in fact, suspected that I was a traitor and was actively plotting against the Government. I was aware that the security police watched me and checked on my movements: my office and even my home were bugged. The secret police would naturally assume that, once in Helsinki, I would defect and work against the regime.

Thus, when I wrote a letter to Lotar Rădăceanu, a member of the Political Bureau of the Communist Party, who was dealing with the selection of the delegation, suggesting that I should be included, I felt I had a very slim chance of succeeding. Rădăceanu had been the leader of the Social Democrat Party before it merged with the Communists. He was an old friend of mine. I was very pleasantly surprised to receive a reply stating that my suggestion would be seriously considered and, a few days later, I was informed that I would be a member of the delegation.

This was a very significant development. It symbolized a partial change in the attitude of the Government as a whole towards me. I had previously won the friendship and goodwill of some important personalities, particularly President Groza, but such personal friendships could not fundamentally change government policy. Now the door was being left slightly ajar for an historic reassessment. Years were to pass before this could happen, but I have always considered my trip to Helsinki not only as a gratifying event in my own life, but also as a landmark in the history of Romanian Jews. Yet the security services were still not ready to adopt a new attitude.

Travelling by train to Helsinki would have involved desecrating the Sabbath. I, therefore, insisted on travelling by air to Moscow and, from there, going by train to the Finnish capital. When I got on the plane, I noticed a man who pretended to be a journalist, but whom I immediately recognized as a security agent. When I boarded the Moscow–Helsinki train, the man was in a compartment near me. On arrival at the Helsinki railway station I was met by the Romanian Ambassador, Acs (a Jew who now lives in Israel). He offered hospitality at the Embassy both to me and to the fake journalist. I was never alone: when I went for a walk, the Ambassador and his wife insisted on accompanying me. The Ambassador's car and his personal driver were put at my disposal. The fiction was that the Embassy was honouring me with all this attention, but I was actually under constant surveillance.

Had I really wanted to defect to the West, all these precautions would have been useless. The Government trusted me to the extent of allowing me to go abroad; the security services suspected me, but their measures against me were so transparent that they were bound to discredit them. My sister Bracha, the wife of Rabbi Dr Gottlieb of Glasgow, had learned that I was in Helsinki and immediately boarded a plane to see me. On arrival, she telephoned the Romanian Embassy and asked to speak to me. The man who answered the phone subjected her to a prolonged interrogation. How did she know where I was? Why had she come all the way from Scotland? When had she left Romania? He then told her curtly that I was not in the building and that he did not know where I was. Bracha, who had become very anxious about my safety, spoke to the president of the Helsinki Jewish community, Davidkin. Immediately rumours spread that I was being held prisoner in the Romanian Embassy and that the staff was denying that I was there.

I knew nothing of this commotion. On the following day, Sorin Toma, a former editor-in-chief of *Scînteia* who was a leader of the delegation, surprised me by asking, 'Why are you staying at the Embassy?' 'Because I was invited,' I replied. Toma then telephoned the Ambassador and, in a voice shaking with emotion, told him to set me free. 'The Chief Rabbi is free to stay where he wishes, to walk where he wants and to do what he likes,' he stormed at the Ambassador. I protested that I was satisfied with my accommodation and that there was no need to change it. Only when Toma explained to me what had happened to my sister, and told me about the rumours that had spread, did I fully understand his concern. He assured me that nobody would now interfere with my activities. My sister would come to see me very soon. His promise was quickly fulfilled. The meeting with my sister, after so many years of separation, after so many dangers and miracles, brought tears to our eyes. We were able to take long walks together without anyone disturbing us. The Ambassador's car was no longer at my disposal, but this was more a relief than a hardship.

My speech at the peace congress was favourably received. The novelty of a Chief Rabbi speaking at such a congress inevitably led to many requests for press interviews. I was also invited to preach at the main synagogue in Helsinki during the Sabbath morning service. I learned that the leaders of the Romanian delegation, who could not but feel some nervousness in regard to my speeches, were pleased with my remarks.

On the following day, I received a message that the Chief Rabbi of Sweden, Dr Kurt Wilhelm, wished to meet me. Our meeting was to prove of importance to the future of Romanian Jews as he was to make the first breach in the Iron Curtain dividing the remnants of European Jewry. He was a distinguished-looking, highly cultured man, who had a warm and gentle character. He was deeply devoted to the Jewish people. Although his background was that of a German Jew and mine that of an *Ostjude* (Eastern European Jew) – the contempt felt by some German Jews for the *Ostjuden* was notorious – we immediately became friends. We sensed that we were in harmony with each other and we seemed to understand each other perfectly the moment we met. My attitude towards him was not affected in the slightest degree by the fact that he was a quasi-Reform rabbi: normally I found it difficult to make friends with Reform rabbis. We realized with a sense of wonder that we held the same views on many problems and about many people, as well as about the issues which had to be dealt with. On that day in 1955, we laid the foundation of a co-operation which was to have, I believe, historic results.

24 *A Sabbath in Moscow*

When the peace congress ended, more than 2,000 delegates booked seats on flights from Helsinki to other capitals. Our Romanian delegation arranged to travel by train for three days, including Saturday, from Helsinki to Bucharest. I told the leaders of our delegation that, once again, I would not be able to travel by train, as it would involve the desecration of the Sabbath. I realized that the person who was responsible for ensuring that I returned to Bucharest and did not remain in the capitalist world was Aurel Duma (later a deputy Minister for External Affairs) and I could see the fear in his eyes lest I defected. If this happened, he would be ruined.

However, the man who dealt with my travel problems was Toma, who said to me frankly, 'I have been ordered not to return to Bucharest without you. You cannot stay on here after we leave.' I explained to him that I could travel by plane to Moscow and return from there to Bucharest. I saw a chance of remaining in Moscow for a few days and of studying the conditions of Russian Jews. During the Stalinist period, we in Romania had had no possibility of corresponding with other Jewish communities and rabbis – not only in the West, but even in the Communist world. Visiting a foreign country was also out of the question. My trip to Montreux was the one exception, which occurred during the unique period of Soviet support for Israel. The official theory was that there was no Jewish people and, therefore, Romanian Jews could not have links with Jews in other countries.

Toma argued vigorously with me, but, when he realized that I was adamant, he approached the Soviet delegation, who had an aeroplane at its disposal. Toma explained the problem to the Russians and managed to obtain two seats on the Soviet plane – one for himself and one for me. Duma came to the airport to make sure that I left for Moscow. I could see the great relief he felt when he saw me boarding the plane.

When we arrived in Moscow, on a Thursday evening, and checked in at the Hotel National, Toma took out my passport and plane ticket and said, 'Chief Rabbi, your plane leaves tomorrow morning for Bucharest.' I replied that I could not travel on the morrow because it was Friday. I then added, 'I won't travel by air on the Sabbath.' Toma at first thought I had made a mistake and would correct myself, as what I had said appeared illogical. When I repeated the words, he said with rising irritation, 'I know you don't travel on the Sabbath, but tomorrow is Friday!' 'I don't travel on Fridays, either,' I responded. 'One never knows what may happen. If the plane were delayed by some problem, I would be forced to desecrate the Sabbath.' I then added, 'What does it matter to you if I stay longer in Moscow? What are you afraid of? We are no longer on the other side. We are now in the Soviet Union. You have fulfilled your mission and ensured my return to Bucharest. I shall remain at the hotel at my own expense.' Toma again argued with me, but in the end gave in. He knew that he could not take me back to Bucharest by force. He probably attributed my insistence on remaining a few days in Moscow to my keen wish to stroll about the Soviet capital.

On Friday morning, I rang the Romanian Embassy and informed an official there that I wanted to pay a formal visit to the Chief Rabbi of Moscow and to participate in the Sabbath religious services at the main synagogue. His answer was deliberate and icy, 'Chief Rabbi, please don't forget where you are. Your schedule in Moscow will be drawn up by us. You must not call on the Chief Rabbi of Moscow, nor must you go to the synagogue. We will send a guide today to take you to the agricultural exhibition and to the Lenin–Stalin mausoleum.'

'I am sorry but I cannot accept this,' I told the official. 'Patriarch Justinian has paid an official visit to the Patriarch in Moscow, yet you tell me that I am not allowed to call on the Chief Rabbi! In any case, you have no right to prevent me from saying my prayers at the synagogue. You rightly say that we are on Soviet territory. Therefore, it is up to the Soviet authorities to make a decision about my activities. I am merely requesting that you convey my wishes to the Soviet Foreign Ministry. I will naturally accept their decision.'

For a few moments there was silence on the line. The official was obviously puzzled about what he should do. Perhaps he was consulting another, higher placed official. Finally he said, gruffly, 'We'll be sending you a guide.' The guide duly arrived at ten o'clock and we went to the agricultural exhibition. When I returned to the hotel at six o'clock, I found several messages from the Soviet Foreign

Ministry, informing me that Chief Rabbi Schliefer would expect me at the synagogue at eight o'clock in the evening.

I deliberately arrived half an hour early, as I wanted to see by myself how the synagogue was functioning. In the courtyard there were a number of elderly Jews sitting on two long benches. When they saw me, they stood up, but not one of them came to greet me, to ask me who I was, to wish me the traditional '*Shabbat Shalom*', as would have happened in any other synagogue in the world. It was clear to me that these Jews feared any contact with a foreigner, even a rabbi. This fear was the result of bitter experience.

I went through the courtyard and opened the door of the synagogue, but could see no one inside. I turned round and went up to the Jews in the courtyard. 'Where is the rabbi?' I asked them. None of them said a word, but they pointed their fingers to the back of the synagogue. The Chief Rabbi had a room there for the Sabbath. I opened a door and found myself facing Chief Rabbi Schliefer and one of the synagogue wardens. Though surprised at my sudden appearance, the Chief Rabbi received me amiably. I was impressed by his serene face and keen eyes. Later, when we became friends, he revealed that he had been at Jukovsk, a health resort about fifty kilometres from Moscow, when an official arrived on Friday afternoon and took him back to the capital. He was told that an important guest had arrived in Moscow from abroad and that he must meet him at the synagogue. The congregation was not informed. When we entered the synagogue for prayers, I saw that three-quarters of the seats were empty.

Afterwards, the Chief Rabbi invited me to dinner, but it was not a very convivial occasion. It was obvious that he did not trust me. Nor, to tell the truth, did I trust him. We both suspected each other of being an agent of the regime and, therefore, spoke very guardedly. However, towards midnight I decided that I must take a risk and ask him some delicate questions. Was there religious education for Jewish children? Did the community have Talmud Torah classes and *yeshivoth*?

Chief Rabbi Schliefer heard my questions, but did not answer them. I described the conditions under which Romanian Jews were living and how we had managed to establish Talmud Torah courses. I referred obliquely to the settlement of Romanian Jews in Israel. He listened, but remained silent.

When I entered the synagogue next morning, he surprised me by saying, 'This morning you will have the honour of preaching to our congregation. You will be the first foreign rabbi since the revolution to speak here.' While thanking him for the invitation, I asked him, 'Why did you not inform me last night that I would have this honour? You are a preacher yourself and must know that one has to prepare a sermon.' Chief Rabbi Schliefer smiled and said, 'How could I inform you last night when I myself did not know that you would be allowed to preach here?' Clearly, he had been informed only that morning by 'higher circles' that I could address the congregation.

The synagogue was crowded with about 1,500 to 2,000 people when I rose to speak. The congregants were mostly middle-aged or elderly. I saw very few young faces. They listened in complete silence, but this was not a sign of apathy. I noticed that they listened intently, but were afraid to reveal their inner thoughts in case they fell victim to informers, who must have been present.

Speaking in Yiddish, which I was sure most of the congregants understood well, I somehow weaved into my comments on the Torah the problem of Jewish education and Talmud Torahs. I pretended to be ignorant of the fact that religious education was forbidden in the Soviet Union and that offenders were punished by law. As a loyal patriot, I praised the Romanian Government for granting Romanian Jews the right to teach their children the prayers and the Bible in Hebrew. I extolled the virtues of the Hebrew language, knowing, of course, that the Soviet Government forbade the teaching of Hebrew. I also spoke of the Romanian Jewish communities and their institutions, which were tied to our Jewish faith and our Judaic culture. I, therefore, praised my Government for having given these rights to us, because I knew that in Russia not a single organized community existed.

My sermon had the desired effect. The congregants understood the point I was driving home. 'So it is possible to have Talmud Torahs in a Communist country!' many of them exclaimed as they crowded around me afterwards. The fear of the informers seemed to have vanished. The congregants even went on the offensive. When one man came up to shake my hand, a group of people shouted out in unison, 'Don't have anything to do with him. He is a *moosser*.'

During lunch, Chief Rabbi Schliefer was also more forthcoming. Now convinced that he could trust me and, not being inhibited by the presence of any other person, he began to question me. How did I manage to establish Talmud Torahs in Romania? How did I get permission to practise *shechita*, to bake *matzoth*, to keep so many synagogues open? He was avid for information. He described to me his and Soviet Jewry's sad experience. He was the disciple of the great Chief Rabbi of Moscow, Yaacov Mazo, and had become Rabbi of

Alexandrowsk. In the 1930s, years of an immense anti-religious drive by Stalin, rabbis and Jewish leaders were deported to Siberia. Most of them never returned. Not wanting to share their fate, Rabbi Schliefer cut off his beard and *payot* and started work as an accountant. He avoided deportation, but he was wrong in his belief that the security services had lost track of him. In 1941, he was summoned by the NKVD and ordered to reopen the main synagogue in Moscow. The German invasion of the Soviet Union had started and the authorities were keen to win over Western opinion by showing that there was religious freedom in the country. Rabbi Schliefer begged the authorities to leave him alone and not force him to take part in a charade, but they insisted. For months he came daily to the synagogue and unlocked the big doors, but the synagogue remained completely empty. No Jew dared to enter it. Everyone feared that the NKVD had set a trap for unwary Jews.

Sighing deeply, Chief Rabbi Schliefer spoke of his profound distress at not being able to achieve anything worthwhile for Judaism in the Soviet Union. He was resigned to this failure and could see no possibility of improvement. He warned me repeatedly that, sooner or later, I would become a victim. He spoke about the terror felt by Russian Jews during the last days of Stalin's life and their fear that they might be deported.

I considered Chief Rabbi Schliefer a great, but tragic figure. He had a profound knowledge of the teachings of the Torah and the works of the various commentators, yet he felt helpless when confronted by the power of a huge, atheistic state. This made him a very sad man. I felt that he was too pessimistic. On the following day, Sunday, he invited me to officiate at a wedding. The bridegroom, who arrived in the synagogue in civilian clothes, was an officer in the Soviet army. That such a man would want to be married by a rabbi in a synagogue was to me a hopeful sign for Soviet Jewry.

Chief Rabbi Schliefer and five other Jews came to the airport to bid me good-bye. As I walked up the steps to the aeroplane, they shouted, '*Leshana Haba B'Yerushalyim* [Next Year in Jerusalem]', a traditional blessing. I was deeply moved. Only two years after Stalin's death, Russian Jews were beginning to voice openly their love for Zion.

I concluded my first Moscow visit, repeating to myself the words of the Jewish national anthem: '*Odlo avda tikvateinu* [Our hope is not lost]'.

25 A First Rift in the Jewish Iron Curtain

*R*eturning to Bucharest, I began to consider the possibility of inviting Chief Rabbi Wilhelm to Romania. I noticed that the contacts I had made with Western personalities in Helsinki were viewed with interest in official circles in Bucharest. The authorities appeared impressed by the favourable notices which my speeches were given in the Western press. Even a Communist member of the Canadian Parliament, Zalzberg, wrote a complimentary account. I also realized with relief that my house was no longer being watched by the security police, nor was I being followed by their agents. I considered that the chance of my being arrested had receded. Apparently my behaviour in Helsinki and my willingness to return to Romania had convinced the authorities that I was not an enemy working against the regime.

I considered that, in such a climate, a visit by Chief Rabbi Wilhelm could prove very useful. The gates of the country still remained closed to *aliyah* to Israel, and thousands of Jewish families were still torn apart and yearning to be reunited. Occasionally a Jew might get permission to leave, but this was very rare. Moreover, while many imprisoned Zionists had been set free, others, particularly members of the Revisionist (right-wing) group, were still in captivity. And none of the freed Zionists had been granted permission to leave for Israel.

When I was told that Chief Rabbi Wilhelm could visit Romania at my invitation, I felt very gratified. My satisfaction grew when I noticed that the authorities were attaching considerable importance to the visit. The Chief Rabbi of Sweden was seen by them as a means of winning over Western public opinion at a time when Romanian leaders were increasingly thinking of a more independent domestic and foreign policy, free from the shackles of the Soviet Union. Although it was some time yet before Khrushchev revealed to the 20th Congress of the Soviet Communist Party the full extent of Stalin's murderous policies, Romanians were fully aware of the dictator's terror, which had claimed the lives of millions. The Romanian leadership was seeking new guidelines in its relationship with the Soviet Union. Chief Rabbi Wilhelm's visit fitted in well with this revaluation.

For us Romanian Jews, the forthcoming visit by the Chief Rabbi of Sweden had a much more emotional significance. We awaited his arrival with extraordinary eagerness – almost as if he were some kind of Messiah. He represented our first link with our brethren in the West. We all attached immense importance to his arrival. It was to be the first rift in the Jewish Iron Curtain.

Minister of Cults Constantinescu-Iaşi personally supervised the arrangements for the Chief Rabbi's visit. Curiously, we Jews benefited from the exaggerated power which the Romanian authorities attributed to 'international Jewry', of which Dr Wilhelm was seen as a representative. Despite the fact that a third of the Jewish people had been killed by the Nazis and European Jewry had almost been wiped out in the Holocaust, Romanians still believed that Jews were a powerful force. Stories from the Tsarist anti-Semitic forgery *Protocols of the Elders of Zion* had penetrated deeply into the minds not only of the Romanian people, but also of the senior Communist Party activists.

When Chief Rabbi Wilhelm arrived with his wife in Bucharest, he was received with enthusiasm by the Jewish communities and with respect by the authorities. The Minister of Cults, who could be so rude to me, was amiable and hospitable to the Chief Rabbi. He made every effort to ensure that the Chief Rabbi would leave the country with a favourable impression of Romania. Meanwhile, I saw an opportunity of organizing public religious celebrations – something impossible at the time. I knew that such celebrations would enrich the religious life of the communities beyond limits. Reminding the Minister that Chief Rabbi Wilhelm would be in Romania during the festival of Purim, I pointed out that it would be embarrassing if he wished to attend a children's celebration and was told that this was not permitted. 'You will organize a celebration,' the Minister immediately replied.

I eagerly accepted the challenge. The Communist–atheist leaders of the Jewish community had to look on in bewilderment and dismay as we held numerous rehearsals for the celebration of Purim, for the first time since 1948, when the Communists began to take over our communities. The festivity proved immensely successful. Over 1,500 people crowded into the Great Synagogue in Bucharest. The enthusiasm of the children and the elders was overwhelming.

As soon as Purim was over, we began rehearsals with the children to celebrate Passover. The main event was, of course, the *Seder*, the meal at which the children ask questions about the Jewish people's deliverance from the ancient Egyptians and stories and prayers are recited from the *Haggadah*. The *Seder* can be both a family and a communal event. It is rich in religious symbolism and thus anathema to Jewish atheists. Bacal tried to stop the rehearsals. I told him curtly, 'Mr Bacal, what is acceptable for Purim must also be possible for Passover. If this were not so, it would mean that what we did was a charade to impress foreigners.'

I ignored all the protests of the Jewish Communists. I informed the Ministry of Cults about the Passover rehearsals, but did not wait for a formal approval; none came. The children's *Seder* also took place at the Great Synagogue in the presence of a packed congregation. It was a huge success. Seeing how much these celebrations added to the quality of Jewish religious life, I also began to organize public celebrations of Chanucah. I did more. I started the now well-established system of visiting all the Jewish communities in the country and joining with them in the celebrations. Thousands of children sang, recited and danced. They rejuvenated an ageing community. Public celebrations of Purim, Passover and Chanucah became powerful forces for Judaism in Romania. The authorities never formally approved the celebrations, but neither did they hamper them.

An able and sensitive man, Chief Rabbi Wilhelm knew how to exploit for the sake of Romanian Jews the favourable climate that he found in the country. Speaking at the Choral Temple, he praised the Romanian Government for the religious liberties granted to the Jews. The authorities were pleased with his words. Having endured so much criticism from Israel and Jewish circles in Western Europe and the United States, the Romanian leaders were gratified to find an influential Jewish voice offering friendship.

Dr Wilhelm was received by President Groza, Vice-Premier Alexandru Bîrlădeanu and Patriarch Justinian. Everywhere he made a favourable impression. He was precisely the most suitable Jewish envoy for that period in Romania. The really vital audience was with Bîrlădeanu, who had been asked by the state and party leadership to discuss with Dr Wilhelm the major problems of the Jews. I was present at that audience and vividly recall how Dr Wilhelm raised the most delicate problems affecting us, with the skill of a trained diplomat. He brought up the question of the 60,000 Jews who had for years been waiting for permission to leave for Israel in order to join their parents or children. There was the problem of the Zionists held in prison. What was going to be their fate? Could those Zionists who had regained freedom be allowed to leave for Israel? Would the Romanian authorities allow the American Jewish Joint Distribution Committee to help the many thousands of poor Jews?

Bîrlădeanu listened carefully and responded in a friendly manner, half-promising to do what Dr Wilhelm had requested. But he emphasized that it was essential for the attacks on Romania to cease. The climate between world Jewry and Romania had to improve first. He congratulated Dr Wilhelm on his attitude.

Dr Wilhelm's remarks were reported in the world press and caused a major surprise. He spoke of having seen synagogues packed with Jews, of Talmud Torahs crowded with eager young pupils. He did not have to exaggerate. The truth was as he described it. There was an intense Jewish life, despite the attempts of the Jewish Communists in the CDE to wreck it. Until Dr Wilhelm spoke out, it was axiomatic that every reference abroad to Romania should be critical. Every newspaper, Jewish and non-Jewish, appeared affected by the Cold War propaganda. Jewish criticism seemed to be particularly harsh. Dr Wilhelm broke with this ritual and many people did not like it. The knights of the anti-Communist crusade in Israel and the West were dismayed. They attacked him, but his reputation for sincerity was so great that their criticism was totally ineffective. People took notice of his words.

Dr Wilhelm's visit added to our community's prestige. As it was dominated by the CDE, Jewish intellectuals, writers and scientists had no links with it. Only the writer I. Peltz came regularly to synagogue. The others apparently believed that only by embracing anti-Zionism and atheism would they improve their standing in general Romanian life. They bowed their heads in submission. They changed their Jewish-sounding names into gentile ones. The Jewish community was portrayed as a reactionary group of people whose outlook the CDE was trying hard to change. Such a community had to be avoided by men who sought promotion and the Government's approval.

When Dr Wilhelm arrived, the authorities realized, even without my prompting, that he was bound to inquire about the Jewish intellectuals. Where were they? Could he be told that there was no organized Jewish framework for them, that they shunned their own community? Realizing that such an admission would damage Romania's reputation, the authorities ordered Jewish writers, scientists and artists to attend the strictly kosher dinner organized in Dr Wilhelm's honour at the Athénée-Palace Hotel.

Dr Wilhelm established a bridge between Romanian Jews and the Jewish world in the West. It was a very narrow bridge, but it raised many hopes. In Romania itself it encouraged us to struggle with greater vigour for the freeing of the Zionists who were still in jail. We pressed for the *aliyah* of those who had been set free. We managed to obtain semi-official approval for the Talmud Torahs, thus decreasing the risk to the teachers, parents and children. We gained greater confidence in fighting the atheists of the CDE. My own position as Chief Rabbi appeared strengthened by Dr Wilhelm's visit. I no longer dreaded becoming a Prisoner of Zion. I was already known abroad and this would make any arrest counter-productive. Moreover, I had proved how useful I could be to the country. We had not yet obtained the great single concession we were seeking – free emigration of the Jews to Israel – but for the first time we began to feel some hope. And the concessions we did obtain were significant. Those world Jewish figures, who had used Cold War tactics to force the Romanian Government to make concessions and had failed, noted the result of the Wilhelm–Rosen alliance and were impressed.

The depth of Dr Wilhelm's devotion to the Jewish people can be gauged from one sad fact. At the time, his son, aged twenty-two, was critically ill. His doctors had diagnosed that he had cancer and had only a short period to live. Dr Wilhelm agonized over whether he should remain in Stockholm or fulfil his promise and visit Bucharest. To make matters worse for him, he was suffering from a heart disease, which meant that he could not travel alone to Romania and would have to be accompanied by his wife. Hearing that so much depended on his visit to Romania, Chief Rabbi Wilhelm set out on his journey with his wife, leaving their son in hospital. This was a heartrending, heroic action performed by a true Jewish leader. It was no less than a sacrifice. When Dr and Mrs Wilhelm returned to Stockholm, they were informed that their son had died.

I cannot conclude this chapter without mentioning one important 'detail': everything connected with the Wilhelm–Rosen action was inspired and initiated by certain groups in Israel. It is also certain that we surpassed enormously the scope of our 'mission', thus bringing about a radical improvement in the whole relationship between East and West concerning the Jewish problem.

Later on we will see how things developed in the right direction. Wilhelm's visit was, indeed, the first rift in the Jewish Iron Curtain.

26 *Rabbinical Visits Lead to Unexpected Results*

Within four months, I received an official invitation from Dr Wilhelm to visit his community. I was, of course, eager to accept, but I felt that I could also obtain some concessions from the Romanian authorities. I was aware that they would favour my going to Stockholm because such a visit would further improve Romania's image in the Western press.

I immediately asked for an audience with Deputy Premier Emil Bodnăraş. He was a Ukrainian by birth – his original name was Bodnarenko – and he hated the Russians. He had been born in Cîmpulung, a Bucovinian town, which had a large Jewish population and he claimed to know a number of Yiddish and Hebrew words. Once pointing his finger at his brow, he said to me, 'You know, Chief Rabbi, Jews have *tsimmes*!' In Yiddish *tsimmes* is the name for a very highly flavoured Sabbath dish. What he meant to say was *seichel* (cleverness). Bodnăraş's knowledge of Yiddish was far more limited than he suspected.

He was, nevertheless, a very astute man, who now occupied a powerful position in the Romanian party and Government. He had had a long career as a Communist activist, having become a committed Communist while serving as an officer in ex-King Carol's army. Fearing arrest, he had escaped to the Soviet Union. During the Second World War, the Russians sent him back to Romania, where he organized anti-government and anti-German fighting groups. With the Russian successes in the war and the Romanian switch of alliances, he was able to emerge from the underground. It was Bodnăraş who took Marshal Antonescu into custody at the royal palace, at the King's request.

Being responsible to the Romanian leadership for the armed forces, the administration of justice and the Cults, Bodnăraş dealt with the problem of the Jews. His personal attitude to the Jewish question was to have a profound effect on the fate of our communities. He wore the uniform of a general but spoke with the bluntness of a soldier. His views on the Jews were totally different from those of Ana Pauker. She, a Jewess, believed that Romanian Jews were Romanians and were entitled to all the rights of Romanian citizens; but that those who wanted to leave for Israel were traitors. Bodnăraş thought Ana's approach totally mistaken. His attitude to Jews who wished to leave for Israel was '*mazel tov* [good luck]!' Such an emigration would benefit them and would also be good for Romania. I once said to my wife, 'It is our good fortune that he wants to get rid of the Jews.' However, even Bodnăraş did not think in terms of total, mass Jewish emigration, as will be shown later.

I shall have to return to Bodnăraş several times in this story, because his interventions were crucial for us. Had it not been for this powerfully built man, I believe that Romanian Jews might have suffered the same fate as Russian Jewry. It was he who, with caution and able tactics, regularly backed my efforts to resume *aliyah*. He, too, risked being 'unmasked' as a 'Zionist agent'. It was due to him that I was able to travel abroad and establish bridges with our Jewish brethren. He could talk bluntly to me, but he was ready to accept bluntness from me in turn without feeling offended. It was he who understood the advantages of a policy 'favourable to Jews' and what Romania could gain by adopting such a policy.

When I went to see him about my trip to Stockholm in June 1956, I pointed out that people there would ask me about the imprisoned Romanian Zionists. Could he not give me a promise that they would be released? This would greatly enhance my visit to the West and would promote favourable comments about Romania in the Western media. Bodnăraş replied that provided the Zionists did not speak against the Romanian Government, and provided my trip to Stockholm proved successful, the imprisoned Revisionist Zionists would be released. 'Have a little patience,' he said. 'We'll keep our promise.'

He did keep his word. Shortly after my return from Stockholm, the Revisionists Edgar Kanner, Jakerkanner and others were released. Bodnăraş apparently thought that my trip to Stockholm had proved useful.

At that historic meeting with Bodnăraş, I had also requested emigration passports for A. L. Zissu and Moshe Benvenisti, the top leaders of the Zionist movement in Romania, who were already free.

In my presence, he had summoned an official and ordered the passports to be issued.

Plucking up courage, I demanded passports for the other 200 Zionist leaders, so that they could leave for Israel. He again answered that it depended on the results of my Stockholm visit: 'If your trip is a success, your requests will be granted.'

I did not want the audience to come to an end without once more raising the general problem of *aliyah*. Again I heard him saying '*mazel tov*' and then, 'Have a little patience, Chief Rabbi; it depends on an improvement in our relationship with the West. You can do a lot for us in this respect.'

My visit to Stockholm also had an unexpected outcome for our religious life. I gave an interview to the famous London *Jewish Chronicle*, the oldest Jewish newspaper in the world, in which Theodor Herzl had first propounded his theory of a Jewish state in Palestine. In this interview I kept strictly to the facts, stressing that we had Talmud Torah classes and two *yeshivoth*.

I was telling the truth: fifty-six students were attending the *yeshivoth*, day and night, in Arad and Satu-Mare. What I did not say was that the CDE leaders vehemently opposed them. They instructed their men not to give a penny to the *yeshivoth*, so that all the expenses had to be covered by our own fund-raising. We faced dangers, pressures and financial difficulties in supporting the *yeshivot*. Students had to be distributed among many Orthodox homes and had to eat '*teig*' (i.e. going daily from one to another to have lunch or dinner), because there were no hostels or restaurants for them, and they were in permanent danger. Nevertheless, although all this '*yeshivoth* enterprise' was illegal and a political 'crime', neither the police nor the Ministry of Cults interfered.

Therefore, my statement at the interview was truthful, but the situation had to be improved.

I had a similar interview with the Swedish newspaper *Svenska Dagbladet*. My reference to the Talmud Torahs, *yeshivoth* and Jewish religious life made a very considerable impression on the newspapers.

Official receptions took place, at which representatives of the Swedish Government and the Israeli and the Romanian Ambassadors participated. The whole atmosphere became very favourable to Romania.

While still in Stockholm, I was informed that a delegation of the Rabbinical Council of America, composed of Rabbis Hershel Schechter, Gilbert Klaperman, David Hollander and the late Rabbi

Adelman, intended to travel to Romania after visiting the Soviet Union. I was asked to come home to greet the delegation. Returning to Bucharest immediately, I went to see the Prime Minister, Chivu Stoica, an evil man. I felt that since he had become Prime Minister in 1955, our status had tended to worsen. I showed him a copy of the *Jewish Chronicle* and the *Svenska Dagbladet*.

'You have won the capitalist press over,' he remarked.

'Prime Minister,' I responded, 'I have to reveal a secret to you. Can you see what is printed here in the *Jewish Chronicle*? It states that we, in Romania, have two *yeshivoth*. When the rabbis from America arrive, they will discover that these *yeshivoth* do exist, but only illegally. They have no premises, nothing. When the rabbis look at the *Jewish Chronicle*, they will naturally ask, "Where are the *yeshivoth*?" I will have nothing to show them. What should I do, Prime Minister?' I described the real picture: no hostels, no canteens and no money.

'I have taken a note of your remarks,' Stoica replied coolly. His response promised little, but he was to take me totally by surprise.

My meeting with Stoica took place on a Friday. The next Monday, on the eve of Tishah B'Av (a fast and mourning day), the American rabbis arrived. I warned them immediately not to discuss vital matters in their rooms, in which, I was sure, hidden microphones had been installed. In order to speak freely, we went for walks. On Wednesday, we travelled to Iaşi, where thousands of people crowded into the large synagogue. We then left for Arad, where we arrived on Thursday. According to my interview in the *Jewish Chronicle*, there was a *yeshiva* in the town, which the rabbis would obviously want to visit. I trembled when I thought what they would see, or rather not see, and what they would think.

We went to a building which had belonged to the Jewish community, but which had been taken over by the authorities, who had turned it into the offices of the anti-aircraft defence command in 1948. When I entered the building, I stood open-mouthed in astonishment. The centre had been transformed within a few days into a *yeshiva*. There were classrooms, dormitories for fifty people, a library and a synagogue. There was even a kosher kitchen and a restaurant. I stared at all this and could not believe my eyes. I saw the pleasure in the eyes of the American rabbis. This was a real *yeshiva*, of which any Jewish community could be proud. To find it in a Communist country was, indeed, gratifying.

Only later did I learn that, after my conversation with the Prime

Minister, a veritable army of workmen had descended on the building. Working day and night, they had accomplished their task within days. After the departure of the rabbis, the authorities wanted to close the *yeshiva*, but my protests were so loud that they desisted, and it remained open until 1965, when the principal and all the teachers left for Brooklyn, New York. They were all followers of the Neturei Karta, the extreme Orthodox anti-Zionist group.

That *yeshiva* produced many rabbis, ritual slaughterers and cantors and was a real 'home of the Torah'. However, it is necessary to underline a certain phenomenon which occurred here and is of great significance. During the years 1948–56, my struggle for a *yeshiva* had been opposed by the CDE. When they finally agreed, two of their conditions were: no Hebrew language and no history of the Jewish people, both being considered as 'Zionist propaganda' by the CDE. In the end, in the new political circumstances, under pressure from the Government, Jewish history and the Hebrew language were included in the syllabus.

Very surprisingly, these topics were also opposed by the Orthodox Chassidim in Satu-Mare, with their rabbi, Paul Miller, refusing to accept them. 'History, Chief Rabbi, history? What does history mean?' Rabbi Miller asked.

Despite the fact that it is impossible to understand the Talmud without knowing our history, despite the fact that the whole Tanach (Bible) is written in Hebrew, they refused to teach history. '*Les extrêmes se touchent* [Extremes meet]': this French proverb was painfully confirmed on that occasion.

Ezra Fleischer, a brilliant scholar and poet, my 'partner' in our Hebrew and Romanian journal (see page 165), went to Arad to teach at the *yeshiva*, where he suffered a great deal on account of both kinds of fanaticism – right and left. He, too, could write a 'best-seller' on his activities at the *yeshiva*!

After our visit to Arad, we were received by Vice-Premier Bîrlădeanu. As we were involved in an animated discussion, I noticed that the time for *Mincha* (afternoon prayer) had arrived. As I had always insisted that the authorities should respect the religious needs of the Jews and especially the rabbis, I remarked to Bîrlădeanu, 'Mr Deputy Prime Minister, we are all rabbis and we have a duty to recite our prayers now.' He looked startled, but not in the least offended. He left the room and we began to recite our prayers. After a while, he returned, noticed that the prayers were over and we resumed our discussion. This must have been the first time ever that a Jewish religious service was held in the room of the Deputy Premier of a Communist republic.

On 23 August 1956, my wife and I were, as usual, the guests of the Government at a reception given on the anniversary of the victory over Fascism in August 1944. There, Bodnăraş approached us and, in a very friendly manner, thanked me for my successful activities in Stockholm. Then he said, 'I have not forgotten what I promised you. Please, have a little patience. In a short time, I will fulfil my promise.'

Eight days later, on 31 August, my wife and I were invited to a reception given by the Government in honour of a visiting Indian woman minister. It took place at the Military Club in Bucharest. As we were walking up the marble stairs, I saw at the top a group of the country's leaders: Gheorghiu-Dej, Bodnăraş, Stoica and Apostol who, I think, was a deputy Prime Minister. As we came closer to the group, I greeted the leaders, each of whom acknowledged the greeting with a gesture. The one exception was Bodnăraş, who responded in a loud, gruff, aggressive voice, 'I have given you your Zionists. Let them go to your *Wondertopf* [pot of miracles]. Your cup is now overflowing!' His outburst was heard by his colleagues. As he said these astonishing words, he turned his back on me and walked away.

I stood dumbfounded. I was totally confused. So was my wife. We felt shocked by the crudeness of his inexplicable behaviour. But after taking a few steps away from the leaders, I was struck by the words he had used. 'Did you hear what Bodnăraş said?' I asked my wife. ' "I have given you your Zionists!" This must mean that they can leave. By "*Wondertopf*" he meant to refer sarcastically to Israel. He seemed to be rude, but it is what he said that really matters. He has given us great news.' I was overcome by sudden excitement, but at the same time I still felt anxious. Never had Bodnăraş used such a contemptuous and hostile tone of voice when speaking to me. And I had to remember that he was a very powerful person indeed.

Half an hour later, Bodnăraş, who was the host at the reception, invited seven or eight people to join him and his Indian guest of honour in another room. My wife and I were among those invited and I found myself sitting at the table next to him. He spoke to me in a very cordial manner. I looked at him in surprise and asked him why he had spoken so bluntly before. He saw that I was upset and confused. He laughed heartily, as if I had told a good joke, and said, 'What is important is that your request has been granted. You can forget about the rest.'

I immediately realized what had happened. Bodnăraş had adopted a fake, hostile attitude towards me in the presence of his colleagues. He knew well that any minister, however powerful, who released the Zionist leaders from prison and granted them permission to leave for Israel would arouse suspicions. A rival might accuse him of imperialist deviations or of becoming soft on Zionism. Although there was a new climate in Romania, the echoes of the anti-Jewish and anti-Zionist Slansky trial in Prague had still not totally died down. Bodnăraş felt that he had to be careful. He was amused that his play-acting with me had been so convincing.

As soon as I left the reception with my wife, I contacted Leon Itzkar, one of the Zionist leaders who was a reliable and devoted man. In a voice brimming with happiness, I told him to prepare lists and personal data of Zionists who wished to leave for Israel. A few days later, Itzkar, together with the lawyer Littman, sent me a list of more than 200 names, with their personal data, and I gave it to Constantinescu-Iaşi and to Professor Dumitru Dogaru, who was to be his successor as Minister of Cults. The Zionists named were given passports and told that they could leave.

The good news had come so suddenly that not every Zionist leader believed it was true. Some suspected a trick. Mendelovici, a former editor of the Zionist journal *Renaşterea*, remained extremely suspicious. But, finally, even he was convinced and he sailed for Israel. Other Zionists, who saw the urgency of the situation, were able to leave Romania for Israel. But there were some who delayed their departure, either for personal reasons, or because they thought the door would be kept open for them. They made a sad mistake. One month later, on 23 October 1956, the Hungarian crisis which led to the revolution broke out. Almost at the same time, the Suez crisis erupted. As a consequence of these dramatic events, the emigration of Zionists to Israel was brought to a halt.

27 Budapest and Suez

*I*n July 1956, following a very unpleasant experience, I decided to avoid travelling by air. My wife and I had visited my sister and brother-in-law in Glasgow. This was an entirely private visit and the authorities had raised no objections to my returning to Romania from Stockholm via Glasgow. After our family visit, we went to London by train and caught a plane travelling to Bucharest via Zürich. When we were over Switzerland, the plane began to shake and tumble. It seemed to be out of control. The pilot made desperate efforts to avoid a crash. Apparently, one of the engines had failed and a disaster seemed imminent. We were thrown against the side of the plane and some passengers even hit the ceiling. In front of me, a father was urging his son to recite prayers. I myself was reciting psalms and praying for deliverance. We did not crash. Showing great skill, the pilot managed an emergency landing in Geneva. Without saying a word to my wife, I silently made a promise to myself that I would never travel by air again.

When, in October that year, I made arrangements to go to Paris for the unveiling of the Tomb of the Unknown Jewish Martyr, a celebration initiated and created by Isaac Schneersohn, I decided to go by train, in fulfilment of my promise. This time my wife was not accompanying me and my travelling companion was Ludwig Bruckstein, an author and then a committed Jewish Communist and atheist. A number of rabbis came to the Bucharest railway station to see me off. As the train was about to leave, Rabbi Portugal put his hands on my head and blessed me. This was a dramatic gesture, witnessed by the wife of the Italian Ambassador in Bucharest and two Italian diplomats, who were travelling on the same train and were looking out from a window of the same sleeping-car.

On arrival in Arad, for a short stop, the train was met by Rabbi Dr Schönfeld and several secular community leaders. After greeting me, they whispered that the BBC had reported that morning that a revolution had broken out in Budapest. Our train was scheduled to travel via Budapest to Paris, and so this unexpected news should have alarmed me, but I displayed ridiculous naivety. 'So what is the problem?' I asked. 'Our destination is Paris and not Budapest.' Dr Schönfeld and the other leaders must have been very surprised – and perhaps a little disturbed – by my response.

When we reached the Hungarian border, the train stopped for rather a long time. Becoming concerned, I asked the customs officials, 'Is there anything new?' I did not think it wise to mention the reported BBC broadcast. I was assured that everything was all right. Soon, the train moved slowly forward and we entered Hungarian territory. But at the next station I noted with surprise and increasing concern that no one boarded our train, which was carrying only six people. Nor did any official arrive to arrange our sleeping berths. The dining-car was closed, and there were no cooks, no attendants and no guards. Only the engine-driver remained on what had become a ghost train. Now thoroughly alarmed, I was convinced that the BBC report must be true. In our ignorance, we were travelling towards a possibly dangerous turmoil. Other people, including the railway staff who had abandoned the train, were wiser.

After consulting Bruckstein, I went to speak to the Italian Ambassador's wife. I had seen her at several diplomatic receptions, but had never spoken to her. I still avoided conversations with foreign diplomats, even after travelling abroad, as I had no desire to attract the attention of the security police. But now I felt that she must be told the stark truth. 'There is a revolution in Hungary,' I told her. She opened her eyes wide and asked me to repeat what I had said. As I did so, she burst out laughing, almost uncontrollably. She eventually translated my words into Italian for the benefit of the two Italian diplomats.

'Please forgive me for laughing,' she said, 'but there are no revolutions in Communist countries. Don't worry. Somebody must have told you lies.'

I did not react to her comments. They were obviously misguided, but I knew I would not convince her that she was wrong and that we were in a perilous situation.

I went back to my compartment to await events. The train sped forward, coming ever closer to the centre of violence. After midnight, it stopped near a station at Rakos, about twenty kilomètres from Budapest. Suddenly we heard the unmistakable sounds of cannon fire and bursts of machine-gun fire rattling. The lights went out. We all rushed out of the train and threw ourselves on the damp ground. Instead of laughing, the Ambassador's wife was now sobbing. We all feared that the train would be hit and go up in flames, and that we would then be the target of the gunfire.

I felt somebody creeping towards me in the darkness and then a hand touched my shoulder. Peering at the figure, I saw one of the two Italian diplomats, who was shaking with fear and murmuring, '*Il uomo sancto* [the saintly man]'. At first I did not understand what he was referring to, but then I guessed that Rabbi Portugal's blessing had greatly impressed him. He said to me in a shaky voice, 'Chief Rabbi, this holy man blessed you. Let's hope that his blessing will save all our lives.' It was a statement with which I fully agreed.

After lying prostrate on the ground for what appeared an eternity, we heard the engine-driver's voice asking us to get up and return to the train. The firing had subsided and he felt that he could now continue to Budapest. We trudged back to the train, our clothing and faces caked with wet earth. The train moved forward slowly, very slowly. It was already dawn when we reached the main Budapest railway station, which was totally deserted and no wonder: a major battle appeared to be going on around the station. We had driven right into the centre of the fighting.

We huddled together, naively seeking protection from the railway cars. Although we had no food or water, we decided that we must not leave them. We stayed like this for twenty-four hours. During the night, a group of youngsters, carrying guns and flashlights, jumped on the train and demanded to see our identification papers. They seemed to be satisfied that we were not enemies and left. At dawn, a car arrived from the Italian Embassy and, while we stood watching with envy, took away the Ambassador's wife and the two diplomats. The Embassy had become alarmed about them, having apparently received an urgent message from Bucharest. A Swiss citizen was also picked up by his Embassy. What about the Romanian Embassy in Budapest? Surely, it too would respond swiftly when it heard that its Chief Rabbi and a well-known writer were in a desperate plight. I asked the engine-driver to telephone the Romanian Embassy and request that a car be sent to the railway station to take us away. He managed to get to a telephone and rang the Embassy, who told him that no car could be sent. I asked him to ring again. He did so and received the same answer. It was a brutal refusal to our appeal for help.

Realizing that our situation was now desperate and that our only chance of survival was to be swiftly evacuated from the train, I asked the engine-driver, who was a very brave and helpful man, to telephone the Israeli Embassy and to tell whoever answered that the Chief Rabbi of Romania and a Jewish writer were trapped at the railway station and urgently requested the Embassy's help. Within half an hour, a car appeared at the station. When Bruckstein saw it, after hearing that the Romanian Embassy had refused to help us, he burst out crying. It was the beginning of his 'change of mind'.

As soon as we reached the Israeli Embassy, I telephoned the Romanian Embassy and asked to speak to the Ambassador. In a stern voice, I warned him that he personally would be held accountable for my life, because the Embassy had refused to assist and protect me. This warning was effective. A car arrived shortly afterwards and took us to a guest-house belonging to the Embassy. But we could hardly have been placed in a more dangerous and exposed place. To our horror, we discovered that we were in the middle of the fighting area. Near us was a students' hostel, in which revolutionaries had barricaded themselves. Across the street were barracks where heavily armed Russian soldiers were in force. For eight days and nights we were penned up in the guest-house, bullets constantly crashing through the windows. We kept rushing to the cellar because that was the only spot where we felt comparatively safe. To add to our worries, we began to be short of food. Somehow the telephone was still working and I managed to contact the elderly Chief Rabbi of Budapest, Rabbi Benjamin Schwartz. A truly brave man, he appeared personally at the guest-house with some kosher food. Had it not been for the Jewish community of Budapest, we would have starved.

After a week, the firing gradually died down and we ventured outside. On the boulevard nearby, where once a huge monument of Stalin had stood, only two enormous metal boots remained. The figure had been cut off just above the boots and dragged through the streets by the excited crowds. They spat at and derided the figure, but their exultation did not last long.

With us, at the guest-house, was Madame Costache, the wife of the Secretary-General of the Romanian Ministry of the Interior. She was suffering from a nervous disorder and had come to Budapest for treatment. She arrived precisely when the fighting was at its fiercest. However, while we were panic-stricken, Madame Costache was always calm and serene, walking about in a dressing-gown and picking up bullets from the floor.

In contrast, Bruckstein had become increasingly nervous. Having abandoned his atheism, he constantly prayed and recited Hebrew psalms. He came to believe that only I could save his life. Once, when bullets crashed through the window, I hid under the bed. He immediately followed me and, desperately afraid, clung to me. He whispered, his body shaking, 'What will become of us? When will we get out of this?' I tried to calm him and told him that I was sure that Madame Costache's husband was making every effort to evacuate her from this danger spot. He would show us the way to escape.

One morning, I saw Madame Costache on the stairs of the guesthouse. She was smartly dressed and in very good humour. When I greeted her, she smiled amiably at me. I asked her what would become of us. 'There is no problem any more,' she replied. 'I could leave today if I wanted to. A plane loaded with medicines has arrived from Bucharest. The people at the Embassy say that it could take me home, but it has no seats. So I have decided to await an airliner. I don't want to travel on a freighter.'

This was the best news I had heard for a long time. I knew that I had to act quickly as the opportunity could not be missed. I telephoned the Romanian Embassy and insisted that a car be sent to take me and Bruckstein to the airport and that we should be permitted to fly back to Bucharest on the freighter. It was a most uncomfortable flight as we had to sit on the floor of the aircraft. Moreover, because the plane had to fly very low, so that the Red Cross sign on it should be visible on the ground, the flight was also very bumpy and uneven. But we did not mind the discomfort. We were happy to be escaping a nightmare. When we landed in Arad, we were immensely relieved. We felt new-born. For Bruckstein the events in Budapest did, indeed, mean a new birth. He became a Zionist, joined the ranks of those wishing to emigrate and, eventually, with a sense of excitement and renewal, went to live in Israel.

As for myself, I now travel uncomplainingly by air. It is safer.

Almost at the same time, when Israel, France and Great Britain became involved in what became known as the Suez War, intense pressure was put on me to join in the public attacks on the Jewish state. A meeting of the National Committee for the Defence of Peace was convened to brand Israel as the aggressor in the war with Egypt. The head of the committee was Sanda Ranghetz, a Jewish Communist. Among its members were leading artists, writers and scientists. But if the Chief Rabbi could be made to launch the condemnation of Israel, the effect would be particularly strong. Sanda Ranghetz knew that I had always refused to condemn Israel and Zionism, but now thought that the pressure would be too great for me to resist.

She arrived at my home and began to press me to make the main speech at the meeting. I said to her, 'You are defending Gamal Abdul Nasser because you say he is the victim of Israel, the aggressor. I am told that in the Israeli Parliament, the Knesset, there are several Communist members. There is also a legal Communist Party in Israel, with such members as Moshe Sneh, Samuel Mikunis and Esther Vilenska. But in Egypt, the country which you are defending, the Communists are in prison and suffering from state terrorism. Tell me, please, are you asking me to condemn a government which treats the Communists well and to defend a government which imprisons and tortures Communists?'

Madame Ranghetz became angry and began to threaten me. Noting that I remained unperturbed, she asked, 'What do you intend to do?' 'That is my concern,' I replied. 'Write your speech and let me see it,' she burst out furiously. 'I won't write any speech,' I told her. She rushed out of the house, threatening that I would pay a heavy price for my conduct.

I did deliver a speech at the meeting of the Committee, but it was not one that delighted Madame Ranghetz. I spoke at length about the need for peace, but I did not single out Israel for condemnation. Members of the audience, who knew that Israel had been the target of numerous Egyptian terrorist attacks, appreciated my remarks and my refusal to join the detractors. Mihail Sadoveanu, Romania's greatest writer, who was the president of the Committee, said to me, 'People are congratulating you on what you have said. I congratulate you on what you have *not* said!'

28   *A Miraculous Magazine Is Born*

A unique role in my long struggle for Jewish religious and cultural rights in Romania has been played by our communal–international newspaper, *Revista Cultului Mozaic*. Its birth was the subject of a bitter fight with the Jewish Communists. Even its name caused irreconcilable differences, which were never resolved. My opponents rightly saw the planned publication as a powerful weapon in my hands, as I tried to keep the flame of Judaism alive in the country and establish contacts with Jewish communities abroad.

After eight years of struggle, the Government granted me approval in October 1956 to start the journal and I brought the matter before our Federation leadership. They immediately looked for opportunities to prevent or to delay its appearance and, if that proved impossible, to stifle its influence and effectiveness. When I suggested that the journal should be named *Menorah* (a seven-branched candelabrum), the response was that this was the nationalist symbol of the State of Israel. I proposed an alternative, *Sinai*, which also proved unacceptable. To ordinary religious Jews, Sinai was a place where the Israelites wandered after escaping from Egyptian slavery and, more important, where they received the Ten Commandments, but the Jewish Communists argued that the name would remind readers of the Suez War and imperialism. Realizing that these objections were not genuine, but were merely an attempt to stop the appearance of the journal, I decided that the best solution was not to give it a title at all, but to say that it was the organ of the Jewish religious people of Romania. And so it eventually appeared and, till today, is printed bi-monthly under the title *Revista* in Romanian, *Ketar-Eit* in Hebrew and *Journal* in English. Of course, after so many years, nobody would stop me giving it a name, but I think that, for historical reasons, it is more useful to let it remain as *Revista*.

On the day that the new journal was born, there were still 300,000 Jews in Romania, but the Jewish Federation would not allow more than 2,000 copies to be printed. Today, when there are no more than 22,000 Jews in Romania, we are printing 10,000 copies of the journal, all of which sell out regularly.

The Jewish Communists used every conceivable and inconceivable method to sabotage the appearance of the journal even though the Government had given its formal approval. Later, when I became president of the Federation, I was able to read all the memoranda and letters in which the leaders voiced their concern about the new journal and thought of ways to strangle it. Delay and confiscation were two methods. Every article and report intended to appear in the journal had to be submitted for censorship by the Federation leadership. Bacal was made responsible for this task and he tried to make us despair of ever achieving any success with the publication. The agreement was that he should return the reports and articles within a fortnight, but he would keep them for a couple of months or even more. When they eventually left him, they had to be sent to the Ministry of Cults for another month for further perusal and further censorship. Our journal was originally supposed to appear every fortnight, but, in reality, it normally took two or three months to bring it out.

How did the censorship 'work'? If an article had a religious content, it meant that it was 'religious propaganda' and, therefore, might be forbidden. If it had a national tendency, it was 'Zionist poison' and, therefore, was not admitted. If it had some political hints, the answer was 'Don't interfere in our politics.'

When at long last I looked happily at the finished copies of *Revista*, I underwent additional frustration. I felt like a mother who sees strangers taking her new-born child away from her. The Jewish Communists withdrew many copies and destroyed them. They sent others to provincial centres with orders to their employees neither to sell them nor to distribute them to the Jewish communities, but to hide them in the cellars.

In such circumstances, it seems almost miraculous that the journal survived. What saved it, what made it grow stronger and flourish, was the fierce determination that I and my supporters displayed in keeping it alive. Foremost among my aides was Professor Ezra Fleischer, now of the Hebrew University of Jerusalem. Fleischer, one of the most important Jewish scholars in the world today, an expert in medieval Jewish poetry, had worked at the Israeli Embassy in Bucharest, had been arrested for being a Zionist and had spent three years in prison, but neither hardship nor prison could break his spirit or dampen his enthusiasm for Zionism and Israel. He 'wrote' poems in prison, without a pencil or paper. He knew his poems by heart and, after his liberation, when his *Gog umagog* epos, under the pseudonym E. Gole, was printed in Israel, the anonymous poet from behind the Iron Curtain was awarded the National Poetry Prize of Israel.

Fleischer offered to become my assistant in bringing out the journal and defeating the tricks of the Jewish Communists. He helped to make *Revista* one of the finest publications of its kind in the world. With its mixture of news, articles on religious and cultural subjects, learned dissertations on the Bible and Talmud, photographs of gatherings and of our youth on festive occasions, the journal fulfilled an urgent need. Its reputation spread very quickly and widely. I was pleasantly surprised to learn that among the subscribers were leading members of the Romanian Parliament.

I obtained the collaboration of important personalities from abroad, such as the Chief Rabbis of Britain (Dr Israel Brodie), of France (Dr Kaplan), of the USSR (Dr Schliefer), of Sweden (Dr Wilhelm) and of Czechoslovakia (Dr Sicher).

We published our journal in three languages: Romanian, Yiddish and Hebrew; later we added English. This feature gave us an opportunity to influence large numbers of people throughout Eastern Europe as well as in the English-speaking world.

Our Hebrew section was of great significance. It was the only one that appeared throughout Europe, including the West. You can hardly imagine the joy with which it was received by thousands of devoted Jews in the Soviet Union. We sent several hundred copies of the journal to subscribers there; each Hebrew page was then copied by the thousand and distributed to eager readers. I received thousands of touching letters from the most far-away places in the Soviet Union. Each letter was a hymn of joy. It was as if we had given food to the starving. And, indeed, we were providing a soul-saving service. The Soviet Government opposed the teaching of Hebrew and went to great lengths to stamp it out. Jews who taught Hebrew were actually jailed under false indictments. Yet our Hebrew paper was allowed legally to enter the Soviet Union and to be distributed. I believe it did much to keep up the morale of all Jews seeking to maintain their Jewish identity. Our paper's appearance in the Soviet Union can be described justly as one of the many miracles that has helped our people to survive.

On the occasion when I met the Vice-President of the Council for

Religious Affairs of the Soviet Union, Titov, in Moscow, he told me, 'Look at your paper. You think that we are not aware that you are sending it to our citizens? Of course we know about it and yet we do nothing to prevent it. Why? Because you are not attacking us. We have nothing against *Revista*'s educational and religious work.'

An Israeli diplomat once told me, 'On a Saturday afternoon I went to the Leningrad synagogue and there I saw forty to fifty Jews sitting and listening to one of them reading *Revista*.'

Our news items from the whole Jewish world, including Israel, used to be for dozens of years the only legal source of information for Soviet Jewry.

The president of the Jewish community of Kishinev, who was our guest for a Chanucah tour, told me a year later when he revisited Bucharest, 'I returned home and went to the woman in the town hall who was responsible for buildings. As the Jewish community has no legal existence, the synagogue depends on "the buildings section". I showed her *Revista* with two pictures of Bar-Mitzvah ceremonies in it. Since 1940, not one Bar-Mitzvah has taken place in Kishinev, a town with around 50,000 Jews. I asked the girl to allow us to follow the Romanian example and to authorize us to have Bar-Mitzvah classes. When I tried to explain to her what a Bar-Mitzvah meant, she interrupted me by asking if, on such occasions, we drank alcohol. I assured her that we did not. Thereupon she gave her approval for Bar-Mitzvah classes. And so it is thanks to your *Revista* that we now have dozens of Jewish children passing through Bar-Mitzvah ceremonies.'

Our Yiddish section also played an historic role. Large numbers of Jews in the Soviet Union still speak Yiddish. For them a journal which contained genuine Jewish news and fervent religious articles was a momentous occurrence. They had come to distrust Yiddish publications because they were filled with anti-Jewish, anti-Zionist and anti-religious propaganda. Our journal was like finding water in the desert. This was equally true for the Jews of Latvia, Estonia and Lithuania, where there had always been a strong attachment to Yiddish in the Jewish communities. Vilna, the capital of Lithuania, was known as the Jerusalem of Lithuania because of its rich cultural heritage of Hebrew and Yiddish scholarship. Yivo, the World Organization for Yiddish, had its headquarters there between the two world wars. Few Jews survived the Nazi massacres and many of those who did emigrated, but there were still considerable numbers of Jews in the three 'countries' who remembered and loved Yiddish. Our journal gave them great joy. Their letters are proof of that.

Our Romanian section proved a most valuable link for all Romanian Jews in the country and outside it. It sustained their courage and endurance. Copies went to our brethren in Bessarabia and Bukovina, which were once part of Romania, but were now absorbed into the Soviet Union. It is not difficult to imagine what effect our paper would have on the Jews who had suffered so much there.

I have no greater satisfaction than to visit our archives and read the letters and messages we have received over the years from our grateful readers. Sometimes the writer would be a lonely Jew living in a far-away town in the Soviet Union, who might be ill and poor, but who would write to tell us that we must never stop sending him the journal because it was the very breath of life to him. A Jew in Novosibirsk or Tashkent would write and tell us of some particular piece that he found interesting. And though our community grew smaller and smaller as its members left to settle in Israel, our journal grew in strength. It now finds its way to the Romanian Jews in Israel, who can read it in Romanian, Yiddish and Hebrew. The 10,000 copies that we print are sent all over the world. We have now got a very devoted English readership, too.

When I think of all our struggles for Jewish life in Romania and in Eastern Europe generally, I cannot help feeling that among our greatest and most significant achievements was the publication and promotion of our nameless journal, animated by such a wonderful and miraculous power.

29 *The Father of Orphans*

*A*n ascetic face, a body as thin as a lath, a baby's naive eyes, a lovely serene smile, a man so frail that one feared that a sudden wind would lift him off his feet: this to me was the Rebbe of Sculeni, Rabbi Zisse Portugal. He was unquestionably a *Tzaddik*, a saintly man. His wonderful character and noble behaviour encouraged me in my work and brought solace to many thousands of suffering Jews.

When in pain and exhausted and forced to take a few hours' rest, Rabbi Portugal would instruct his family, 'If somebody brings a *pidyon* [a gift], please don't wake me. But if a needy man comes and asks for a *neduvah* [a sum of money], please call me. I want to hear from the man's own lips what grieves him. I may be helpful to him.'

Rabbi Portugal, who was then living in Czernowitz, went to Transnistria immediately after the war to assist those who had survived. Eighty thousand Jews had died from disease and cold. The children who had lost their parents were starving and had no shelter. They appeared doomed to die a slow and painful death. The Rebbe gathered 200 orphans from the streets and took them away with him. Somehow he found food and lodgings for them. He proclaimed, 'These are my children.'

After a while, he brought his family and the children to Bucharest. Running from one institution to another for help, he managed to find a home for all of them. Their plight touched people's hearts. The children loved the Rebbe and his kindly wife, who showed a rare sensitivity in dealing with them. A small example will illustrate this. A well-wisher sent a wristwatch as a gift. Rabbi and Mrs Portugal had a son, Shrulikel (who became Rebbe after his father's death), but they decided not to give the watch to him but to one of the orphans, Hershele, because they wanted to avoid giving the orphans the impression that they were favouring their own son. 'I am sure

Shrulikel will understand why we did not give him the watch,' Mrs Portugal said.

The 1948 decision by the Government to nationalize all schools, kindergartens and children's homes was a disaster for the Rebbe. The CDE leaders, always more zealous than the authorities, were eager to hand over all Jewish institutions to the state as proof of their intense loyalty. Nobody felt strong enough to resist their efforts, except for Rabbi Portugal. 'My children must eat kosher food, observe the Sabbath, be true Jews. What will become of them if they are taken to non-Jewish homes? Do you want to baptize them? I will never allow it,' he told the Jewish Communists.

His protests proved unavailing. One morning, the police arrived, forced the screaming children into lorries and drove them away. They were taken to a non-Jewish home in another part of the city. The authorities apparently thought that this was the end of a troublesome matter, but they were wrong. When the director of the non-Jewish home arrived to inspect his new charges, he could not find them. They had all mysteriously disappeared. The police turned up in force at Rabbi Portugal's home and searched every room for the children, but none was found. However, they searched the local parks and squares and caught several of the children there. They fought and screamed, 'Leave us alone. We want to remain Jews!' The police were made to look ridiculous as they chased the frantic children. They had to bring in reinforcements and finally rounded them all up. It was a sad sight. For Rabbi Portugal it was a painful tragedy.

The authorities followed this up by arresting Rabbi Portugal in July 1949. My marriage had taken place a fortnight earlier and thus my honeymoon was overshadowed by this event. Romanian Jews were dismayed by the arrest of the beloved Rebbe. As, in those early days of the new regime, it was still possible to vent one's indignation openly, a delegation of rabbis, led by me, went to see Bercu Feldman. He received us in a friendly manner, but when we asked for Rabbi Portugal's release from prison, he replied, 'You rabbis believe in heavenly reward and punishment. A man is rewarded for his good deeds and punished for his sins. Well, this is precisely how we are treating Rabbi Portugal.'

'What sins has Rabbi Portugal committed?' we asked in astonishment.

'You will learn in due course,' he replied.

We went away dispirited and anxious. We sent an appeal to the Deputy Minister of the Interior, Mr Jianu, who – we understood – was dealing with the case, but we received no reply. However, two months later, to our great relief and surprise, Rabbi Portugal was set free. No charges had been made against him. The aim of the arrest had obviously been to intimidate religious Jews and to force them to give up the struggle over the orphans. But Rabbi Portugal would not give up the fight. He somehow managed to smuggle a few of the children into his house and keep them away from the state-owned home.

Rabbi Portugal's release was as much a surprise to Feldman as to us. When I had gone by myself to see him, to intercede for the Rebbe, he had replied curtly, 'Jianu has summoned me and shown me your letter to him. You have made a mistake in interfering in a very serious affair. I advise you not to repeat it.' He then added solemnly, 'Rabbi Portugal will never see daylight again.'

To this day I remember how shocked I was. I went to my parents' house, where my wife was. She saw that I was distraught and asked what had gone wrong, but I could not make myself tell her the sad news. However, when we arrived at our flat, I heard the telephone ring. When I picked up the receiver and heard Rabbi Portugal's voice, I was amazed. I could not believe my ears. He finally convinced me that it was, indeed, he. He was ringing to thank me for my efforts to free him. Hardly forty-five minutes had elapsed since Feldman had spoken to me. It was clear that, with all his power, he was not so much in the confidence of the Government as he pretended.

I asked Rabbi Portugal how he had managed to have enough to eat to survive in prison in view of our repeated failures to send him kosher food. 'It was the brown bread which I received that kept me alive,' he explained. 'I became very weak and the doctor came to see me. He decided that the few coins I possessed should be used to buy grapes for me. This was a truly wonderful event. I had a bit of bread for the Friday night *Kiddush*. As I had no wine for the Saturday evening *Havdala* [prayer marking the end of the Sabbath], I pressed the grapes. These grapes were my salvation. Otherwise, I would not have been able to make *Havdala*.'

Tales of the Rebbe's goodness spread far and wide. Jews came from all over the country to pour their hearts out to him. They sought his advice and blessing. He himself began to travel, spending every Sabbath in a different community. Thousands of Jews gathered in the towns and villages to greet him and participate in huge communal meals with him. They found comfort in his words, his kindness and his love. He kept none of the money given by his followers. In fact, he had so little money on him that, at the end of every long journey, he would send a telegram to Bucharest requesting the amount for his fare back home.

During the terribly cold winter of 1954, when Bucharest lay under several inches of ice and snow, I visited Rabbi Portugal's house. It was freezing cold there. Apart from Rabbi and Mrs Portugal, there were children in the house. I was very concerned for them and made a special effort to send them a truckload of firewood. A few days later, I went to see Rabbi Portugal, expecting to find a cheerful, warm house, but there was no fire burning in the grate and I could see no firewood. 'Where's the wood I sent you?' I asked, surprised. 'I gave it to the poor. Their needs were greater than mine. I could not leave them to freeze in the cold,' he replied.

Although freed from prison, Rabbi Portugal was still harassed by the security services and the CDE. They tried to frighten Jews away from his synagogue. I did my utmost to support him in his work and to defend him. In return, Rabbi Portugal backed me enthusiastically in my battles for Talmud Torah and other religious needs. Our backgrounds were different, but we became brothers in spirit.

Rabbi Portugal was particularly anxious to help the families of the thousands of Jews who had been detained for various economic offences. The 'closed gates' of Romania, from 1952 to 1958, took by surprise thousands of strictly Orthodox Jews – *'shomrei Shabbat'* – who, because they did not work on Saturdays, were unable to obtain employment and, therefore, resorted to various expedients, dealing in forbidden foreign currency, gold, etc. Most of them were sent to prison and spent many years there. Without Rabbi Portugal's help, most of their families would have starved. He was not concerned whether those detained were guilty or innocent. Indeed, many Jews who had become destitute because of the Government's harsh economic measures committed currency offences. But the Rebbe felt that their innocent dependents should not be punished. Some people took advantage of his childlike goodness and swindled him. But he never became disillusioned and never sent anyone away without giving him a helping hand. Because of his activities, the police constantly watched his house, hoping to find incriminating evidence against him, but they never did. Nor could they.

I recall a rather amusing episode in connection with him. When the American rabbis visited Bucharest in July 1956, they had a long conversation with Rabbi Portugal. It occurred on the night of *Tishah B'Av* and the discussion went on until two or three o'clock in the morning. When Rabbi Portugal was arrested again in April 1959, the interrogator asked him what the subject of his conversation with the American rabbis had been. He replied that they had discussed issues connected with the Torah. Puzzled, the interrogator said, 'I don't understand what you mean. Were you not trained to become a rabbi and did you not pass a final examination?' 'Yes,' Rabbi Portugal replied. 'And did not the American rabbis study and pass their rabbinical examinations?' 'Yes,' was the answer again. 'Then, if all of you passed the examinations and are rabbis, why did you need to discuss the Torah any more?' Very often in my sermons, when I want to explain the difference between our outlook on culture, on science, on the Torah and the outlook of others, I use this dialogue between Rabbi Portugal and his interrogator.

His second arrest took place in the spring of 1959, after the borders closed again on 25 February. Thousands of Jews who had sold their furniture and lost their jobs, whose children had been expelled from schools and universities and who were waiting for their exit visas, were faced with no prospects other than starvation and being designated 'enemies of the country'. A few hundred Jews of various categories, suspected of being Zionist activists, were arrested. Among them were Rabbi Zisse Portugal and his son Shrulikel. The police searched his house throughout the night and the small amount of money that was found was taken away. In the house there remained two women, Shrulikel's children and several adopted children. They were all totally penniless. The old Rabbi Portugal's wife was a woman of high principles, who could not bear to be in debt. Two weeks before the arrests, the Rebbe had borroweed 3,000 lei from one of his devoted followers, a Mr D. Haimovici. Somehow, the police had not found the money in the house. Immediately after the search, she asked Rabbi Saul Kahane, the *shochet*, to return the money to Haimovici and to thank him on her behalf. Of course, we made sure that the families of the two rabbis did not starve.

I decided that I must appeal directly to President Maurer, who had taken over in 1958 and whom I considered both a clever and a courageous man. It was Maurer who gave the famous answer to Khrushchev, when the Soviet leader appeared to be interfering in Romania's internal affairs. 'Sir,' he said to him, 'in Romania we are masters of our own house.' Before becoming President, he had been Minister of Foreign Affairs and so his knowledge of the government machinery was considerable (later on he would be the country's Prime Minister for a long while). Unlike Bodnăraş, who liked to talk and attempt to convince me that his arguments were valid, Maurer was prepared to listen. When I said that I admired his patience, he remarked, 'I consider myself the highest judge in the country and a judge has to listen.' But though I presented him with a written statement and explained in detail the personality of Rabbi Portugal and the high esteem in which he was held in the Jewish world, I failed to make any impression on him. Nor did my argument that a junior official had made the mistake of arresting a saintly, innocent man and that it was, therefore, urgently necessary to free Rabbi Portugal before the matter became public, prove any more effective.

'We know perfectly well who Rabbi Portugal is and what prestige he has,' Maurer replied. 'We, the leadership, and not some police officer decided that he should be arrested. We have thought the whole thing through. The fact that we took the decision to arrest him also means that we have considered the risks.'

Even sending food parcels to Rabbi Portugal was ruled out by Maurer. 'We were once in prison, too, and we know very well that a letter or other object can be slipped into a parcel,' he said. The Interior Minister, Drăghici, also opposed my requests that *matzoth* and other Passover food should be taken to Rabbi Portugal during the festival. Curiously, an official came and asked me for sugar for him, but refused to take him *matzoth*. The prospects for the Rabbi appeared very gloomy. He was the victim of a complex conspiracy.

He later described to me, with tears running down his cheeks, how distressed he was to discover that he did not know when Passover began. Despite the fact that he was imprisoned only two weeks before Passover, he had lost count of the days in the basement cell, where there was no light. Only on the last day of Passover was he given the sugar and told of the festival. Sobbing, he said that the guards had bound him hand and foot, forced his mouth open and pushed food through a tube. 'They made me eat *trefah* [non-kosher food],' he sobbed.

Rabbi Portugal and his son were beaten up and tortured in prison. Hair was torn from their beards. Young Rabbi Portugal told me, 'The interrogators took a Sepher Torah and tried to force me to swear on it that I would tell them the truth. They then beat and tortured me until I lost consciousness. When they poured water on me, I regained consciousness. This was the system they consistently used.

'One day, a group of people came to see me. They asked me if I was willing to talk. When I refused, they started to torture me and I fainted more than once. Then they poured water on me and I revived, but I still refused to talk.

'This was repeated a number of times. I had never previously suffered so much. I believed I was going to die. I told the torturers to stop and to take me to the group of people who were waiting in another room. I said that I had something to tell them. The men stopped beating me, washed and dressed me, and led me before the security leaders. Believing that I was now ready to "confess" and say exactly what they required, they smiled at me. Finally they asked me what I wanted to tell them. I said that, as I was going to die, I desired to mention my last wish: I wanted to be buried in a Jewish cemetery. These words infuriated them. I was immediately hauled back to the cell and the tortures were resumed in an even more savage manner.'

His father's interrogator was a Russian, who tried for month after month to force him to confess to non-existent crimes. It so happened that the Rabbi had a wonderful gift for composing tunes to words in the Bible. These tunes have become famous in the Jewish Orthodox religious world. 'Once, I was being interrogated,' the Rabbi recalled to me, 'and I felt totally exhausted after hours of physical and spiritual suffering. I thought that I was about to collapse. Suddenly a sweet melody sprang up somewhere in my soul. As the melody flowed softly, I fitted it to the final words of Psalm 109: "With my mouth I will give great thanks to the Lord; I will praise Him in the midst of the throng. For He stands at the right hand of the needy, to save him from those who condemn him to death."

'These sublime words, mingled with the melody, truly reflected my state of mind, for I had only one hope that I could cling to. And the melody began to dominate me entirely. I no longer heard the interrogator's harsh questions. I was in a different world. The Russian, noticing that I made no response to any of his questions, started shouting at me. However, the louder he shouted the more I concentrated on my melody, because I feared I would lose it. I shut myself off entirely from the Russian. He rushed at me in a frenzy and began to pull at my hair and beat me about the face. Blood ran down my cheeks, but I still held on to the tune, the *niggun*. In the end the Russian gave up in disgust and left the cell, murmuring threats. My *niggun* had emerged victorious.'

One evening, the Russian interrogator concluded his work and read out to the Rabbi the full indictment, which enumerated a large variety of crimes, under the general heading of treason or spying. The most fantastic accusations followed one another. Those who had hatched the plot against the Rabbi were determined to find him guilty, even if total fantasy was used.

As is the custom in such cases, the interrogator asked him if he had anything to say in his own defence. The Rabbi responded by asking a question, 'Do you believe in God?' The man opened his mouth in astonishment and then became angry. 'How dare you make fun of me?' he shouted. 'You know very well that I am a Communist and atheist and yet you ask me such a question?'

Ignoring the outburst, the Rabbi asked calmly, 'Why don't you believe in God?'

'How can you expect me to believe in your humbug?' the man replied. 'What proof have you got that God exists? You have no proof and there is no proof. That is why I don't believe in any God.'

Still calm, the Rabbi replied, 'You don't want to believe in God because you say I don't give you any proof of His existence. Yet you want me to believe all the lies you have read out to me without providing any proof.'

Nevertheless, the indictment against the saintly Rabbi and his son was drawn up, but their enemies did not triumph. The political situation changed and they were both set free in August 1959, immediately after *Shabbat Nachamu*, the Sabbath of Consolation. The same week a daughter was born to young Rabbi Portugal and was named Nechama – 'Consolation'. A few months later, the Rabbis, father and son, and all the members of their families left Romania for the United States. Old Rabbi Portugal was not a Zionist, but I think that what prompted him to leave for the US and not for Israel was his belief that he could achieve much more for the Jewish people in America than in Israel.

He was like a brother to me. He never forgot our common struggle, our common sufferings and dangers. He continued for many years, up to his last day, to dedicate all his life to helping people in need and to bringing out of prisons Jews sentenced on various charges.

In New York I was his guest on many a Sabbath. Several years before his death, he went blind. Still, he used to write letters to me. On the back of each page the words were typed, since his handwriting would have been completely illegible to me. He told me that his love for me was the reason for this procedure.

Hundreds of children, coming from the Soviet Union to Israel without any Jewish education, now find in the Holy Land dozens of institutes teaching the Torah. Their name is *Chesed Leavraham* and their founder was the noble and saintly Rabbi Portugal. May the memory of this 'father of orphans' be blessed for ever.

30   *On the Offensive*

By 1957 my struggle with the CDE leaders was reaching a climax. An unexpected development was to prove useful in this fight. The time for elections for a new Parliament was approaching and a new structure was given to this forum: the Council of Socialist Unity. Besides the members of the Communist Party, it comprised personalities who did not belong to the party: scientists, artists and other people working in the field of culture, as well as representatives of the various denominations. The Patriarch of the Greek Orthodox Church, the Bishop of the Roman Catholics, the Bishop of the German Protestants and of the Hungarian Lutherans, and the Chief Rabbi of the Jewish Communities were asked to stand for Parliament. So they did, and they were included in the list of candidates. I became a candidate in the Bucharest district which, before the Second World War, had been inhabited mostly by Jews.

I made a number of speeches to the residents in my area. Wearing my full rabbinical canonicals and with my prominent Magen David on my chest, I spoke to the people, stressing how the Romanian Government had stopped the persecution of Jews and was allowing full religious freedom. I was duly elected a Member of the Romanian Parliament, which I have remained to this day. My election was a bitter pill to the CDE. Feldman, Bacal and the others knew very well that the fact that I belonged to the Grand National Assembly inevitably enhanced my standing in the country and made it more difficult for them to topple me.

However, they were determined to intensify the struggle with me and, if possible, bring it to a head. Their resolve was strengthened by their desperation, because they were now operating under a double anomaly. Officially the CDE no longer existed since it had been disbanded in 1952, along with all the 'committees' of the national minorities – Hungarian, German, Serbian, etc. But it had continued to control the Jewish communities as if no such decision had been taken. The communities still knew the Jewish Communists by this name and that is why I have kept on referring to it. I suppose the authorities turned a blind eye to the anomaly, because they did not see any alternative and because the CDE leaders made various promises which obviously were not being, and would never be, fulfilled. They had failed to convince the Romanian Jews, despite threats, arrests and inducements, to give up their passionate yearning to settle in Israel, and they had been ridiculed in their efforts to turn the Jews into atheists.

Feeling their position weakening and frightened of the spectre of losing their privileged jobs, the Jewish Communists in the CDE concocted a major plot to destroy me. I suppose they noted my improved standing in the country and felt that they had to strike quickly. I realized they perceived me as the one major obstacle to their plan to destroy Jewish religious and communal life, while at the same time strengthening their own positions. If I was branded as an enemy of the regime and of the Romanian people, they could still have me removed. With me out of the way, they reckoned they would be able to smother all other opposition.

An invitation which I received to visit Britain in May 1957 gave the CDE an opportunity to pour poison into the ears of the Romanian leadership. The invitation came from Chief Rabbi Israel Brodie, Barnett Janner (later Lord Janner), president of the Board of Deputies of British Jews (the Jewish representative body), and the Marchioness of Reading, president of the British section of the World Jewish Congress. The CDE reckoned on manipulating the considerable anti-British feeling which had been aroused because of the attack on Egypt in the Suez War. However, whilst some ministers in the Cabinet felt that Romania should adopt a critical stand against Britain, there was also a certain feeling in the top leadership that Romania should not follow the Soviet line, which was particularly hostile to Britain. The idea of an independent Romanian foreign policy was becoming increasingly attractive. Without understanding the reasons at that time, I became a 'partner' in a high political game.

When I first informed the Government of the British invitation, I was told that I could go. I made all the preparations for the journey and informed my British hosts of the date of my departure. But on 20 May 1957, the very day of my departure, when all the luggage was packed and many synagogue leaders were ready to see me off at the airport, I was called to the new Minister of Cults, Dogaru, who told me bluntly, 'Sir, you are not going to Britain.' I was shocked.

Whether I visited London at that time or not did not matter very much. What was of vital importance was the use I wanted to make of such a visit. I intended to try again what I had done during my stay in Stockholm in 1956. I wished to use my British contacts to ensure that the remaining Zionist leaders who had been unable to leave Romania before the Suez crisis (September and October 1956) should receive their exit visas. I also wanted to try once more to obtain the 'opening of the gates' – free *aliyah* for divided families. In the years 1952–8, 60,000 such requests were refused. I also feared that some circles in the Government were planning to re-arrest the Zionist leaders who had remained in the country, because they needed them for another 'political show'. My fears were shared by Marco Cohen, a distinguished lawyer, who was my link with the Zionists. He himself had spent many years in prison under the accusation of being a 'Zionist spy'. When he heard that my visit to London had been cancelled, he had a heart attack. He, too, felt that the Zionists were facing a catastrophe. He understood that the authorities could hardly carry out arrests and, at the same time, have me visit a Western country where I would inevitably be asked embarrassing questions. It was vital to reverse the decision banning my visit.

I contacted Max the barber and asked him to inform President Groza of the sudden cancellation of my trip and of my distress at the decision. I transmitted the letters and telegrams which had arrived from London, the receptions, meetings and various other points of the schedule that had been decided upon, and I stressed the bad impression that such a last-minute cancellation would make on public opinion in the West.

Early on the following day, I received a message from President Groza, informing me that my visit to Britain would go ahead. A few minutes later, Bodnăraş rang me up, confirming the decision. I learned for the first time that the CDE leaders had reminded the Government that I was travelling to Britain with my wife and, therefore, would probably not return to Romania. When told that I had returned from visits to Helsinki and Stockholm, Bacal had replied cleverly, '*Once* is quite enough for not coming back.' Bacal himself later admitted that he had given this 'opinion' to the Government. My approach to the President had led to the reversal of the decision to ban my trip, which was a significant blow to the already tarnished standing of the CDE.

As all my efforts to obtain exit visas for the remaining Zionists had been unsuccessful before my departure for Britain, I decided on another desperate gesture. On the eve of my departure, I handed to my secretary, Rabbi Guttman, a closed letter to be given to Bodnăraş. In it I complained that I was going to England 'empty-handed' and I implored him to give me, if not all the Zionists, then ten of their leaders. My criterion for choosing them was simply to take the leaders of all the Zionist factions, thus avoiding another possible 'show'. I indicated Dan Ieşanu and Dr Theodore Loewenstein from Mapai, Osias Ebercohn and Marco Cohen from the Centre, Marc Abir, a young Zionist suffering from cancer, Edgar Kanner and Jakerkanner from the Revisionists. (I cannot recall the names of the other three.) Bodnăraş approved my request in my absence. When I returned from England, these men had already left the country.

The visit to Britain, however, was to cause me major problems and to give the CDE an opportunity to attack me. When Barnett Janner welcomed me in a London hotel in the presence of the press, he launched into an open attack on Romania's attitude to the emigration of Jews to Israel. I was taken aback by his words. He had not consulted me before speaking. If he had, I would have done everything possible to prevent him from voicing any criticism, because I knew it could do only harm. Now it appeared as if Janner had co-ordinated his criticism with me and that I was deliberately lending myself to a propaganda offensive against Romania. I immediately realized that a damaging mistake had been made and that a weapon had been presented to the eager hands of the CDE.

I was touched by the warmth with which I was received by British audiences – and by the French when I stopped over in Paris on the way home – but when I arrived in Bucharest I encountered a chilly atmosphere. Bacal had orchestrated a successful campaign against me, and I was accused of leading an international Zionist campaign against the Communist regime of Romania. Some Romanian circles appeared to be ready to believe this falsehood.

It was not only my life that was in danger. The fate of a whole population depended on who would win the battle. If it were the CDE, then tens of thousands of Jews would disappear as Jews, the Zionists would be returned to prison and Jewish education would be destroyed. I had no choice. I felt that the time had come for me to engage in an open battle to save my community.

I simply had to go on the offensive. Defending myself would not prove sufficient, even though I was totally innocent of the charges thrown at me. I also knew that my counter-offensive had to be directed at the Jewish Communists, who were my main opponents. My offensive was based on a single question: 'What are you doing here in the Federation of Jewish Communities? You are Communists and atheists. We are religious communities. If you are atheists, you are lying to us. If you are religious, you are lying to the Communist Party. So what are you? What do you want?'

The Jewish Communists had provided Jewish communal funds for the Communist newspapers, *Unirea* and *Ikuf-Bletter*, and for the Jewish State Theatre. I went to the authorities and said to them, 'Look what they are doing with our money.' I began to organize the Jews of the communities against the CDE. They, in turn, accused me of organizing a counter-revolutionary movement. The conflict was becoming increasingly bitter.

It was fortunate for me that I had an unexpected ally in the person of the Minister of Cults, Dogaru. He was not pleased with the attitude of the Jews who, in contrast to the other religious groups, did not look upon him as the main authority because they were controlled by the CDE. Dogaru did not, therefore, respond to the CDE's wild charges against me.

Dumitru Dogaru, who had succeeded Professor Constantinescu-Iaşi at the beginning of 1957 and remained at the post until 1975, was even more influential in my struggles and in the fate of our communities. He was a professor and a distinguished intellectual. At first he sided with the CDE, or so it appeared, but he was actually playing a double game by seeking to sharpen the conflict between me and the CDE. I suppose he was playing a variety of the old game of 'divide and rule', and he certainly had a special talent for this. However, he gradually came to the conclusion that I was not an enemy of the regime and could even be useful. At the same time, his dislike and distrust of the CDE grew and he considered them a danger to the country. At first, when faced with a major problem, I used to seek the help of Maurer or Bodnăraş. When I noticed, however, that Dogaru was changing his attitude towards us, I began to take my problems to him. He became our skilful channel to the party and state leadership.

Yet his assumption of the Cults post coincided with a most disturbing development for Romanian Jews. While the gates of the country remained closed to *aliyah* to Israel, many Jews began to be dismissed from their state jobs for no other reason than that they were Jews. This followed a secret circular sent to all government offices and state-controlled concerns providing a new definition of nationality. It was a complex definition, but it basically deprived Jews of full nationality rights. I saw one of these secret circulars, which had been sent out by the president of the Union of Carpenters, Vasilichi, who was not himself an anti-Semite. The circular gave instructions for the dismissal of a certain percentage of the workers. The criterion had to be 'national structure', which meant, in the old anti-Semitic vocabulary, *numerus clausus*. The aim was not to dismiss all Jews, but to limit the number of those with jobs.

I was profoundly shocked by this circular, but I had no possibility of making use of it, for it was a 'secret official document' and the man who showed it to me was risking his life. I heard that thousands of Jews had lost their jobs, but each dismissal was explained away as being due to over-staffing or lack of work. However, I eventually obtained the proof I needed. A Jewish engineer named Usher Weinrauch, who had been working at the Ministry of Chemical Products, came to see me. He told me that he had been summoned by an official and dismissed on the spot. When he protested, he was told, 'We have too many Jews here.' Ironically, the Minister, Mikhail Florescu, was himself a Jew, whose original name was Iacobi. He had founded the country's petro-chemical industry and was a friend of mine when we were students.

I asked Weinrauch if he was prepared to put the allegation in writing. Without hesitation he agreed to do so. Within a short time he handed me a letter giving a full description of the treatment he had received. It was a very brave action, indeed. Openly to accuse government authorities of pursuing an anti-Semitic policy was very dangerous and created a great risk for the author of such a letter.

Indignant and distressed, I wrote a sharp letter to the Minister, demanding an immediate investigation. I pointed out that Weinrauch was accusing the Communist Government of Romania of pursuing racist policies. I then added, 'If this man is telling a lie, he should be punished. If what he is saying is true, the Government has a major problem. The most elementary laws of the country have been violated and those responsible should be severely punished.'

A few days later, I received a reply from the Minister, which accused Weinrauch of being neglectful and of other vague shortcomings. There was no response to the main point of my letter – the allegation of official racism. When I met Florescu at a meeting of the Romanian Parliament, he appeared embarrassed. Suddenly he remarked to me, 'Chief Rabbi, I think you are making a mistake in defending that man. He is a wretch and does not deserve your protection.'

'Minister,' I replied, 'I did not know the man before he approached me. It is not vital to me whether he gets his job back or not. I am not defending him. This is not the question at all. What is vital is whether his allegation is true or not. You have not answered me. Is it or is it not true that there is a new policy based on national structure? Is it or is it not true that a Jew can lose his job only because he happens to be a Jew?'

Florescu remained silent. He smiled weakly. I walked away from him without saying another word. His silence had given me all the answers I needed. I asked Weinrauch if he wanted to complain to the highest authorities in the land. I pointed out to him the risks that he would be running. To accuse the Communist regime of racial discrimination could be considered a major crime. He replied that he was not afraid of the consequences. He knew that he was right and had been treated unjustly.

I helped him to draw up a petition to the Prime Minister, Chivu Stoica. The content and the style of the petition were calculated to annoy the authorities. The final sentence stated: 'As all my demands to be restored to my former position appear to be in vain, I kindly ask you to authorize my departure for Israel, a country in which I will not come up against the obstacle of "national structure" and where I will be able to work in accordance with my merits and abilities.'

I sent the petition by special messenger to the Prime Minister, with a covering letter in similar terms to the one I had addressed to Florescu.

About a week later, the engineer received a note inviting him to go to the Prime Minister's office. I feared that this was a ploy to have him arrested when he arrived. However, he was met not by police, but by the Prime Minister's officials, who took him to his private room. It was in every way a rare honour for a humble, unemployed engineer.

As he entered the room, he noticed that Prime Minister Stoica was holding a petition in his hand and reading it. Having finished, the Prime Minister looked up and asked, 'Do you stand by what you have written here?' 'Yes,' Weinrauch replied promptly. 'You can leave the country,' the Prime Minister told him. Having said these unexpected words, he made it clear that this was the end of the interview and Weinrauch, somewhat startled, was ushered out.

When he described to me what had happened at the 'interview', I realized that we were witnessing a turning-point in the situation of Romanian Jews. The Government no longer considered as an enemy a man who accused it of unfairly depriving him of his livelihood. Instead, it told him that he could leave the country. And, meditating on the implication of this permission, I said to myself, 'This means that other Jews will be able to leave, too. The gates of the country are being opened. *Aliyah* can begin once again.'

Weinrauch was given a passport and allowed to leave for Israel, and we began to await the happy news of the resumption of *aliyah*. His departure was like 'the dove leaving the ark'. The gates had been closed since 1952, and now one man had been permitted by the Prime Minister himself to go to Israel. A new situation was arising.

31   *Who Likes Fish?*
The Gates Open
and Close Again

When Romanian Jews heard on Yom Kippur, 1958, that they could register for emigration to Israel, the effect on them was electrifying. Now, suddenly, they would be able to rejoin their loved ones and start new lives. So overwhelming was the feeling of joy, excitement and relief, that even ultra-Orthodox Jews in Satmar took off their *tallitoth*, put down their prayer books, left the synagogues and began to queue up at police stations for exit permits.

These dramatic scenes were repeated all over the country. Every day thousands of Jews gathered in Bucharest outside the central police station. The queues stretched for miles. It was an awesome sight. And as soon as the Jews obtained the necessary exit papers, they hurried to find seats on the next flight to Israel. Many Jews did not wait to sell all their belongings, believing that they would obtain all their needs in the Jewish state. The degree of their trust in Israel was astonishing. The scenes were reminiscent of Messianic times. Foreign newspapers and television stations widely reported on this phenomenon.

There had been an historic change in Romanian government policy. For many years, the authorities had held strongly to the view that Jews were needed by the country: Jewish workers, intellectuals, artists, politicians and even merchants were seen as being essential to the progress and prosperity of Romania. Jews had played a leading role in the Romanian Communist Party when it was still illegal, so it was not surprising that some of them now occupied high state positions. This, in my view, was not a desirable development, because it gave the impression that Jews were controlling the country.

Anxious to persuade the Jews to remain in Romania, the authorities were prepared to provide living conditions that would remove the need to emigrate. They clamped down on any manifestations of anti-Semitism that might have frightened the Jews. Yet all these efforts proved unavailing. From 1948 until 1952, when the gates were closed, about 100,000 Jews left the country for Israel.

Gradually, the authorities began to change their policy towards Jewish emigration. A number of factors, both internal and external, prompted the radical transformation. There was a greater emphasis on Romanian nationality as the Romanian leaders sought to disengage themselves from the Soviet embrace and proclaim their national independence. Jews were signifying that they did not see their future in Romania, but the authorities still did not know the full extent of the Jewish desire to leave. They assumed that, if a comparatively small number left, they could easily be replaced by Romanian nationals.

Understanding the psychology of the leadership, I had adopted an approach which I knew could at times be misunderstood and controversial, but which – I was certain – would be to the benefit of our Jewish communities. I saw Romanian Jews as guests in the country: entitled to the rights of citizenship and to full human rights, but still guests. People in the West may find this view incomprehensible, coming from a Chief Rabbi. Conditions, I know, are different for Jews in Britain, the United States, France and other countries, but Jews in Romania did not want to build up the country. They wanted to become part of the new State of Israel and to build it up with their sweat and tears – and not with donations from afar. There were historical reasons for this attitude. And the Jews proved by their actions and sacrifices that I understood their innermost desires.

I thus evolved a double-edged policy. Firstly, I had to obtain full religious freedom and all the services which made this freedom meaning-ful: there had to be synagogues, Talmud Torahs, *mikvaoth*, cultural centres and old age homes. When he thought of emigrating, the Jew's eyes had to be turned towards Jerusalem and not to New York. He had to think of living a full Jewish life rather than of the material benefits of the capitalist world. And, secondly, I had to obtain the right for Jews to leave Romania and to settle in Israel. These great rights could only be obtained with the Government's approval. Jews had to have the right to be equal with others and yet, at the same time, be different.

Knowing that I had the fate of hundreds of thousands of people in my hands, I agonized on the policy I should adopt. Would I succeed if I began to fight the Government, if I started a campaign of 'Let My People Go', of smashing windows and of demonstrations? I knew that these tactics would quickly lead to disaster for the many thousands of people who looked to me for help. I knew I had no right to play with the lives of a community of over 300,000 people.

After many sleepless nights, I came to the conclusion that, if I was to bring salvation to the Jews of Romania, if they were to avoid the fate of Russian Jews, I had to win the sympathy of the Romanian authorities. I had to convince them that Zionism was not their enemy. I had to demonstrate that both Jews and Romanians shared a common interest. I recall a saying by Charles de Gaulle: 'I have no friends, I have no enemies. I have only interests.' This approach applied particularly to the Romanian authorities. To do my utmost to avoid a clash, to be able to find out our common interests, to harmonize our interests with theirs and to apply a policy of give and take – these were my main purposes.

Millions of Jews were living under Communist regimes and their fate was dependent on the goodwill of the Communists. We had to ensure that these Jews survived, as we could not afford to lose any more, having already lost six million in the Holocaust. We, therefore, had to act responsibly.

Painfully and gradually, I began to convince the Romanian authorities that it was as much in their interests as in ours to allow emigration to Israel. I was ready to co-operate with them, but I made one fundamental stipulation: no concession in regard to Zionism and *aliyah* to Israel.

Delighted and happy though I was at the news that Jews were once again registering for emigration to Israel, I was puzzled by the methods adopted by the authorities. When I received detailed reports of emigration queues in the streets, my puzzlement turned to concern. Why had the authorities deliberately encouraged all Jews to register? Why had it all been done in such a public manner?

I considered the matter of such importance that I sought an interview with President Maurer on 1 October 1958. I started the conversation with a question, 'Mr President what is happening? Why is there a queue of Jews in front of the former police headquarters in Calea Victoriei? Is it aimed at supplying sensational material for the foreign press?'

'What kind of question is this?' the President responded. 'You have been writing petitions and sending complaints to us for years, requesting us to allow emigration to Israel. And now that we are doing precisely what you wanted, you come here and ask what is happening!'

'You are right, Mr President,' I replied. 'But please allow me to explain why I have called on you. You have, indeed, decided to open the gates and we Jews are very grateful and happy. But why do the authorities need mass registrations? There are already 60,000 applications for permission to leave for Israel, submitted by parents who want to be reunited with their children and by children who want to rejoin their parents. Why are the authorities not dealing with these cases first? Why do they need thousands of other applications? And why is there only one registration station for the whole of Bucharest? And in the very centre of the city! I am sure that you, Mr President, are well aware that such registrations usually take place at small stations on the outskirts of the city.'

I then said that I hoped he would not object to my telling him an old Jewish joke. After the service in synagogue one Friday evening, the rabbi invited, in a loud voice, all those who liked fish to come to his house that very evening. Many people turned up expectantly at the rabbi's house. He was sitting at the table and eating fish, obviously enjoying his meal. He asked the visitors to sit down. They did so and waited to be served with fish, but none came. The rabbi continued to eat, oblivious to the surprised looks on the faces of the visitors. Eventually, they could not help voicing astonishment at his behaviour. He looked at them steadily and remarked, 'Did I say that I was going to give fish to anyone? Certainly not. What I said was that I wanted to know who liked fish. Now I know and I thank you.'

After telling the story, I said to the President, 'Is it by any chance possible that the reason for all these registrations is that you wanted to know how many Jews wished to leave for Israel, just as the rabbi wanted to know who liked fish?'

President Maurer smiled, but did not reply.

However, thousands of Jews received permission to go and, provided with passports, they soon left for Israel. But, to our utter astonishment and horror, Kol Israel (Israel Radio) began to broadcast every night violent attacks on the Romanian authorities. These broadcasts made our blood run cold: they were so illogical, so inexplicable. One would have expected lavish Israeli appreciation of the Romanian decision to allow Jews to leave the country for Israel for the first time in several years. Instead, there were these daily attacks. Why? I asked myself in despair.

As I listened to the Israeli denunciations of Romania, the words of the famous Berdichever Rebbe, Leivi Yitzhak, came to my mind. During a particularly difficult period of his life, when he and his community were suffering blow after blow, he exclaimed, 'Oh, Lord Almighty, I no longer understand the manner in which Thou rulest over this world. Thou must, therefore, make a choice. Either Thou rulest the world in keeping with the mind, the logic Thou hast bestowed upon us, or give us, O Lord, another logic, so that we be able to comprehend Thy rule over the world.'

Indeed, I tried desperately hard to understand why Kol Israel was launching these attacks, but I could find no explanation. I feared for the consequences. Hostility was bound to be met with hostility. The fate of thousands of Jews would be affected. An unnecessary catastrophe was being created.

When the first Romanian response came, on 25 February 1959, it nevertheless managed to shock me. *Scînteia* carried on its front page a virulent anti-Zionist onslaught. No such attack had appeared in a leading Romanian newspaper since the days of Beria. A worse event occurred on the following day. The Romanian Government announced that it was suspending the emigration of Jews to Israel. Thousands of exit permits which had already been issued were cancelled. Hundreds of Zionists were taken into custody. Young Jews were expelled from schools and universities.

Panic and despair seized the Jewish communities. Many thousands of people who had already given up their jobs and sold all their belongings, waiting to leave for Israel within days, were facing total ruin. They would have to live in the streets, destitute.

Six days after the dreadful *Scînteia* article and and five days after the horrifying suspension of emigration, President Maurer agreed to receive me again. I began this particularly urgent meeting with the words, 'I was right, Mr President. You wanted to know exactly who liked fish, did you not?'

The President smiled and said, 'I remember everything you told me when we last met, including the joke about fish. Then I was unable to give you an answer, but I can do so now. Yes, Chief Rabbi, we wished to end our Jewish problem. I personally did not want to feel like a prison governor who cannot travel abroad for fear of being attacked and accused of holding innocent people in prison. My colleagues and I, therefore, hit on the idea of starting the registration of Jews to find out how many of them really wanted to leave. We expected 10,000 to 20,000 applications, but we received 130,000. Yes, 130,000! Who could have imagined such a figure? What terrible harm have we done to the Jewish people that they wish to leave in such huge numbers? We saved your lives, we granted you equal rights. Why should there be such a flight, worse than when the Jews were under the Fascists?'

I interrupted the President, by saying, 'We did not have a country of our own at that time. Now we have one.'

The President continued in a grave, sad voice, 'There are other problems which we cannot understand. I was once a practising lawyer and I have always worked with Jews. As you know, I have many Jewish friends. I know that you are an intelligent people. But what kind of leaders have you got now? Nasser's Ambassador comes to us and protests against the departure of Romanian Jews, claiming that we are sending soldiers to Israel. We reply that this is not true, that only old and handicapped people are leaving. The Ambassador then says to us, "Whom should I believe, you or Ben-Gurion and Golda Meir? Every evening they broadcast precise details of how many Romanian Jewish engineers, doctors and young professionals have arrived in Israel." '

After a short pause, the President added, 'We opened the gates of our country so that we should no longer be described in the world press as bandits. But we notice that our gesture has made no difference. Nothing has changed. We are still being attacked and described as bandits. Well, if we are bandits when we keep the gates closed and bandits when we open them, we would rather keep them closed and avoid the problems we have with the Arabs and others.'

These were harsh and painful words, yet I felt that Maurer was right to utter them. Kol Israel and those behind it were cruelly and illogically harming Romanian Jews. I instinctively felt that I should not argue with him, that I should implicitly accept the criticism and seek his advice. 'What is to be done?' I exclaimed, almost involuntarily.

'You must learn not to make so much noise. You are only harming yourselves,' was the President's reply.

President Maurer said these words in a particularly stern voice. Yet they gave me hope. They indicated that the gates might be opened again if the Israelis changed their behaviour.

I rushed to see the Israeli Ambassador and told him what the President had said. I strongly emphasized that I entirely agreed with the President's advice. The dangerous, illogical campaign against Romania by Kol Israel had to be stopped. The Israelis, for once, listened. The campaign ceased and, a few months later, the authorities in Romania reacted. Emigration of Jews to Israel was gradually resumed, although this was no longer a mass *aliyah*; only small numbers left. But the gates were opening once again. That was the thrilling news. And eventually more and more Jews were able to leave. But no one wrote about this *aliyah* or spoke about it on radio or television. A special law was passed by the Knesset in Israel making it an offence to refer to the arrival of Romanian Jews. This emigration acquired a special name – the *sha-sha aliyah* (hush-hush *aliyah*). A bitter lesson had been learned at a heavy cost.

Since 1959, more than 250,000 Jews have left Romania for Israel, with no noise and no publicity. The Romanian authorities have learned who likes fish, and we have learned how to eat fish.

32 *Eating a Little Less* Kugel

*A*s a Chief Rabbi who had to ensure that religious life continued at an acceptable level in every community in the country until all the Jews had left for Israel, I felt anxious about the departure of rabbis and *shochetim*. This had always been one of my main concerns and an intrinsic part of my struggle with the CDE leaders. They made a special point of encouraging the emigration of rabbis because they rightly considered that, without them, Jewish religious life would wither away. Equally important, perhaps even more so, was the presence of the *shochetim*, because without them the blow to religious life would be even stronger and more immediate. Without a *shochet*, a religious Jew can starve.

In a further effort to weaken Jewish communal life, the CDE decided that each town in the country should have only one community, led by a Jewish Communist secular head. A small concession was made that Sephardi Orthodox and Neologue (Reform) groups would be permitted to exist within the communities, but would no longer have total independence. Until then each town had had a number of independent communities, which had undoubtedly given Jewish life variety and strength. The new decision was taken in 1948, a few weeks after my election.

Realizing how dangerous it was, I invited to my house three of the oustanding Jewish sages in the country: Rabbi Joseph Adler of Turda, Rabbi Sofer of Timişoara and Rabbi David Sperber of Braşov. We agreed to oppose the measure. Rabbi Sperber was particularly indignant and spoke angrily and eloquently against it. When Feldman, Bacal and the other CDE leaders heard of this opposition, they tried to make us change our minds. They invited us to a meeting, but made no impression on us. Rabbi Sperber was fierce in his opposition. When an angry Feldman began to threaten him, he said calmly, 'What can you do to me in my old age? You can only make me eat a little less *kugel* in this world.' (*Kugel* is a favourite traditional Sabbath cake.) Sperber's meaning was clear: 'You can shorten my life so that there will be fewer Saturdays and fewer *kugels*, but at my age I am not afraid of such a threat.'

These simple words made a profound impression on me. I was only thirty-six when I first heard them and they were to influence me profoundly in the dramatic struggle for Jewish survival. So I, too, would eat less *kugel* if I stood up for Jewish rights. Compared with this supreme aim, what importance could be attached to life itself? What was its value? That was the message given by the brave Rabbi Sperber.

I must confess that, whenever I faced a dramatic decision, Rabbi Sperber's answer was present in my mind, like the sound of the *shofar* calling us to follow our conscience. In my dialogues with myself, whenever I reached the question, 'What will happen to me if I do or do not do something?', my answer was, 'What can happen? I will only eat less *kugel* in this world.' However, although the risks were bigger than that, for the life of a whole community was at stake, the symbol was always valid.

Rabbi Sperber made *aliyah* and I never saw him again. In April 1962, on arriving in Jerusalem for the first time, I entered the King's Hotel and saw a 'Levaia' (funeral) passing in front of it. It was that of Rabbi Sperber, blessed be his saintly memory.

When the gates began to open in 1958, I realized that I had to watch carefully the departure of the rabbis and *shochetim*. When I first became Chief Rabbi, there were 600 rabbis in the country. Gradually their numbers dwindled as they took the opportunity to emigrate to Israel. I saw Jewish communities facing extinction as a result of internal not external forces. When I asked Feldman to help me retain a sufficient number of rabbis and *shochetim*, he refused. I pleaded that rabbis must not be the first to leave, but he rejected the argument. Feldman eventually suggested that some rabbis would be retained, but nobody must be told that I was responsible for that situation. I replied that I could never agree to such a decision being taken in secret. It would lead to all kinds of harmful rumours and would weaken the communities.

In 1952, I had called a conference of all the remaining rabbis and *shochetim* and told them, 'It is your duty and responsibility to stay behind. I, too, am staying, although I, too, wish to leave for Israel. Let the ordinary Jews go first. After they have gone, we'll go, too.' Some of the rabbis and *shochetim* had protested, because for many years they had dreamed of settling in Israel. My appeal came as an unpleasant request, but most of them, though saddened, realized that I was right. They knew they were indispensable. If they left, the flocks would be without shepherds. Therefore, about 150 rabbis agreed, some with heavy hearts, to remain. A few months later, the gates of the country closed for six years. I truly believe that had these rabbis left Romania, little of Judaism would have remained by the time the gates were reopened. In those dark years, the synagogue became the centre of Jewish life. The rabbis played an historic role in keeping up the spirit of the communities. When they were criticized by the CDE for being so conscientious, they answered that they were afraid of me. I doubt that this was the sole reason. Rabbis in Romania as elsewhere like to display independence, but I undoubtedly tried to introduce discipline in the running of the rabbinate in order to prevent the destruction of the communities.

At one point in 1958, after the gates had been open for some time, I noted with consternation that the number of active rabbis had been reduced to thirty-six.

Having failed with the CDE, I appealed in desperation to President Maurer and asked that he should help me retain the services of the rabbis by not granting them exit papers for the time being. I knew that whilst some of them would understand my action, others would not, and that I would be the object of intense criticism. What right did I have to prevent a rabbi from leaving Romania for Israel? Was I exceeding my duties and my powers? It was an agonizing decision to have to take, but I knew that I was right. I could not think merely of my own popularity with certain rabbis; I had, above all, to think of the welfare of the remaining Jewish communities.

Maurer responded by saying, 'Chief Rabbi, we speak like Jesuits to the various religious groups. They behave similarly to us. We are Jesuits to them and they are Jesuits to us. They are hypocritical to us and we are hypocritical to them. They tell us lies and we tell them lies. It is a kind of diplomacy based on lies. But we will not tell you lies because we consider you as our loyal enemy. We have followed your activities for many years. When you disagree with us, we know it. You don't intrigue against us in private. We assume, therefore, an obligation to be frank with you, too. We are the enemies of religion. Our aim is to destroy all religions, but we have to use suitable tactics. The time for destroying religion has not arrived yet. For the moment we are co-operating with religious groups. However, if your rabbis lose their sense of duty and responsibility and, as a consequence, their communities are dissolved, can you really ask us to try to retain them by force? Don't you think that you are asking too much?'

'Mr President, I understand your point of view, but I want you to understand mine. I am not prepared to continue as Chief Rabbi in these conditions,' I replied solemnly. 'I cannot go on fulfilling my duty without the remaining rabbis and *shochetim.*'

My protest and my threat of resignation had an immediate effect. The problem went to Bodnăraş, who placed an embargo on the emigration of the thirty-six rabbis and 150 *shochetim.* This was not, however, a definitive ban. From time to time I gave my approval for a rabbi and, more rarely, for a *shochet* to leave. *Shochetim* were sometimes more important in certain communities than rabbis.

Some rabbis understood my policy; others did not. One day I received a letter from Chief Rabbi Unterman of Israel asking me to approve the emigration of a *shochet* from Mediaş, in Transylvania. I replied, 'This is the day that I have been expecting. It is a crucial matter for our communities and I don't want to take the responsibility. I therefore ask you, Chief Rabbi, to give a *Din Torah* [a decision in accordance with the Torah]. If you so decide, I shall allow the *shochet* to leave within a day. However, on the following day I will have to close down the Jewish community of Mediaş. Besides, why should this *shochet* leave before the others? I will then be obliged to give the same permission to the others, which will mean closing down all our communities. Please, make your decision, assume full responsibility and I will comply.'

Chief Rabbi Unterman did not answer, so that particular *shochet* did not leave Romania at that time. When I met him a year later, he said to me with a smile, 'You wanted to take the ball from your court and put it into mine!'

'You are the Chief Rabbi of Israel. You have to make a decision,' I replied. But Chief Rabbi Unterman took no action.

However, another *shochet* was to cause me problems and embarrassment. Pinkus Wasserman, of Dorohoi, collaborated with the CDE in the first years of their activities and never asked for *aliyah*. However, one day he came to see me and spoke about his family affairs. He had three daughters and a son, who were in their late teens and early twenties. What would happen to them? he asked in a worried voice. Shortly afterwards he requested that his children should be given papers to leave for Israel. I obtained the exit visas for him, though I was warned by no less a person than Interior Minister Ion Stănescu that I would regret my action.

He was right. Wasserman made a good living and was not short of money. Apart from his salary as a *shochet*, he received $200 a month from the American Jewish Joint Distribution Committee, to encourage him to continue his work. He supplemented his earnings from a most unusual source. The peasants in the area, for reasons which have never been satisfactorily explained, believed that Wasserman could accomplish miracles. They began to bring to him their agricultural produce and poultry in order to be blessed by him. He duly complied and received money and all sorts of produce in payment. He kept an accounts book for this kind of business, which the police found, and the Communist newspapers began a campaign aimed at slandering and ridiculing all rabbis who were 'swindling the poor peasants'. It developed into an attack on our rabbinical dignity. I intervened and was able to obtain the closure of the case after Wasserman promised not to repeat his 'miracles'.

Unexpectedly, he became the centre of a major controversy in the Jewish world in the summer of 1975. My internal and external policies had annoyed some people, who saw a chance to discredit me, or so they thought. The charge was spread far and wide that I was preventing Wasserman from leaving for Israel, where his children were clamouring for him. Outside the Hechal Shlomo centre in Jerusalem, where I was attending a meeting of European rabbis, there appeared a large banner with the words, 'RABBI ROSEN, LET OUR FATHER GO!' Television cameras arrived to film the scene.

I told the rabbis, 'You decide. I am ready to accept your *Din Torah*. If you so decide, all *shochetim* will leave Romania immediately. You will then have to take over responsibility for *kashrut* in the country.'

The rabbis assured me that I was right. In response to telegrams from me, Chief Rabbi Ovadia Yosseph, the Israeli Sephardi Chief Rabbi, confirmed that it was against the spirit of Judaism for *shochetim* to leave as long as Jewish religious communities existed. I also informed the Jewish Agency of the World Zionist Organization that I was prepared to send all Romanian *shochetim* to Israel, provided the Agency took over full responsibility for Jewish life in Romania. I received no reply. Yet the media campaign against me continued in Israel.

When I asked Wasserman if he really wanted to go to Israel, he replied, 'Yes, but only to visit my children.' He said that he wanted to spend a month there. I told him that he could go and that, on his return, he should prepare himself for emigration.

After his visit, I gave Wasserman three months' salary and exit papers for Israel. He looked at me in alarm and began to weep. 'Chief Rabbi, I don't want to leave,' he said, clutching at my hands. He begged me to allow him to remain in Dorohoi. When Israeli television sent a team to Dorohoi to interview Wasserman, he strenuously denied that he had ever asked to emigrate to Israel. 'It was the enemies of Chief Rabbi Rosen who made all the noise,' he assured the TV men.

When the late Leon Dulczin, president of the World Zionist Organization, visited Romania in 1979, I took him to Dorohoi. He asked Wasserman, 'Why are you not going to Israel, to your children?' He replied, 'Why should I go, to be a parasite there? Here I am useful and the Chief Rabbi is my protector.'

That is how history is written . . .

33 *A Visit to East Berlin*

While not able to visit a Western country during that fierce period of my struggle with the CDE, when I felt like a prisoner, I was allowed, in May 1960, to accept an invitation to participate in an ecumenical congress in East Berlin. Aware that there were no *shochetim* in East Germany, I took some kosher food with me. When I arrived in East Berlin, I was informed by a member of the peace committee who met me at the airport that they knew I kept a special diet and that arrangements would be made to ensure that I could strictly observe it during my visit.

As a car took me to the guest-house of the East German Government in the famous Wilhelmstrasse, I could see huge areas of destroyed buildings and houses. The destruction wreaked by the American and British air forces during the war was still evident.

As I was opening my luggage in my room, the president of the committee suggested that I should stop for a few moments. 'I want to show you something that will be of interest to you,' he said mysteriously. He guided me to the balcony and pointed at a small hill in the distance. 'That is Hitler's grave!' he declared dramatically.

In fact, the spot he pointed out was the bunker in which Hitler had spent the last days of his life and where he had committed suicide, as the Russians were entering Berlin in May 1945. His loathsome body, which was partly burned by his aides, was taken away by the Russians and nobody knows where it was buried.

Nevertheless, I was profoundly moved. Seeing the spot where the murderer of the Jewish people, of my brother and my sister and their families, of all the seventy-two members of my mother's family, had himself met his death was an overwhelming experience.

My fellow Jews, the remnants of the famous and glorious Berlin Jewish community, received me with tears of emotion. I visited for the first time the ruins of the synagogue in Oranienburgerstrasse, burned by Nazis during *Kristallnacht* in 1938, when many synagogues in Germany were set on fire by the SS and SA gangs. The lamentations of the Prophet Jeremiah were present in my mind and in my heart: 'Eicha, how was it possible?'

I arrived at the Berlin Jewish cemetery, where I met Martin Riesenburger, the last rabbi of East Berlin. He had only survived the war because his work under the Nazi regime was that of guardian of the cemetery; the Nazis had needed him as an administrator of their 'death empire'. He told me many fantastic stories of survival. I will never forget the grave he showed me, where he had made a *succah*. As it was covered with branches, none of the Nazis had guessed that, instead of death, the '*Torath Chaim*', the Jewish way of life, was being proclaimed there.

At one point during my visit to East Germany, I came to a crossroad. One sign pointed to Weimar and the opposite sign to Buchenwald. How symbolic these signs were of German history: Goethe and Schiller in one direction, Hitler and the extermination camps in another.

The East German authorities made sure that I had kosher food wherever I went. However, there was an ironic twist to their thoughtfulness. I was informed that on Saturday I would be the guest of the Jewish community at Erfurt, who would be responsible for the *kashrut* of my meals. There was a highly emotional scene when I went to the local synagogue for the Sabbath services. Twenty or thirty Jews who had survived the Holocaust wept as I prayed before the Ark. After prayers, I was invited to the Sabbath meal by the president of the local Jewish community.

Everybody wept when I made *Kiddush* (a Sabbath prayer). Candles were burning on the table and there were *challoth* and a bottle of kosher wine. But what happened then came as a profound shock to me.

As we sat down at the table and began the meal, the president's wife brought in warm meat. Knowing that there were no *shochetim* in the area, I asked the hostess where she had obtained the meat from. 'From the butcher,' she replied promptly, without comprehending the terrible thing she had said. She was serving *trefah* meat to a Chief Rabbi! I was stunned. It was a shattering experience for me. Both the president and his wife were so far from the true observance of Judaism that they could serve meat from the local non-kosher butcher to the Chief Rabbi of Romania without knowing that it was forbidden by our ritual laws.

I refused the meat. A surprised and flustered hostess offered to cook me two eggs. I pointed out to her that it was forbidden to cook on the Sabbath. This must have been a second surprise to her and her husband.

On that Sabbath I had to be content with eating fruit and vegetables. Fortunately, I could rely on the East German Communist authorities to provide me with kosher food for the rest of my visit. Such is the irony of Jewish life.

34   *A Clash with Golda Meir*

Although the attacks on Romania had ceased in Israel, I was to discover that the bitter opposition to my approach in dealing with *aliyah* and with the Romanian authorities had not diminished. Besides, certain circles in Israel made sure that this critical view of my activities also existed in the United States.

Following my new, deeper understanding with the Romanian authorities, I was given approval, in 1961, to visit the United States at the invitation of Dr Samuel Belkin, the president of the Yeshiva University in New York. American Jewish leaders urged me not to mention the date of my arrival in the country, because they feared that I would be severely questioned by the press and television stations about conditions in Romania and would not know what to answer. They thought that I would be involved in a public relations scandal.

To their astonishment, I replied, 'On the contrary, let the press come to meet me.' In fact, the press knew exactly when I was coming. Moreover, it was I who took the initiative. On arrival in New York, I went to the press room at the airport and offered to answer any and every question. I told the journalists that I was prepared to convene a press conference. I said to them, 'The problem is that we are living in two different worlds and we have two different propaganda machines. We have both been brainwashed. The difference between us is this: you believe everything you read in the newspapers, and we believe nothing.'

Many people had been very sceptical, but they began to change their minds when they heard that we had rabbis and synagogues, kosher food, Talmud Torah classes and *mikvaoth* in Romania. This came as a total shock. The mass media in the West had hidden the truth for years. I was the first to point out the remarkable details of the existence of a full Jewish religious life in a strictly Communist state. Audiences were astonished.

The Yeshiva University sponsored a coast-to-coast tour and I visited thirty-four towns and cities before leaving for California. Everywhere there was the same gasp of near-incredulity. And when they learned that 150,000 Romanian Jews had already settled in Israel since 1948, with the blessing of the Romanian authorities, the effect was startling. I was overwhelmed with questions. The *New York Times* printed a long, front-page report of my revelations. People believed that Jewish life had already been liquidated in Romania, that not one synagogue existed, and here was a Chief Rabbi denying all those stories. Prominent American Jewish personalities recommended me warmly as an authentic leader and gave me full credit.

Israel's Foreign Minister, Golda Meir, who happened to be in the United States at the UN General Assembly, sent a man to inform me that she wanted to meet me. I was, of course, happy to accede to her wish. I already knew that Golda was a charismatic leader. I also knew that she was a practical person, who liked to deal with complex matters in a straightforward, common-sensical manner. I had decided that, if I ever had the opportunity of meeting Israel's Foreign Minister, I would not hide any problem. I would speak out bluntly about all the mistakes that had been made and about the damage inflicted on Romanian Jews by the misguided policies of the Israeli authorities.

I thought that only God knew if I would ever have another opportunity of speaking freely and openly to one of Israel's most prominent leaders, so it was imperative that I should be very frank. I even had to take the risk of hurting Golda with my story, but she must know the truth. I was the only person who could tell her the truth and I promised myself to do so.

We sat in the house of Dr Itzhak Levine, professor of history at the Yeshiva University. My wife accompanied me. Liova-Eliav, Golda's secretary, was also present.

I kept my promise. I gave Golda a long and accurate report on all that had happened in the autumn of 1958 and the winter of 1959, when the bitter attacks directed against Romania by the Israeli leaders and the Israeli mass media proved catastrophic for Romanian Jewry. I quoted exactly my interviews of 1 October 1958 and 1 March 1959 with President Maurer (see pages 186 and 188). I said that Israel's irresponsible attitude had brought about the closing of the gates, the starvation of thousands of Jews, the expulsion of thousands of youngsters from the universities and the arrests of hundreds of Zionists. Why? What was the logic of such an attitude? I spoke for over an hour. I saw Golda's face growing red and her eyes looking at me with scepticism. As she listened, she became increasingly angry. 'The Romanian Government should award you a special decoration for the services you have rendered them and for the speeches you are making on their behalf in the United States,' she said to me. 'You are disrupting everything. I have come here to save the hungry and persecuted Romanian Jews, but I find that you are proclaiming that life is good in Romania. Is this not sabotaging our work?' She was, indeed, furious.

Trying to keep calm, I asked Golda, 'Don't you want to take all the Jews out of Romania and bring them to Israel? Don't you want synagogues and Talmud Torahs to exist in Romania? Don't you want a strong Jewish life to exist there in the meantime? How can I deny the existence of the synagogues and Talmud Torahs and all the features that go with a religious Jewish life? If I denied their existence, I would be guilty of two crimes: I would be a liar and I would be responsible for their destruction.

'Let us not speak from the purely ethical point of view. Let us speak from the practical point of view. Is not the Government of Israel interested in maintaining Jewish life in Romania, so that the right climate should be created for immigrants to Israel? Please, tell me: what wrong am I doing? Is there any other Jew in Romania who is providing you with a truer picture of events there? And is the Government of Israel not aware that the Romanian authorities have reacted to my speeches in the United States by increasing the number of Jews leaving for Israel?

'If you want *aliyah*, you need Jews. If I do not maintain and develop Talmud Torahs, Jewish education, synagogues and Jewish culture, our people will disappear as Jews and they will not go to Israel. Have your informers told you nothing about the dangers I have faced, and am still facing, on account of my permanent struggle for *aliyah*, for Zionism?'

My words appeared to make no impression on her. The fierce look did not leave her face. She had been filled with too many inaccurate facts about my work to make her change her views in one meeting with me.

For security reasons my wife and I left the Levine house first. Golda stayed behind for a while. According to Mrs Levine, who later became friends with my wife, Golda remarked after our departure, 'I don't believe a word he says.'

My meeting with Golda in New York in November 1961 had unbelievable consequences for me for more than ten years. She was not a person to forget or to forgive. At every step, I felt her fierce look, I saw her red face and her angry eyes. At that time, I had to fight on two battle fronts. Security agents in Romania accused me of being a 'Zionist spy' and some people in Israel also tried to discredit me. Golda, despite her strong position, could not deny the evidence of my work for Israel, for *aliyah* and for my communities. I continued to praise the Romanian Government for having granted us all our religious, national and cultural rights. It was very difficult. I had to ignore all the physical, material and moral pressures, coming from left and right, and to promote my own line of 'give and take'. Whenever I obtained a concession, I had to pay the price by bringing it to the public's attention. When I came with a favourable newspaper editorial, it paid its price: *olim*, Talmud Torahs, youngsters singing and dancing on the occasion of Jewish festivals, kosher food, medicines, clothes, old age homes and more Jewish publications were granted.

Owing to my method, our Jews arrived at Lud in Israel and not in Vienna and became citizens of Kiriat Shmone and not Philadelphia. Thanks to my method, the problem of Romanian Jewry is no longer a problem: ninety-seven per cent are no longer in Romania. They are in Israel and, at the same time, they are Romania's friends. The remaining three per cent have sixty-seven well-organized communities and are continuing *aliyah*. As a result of my method, relations between Israel and Romania improved so much that, in 1967, Romania was the only Socialist country to maintain diplomatic relations with Israel. That was a surprise for many people, but not for me. I can proudly state that the whole outlook on Zionism, on Israel's right to exist and on the Jewish problem was radically changed in the higher echelons of Romania's leadership.

At the same time elsewhere, in other Communist countries, the tactics of 'Let My People Go' and of permanent clashes were bankrupt, resulting in the vast majority of emigrants not going to Israel.

When my wife and I, after the Six Day War, entered the office of President Shazar of Israel, he stood up, came forward, embraced me and said, 'You and not we were right. Your way and not ours was right.'

My visit to the United States, which lasted from November 1961 to April 1962, affected the fate of the Romanian Bishop Trifa, one of the Iron Guard leaders of the murderous Bucharest pogrom, who had managed, by telling a series of lies, to get into America.

As I have already mentioned, I was in Bucharest during the pogrom and saw with my own eyes the manifesto, signed by Trifa, calling for attacks on Jews. I heard with my own ears Trifa's voice on the radio saying, 'We'll kill every Jew. The Jew will not escape us, even if he hides himself like a snake in a hole.' Trifa was an active leader of an Iron Guard student group and one of the most venomous. When the Iron Guard failed to topple General Antonescu at the time of that pogrom, Trifa fled to Germany, where he remained until 1944. He told the Americans that he had left Romania in 1944, claiming to be a 'displaced person', a victim of Communism. He denied that he had ever been a Fascist. He had prospered in the Christian Orthodox community and risen to be an influential bishop. My accusations against him, backed as they were by eye-witness evidence, came as a shock to him.

I challenged Trifa, declaring, 'I am a priest and he is a priest. If he claims that I am not telling the truth about him, he should summon me for a hearing before an ecclesiastical court. I am ready to prove that he is a war criminal.' Trifa did not respond to my challenge.

With the aid of Robert Kennedy, then US Attorney-General, and Philip Klutznick, the US Ambassador to the United Nations, I was able to bring the matter before the highest circles in the US administration. I was also able to persuade Congressman Halpern to denounce Trifa's crimes and lies in Congress. I called a press conference and appealed directly to American public opinion; after that, in April 1962, I called a large press conference in Tel Aviv.

However, Trifa, like other major war criminals, had powerful allies. I learned to my sorrow that he had obtained the protection of the American Central Intelligence Agency, who had recruited East European personalities in the fight against Communism. As the CIA had brought Trifa to the United States, the agency did not want him to be expelled from the country. Trifa was also protected by the Romanian Orthodox Church in the US, which had over 100,000 members in Detroit and Cleveland, Ohio.

Trifa's lawyer questioned me when I testified against his client in the US Department of Justice. He asked me, 'Did you see Bishop Trifa kill Jews?' 'No,' I replied, 'but I did not see Hitler kill Jews either.'

Despite his protectors, after many years Trifa eventually lost his case. The evidence against him was too strong. He was stripped of American citizenship and deported to Portugal, one of the very few countries willing to accept him. He died there a few years later.

Having won the appreciation of the Romanian authorities, I felt that the time was right for a visit to Israel. I had hardly ever thought that such a dream could be fulfilled. During the years of Stalinist terror, my wife and I were certain that we would not be able to save our lives and that we would never see the Holy Land. Now, I decided, I must try to obtain 'the impossible'.

I went to see the Romanian Ambassador in Washington and told him, 'I want you to allow me to visit Israel, where the remains of my father are buried.' The Ambassador cabled to Bucharest for instructions. The affirmative reply came from Gheorghiu-Dej personally.

I got in touch with Meir Rosenne, Israeli Consul in New York (later Ambassador to the United States), and asked for a visa. He did not grant me one, but sent a cable to Jerusalem, asking for instructions. Apparently, he foresaw some problems. Having received his instructions, he warned me, 'Our advice to you is not to travel to Israel. It's dangerous.' He added mysteriously, 'Nobody has returned to Romania from Israel. Don't go.'

Startled and angered by this reply, I said, 'Thank you, but I know my own interests best. I want to go to Israel.' Rosenne checked again with Jerusalem and the reply was the same. I told Rosenne, 'I am a Jew and I am entitled to an entry visa. You cannot deny me the right to visit Israel.' 'We are not giving you a visa,' he replied.

Five or six times, I received rejections to my request. It was an incredible situation: the Government of Israel refusing a visa to the Chief Rabbi of Romania. I could only assume that certain circles in Israel, annoyed at my confrontation with Golda Meir, were taking revenge on me. I could not possibly accept such a ban. I told Rosenne, 'Let the Government of Israel know that my right to obtain an Israeli visa does not depend on them. It depends on the Torah. I have the same rights as any member of the Government. Nobody has the power to stop me from stepping on the soil of Israel, our Holy Land.'

I intended to travel with my wife without a visa, and we made all the necessary preparations. However, at the very last moment, we received visas. We arrived in Israel on 2 April 1962. As the aeroplane circled above Tel Aviv, Hebrew tunes were played over the loudspeaker. We were so happy that we both burst into tears, but we were soon to be shocked, too.

When we left the aeroplane and went through the main reception hall into the exit hall, we were suddenly surrounded by half-a-dozen security men, who insisted on opening our luggage and examining every item thoroughly. My wife and I stood in shocked amazement as the search went on for three hours, well past midnight. We knew that relatives were waiting at the airport to welcome us and we wondered what they would be thinking. It was an intolerable situation. I demanded that the luggage should be returned to us. The security men had not been able to discover anything illegal, but now came another demand: 'We require a certificate of vaccination.' We had none. Nobody else on our plane had been asked for vaccination certificates. However, when we told the men that we had no certificates, they immediately replied, 'Then you cannot enter Israel.'

I realized that I had somehow to inform the Israeli public of what shameful things were being done in their name. I told the security men that they could not prevent me from telephoning to Tel Aviv. While they hesitated, I went to the telephone and began to call up national newspapers. I told them of my incredible predicament and invited them to a press conference at the airport. I remember that the first newspaper I contacted was *Ma'ariv*. My calls were evidently monitored by certain circles, who obviously did not relish a public scandal. Within five minutes, our passports were stamped and we were at long last permitted to leave the airport. Next day, President Ben-Zvi and the Speaker of the Knesset, Kaddish Luz, invited me to see them. Leading politicians, such as the Minister of Religion, Dr Warhaftig, and the Minister of the Interior, Moshe Shapiro, came to see me. They were distressed to hear how my wife and I had been treated.

I was also invited to travel all over the country and I joined the religious kibbutz, Javneh, for Passover.

We delayed our departure from Israel at the express wish of the Romanian Government, who wanted me to carry out further investigations into the Trifa scandal. There were witnesses and documents in Israel, and it was important that I should examine them. Romanian Jews knew only of the postponement of my return, but not of the reasons. Naturally rumours spread. Hundreds of people turned up at Bucharest airport to greet me on my arrival, many of whom were curious to know whether I would really return.

The Romanian authorities were very pleased with the new image of Romania I was able to present to the American people during my visit, which was described as a tremendous public relations success. Gheorghiu-Dej later remarked to me, 'We have had fourteen ambassadors and 300 diplomats in the United States since 1945, but all of them together did not do as good a job for us as you did, Chief Rabbi.' The good relations I had established with the Romanian leadership, their awareness that their interests coincided with ours, were decisive factors in the promotion of Jewish emigration to Israel. In the fifteen-year period from 1961 to 1975, no fewer than 150,000 Jews left

Romania for Israel, quietly, without making any noise whatsoever. The US State Department also made it clear that my visit had helped to improve US–Romanian relations. This was to prove of considerable importance for the Romanian economy and for the country's image abroad, at a time when Romania was moving towards independence and towards improved relations with the West.

Minister Pungan, who was then the 'number two' (but actually the leader) at the Romanian Embassy in the United States, was my link with Gheorghiu-Dej. He believed that the radical improvement in relations between the US and Romania was partly the result of my work during the five months of my American visit. I hope so.

The climax of the improvement in US–Romanian relations was to be reached in the years 1975–88, when the MFN (Most Favoured Nation) status was granted to Romania (see pages 245–59).

But let us return to Golda. Years passed. I met her on various occasions, but her look did not change, nor did her negative opinion of me. However, she did send me a message of congratulations on the twentieth anniversary of my Chief Rabbinate in 1968, through Chief Rabbi Goren. And then suddenly, she came to Bucharest in May 1972 to meet President Ceauşescu.

When she entered the Choral Temple on Friday evening, many thousands of Jews crowded in the Temple, the courtyard and the neighbouring streets. More than 100 boys and girls welcomed her, singing 'Shalom aleichem'. Golda was astonished. Sitting next to me, she began to cry when our children's choir sang 'Yerushalaim shel zahav'. Her picture, with the caption 'Golda wipes her tears in Bucharest', appeared in all the Jewish newspapers.

In my sermon given to honour Golda, I reminded her of the following joke:

'In the first decades of our century, many Jewish "speakers" of Keren-Kayemeth [the Jewish National Fund] used to travel to Eastern European *shtetlech* to make Zionist speeches. One of them, who had never been to Palestine, used to give to his audience all kinds of details concerning the beauty of the land, of its architecture, etc. After twenty years of such activity, he decided to make *aliyah*. When he arrived in the Holy Land and travelled about the country, he exclaimed, "I didn't know that all the lies I used to tell in my speeches were true." Madame Golda,' I continued, 'look around the place and you will see that the lies that I was supposed to have told you are all true.'

Her attitude changed radically and she became an enthusiastic 'believer' in me. At the reception given by the Israeli Ambassador, her eyes were no longer cold and cynical; she looked at me with respect. As far as I was concerned, she was a different Golda.

When she went back to Jerusalem, she was informed that I had been elected president of the Museum of the Diaspora (*Beit Hatefutzot*) and that I was preparing to leave Romania to start my new job.

Nahum Goldmann told the following story, at a meeting of the Governing Board in July 1975, in Geneva: 'One day, Golda Meir rang me up. She said, "Nahum, *Hishtagata*? [Nahum, are you mad?] You want to take this man out of Romania. Do you know what kind of vital work he is doing there? How can you take such a responsibility and deprive Romanian Jewry of their leader?"

'I answered, "I am glad to hear that you have such an excellent opinion of Chief Rabbi Rosen." '

When I saw that things were becoming complicated and that Golda's new feelings towards me could damage my projects (I was then determined to accept the new job), I visited her in her office in Jerusalem. We spoke in Yiddish. I told her, 'Madame Golda, for more than ten years you were my *mitnagedet* [opponent] and right now, when I want to accept your criticism and leave Romania, you have become my *Chassidiste* [believer], my admirer, and are interfering with my plans. If for such a long time I was not the right man, how do you explain the fact that I have now suddenly become indispensable?'

She delivered a whole speech with all kinds of compliments. 'It is your duty to remain there for another two years,' she concluded.

We became very friendly and, when she was no longer Prime Minister, she invited me to her home in Ramat Aviv. We had a long discussion on the combination of the two elements of nation and religion in the definition of a Jewish entity.

This was my clash with Golda. I withstood the storm raised by her bad impression of me at our 1961 meeting, and I consider this chapter of my life as being a decisive one.

35 *The Beginning of a New Era*

A few days after my return from my US–Israeli trip at the end of May 1962, the leaders of the CDE were ordered by the Government to organize a solemn dinner in my honour. All the community presidents in the country were invited and told to eulogize me and my 'patriotic services' rendered to the country. I was amazed. Yet, at the same time, I felt a marvellous sense of revenge sitting there and listening to the praises of my enemies, who had wanted to kill me.

The impact of my visit to the United States and Israel was tremendous. The Government fired all the *Jewseks* whose struggle against Zionism and *aliyah* had failed and gave me the leadership of the Federation (Bacal had died in the meantime).

All at once, the Jewish population was not considered necessary any more. Jews were no longer irreplaceable. A new generation of Romanian scientists, doctors, engineers, specialists, artists and writers were ready to take over. At the same time, the Jewish population demonstrated that it was determined to go to Israel. Stalinist terror, imprisonment, CDE propaganda and all kinds of skilful methods of persuasion had failed to make them change their minds. In 1958, 130,000 Jews registered for *aliyah*.

'There is nothing to be done. We have given up trying to persuade the Jews to stay,' Bodnăraş said to me. 'You have turned your backs on us. We have saved your lives, we have given you all the rights that you never had in this country, but you are a "nomadic" people.'

I interrupted him, 'Therefore, in order no longer to be "nomadic", we need a home, a country of our own, which is Israel.'

Bitterly disappointed, the Government reacted by dismissing tens of thousands of Jews and expelling Jewish students from universities.

Bodnăraş, answering my protests, said, 'You know that education in our schools and universities is free of charge and that we, the

Socialist state, cover all expenses. You are asking us to train, at our own expense, doctors and engineers for Israel. That is too much!'

Eventually, the Government accepted the fact that Jews were 'a lost capital' in political business and could, therefore, be 'given' to the Rabbi.

But, alas, the very moment at which the Government agreed to set up a new leadership of the Federation and of the communities, I fell ill. A shadow was spreading over my right lung and, according to the first diagnosis, it was lung cancer.

Although I did not feel any pain, from the moment I was aware of the diagnosis, I remained isolated in my home, refusing to see people. Week after week, month after month, the best specialists in Romania advised that the lung be excised, but I refused because I wanted to consult Western doctors first. I knew very well the high level of medicine in Romania, but I would not agree to undergo any operation before being examined by other doctors abroad. My logic was that if the diagnosis of lung cancer was confirmed, an operation would be useless. Paradoxically, the Government, which had allowed me to travel quite often, refused this time, for fear that it might be considered a lack of trust in Romanian physicians.

After speaking to my doctors, Bodnăraş decided to prepare a successor. Rumours were going around that I was done for and I myself did not see any chance of survival.

For eight months (January–August 1963), I was in this situation and my wife had to face this trauma. In the end, I received an exit visa and went to consult specialists in Zürich, Paris and Lausanne.

The fact that, after eight months, I was still alive invalidated the first diagnosis. The foreign doctors admitted that in their Romanian colleagues' place, at the beginning of the illness, they, too, would have made the same diagnosis. However, there seemed to be no explanation for my illness.

The shadow is still there now, after twenty-six years. In the meantime, all my doctors have died and I have become a 'miracle' for every radiologist who X-rays my lungs and sees the shadow!

On returning home and declaring myself to be in good health, I went back to work and, in January 1964, I became president of the Federation. All the Jewish Communists had to leave the Federation and the communities.

The new leadership consisted of myself as president; Emil Schechter, a lawyer and former president of the Dorohoi community

209

(who is now secretary-general of the Federation); Daniel Segal, a lawyer and former president of the Husi community; and Martin Balus, another lawyer and former president of the Fălticeni and Iaşi communities.

A new era began. One of my first decisions was to reorganize the whole educational system, to extend the network of Talmud Torah classes and to introduce a legal, financial control.

During the era of the CDE, many financial irregularities had occurred and Dogaru, wanting revenge, asked for an investigation into its administration. I refused to comply and for months allowed Friedman and Streissfeld to continue to use their offices. I did not fire them and·thus gave them the possibility of destroying evidence so that they could avoid being tried in court. At the end, the Federation's bank account amounted to 15,000 lei, which was not enough to pay the salaries in the first month of my administration.

Up till then, our canteens in Bucharest and our villas in the Carpathian Mountains and on the Black Sea coast were all non-kosher and, therefore, no religious Jew could benefit from them. During one of my struggles with the CDE, I remember spending a whole night arguing with the other fifteen members of the Federation Presidium, trying to obtain kosher meals for them.

Bacal, claiming that I was trying to introduce terror into Jewish life, said, 'I am an atheist and you want to force me to eat kosher food.'

I replied, 'It is you, and not I, who want to force others to act against their beliefs. You, the atheist, can eat everything that is kosher, whilst we, the religious ones, cannot eat your food.

'Secondly, all this food is bought with the money from religious contributions [donations in synagogues, *matzoth* for Passover, etc.], and you are using these sums to prepare food that we, the donors of the money, are forbidden to eat.'

My arguments had not been successful and I had been helpless. Now, overnight, all the restaurants run by the Federation were made kosher.

'*Lo Amut*', God had granted me life and I had to pay Him my debt. 'I shall not die, but live, and declare the works of the Lord' (Psalm 118: 17).

36 *Yigal Allon and the 'Rosen Shock'*

W hen Yigal Allon, a one-time Foreign Minister and one of the outstanding generals of Israel's War of Independence in 1948, concluded a visit to Romania, he told me, 'Now, I have to make something clear to you. Before my departure for Romania, one of your "friends" warned me to be cautious, saying that you have a special method of shock-treatment for foreign guests: when we enter the synagogue, you immediately give us a "shock" and we fall under your influence and are lost.' Allon laughed and added, 'I was cautious, but I congratulate you on your "shock-power". It's your boys and girls – nobody can resist them.'

Who were these youngsters? How did they appear in Romanian Jewish life?

As I have already mentioned, a strong wave of assimilation dominated the Bucharest community after the expulsion of the great scholar Rabbi Meir Leibush Malbim. As a result, Jewish traditional life and Torah studies were utterly destroyed. For many years the assimilationists, who were ignorant of Judaism, led the institutions in a negative direction. Therefore, before the Holocaust, Bucharest had more than 150,000 Jews, but only one Talmud Torah in Mamulari Street with ten to fifteen pupils. Nobody took any initiative to bring the new generation back to the Torah.

When I became Chief Rabbi, most of the congregation at the Choral Temple did not know the *Alef-beit* (elementary Hebrew letters). At prayers during the week, only two or three congregants put on *tefillin*. A *Kaddish* prayer written in Latin characters had provided the majority with the opportunity of paying homage to the deceased.

In these circumstances, the CDE began its campaign against Talmud Torah. While they had to face some resistance in Transylvania, in Bucharest the situation was such that they had no opponents.

I had to start the 'mission impossible' of bringing back to Judaism a generation of boys and girls, who had been educated in their homes as non-Jews and in their schools as atheists and, as a whole, who had ignored everything about their people, their religion, their tradition and their language.

A group of good and devoted Jews, presidents of synagogues like Joseph Feuerstein from Yeshiva Torah synagogue, Moshe Braunstein from Malbim synagogue and others, risked their lives and fought, day and night, against the leadership of the community in order to promote Talmud Torahs.

By the end of 1949, starting from the one Talmud Torah which existed in July 1948, we had established eighteen other such schools. Year by year, all over the country, these wonderful children came back to us, despite the fact that in their schools they had to suffer being denounced as Zionists.

Whenever I am at a *Seder* meal, with over 300 guests, and sixty to seventy boys and girls singing songs from the *Haggadah* and listening to my explanations until two o'clock in the morning, I see before me a real image of redemption.

At one of these Passover dinners, the following occurred. There is a tradition that at the beginning of the dinner a child 'steals' one of the three *matzoth*, called the Afikoman. Late at night, at the end of the *Seder*, the leading person at the table, most commonly the father of the family, asks for the Afikoman. The child can 'blackmail' him, raising conditions and demanding gifts or other things as the price for returning it.

When I asked, 'Who has stolen the Afikoman?', sixty boys and girls answered in a single voice, 'We have.' 'And what do you want as a price for giving it back?' 'We want *Leshana Haba Biyerushalaim* [Next year in Jerusalem].'

There were students who had not undergone circumcision, an essential prerequisite of every male Jew, normally carried out on the eighth day after birth. Their parents had deliberately rejected circumcision because they were eager to abandon Judaism. Now these boys were twenty or twenty-one years old and, insisting on regaining their Jewish identity, they asked to be circumcised. I sent them a *mohel* (a specialist in circumcision) and a Bar-Mitzvah teacher, since they had not passed this exam at the age of thirteen, like every other Jewish boy. I attended one Bar-Mitzvah celebration, and the teacher, noting that I was not entirely satisfied with the degree of the boys' Hebrew knowledge, remarked, 'Please don't be upset with me, Chief Rabbi. In all my life as a teacher I have never heard of anyone having only a three-week interval between *Brit Milah* [circumcision] and Bar-Mitzvah.'

In view of the absence of rabbis in so many of our communities outside Bucharest, I made it a custom every year to travel to all parts of the country on the occasion of Chanucah in December. Joined by hundreds of smiling, happy boys and girls, we set out in a caravan, a 'Chanuciada', to visit the small communities in villages and *shtetls*. An accompanying choir and orchestra makes our journey particularly enjoyable. We all have a great time.

We have learned from American Jews how to prolong Chanucah. This festival lasts, traditionally, for eight days, but we have made it last for up to fourteen or fifteen days. I remember that when I went to the United States in 1961, I was invited to a Chanucah festival at Madison Square Gardens, in New York, attended by 25,000 Jews. Golda Meir gave an inspiring speech. For me, coming from behind the Iron Curtain and visiting the US for the first time, it was a very moving occasion. However, a few weeks later I was invited to another Chanucah festival. I was astonished. My astonishment grew when, in the middle of January, I was told that there was yet another Chanucah festival! When I pointed out that Chanucah had long gone, the reply was, 'For reasons of fund-raising, Chanucah in America lasts for three months.' It was meant to be a joke, but the statement had a lot of truth in it.

In Romania, I extended the Chanucah celebrations not for the sake of fund-raising, but for soul-raising. I normally visit thirty-six communities, travelling day and night, sometimes through snow, ice and fog. On one such trip I was accompanied by the American Chargé d'Affaires, Mr Kayser, and Rabbi Menachem Hacohen, an Orthodox member of the Knesset. Our plan was to visit the Jews of Ploeşti at six o'clock in the evening, on the way back to Bucharest. However, because of fog and snow, we were greatly delayed. It was suggested to me that we should not stop in Ploeşti, as it was already midnight, and should proceed directly to Bucharest, but I told our driver to try to reach the Ploeşti synagogue. I was very pleased with my decision. The synagogue was packed with men, women and children, who greeted us with immense enthusiasm. It was icy cold in the great synagogue and they had waited for more than six hours. I was deeply moved by the faith of these simple, honest people. We celebrated Chanucah with them in an atmosphere of unbelievable joy.

In another year Shlomo Lahat, the Mayor of Tel Aviv, came with his wife to celebrate Chanucah with us. They were accompanied by all the deputy mayors, Itzhak Artzi, Bassok and Yigal Griffel. They spent fourteen days going from town to town and participated in marvellous celebrations with thousands of Jews.

In contrast to the normal experience of other countries, we were able to make the Jewish community younger as the years passed. More youngsters joined us than old people died. Who were these youngsters? The great majority of Romanian Jewry had gone or was planning to leave for Israel. Everybody connected with Jewish religious observance had settled or was settling in the Jewish state. Those middle-aged or young Jews who decided to remain were mostly anti-Zionists, atheists and assimilationists, who did not want any share in the Jewish destiny. Yet it was their children who came to us, who made us young.

Speaking of youngsters, I will never forget the first appearance of our youth choir in the Mann Auditorium in Tel Aviv in 1982. More than 3,000 people were present in the packed building, most of them former pupils of our Talmud Torahs who came with their children. What can give greater satisfaction than to see such people in Israel? In Haifa the choir could not find a big enough hall, so the concert took place in a communal park facing City Hall.

I went over with them to the United States, at the invitation of the Holocaust Committee of the White House. They sang at Madison Square Gardens and on Capitol Hill in Washington. It was a tremendous success, which was repeated in Paris, Strasbourg, Zürich and Berne.

Really my friends were right: Yigal Allon had to be cautious. The 'Rosen shock' was very strong. Through it an entire Jewish generation in Romania found its way back to Judaism.

37 *The Mysterious Death of Charles Jordan*

O ne of the accusations against me was that I wanted to engineer the return to Romania of the American Jewish Joint Distribution Committee. Why such an aim should have been considered reprehensible was difficult to understand. The Joint was, and is, a magnificent charitable organization, which has saved the lives of millions of people. I say 'saved' because, without the Joint, they would have died from starvation or malnutrition. The Joint also gave hundreds of thousands, if not millions, of Jews dignity and hope.

Alas, the Joint was caught up in the turmoil of the Cold War. In 1949, Romanian Jews were dismayed to learn that a law had been enacted stopping the activities of the Joint in this country. Its warehouses, packed with food, clothing and medicines, were raided by the Communist leaders of the Federation of Jewish Communities and the contents distributed mostly to non-Jews instead of to those for whom they were intended.

Although the 1953 'doctors' plot' in Moscow, in which the Joint was said to be implicated, was shown to be a total invention and the doctors were freed, the Joint was not entirely and officially cleared. All that happened was that the Soviet authorities ceased describing it as a criminal organization.

Noting this development, I began to plead with the highest authorities to allow a similar Joint group to start working in Romania. Daily, my wife and I were distressed to see the terrible poverty which afflicted thousands upon thousands of families. We noted with particular horror the starving and deprived old people.

There were two main categories: the first was that of Jews who had returned from Auschwitz or from Transnistria without their families. They were ill and lonely, and wanted to begin a new life in Israel. However, with the ups and downs of *aliyah* to Israel, they often had to wait many years before receiving the miraculous exit visa. In the meantime, they grew older. It was soon too late for them to go to Israel, a country that needed strong young people, and they had to remain in Romania without jobs, without pensions (they had not sought work while waiting for a passport) and without anybody to help them. The second category was that of parents whose children had left for Israel and who had remained in Romania, without any help from their children. As the years passed, tens of thousands of people became more and more destitute and unhappy. Would they survive? This depended on us, on our energy and on our struggle to save them. Time was running out. The question in Romania in those years was whether the Joint might not arrive too late.

My requests were rejected. The authorities argued that the Joint was an imperialist organization, as well as being Zionist, and that they did not want its money. However, my visit to the United States in 1961–2 convinced the authorities to adopt a different stance. They had greater confidence in me than before and were ready to reconsider the ban. It took some time, but finally in 1964, I was informed that the Joint could come in under certain conditions.

When I visited Poland to attend the unveiling of a memorial at the Treblinka death camp, I made a special point of going to Warsaw to meet Charles Jordan, head of the Joint, who was also in the country. He was surprised at the Romanian Government's decision. At first he found it difficult to believe. I had to repeat the statement several times before he was convinced. But then he raised the question of the exchange rate between the dollar and the Romanian lei. He wanted the rate for the dollar to be fifty per cent higher than the official rate, but the Romanian authorities rejected his demand.

I was very disappointed by this unexpected setback. I felt considerable distress at the fact that, while the Joint was haggling over how many lei could be obtained for a dollar, the Jews of Romania were starving. It occurred to me that the Joint had been taken by surprise by the Romanian decision and did not possess sufficient funds to undertake extensive activities in another country. In the meantime, we made preparations in Romania for drawing up a complete list of our future 'customers'. The utter poverty of thousands of people was unbelievable. We spent days and nights going from one to the other. It was impossible to wait till the discussions on the exchange rate were over.

I warned the Government that the Joint was using pretexts not to start working in Romania. The Romanians had to take the initiative to break the impasse. They responded by agreeing to an exchange rate for the dollar which was twenty-five per cent higher than normal, but they insisted that an agreement could be signed only if I brought in $200,000 a year.

I travelled to the United States and managed to obtain $600,000 dollars. As a result, the Romanian authorities agreed to add a rate of 15 lei to the dollar. That meant twenty-five per cent more than the official rate for gifts, which was 12 lei. The general official rate was 6 lei per dollar. The Joint would have been prepared to accept a rate of 18 lei. Yet the haggling continued. It took three long years before we could come to a satisfactory arrangement with the Joint.

I held many meetings with Charles Jordan and said to him more than once, 'We have no agreement, but people are starving all the time.' We were desperately short of funds and out of this desperation an idea occurred to me. I said to Jordan, 'Please send me large quantities of wine and brandy.' He looked startled. Why should we need so much wine and brandy? I told him that I had a sound reason for my request. The Joint, therefore, arranged to send us 400,000 bottles of wine and 200,000 bottles of brandy every year. I managed to convince the Government that we needed that quantity for religious purposes (*Kiddush* prayers), so that we did not have to pay any customs duties. We then sold the alcohol and, with the money that we made, we were able to help out starving and destitute families. It was a very good arrangement, indeed. Let us not forget that this arrangement could not have worked if the Romanian Government had not exempted us from paying customs duties.

After we had finally reached an agreement for the Joint to begin operating in Romania, Jordan informed me in 1967 that he wished to attend the Passover *Seder* at my home. He was not a religious man, but a very good and sincere Jew, and I was delighted to have him as our guest for the festive meal. Together with the leaders of the Federation, we spent an unforgettable *Seder* night, which lasted until three o'clock in the morning. When he left Romania, he told me that he planned to spend his vacation here.

A few months later, Jordan visited Israel after the successful Six Day War, at the invitation of the then Israeli Prime Minister, Levi Eshkol. Newspapers reported that Eshkol had invited several rich and influential Jews from all over the world to discuss with him the means of obtaining new, massive supplies of arms for the Jewish state. After this well-publicized meeting, Jordan travelled again to Bucharest.

He arrived at Bucharest airport on a Friday afternoon in August, with his wife and his nephew, and told me that he wanted to spend the weekend in Romania and then go to Budapest and Prague. The Czechs had given him a visa, but the Hungarians had only given one to his nephew, not to him.

After attending a service in our synagogue on Friday evening, Jordan waited in the street for a taxi to take him to his hotel. With him was Emil Schechter. As they stood in the street, a car stopped near Jordan with a man and a woman inside. The man asked Jordan where the Athénée Palace Hotel was. As Jordan was staying at this hotel, he replied, 'If you give me a lift, I will show you.' The man and woman invited him to enter the car and hurriedly closed the door.

Schechter, surprised and alarmed by the couple's behaviour, tried to open the door and partly succeeded. 'Who's he?' the man asked. 'He's my friend and if you don't allow him to get into the car and come with us I won't go with you,' Jordan replied.

Reluctantly, the man opened the car door and Schechter got in next to Jordan. No one spoke during the trip to the hotel. On arrival there, Jordan and Schechter got out, as did the couple. The man remarked that he and his companion were tired as they had driven all the way from Belgium. Schechter was surprised to note that they did not appear to have any luggage and that, despite the long journey, the car was quite clean. He was puzzled. The car, however, did have a foreign number plate.

When it became clear on Saturday that the Hungarians were not going to grant Jordan an entry visa, I said to him, 'Why go to Prague? Instead, let me take you to a Black Sea resort. We'll provide you with a good hotel and you will rest for a few days.' I noticed that the idea attracted him, but he then asked me, 'How will we get to the Black Sea?' 'By car,' I replied. 'How long will the journey take?' I told him that it would take about four hours. 'Four hours!' he exclaimed. 'My wife won't be able to sit for four hours in a car. Sorry. We cannot accept your offer. We'll travel to Prague.' At that moment, by this answer, Jordan decided his fate.

I tried to persuade him to change his mind, but he stuck to his resolve to go to Prague. This decision was to cost him his life.

That Saturday evening I invited Jordan to a fish dinner at a Bucharest restaurant. At a table near us I noticed a strange trio – a very elegant, dark man, tall and impressive-looking, an elegant, white woman and a black man, rough-looking and ill at ease. It was obvious that he did not belong to the same social class as the couple. Their presence together was unusual. All three kept looking at our table without exchanging a word. Later I came to attach significance to them as I had a feeling that they had played a role in Jordan's fate.

Taking Jordan back to his hotel, I noticed that he was in a very good mood. He told me that he would like to spend the following day on a trip to Poiana Braşov, the lovely holiday resort in the Carpathian Mountains, near Bucharest. My wife was there on vacation, and the Jordans wanted to meet her. He would return to Bucharest in the evening and prepare for his journey on the Monday to Prague. Schechter was to accompany us.

I was delighted with Jordan's idea and immediately began to make arrangements for the trip. As I wished to speak to him about the work of the Joint in Romania, I arranged that he should travel in my car, whilst his wife went in another one with Schechter.

When Jordan entered the car at nine o'clock in the morning, I asked him if he had slept well. He assured me that he had slept very well indeed. I thought about this answer throughout the subsequent journey.

As the car drove away, I began to speak to Jordan, because it was necessary that I should clear up a number of important matters. Jordan, usually a very attentive and polite person, appeared at first to give me all his attention, but after a few minutes I noticed with surprise that he had closed his eyes and was falling asleep. It was clearly not a normal sleep. He seemed to be uncomfortable and breathing with difficulty.

I was naturally embarrassed by his behaviour but, out of courtesy, tried to pretend for some time that I was not aware of it. Jordan kept waking up and falling asleep. Trying desperately to keep awake, he looked at me apologetically. 'I don't know what's happening to me,' he said in a crestfallen voice. I asked again if he had slept well and he said that he had slept the whole night. He added, 'Throughout the year I travel by aeroplane day and night and I can sleep when I want to. I can also keep awake when I wish. I have never been like this before.' He was obviously distressed.

On arrival at Sinaia, a town some distance from Braşov, Jordan asked the driver, Stoica, to stop and to signal to the second car to do the same. Mrs Jordan, sensing that something was wrong, got out of her car and came over to her husband. She asked him if anything was wrong and he replied in a low voice, hoping apparently that I would not hear, 'Something curious has happened to me. I have no idea what it is. Let's go and have a coffee in the hotel over there.'

He climbed out of the car with some difficulty and began walking unsteadily to the little hotel. We all joined him and his wife. I noticed that he swallowed two cups of coffee as if he were taking medicine. On the way back to the car, he breathed in the air heavily. It was strange. He behaved as if he had been running and was short of breath. Stoica, a very shrewd and experienced man, whispered to me, 'This man is under the influence of drugs.' I was appalled: for a man of his ability and stature to have a drug problem was shattering.

We went on to Braşov, where we spent a pleasant day. Jordan gradually became more like his normal self and I was able to speak to him during the journey back to Bucharest. On the following morning we took him and his wife to the airport and they left for Prague.

The Jordans spent the Wednesday of that week visiting historic sites in the city. There was much to see and it was already nine o'clock in the evening when they returned to their hotel. Tired, Mrs Jordan told her husband that she would go up to bed. Jordan, who had noticed a newspaper kiosk nearby, said that he would go out for a moment and buy a newspaper. As it was summer and warm, he took off his jacket before going out.

Mrs Jordan expected him to return within a few minutes. When he did not, she became anxious. When more time passed and he had still not come back, she was highly alarmed and informed the police. But they could not find him: he had mysteriously disappeared.

Hearing on a foreign radio about Jordan's disappearance, I was profoundly shocked. I rushed to see the Minister for Cults, Dogaru, and begged him to help in the search for Jordan, whom he had met only a few days earlier. He responded by saying, 'Chief Rabbi, nothing happens in a Socialist country without the blessing of the state – not even a crime.'

The next day Jordan's body was found in the River Vltava.

A few weeks later, a Belgian Jewish scientist arrived at Bucharest airport. As he left the aeroplane, two Romanian security men came up to him and told him that he should not feel concerned if he noted Romanian secret service men following him wherever he went in Bucharest. This was meant for his protection. The Romanians apparently knew that there had been a plan to kidnap Jordan in Romania, and they now wanted to make sure that the Belgian scientist was not also a target of kidnappers.

Only later did I learn what really happened to Jordan, and why the Romanian authorities were so concerned about the Belgian scientist. The Egyptian secret service had read the reports of the special meeting in Jerusalem at which Jordan had participated. He was considered one of the most important figures at the conference. When they learned that Jordan was travelling to Bucharest, the Arabs devised a plot to kidnap him and try to obtain from him full details of the Jerusalem discussions. The Egyptians considered it vital to their security that they learn precisely what military plans the Israelis were drawing up. Jordan could provide essential information.

The Egyptian agents traced Jordan's every step. They tried to kidnap him from his room at the Athénée Palace Hotel in Bucharest, but failed. A second kidnapping attempt was made when Jordan stood in the street waiting for a taxi. They would have succeeded had it not been for Schechter's alertness. They then put drugs in Jordan's meals, hoping that they would find an opportunity to take him away half-conscious, but his wife was always with him. This was the reason for his strange behaviour during our journey to Braşov.

Arab agents then followed him to Prague and discovered where he was staying. According to the chief of the Czech secret service, who defected to the United States after the Dubcek crisis in August 1968, the Egyptians saw their opportunity for kidnapping Jordan when he stepped out of the hotel to go and buy a newspaper. Several men seized him and bundled him into a car, which drove off at full speed. But they were not fast enough to escape the attention of the Czech security agents who were watching the hotel. The Czechs followed the car and saw it enter the courtyard of the Egyptian Embassy.

As a foreign Embassy was involved, the Czech agents sought the advice of higher authorities. The problem was quickly conveyed to President Novotny, who ordered that no action should be taken: the agents should watch the Egyptian Embassy all the time and note who went in and out.

At two o'clock in the morning, they saw the door of the Embassy open. A group of men, apparently the same ones who had kidnapped Jordan, appeared, carrying a big box. Stealthily, they put the box into a car and drove away. The Czechs followed them and saw them stop near the River Vltava. The Egyptians carried the box to the bank of the river, took out a body and threw it into the water. The body was that of Charles Jordan.

Apparently, the Egyptians had not planned to kill him. They had wanted to obtain information from him and then to dump him somewhere in the city, but Jordan, a man of strong character, struggled with his kidnappers. Trying to quieten him down, they hit him and killed him.

Charles Jordan lost his life in the fight to save the lives of his brothers in need. May he rest in peace!

Romanian Jews owe a great debt to Charles Jordan. After a somewhat hesitant start, the Joint brought about a transformation in the life of Romanian Jews. As I have already said, when the Joint programme began in 1967, they suffered from terrible poverty and deprivation. My wife regularly visited the hovels in which many Romanian Jews lived. After each such visit, she was on the point of collapse. The suffering of the Jewish people was almost indescribable. Families did not have enough food to eat and some seemed to be on the point of dying from starvation. Particularly horrifying was the sight of families living in caves. Their inhuman conditions brought tears to my wife's eyes. The sight of the emaciated bodies of the children still haunts my wife today.

Undoubtedly the Joint saved – and continues to save – the lives of many thousands of Jews. Jordan showed the way to tackle this terrible problem and his successors have followed with equal understanding. They have helped us with a minimum of bureaucracy. We have come to a very workable agreement which avoids complexities. The total annual Joint budget for Romania amounts to about $4,250,000. We, the Romanian Jewish communities, meet twenty per cent of the budget. In addition, we look after the religious needs of the congregations. The Joint is only responsible for the social needs. The slogan that we and the Joint use is very important: no beggars. No one is made to feel ashamed that they are the recipients of charity. Every Jew and Jewess can retain his or her human dignity.

We make sure that the sums of money which the Jews receive are adequate for a simple and dignified life. No Jew over sixty receives less than 1,500 lei a month. A married couple gets 2,500 lei. They receive the money by post and do not have to stand in queues for it. We make them feel that they are entitled by right to these payments. If the payments do not come on time, I receive letters of complaint, saying, 'Chief Rabbi, you have received your salary but where's mine?'

With the Joint dollars we buy first-class new clothing, shoes, sheets and bedding, and stock them in our shops. The quality is higher than in ordinary shops because the products are meant for export. A points system has been instituted for members of the communities and those who obtain the requisite number of points can visit one of our shops and obtain what he or she needs. In addition, nine times every year we send out food packages to specially needy members of the communities. Each food package contains two bottles of oil, two kilos of sugar, thirty eggs, tins of kosher meat and fish, cheese, soap and other essential items.

We also established eleven kosher restaurants, which serve about 4,000 people daily. I must stress that these are real restaurants and not canteens. Nobody knows who pays the full amount for their meals and who does not. Even those who are under the impression that they are being charged the full amount are mistaken: they are heavily subsidized. We have created a situation which encourages people who normally shun all kinds of charity with horror to come to our institutions and enjoy the company of fellow Jews in a Jewish atmosphere.

For those Jews who are ill, bedridden and unable to have their meals at our restaurants, we have established a meals-on-wheels service. Every morning at eight o'clock, ten trucks leave our central depot in Bucharest with 1,200 warm, freshly cooked meals for the homes of the bedridden. We also have a number of doctors who regularly visit these unfortunate people, who are provided with the necessary medicines. For the old, ill and isolated, we provide a lifeline. No more humane and vital service can be imagined. It is with a special pride that I can say that this wonderful service owes its existence to the initiative of my wife.

Our old age homes are an important part of our social services. In Bucharest there are the Amalia and Moses Rosen Home and the Balus Home, both really splendid institutions. There are old age homes in Arad, Timişoara and Dorohoi. In the summer we provide opportunities for our poor and elderly people, as well as for our youngsters and students, to spend holidays at Braşov and on the Black Sea. We can accommodate 450 people at a time.

No Jew in Romania now suffers from hunger, no Jew is inadequately dressed and shod. We do not see ourselves as the recipients of charity. When a large consignment of second-hand clothing arrived in Bucharest, following the earthquake, we sent it back. When I visited the United States, I remarked that the difference between Romanian and American Jews was that Hitler's arm had been too short to grasp the United States. Romanian Jews suffered because they were Jews. They lost their families and became old and poor. It was, therefore, the duty and privilege of American Jews, who fortunately escaped Hitler's death camps, to help their brethren in Romania to live out their lives in dignity.

38 *To Continue or Not with My Mission in Romania?*

*T*he problem occurred on my first American trip in November 1961, when an invitation was extended to me by Dr Belkin, the president of the Yeshiva University, to visit the United States. As I have already mentioned, it happened at a moment when Romania was interested in obtaining favourable American public opinion, so the Government's answer was that I could accept the invitation, but that I could not be accompanied by my wife.

I, therefore, went to see Bodnăraş, who was the one who dealt with such problems. I spoke to him, as usual, openly and frankly. 'Why won't you let me be accompanied by my wife? Are you afraid that I will not return to Romania? I will never just disappear and abandon my community. I am aware of all my responsibilities and I will never disappoint my people. Of course, my ideal is to settle down in Israel one day. I have never made a secret of this intention, but, when I decide to do so, I will make it publicly known in advance. The Romanian Government and my community will know if I decide to leave.'

Bodnăraş answered, 'I fully agree with you. Let's make a gentlemen's agreement: we will not try to stop you when you decide to leave the country, but you will not do so without our prior knowledge.'

During our American trip, there was intense pressure on me from my mother and my sister, who were afraid of what might await me on my return to Romania. Rabbi Portugal, who had had such a terrible experience in prison and knew that the security men wanted to destroy me, implored me to stay abroad, viewing my return as suicidal.

Only one man – the Lubavitch Rebbe in New York, Rabbi Menachem Mendel Schneersohn – advised me to return. My wife and I went to see him at his residence on Eastern Parkway in Brooklyn, and we talked nearly all night about various Jewish topics. Pointing to my personal problem, he told me stories from his own experience in Soviet Russia, stressing how important the mission of a Jewish leader is in such circumstances.

'My final advice to you is to go back,' he said, and added a remarkable sentence, which I will never forget: 'We know very well of your activities. What you do in one hour in Romania, we won't do in a lifetime.'

The Rebbe is an extraordinary personality, who combines Jewish culture and learning with a deep knowledge of the world. A naval engineer who graduated from the Sorbonne University in Paris, he has hundreds of thousands of Orthodox and modern followers from all over the world, who admire his wisdom. That night he encouraged me to resist all the pressures and to respect my agreement with Bodnăraş.

Later, in 1968, during the Czechoslovakian crisis, I was in London on my way to Argentina as a guest-speaker at the opening of a week dedicated to Yiddish writing. So intense was the Kremlin's anger at the Czech show of independence that Romania feared that it, too, was in danger of an invasion by the Russians. Late at night I heard a knock at the door of my hotel room and was amazed to see the Romanian Ambassador in London, Mr Pungan. He told me that he had a message from the highest circles in Bucharest, the gist of which was: 'Help us. The Russians are going to invade Romania.' This gives some idea of the desperation among the Romanian leadership.

After this dramatic appeal to me, I felt I had to do everything possible to help Romania, even though I doubted that my efforts could prove useful. I contacted an aide of President Lyndon Johnson and impressed on him the danger to Romania's independence. Influential Jewish circles in the United States and Britain also intervened on behalf of Romania. President Johnson decided to act and issued a strong statement. He startled the Russians by telling them that they 'should be careful lest they awaken the dogs of war'. I personally believe that the warning by Johnson stopped the Russians from entering Romania.

When I returned home, Bodnăraş revealed to me how the Moscow Government had informed the Romanians that the armies of the Warsaw Pact had entered Czechoslovakia. At three o'clock in the morning on 21 August, the doorkeeper of the Russian Embassy in Bucharest had knocked at the window of the doorkeeper of the Central Committee of the Romanian Communist Party and delivered an envelope to him.

'Forward this envelope immediately to your boss,' said the Russian envoy.

Two hours later, the Central Committee was in session. In the morning, hundreds of thousands of Romanians assembled spontaneously in the square next to the Central Committee, where President Ceauşescu made his historic statement that Romania would resist and would oppose with armed force anybody who tried to cross the borders.

I told Bodnăraş, 'You know very well that I respect our 1961 agreement and that I have always returned home from my travels throughout the Jewish world. However, this time the situation was different. I did not know who I would find in Bucharest on returning home, you or the Russians. Therefore, I hesitated as to whether I should return or not.'

Bodnăraş replied, 'Chief Rabbi, are you trying to tell me that you would have considered returning to Romania if the Russians were here? God forbid! If the Patriarch were abroad and the Russians entered Romania and he asked me what to do, I would tell him that it was his duty to come back. This is his homeland and he must stand by his people. But if you, Chief Rabbi, are ever in the same position, the first thing you must do is to seek political asylum in a foreign country.'

This opinion from one of the leaders of the country, who was not an anti-Semite and who had spent his whole life as an honest fighter for Socialism, throws light on the real status of a Jew in the Diaspora. Even a Chief Rabbi, who was also a member of Parliament, was still, basically, a foreigner. Bodnăraş was right: my people did belong in Israel.

For 2,000 years, in all the Diasporas in the world, honest gentiles like Bodnăraş have reached the same conclusion: that the home of every Jew is in Israel. This came up in an interview I had with Mike Wallace, the American CBS anchor-man for the programme *Sixty Minutes*. Wallace came to Bucharest to see me at a time when the problem of *aliyah* in general was a delicate one and that of my personal *aliyah* was most sensitive.

I agreed to the interview on one condition: that the problem of *aliyah* was not raised. Wallace agreed. However, while interviewing me during a walk on the streets of the Jewish area in Bucharest, he suddenly asked, 'Chief Rabbi, do you want to go to Israel yourself or not?' This was an unfair and shocking question. Whatever I answered would offend someone. I, therefore, replied, 'For the last 2,000 years, every Jew has dreamed of a day when he would be able to go to Israel.'

In 1965, however, I had begun to think that the time was ripe for me to leave Romania. Asking my good friend, the late Dr Wilhelm, Chief

Rabbi of Sweden, for advice, he had written to me: 'If you had asked me ten years ago, I would have answered you: wait a few years. You have time enough to do it later. If you ask me in ten years from now, I shall answer that it's too late. Forget about it. But now [I was then in my early fifties], my answer is: do it quickly, it's the right time.'

I had overcome enough dangers, had been involved in too many controversies and was still recovering from an illness which doctors feared could prove fatal. Perhaps it was time for a change. I wanted a chance to write. Thousands of biblical and talmudical glosses were waiting to be selected and compiled for study. It was also time to write my memoirs, after such a stormy life. I wanted to rest a little and to recuperate before I finally settled in Israel.

In 1965, I was invited to fill the chair of Chief Rabbi of Zürich. The president of this community, Dr Wreschner, and the leader of the Great Synagogue of the Loewenstrasse in Zürich, Bollag, arrived in Bucharest to make me an official offer and to invite me to Zürich. I accepted and I delivered in Zürich a Sabbath sermon in the synagogue and a public lecture in a communal hall. The *Züricher Zeitung* published a favourable report on my public appearances, and the contract confirming my position as Chief Rabbi and setting out all the technical details was signed by Wreschner.

I agreed to it because I felt that my mission in Romania was near completion. In the seventeen years since I had become Chief Rabbi, hundreds of thousands of Jews had made *aliyah* and the dangers of the Stalinist era had receded. I hoped that somebody else could take over the leadership.

Returning to Bucharest, I informed Bodnăraş of my plans. I was then a parliamentary candidate nominated by the governmental forum of Socialist unity. I asked the Government to cancel my candidacy since I was ready to leave the country. Bodnăraş accepted my proposal, at the beginning, and asked me to write a letter to the Government, stating my wish to change my position. I did so, but after a few days I received a negative answer. Nothing would change: I would remain a candidate and when I decided to go, I could go. Bodnăraş added, 'And now we have to ask you something new. Would it suit you to have a two-year programme of three weeks in Zürich and one week in Bucharest?

'And think, Chief Rabbi. Why consider leaving Romania? Wouldn't that be a kind of uprooting? You grew up in this country: Romanian culture and language are as familiar to you as the air that you breathe. It's your medium, and you are familiar with everything around you.

'I hope that you will ponder things carefully. Don't completely uproot yourself by leaving a country so dear to you.'

I looked at him and answered, 'I understand your point very well. Let us make clear what uprooting means. There are two ways of uprooting a tree, for instance. One is just to take it from one place and move it away to a distant and unfamiliar location. The second is to let it stand in its place and remove the earth from around and beneath it. Little by little, this tree is also uprooted, without any ties to the ground, in spite of the fact that it is still standing. I am like the second tree: most of my people, my family, my friends, the congregants, the rabbis and synagogue officials have left the place, and I, although in the same place, feel uprooted too.'

I believed at first that his offer was a joke, but it was serious. I transmitted the proposal to Zürich. The initial reaction was positive. Dr Wreschner accepted. After a few weeks, things changed again. The problem of bringing the Joint back to Romania became very acute and vital for the poor Romanian Jews.

At the same time, the Talmud Torahs for students were developing successfully, and no fewer than 400 youngsters in Bucharest and hundreds in the provinces were coming twice a week to our lectures, to our Hebrew classes, to our choirs and orchestras. Being in Zürich, I could not possibly maintain and develop this work.

I decided to postpone my Zürich assignment and promised myself that in one or two years I would try again to fulfil my plan to go to Israel.

And so we arrive at my presidency of *Beit Hatefutzot*. It was Nahum Goldmann who proposed, in 1961, in New York, that I became the future president of the Museum of the Diaspora. He pleaded that my public stature, as leader of an important Eastern European Jewish community, made me the right man for such a position.

Goldmann once praised me in a Congress meeting and concluded, 'Dr Rosen is the right man in the right place.' I interrupted him and said, 'Excuse me, I am the right man in the left place!'

As the building of the Museum of the Diaspora was to take a few years, it was agreed that I should remain in Romania in the meantime. This was convenient for me – since my community would not suddenly be abandoned – and for Israel. President Shazar insisted that I should stay another two years. That was at the beginning of the 1960s. In 1972, Golda Meir, coming to Bucharest and seeing what was happening there in Jewish life, asked me to remain for another two years. In 1977, Menachem Begin did the same thing.

And so, after Zürich, the *Beit Hatefutzot* became another *fata morgana* (mirage). Postponing it from one year to another, we arrived at 1973, when the activity of building the Museum became intense. A contract was then signed between me, Nahum Goldmann and Louis Pincus, the chairman of the Jewish Agency. I became president of the *Beit Hatefutzot*. Again I was offered a contract, with all the details of my salary, but again there was another 'detail': that I had to serve another two years in Romania.

It was Pincus who challenged me, during a WJC meeting in Paris, to discuss my future. He said to me, 'Do you want to settle in Israel, one day? I am sure that you do. But do you think, Chief Rabbi, that on the day of your arrival in Israel, the Jewish people will stand up and applaud you for your services? No! The Jews are a hard people. Don't have any illusions. Think of your future. You will not have even a flat – which is granted to every new immigrant. You will be an old man, by then, whose sacrifices will have been forgotten.'

His words startled and also amused me. I was then sixty years old and I still considered myself a young man. I thought his warnings were exaggerated. Laughing, I replied, 'I am not worried. I have confidence in the Almighty.'

Pincus was not influenced by my reaction. At the next meeting of the Board of *Beit Hatefutzot*, he raised the question of my financial situation. Asking me, every two years, not to leave Romania for another two years, meant obligations for the future. He and Goldmann signed a contract providing me with an option on a flat in Tel Aviv, which would be bought by four partners: the WJC, *Beit Hatefutzot*, the Jewish Agency and the Israeli Government. The contract recognized my thirty-five years of work in the service of the Jewish people, and made sure of my future pension rights. It was agreed that during the time that I remained in Romania, my salary would be used to pay for the flat. In 1979, the last instalments for the flat were paid, and so I became the possessor of a home in Eretz Israel.

Looking back on the last twenty-seven years since 1962, when for the first time I faced the crucial problem of whether or not to accept a high position in world Jewish life, or whether to continue my Romanian activities, I recall the words I said to Goldmann at one of our meetings: 'If you want to make a test of who is really a good Jew, you have to put to him the following question. Suppose that you are, again, staying on Mount Sinai and God is again offering you the Torah for 3,000 years.

'When Jews accepted the Torah with the spontaneous statement of

"Naase Venishma" ["We will do and we will listen"], they had no idea what was expected of them for the next 3,000 years, what kind of payment they would have to make in order to remain the people of the Torah, how many rivers of blood and tears they would have to shed.

'Now, in case of a new offer of the Torah, the Jew already knows what awaits him in the next 3,000 years and if he, nevertheless, proclaims his fidelity to the Torah, with a second *"naase venishma"*, then this is the test that proves he deserves to be called "a good Jew".

'So [I concluded], looking back on all the terrible days and nights, on all the sacrifices, on all the pain and sorrows of the last twenty-seven years, and considering all the possibilities, if I had to make a choice and to gain for myself a calm, normal, family life, writing my books and meditating, I would again choose to remain another twenty-seven years in Romania. Nothing, no pomp, no money, no honours can be equal to the great satisfaction of what God has helped me to fulfil in Romania. I am grateful to God for the historical mission he has provided me with.'

Now, in 1990, when ninety-seven per cent of Romanian Jews are already in Israel, and only three per cent are left, when my 'mission impossible' has been accomplished, I draw the same conclusion.

39 Nahum Goldmann Visits Bucharest – The Six Day War

*T*he World Jewish Congress, founded by Stephen Wise and Nahum Goldmann, has played a major role in my life and in the fortunes of Romanian Jews. The WJC became our window to the outside world. As I have already related, I met Goldmann for the first time in 1948 when, as the newly elected Chief Rabbi, I was allowed to visit Montreux and participate in a WJC meeting. That was a unique period, and my contacts with the WJC were severed for several years. In 1956, I was able to establish contacts in London with the late Lord (Israel) Sieff, the Marchioness of Reading and Stephen Roth. In Paris, I met Goldmann again and we became friends. Visits to Romania by American rabbis and many world Jewish leaders helped the Jewish world to gain a more accurate and more appreciative conception of my role. However, I still had the feeling that these important personalities only partially understood what was really happening in Romania and what I was trying to achieve. Only by having a complete understanding of the background to events in the country could one fully appreciate my explanations.

The one exception was Goldmann. Having helped to establish the WJC, he succeeded Wise as president in 1953. From 1955 to 1968 he was also president of the World Zionist Organization, playing a leading role in many developments in post-war Jewish history, notably the reparations agreement with West Germany. Because of his friendly relations with Chancellor Adenauer, he managed to get the amount of reparations increased.

Goldmann immediately understood my aims and my problems. He suggested that I should take the Romanian Jews into the WJC and began to prepare the ground. When he gave a reception in my honour in New York, he invited the Romanian Ambassador and was able to establish contacts with the Romanian Government. I discovered that

Goldmann's reputation in Romanian government circles was high and I, therefore, wrote a letter to the President suggesting that he should be invited to visit Bucharest.

When I received, in 1965, an invitation to participate in a WJC meeting in Strasbourg, I immediately applied for the Government's approval to attend. I felt gratified at the Government's agreement because it was a significant decision. For the first time since 1948, I was able to attend an international Jewish gathering, as the Chief Rabbi of a Communist country. My arrival in Strasbourg caused a sensation in the world press as I was the only representative of a Jewish community in a Communist country. The other Eastern European communities continued their cold war with Jewish international organizations. When I was asked what my role was, I replied, 'I am less than a member and more than an observer' – an accurate enough description. I had to speak carefully because the Romanian Government was understandably nervous about the Soviet Union's reactions.

In the following years I became a full member of the WJC without asking the Government's approval. This was not as reckless as it might seem. On many occasions I took what might appear to be a controversial action without the Government's permission, and assumed all the responsibility myself.

Nahum Goldmann became *persona grata* in Romania and I began to prepare for his visit to Bucharest. His arrival, in April 1967, was an historic event for world Jewry. It marked the return of the WJC to Eastern Europe, though not to the Soviet Union. By a coincidence, an economic delegation led by Pinhas Sapir, the powerful Israeli Finance Minister, arrived from the Jewish state on the same day. Thousands of Jews crowded into the Choral Temple on the Friday evening to welcome these two notable figures. On one side of the holy Ark sat the Israelis and, on the other side, Goldmann. It was an unforgettable sight.

When I opened the Ark and recited the prayer for the State of Israel, Sapir, whom few considered a sentimental man, burst into tears. To hear such a prayer in a Communist country overwhelmed him. He cried like a child when our youngsters sang *Yesh Lanu Eretz* (We have a country).

When Goldmann paid a visit to Dogaru, the Minister of Cults, he was very warmly greeted. Dogaru underlined the world importance of the WJC.

Goldmann replied, 'Don't exaggerate. With our WJC the same thing happens as with the first train. When the train appeared, the Chassidic rebbes didn't understand what made the train run. They went to their rabbi, who, of course, knows everything, and they asked him to explain the source of the engine's power.

'The rabbi asked for an accurate description of this phenomenal machine. "Are there horses?" he asked. "No," was the answer. "Are there human beings pushing the train?" Again the answer was negative. "Then give me other details," said the rabbi. Suddenly, one of the Chassidim exclaimed, "Well, the train makes a great noise."

' "So, it is clear," decided the rabbi, "that the power of the noise makes the train run."

'Yes [concluded Goldmann], we are making a great noise, the power of which enables us to run.'

I had a long discussion with Goldmann about the possibility of sustaining Jewish religious and cultural life in a Communist country. Naturally, Goldmann had some doubts, but I convinced him that, at least in Romania, this was possible. We arranged a banquet in honour of him and his companions on the trip, Dr Riegner, Armand Kaplan and Itzhak Korn, which was held at the Athénée-Palace Hotel on the last day of Goldmann's visit. Though successful, the banquet left me slightly anxious.

There were many speakers and Goldmann could not start his own eloquent and wide-ranging speech until midnight. When he noticed that his speech was not being recorded, he became furious. He almost insulted the organizers of the banquet. It was very embarrassing for all of us. However, he eventually decided to continue and concluded the speech, which he delivered in German, a language he knew fluently. Later, when he had calmed down, I asked him, 'Why were you so angry that there was no tape recording? I could have understood your reaction if this were your first speech, but you have made thousands of speeches.' He replied, 'I was anxious that you should have a tape of the speech to give to Bodnăraş. I wanted him to hear in detail the thesis that it is possible for Jews to live a full Jewish life under Communist rule.'

This incident had an amusing sequel, which Goldmann, with his sense of humour, would have fully appreciated. Two or three months later, I met Bodnăraş and told him this story. Bodnăraş smiled broadly and said, 'Tell Goldmann that he must not worry, we have got the full tape of the speech!'

I had not always seen Goldmann in a favourable light. When he negotiated the reparations agreement with Chancellor Adenauer, I felt so strongly against it that I considered the pact, signed by Ben-Gurion, little short of a crime. Why should Israel make a deal with German killers and take money from them? I asked indignantly. In the Knesset there were furious scenes when the deal was debated and one member, Rabbi Nurock, shouted passionately, 'What is the price of a burnt child at Auschwitz?' I attacked the deal from the pulpit, making a distinction between the Ben-Gurion Government and the State of Israel, and I noticed that the congregation, which had bitter memories of the Nazi crimes, listened appreciatively to my condemnation.

Yet I have to admit that Goldmann and Ben-Gurion were right and I was wrong. I had allowed emotion to cloud my better judgement. Goldmann convinced me that the German reparations were the salvation of the State of Israel, in which hundreds of thousands of victims of Nazism were rebuilding their lives. Even from the point of view of logic, my criticism of the reparations agreement was wrong. The Germans had killed my brother and taken all of his money. Was I not justified in taking some of that money back?

The Goldmann visit to Bucharest brought about an improvement in our situation. It coincided with the positive results of the visits of the Israeli economic delegation. Meanwhile, the Joint had entered Romania, and Passover 1967 was the first festival when needy Jews received massive help.

April 1967 saw the first Goldmann–Sapir–Joint contacts with the Romanian Government. The results of our agreement with the Romanian Communists for many years bore their fruits. Jews were no longer seen as a damaging element, but, on the contrary, as bringing advantages to Romania. Jewish international leaders were no longer viewed as 'enemies', but could be good friends to Romania. Zionism was not an imperialist ideology, Israel was no longer an 'American agent', and a Jew making *aliyah* was no longer a traitor and a spy.

Shortly after Goldmann left Romania, news from Israel threw us all into a state of acute anxiety. Egypt's leader, President Nasser, was threatening to destroy the State of Israel. He had amassed a huge army in Sinai and was marching towards the frontier of the Jewish state. Nearly every Romanian Jew had a son, a daughter, or a close relative in Israel. What would happen to them? Would they be killed or captured? Would the new state disappear and with it the hopes of all Romanian Jews? People listened to the radio throughout the day, hoping for some reassuring news, which never came. At night Jews could not sleep, as doubts and anxieties gripped them. Even non-Jews displayed sympathy for Israel and its plight. Being themselves threatened by a powerful neighbour, Romanians identified with the little Jewish state, which was facing such overwhelming odds against an Arab country several times bigger than itself.

When war broke out in June, Romanian Jews waited and prayed. There was an unnatural silence in Jewish homes and institutions. Then, miraculously, came news of the great Israeli victory. The Egyptian air force had been smashed and the triumphant Israeli forces were marching forward. In Jerusalem, King Hussein of Jordan, whom the Israelis had asked not to intervene in the war, but who had nevertheless joined Nasser in the fighting, was also facing defeat. All of Jerusalem, including the Old City with the hallowed Western Wall, the last remnant of the Second Temple, was about to fall into Israeli hands. There was immense relief and exultation in Jewish hearts.

Israel's wonderful victory won the unstinted admiration of the Romanian people and leaders. Bodnăraş, who was a general and in charge of the armed forces, invited me to his office and congratulated me warmly, as if I were Moshe Dayan, the Israeli Minister of Defence, and not the Chief Rabbi. He said to me, 'I want to tell you that our senior officers are now studying Moshe Dayan's strategy, which brought about such a victory.'

In the joyful atmosphere that followed, a number of jokes were avidly told. I heard the story of a driver who worked for one of the ministers. The driver followed the progress of the Israeli victories with increasing jubilation. He cheered when Israelis broke through the Egyptian lines and applauded when they captured Sharm el-Sheikh. He was ecstatic when they reached the Suez Canal. But, after a few days, the minister noticed that the driver was sad. The minister asked him the reason for this sadness. 'I did not know that the Israelis were Jews,' was the answer.

The Russians in Bucharest were not happy at Israel's spectacular victory. A few days after the war, the Orthodox Patriarch invited me to a ceremony at the historic monastery, Curtea de Argeş. I went there in my full rabbinical regalia, including my Magen David on my chest. When I arrived, I noticed that the Metropolitan of Moscow was among the guests. I was invited to speak and rose from my seat. As I did so, the Metropolitan conspicuously left the hall. Having made sure that I had finished speaking, he returned to the hall and delivered a speech in Russian, denouncing Israel's 'aggression'. But few in the hall understood what he had said. The official Romanian translator did not translate the Metropolitan's words attacking Israel.

The Soviet Prime Minister Kosygin demanded that all members of the Soviet-dominated Warsaw Pact countries should break off relations with Israel. They acquiesced with one exception – Romania. President Ceauşescu told Kosygin, 'I know a state [the United States] which is bombing a Socialist state [Vietnam] every day, yet you, the Soviet Union, maintain diplomatic relations with the aggressor. Why? Is it because this state is a major power? And now that a non-Socialist state [Egypt] has been attacked by a small state, Israel, are you arguing that you can maintain diplomatic relations with the big state because it has so much power, but that we must not maintain relations with a small state because it has hardly any power?'

When Romania did not break off diplomatic relations with Israel, the whole world was taken by surprise. We were not. We knew that it was the result of a radical change in the Romanian approach to the whole Jewish problem.

As a member of the Romanian Parliament, I attended the session after the Six Day War. Everyone was eager to hear what President Ceauşescu had to say. As Romania was the only Communist state which refused to break off diplomatic relations with Israel, the world press showed up *en masse*. It turned out to be a courageous speech. He was not seeking the applause of one or other of the protagonists of the conflict. The President spoke about the necessity of a Palestinian Arab state. He was the first European statesman to make such a demand. He also stressed the rights of the Palestinian Arabs, but, he remarked solemnly, 'If our Arab friends believe that such a Palestinian state will take the place of the State of Israel, then they are totally wrong. Such a state should do everything possible to live as a good neighbour and not as an enemy of Israel.'

40   *Nicolae Ceauşescu*

*T*here is an old Romanian saying that a great many brave people show up after a war. I am reminded of this by what is now happening in Romania since the overthrow of the Ceauşescu regime by the people and the summary execution of the President and his wife. The mass media in Romania abounds with all kinds of people who are proclaiming loudly and forcefully that they played a leading role in the struggle against Ceauşescu. I find such protestations repugnant.

The truth and nothing but the truth is the aim of my memoirs, to which I bear witness before the Almighty and history.

During the twenty-four years of his 'reign', Nicolae Ceauşescu received me no more than eight or nine times. In the past three years I repeatedly asked for an audience, but I received no answer. The reason for this slight was clear to me: Ceauşescu was angry because I objected to his plan to demolish the Bucharest Great Synagogue.

Ceauşescu was possessed with the insane idea of pulling down a large part of our capital city in order to carry out his grandiose rebuilding plan. The demolition squads had reached the former Bucharest Jewish district of Văcăreşti-Dudeşti. Tens of our buildings were demolished, one after the other, including the synagogues in Vînători Street (Aizic Ilie), Emigratului Street, Antim Street, Moşilor Street, the Metzmiah Ieşua synagogue, the Malbim synagogue and the old age home in Negru Vodă Street. Whenever I protested, the Mayor of Bucharest, Olteanu, promised me that this would be the last demolition and that other synagogues and houses of worship would not be touched. But his promises were not kept.

Noticing that the workmen with their demolition tools were

coming close to the Sephardi synagogue in Banu-Mărăcine Street, I sent a protest to the authorities. I pointed out that this synagogue was the only house of worship for our Sephardi congregants as their other synagogue had been burnt down by the Fascist Iron Guard during the 1941 pogrom. When I received no reply and realized that the authorities were determined to demolish the synagogue, I decided to approach the Ambassadors in Bucharest of the United States, Spain and Israel. Together, we worked out tactics for saving at least three other remaining synagogues and buildings - the Great Synagogue, the Choral Temple and the Jewish Museum. We pleaded with the authorities not to demolish the Sephardi synagogue, but our appeals were in vain.

The three Governments sent protests to the Romanian Government. The Jewish press throughout the world denounced the demolitions. The American Senator, Larry Preisler, arrived in Bucharest and had a meeting with Ceauşescu. Preisler warned him that if he went ahead with the demolitions, the American Government would withdraw Romania's Most Favoured Nation status. As this trading concession between the two nations was very important for Romania, the Senator was successful in obtaining an official pledge that the Choral Temple, the Great Synagogue and the Jewish Museum would be left intact. My role in this campaign was quite clear to the authorities.

A few months later Olteanu, who was also a member of the political executive committee of the Communist Party, tried to exert further pressure on me to agree to the demolition of our buildings. In the presence of Theodore Blumenfeld, president of the Bucharest Jewish community, various threats were made to me, but I was not intimidated. I sent letters to Olteanu stating that I would resign from my post if any of the remaining synagogues were touched. The US Ambassador, Roger Kirk, and the Israeli Ambassador, Yosef Govrin, were in constant contact with me over this struggle.

One particular meeting, when the threats reached a new crescendo, is particularly vivid in my memory and was also witnessed by Blumenfeld. It occurred on a Tuesday, three days before Ceauşescu renounced the MFN status - a decision which came as a complete surprise. Nobody knew that he had this in mind.

We were summoned by Olteanu, who said that he was speaking on behalf of Ceauşescu and demanded that I should drop my opposition to the demolition of the Great Synagogue. The building was to be destroyed immediately.

I told him, 'I am struck with consternation at the fact that a clear and public promise by this country's President to spare our last three great houses of worship is not being kept. I intend to resign. In no way will I give my consent.'

Olteanu replied, 'Think the matter over for three or four days. Then I am sure you will give your consent.'

I retorted that this would not happen. But Olteanu, smiling confidently, insisted that I would give my consent, nevertheless. He repeated this assertion several times, and each time I repeated my refusal.

As I stood up to leave, he again remarked, 'Please return next Monday when you will announce your consent to the work.'

I responded by saying, 'You are forcing me to tell you the origins of a prayer which we recite on the Jewish New Year, Rosh Hashanah, and on Yom Kippur, the holiest days of our calendar. It is the story of Rabbi Amnon of Mainz, who had been asked by the local Christian duke to forsake his religion and agree to be baptized. Surprised by this request, Rabbi Amnon said that he would think the matter over for three days. When, after three days, he did not return with an answer, he was summoned by the duke but refused to come. He was taken to the meeting-place by force.

'"Why did you refuse to come here despite my order?" the tyrant asked him.

'Rabbi Amnon replied, "Please cut out my tongue which asked for three days to consider if I should forsake my people or not."

'"No," the duke said, "not your tongue but your legs, which refused to carry you here when I summoned you, will suffer. They will be cut off."

'Mutilated and dying, the Rabbi asked to be taken on a stretcher to his synagogue as it was Rosh Hashanah, There, as he lay dying, he composed and recited the prayer *Unetane Tokef*.'

I told Olteanu that I did not need three days to think over his request. I could tell him now that he would summon me in vain and he could do what he liked.

In the same week, Ceauşescu officially renounced the MFN status. Only then did I understand why Olteanu was so confident that I would surrender. He was certain that, on finding myself deprived of American support once the MFN clause had been cancelled, I would fear reprisals and give in to the authorities' demands. But he was wrong. I stuck to my objections and the authorities felt that they could not ignore them. Thus the Great Synagogue was saved.

Whoever now comes to Bucharest and enters the Văcăreşti district finds an area of many square kilometres of demolished buildings. Only the two synagogues and the Jewish Museum, the last redoubts of Bucharest Judaism, stand intact.

It was my determined opposition to his demolition and rebuilding plans which inflamed Ceauşescu's anger against me.

I also thought it vital for our community to defy Ceauşescu during five years of horrible anti-Semitic attacks unleashed by the group of journalists and writers of Ceauşescu's 'court'. Between September 1980 and 1985 the campaign raged. It was clear to me that despite his public condemnation of anti-Semitism (see chapter 43), no one but Ceauşescu could have given permission to Corneliu Vadim Tudor and his gang to carry out their savage campaign of hatred and incitement to pogroms. Who would have dared without his permission to print in the journal of the Bucharest Communist Party, *Saptamina*, an article by Vadim in which the language of the Nazis was used? Only protection by Ceauşescu's dreaded secret police, the Securitate, would have emboldened Vadim and the journal to print such evil.

When the vicious article appeared, I organized a protest meeting at which 1,000 people were present. This was the first such protest gathering since the Communists took control of the country. Two days before the meeting, I was summoned by first Vice-Premier Ion Dincă. In the presence of Petre Enache, secretary of the Communist Party, and Ion Roşianu, Minister of Cults, he asked me to cancel the meeting. I was told that this demand was being made at the request of Ceauşescu. I refused. During the next two days, I was summoned four times by Dincă, but I stuck to my refusal, despite all kinds of pressures. Our protest meeting duly took place. This was followed by an assembly of all our communities in the country. A written protest, signed by all the presidents of the communities, was sent to the authorities. We were told that we must not publish the protest in our communal journal. However, the protest was pasted on the walls of our synagogues throughout the country.

I appealed to foreign countries and organizations to join in the protests. Greville Janner MP, the British Jewish leader, sent a note of protest to the Romanian Ambassador in London. Edgar Bronfman, president of the World Jewish Congress, sent a protest to Ceauşescu. The Chief Rabbi of France, René Sirat, did the same.

I believe now that it was the secret police that was behind another anti-Semitic booklet, which accused me of being part of a plot to dominate the world. I was in Israel when this booklet was distributed in Bucharest. Yitzhak Shamir, the then Israeli Foreign Minister (and now Prime Minister), asked me to postpone my return home as it was clear that my life was in danger. However, I decided to return to Bucharest. When I protested to the authorities, I got no satisfaction. The head of the prosecution service, Popovici, laughed when I demanded legal proceedings. He made it clear to me that he had received an order not to prosecute the author of the booklet.

When Walter Roman, a distinguished fighter against Fascism, died, the following almost unbelievable verse appeared in the same Communist journal, *Saptamina*. It was signed 'Sima', which was the name of the head of the Iron Guard, the Vice-Premier, in 1941 who had ordered the pogrom against the Jews.

> Moses Shmil is dead
> What a good idea he had!
> Had his Rachel, too, kicked the bucket,
> All our accounts would have been settled.

I sent this verse with a letter of protest to Ceauşescu. Again I did not receive an answer. Walter Roman was the father of Romania's present Prime Minister, Petre Roman.

I also protested strongly over an article by a certain M. Pelin. Under the pretext of analysing the book *Kaput* by the Italian writer, Malaparte, he derided the 11,000 Jewish martyrs of the 1941 Iaşi pogrom – (see pages 278–9). Defying the authorities - and much to their surprise – I brought together several thousand Jews at the Iaşi cemetery on the day commemorating the pogrom. In my speech I strongly attacked the Communist journal in which the article had appeared and demanded that the Government should act against the journal and the author of the article. As a result, Pelin was awarded a scholarship and sent to study in Italy. In fact, he joined an anti-Semitic friend of Ceauşescu's and publishes leaflets full of racial hatred.

The anti-Semitic campaigns were directed against me, probably because I openly attacked them. I was the only one to do so in public. I was accused of being an American spy because I acted with the American Government. I hope soon to publish documents which fully support my assertions.

It was only after Lawrence Eagleburger, Under-Secretary of State at the US Department of State, arrived in Bucharest that the situation changed. He warned Stefan Andrei, the Foreign Minister, that US-Romanian relations would be badly harmed and that American aid for Romania would cease if the anti-Semitic campaign did not stop. The

Romanians had to take account of this warning. I believe that my own life was saved because of this change in Ceauşescu's policies. Certainly the savage attacks on me ceased.

As I describe in the next chapter, I did help Romania to obtain MFN status from the United States. This provided Romania with many hundreds of millions of dollars annually. As a result, my action facilitated the emigration of Jews to Israel.

True *aliyah* to Israel existed before 1975, when I started my campaign to gain MFN status for Romania. Hundreds of thousands of Jews had left in the preceding thirty years, but there were many problems for those who registered for emigration. Many people lost their jobs and their children could be expelled from schools. Moreover, the applications could be rejected. However, once MFN status was obtained, these difficulties were removed. Every Jew who wanted to leave received his papers and managed to keep his job until the departure date. The great Jewish organizations in the United States, such as the World Jewish Congress, B'nai B'rith, the Anti-Defamation League and the American Jewish Committee, helped in my campaign to obtain MFN status for Romania. And MFN facilitated the great humanitarian work of the American Joint Distribution Committee in helping the old, the sick and needy Jews of Romania.

As I have already mentioned, tens of thousands of unfortunate, poor people, who had returned as human wrecks from Auschwitz, were able to enjoy good food and clothing and to receive medical treatment. Young children, whose parents had left for Israel, were given indispensable help by the Joint. And I believe that my ability to establish Talmud Torah schools to educate our youth in a religious and Zionist spirit was made possible by the fact that Ceauşescu and his ministers realized that the Jewish community was an important factor which had to be taken into account.

Moreover, it was a great boon for the Romanian people that millions of dollars poured into the country. The terrible poverty that they suffered was alleviated a little by the receipt of the dollars from abroad.

I still hold to the view that my efforts to obtain MFN status for Romania was in accordance with my patriotic duty. I carried out my duty both to my Jewish brethren and to the Romanian people.

Following the recent revolution and the overthrow of the Ceauşescu regime, a journalist asked me, 'How do you explain the fact that the Jews were treated better in Romania than in any other Communist country? Was this not due to the good relations which you had with Ceauşescu?' This question reminded me of the story told by the great

Jewish humorist, Sholem Aleichem. A woman asked her neighbour to return a pot that she had borrowed. The woman received three answers: 'I have given it back to you'; 'The pot was broken'; and 'I did not borrow any pot from you.'

I told the journalist, 'It is not true that Ceauşescu bestowed all or even most of the privileges which we enjoyed and are enjoying. All the favours or privileges were obtained during the period of Stalin's regime and the subsequent era, long before Ceauşescu came to power.

'One hundred thousand Jews went on *aliyah* to Israel between 1948 and 1952. From 1958 to 1965, when Ceauşescu came to power, several thousand more Jews went to Israel. Ceauşescu only maintained *aliyah*.

'From 1948 to 1965, tens of thousands of children received a Jewish education. Ceauşescu repeatedly tried to prevent this, but his need of the MFN status prevented him from pressing home his wishes and closing the Talmud Torahs.

'Our journal appeared long before Ceauşescu's time - in 1956.

'Our relations with the World Jewish Congress began in 1948.

'Our association with the Joint began in 1964, when I received formal government approval. Three years of negotiations then started and the work of helping the poor began in 1967. Ceauşescu was already in power, but was not yet the absolute tyrant that he became later. It was Prime Minister Maurer who gave approval for the scheme.

'In 1965, when Ceauşescu assumed power, I had already been Chief Rabbi for seventeen years.

'By unleashing anti-Semitism, by demolishing synagogues, by numerous hostile actions, Ceauşescu attempted to deprive the Jews of their rights. The need to maintain good relations with the Americans and my opposition prevented him from carrying out his threats.'

I also told the journalist that the Ceauşescu of the first years of his rule had some positive aspects. He was the only leader in the Communist bloc to refuse to break off diplomatic relations with Israel in 1967. He refused to vote at the United Nations in favour of a resolution equating Zionism with racism. And he opposed the Soviet invasion of Czechoslovakia in 1968. This was a completely different Ceauşescu from the one we saw in the last years of his rule.

I could have given another answer too: should I not have tried to save our Jewish brethren? What Jewish leader or rabbi would not have been prepared to approach even Hitler if by doing so he could save the lives of millions of our people?

I am a rabbi not a prophet. Neither I nor anybody else could have foreseen how Ceauşescu would develop.

The journalist mentioned the fact that I had been a Member of the Romanian Parliament. There was no special significance in this membership. In the period between the two world wars, it was customary for the heads of the various religious denominations to be members of the Senate. This position was confirmed and reintroduced in the Grand National Assembly in 1957 and had nothing to do with Ceaușescu. The Patriarch of the Romanian Orthodox Church, the Catholic Bishop, the Hungarian Protestant Bishop, the German Protestant Bishop and the Chief Rabbi were all Members of the Romanian Parliament. When Ceaușescu came to power, the custom was well established and he retained it. Unlike the Patriarch and other heads of religious groups, I never made a speech in the years during which I was a member of the Grand National Assembly.

My relations with the Ceaușescu of the last decade can be seen from his behaviour at the time of my celebration of forty years as Chief Rabbi and fifty years as a rabbi. The celebration took place in Jerusalem in June 1988 in the presence of the Prime Minister, Yitzhak Shamir, and Foreign Minister Shimon Peres. The Romanian Ambassador in Israel, Bituleanu, was invited to the celebration and he accepted. At his own request, an invitation was sent to the Minister of Cults, I. Cumpănașu. At the very last moment, Ceaușescu forbade them both to attend; he did not even allow them to send their congratulations. I received many messages of congratulations from abroad, including from President Herzog of Israel and President Reagan. Only the President of my own country remained silent. No message came from him.

When the Federation of Jewish Communities organized a festive dinner in my honour and a service at the Choral Temple, Cumpănașu was unable to confirm whether he would be present. When he did arrive, he made a brief, formal speech and did not mention any of my achievements.

It is sad to have to state that Ceaușescu's behaviour in the last years of his rule reminded me of Nero. He was cursed by an entire nation upon whom he bestowed misfortune and grief.

41 *Fighting to Support Romania*

D espite the fact that Israeli leaders were voicing appreciation of my services as Chief Rabbi and as president of the Federation of Romanian Jewish Communities, certain interests in Israel were still unhappy with some of my initiatives. This occurred particularly during my prolonged efforts to help the Romanian economy by using the goodwill that I had obtained in the United States. I was placed in an intolerable situation. The attitude of some Israelis puzzled and bewildered me.

The Government of Romania was very anxious to increase its exports to the United States and gain badly needed dollars, but it knew that Romanian products had little chance of reaching the American market if they had to meet the high customs duties. The situation worsened when other competing countries had the advantage of being absolved from paying duties under the provisions of the MFN clause adopted by the US Government. When the Romanian Government tried and failed to get this all-important concession, it appealed to me for assistance. I naturally did everything in my power to be helpful.

I appealed to Jewish organizations to intercede on Romania's behalf. I also championed Romania's cause at public meetings, when I was invited by the United Jewish Appeal to undertake a lecture tour throughout the United States in 1975. I was delighted when the US Government changed its mind and granted Romania MFN status. Romania thoroughly deserved that distinction: MFN status was meant to encourage developing countries which showed initiative and which displayed a regard for human rights. Romania, which under-stood so well the Jewish dream and which showed so much national independence, could then pass this test with top marks.

Israel should have been pleased with my success. After all, Romania had allowed hundreds of thousands of Jews to settle in the Jewish state. And emigration was continuing. Moreover, unlike the other Warsaw Pact countries, Romania was insistent on maintaining diplomatic relations with Israel.

When the United Nations voted in favour of the shameful resolution identifying Zionism with racism, Romania was the only Communist state which did not support the motion. The two big Communist powers, Soviet Russia and China, supported the resolution, but Romania did not.

Taking into consideration the fact that Hungary and Poland enjoyed MFN status, even though they had broken off diplomatic relations with Israel, did not open the gates for *aliyah* and had voted in favour of the UN resolution, I felt it was a matter of justice and ethics for Romania to obtain MFN status as well.

Imagine, therefore, my surprise at the attitude of the Israeli Ambassador to France, Asher Ben-Nathan, whom I met in Paris on my way home to Bucharest. Knowing that it was not easy to have a confidential meeting with the Israeli Ambassador in Bucharest, I decided to use my Paris stay to let the Israeli Government know about my activities in Washington. I expected Ben-Nathan to be delighted that a Jew had been able to render such services to Romania. This, in turn, would mean that Romania would adopt an even more favourable attitude towards Jewish emigration to Israel. On the contrary, Ben-Nathan was critical of my endeavours. I was stunned. When I arrived in Bucharest and saw the Israeli Ambassador, Yochanan Cohen, he too expressed criticism about my work for Romania. I could not obtain a reasonable explanation for this approach.

This attitude was really beyond all comprehension. Why should any Jew or Israeli oppose the granting of MFN status to Romania, a friendly country? It was illogical. When I later learned that certain circles in Israel were actually conducting an organized campaign against the granting of MFN status to Romania, I was totally astonished. But even if such a policy had to be adopted for some unfathomable reason, should Israel's diplomats not have consulted me? Should they not have asked us what the consequences would be for our community of such a hostile attitude towards Romania?

Moreover, this was not a decision taken at ambassadorial level. Cabinet ministers had become involved, persons of character and common sense, on whose judgement the fate of the Jewish state depended. One of them was Pinhas Sapir, the Finance Minister, whom I had met for the first time at the Choral Temple in Bucharest in April 1967. A few months later, when my wife and I arrived in Israel, he came to see me in the house of my friend Itzhak Korn and expressed his feelings of admiration for my work. In 1975, I met him again in Australia, when I was invited to speak on Holocaust Day in Melbourne. Sapir had arrived there to speak on Israel's Independence Day, a few days later. When he saw me at this event, he said to me angrily, 'What have you done? Goldmann is also going to support the granting of MFN to Romania.'

For a moment I could hardly answer. This was the same man who had wept in the Choral Temple, realizing how we Romanian Jews had kept alive our love for Judaism and Israel. I said to Sapir, 'What do you want from me? I am not Goldmann.' Sapir later apologized to me for his outburst, but I wrote him a sharp letter, nevertheless. I stressed that anyone who campaigned against Romania obtaining MFN status was adopting the attitude of an enemy of Romania. No country had less reason to act as Romania's enemy than Israel, and no Israeli leader could decide on such an attitude without consulting us.

When I arrived back in Bucharest, I was asked to see the Foreign Minister, George Makovescu, a friend of the Jews who had a fine record of fighting anti-Semitism. He said to me, 'Chief Rabbi, what is it that you want from us? The Israelis are saying that there are 100,000 Jews in Romania and that 30,000 want to leave but that we are not allowing them to do so. Is it not your duty to tell the truth? We are not asking you to use anything more than the true facts.' The Minister was, understandably, very upset. I promised that I would grab the first opportunity to tell the world what the truth was.

I left for London to attend a meeting of the WJC. In London, I had a chance of discussing the matter with Philip Klutznick, president of the WJC and a very distinguished American who served the US administration as a Cabinet minister and as a member of the US delegation to the United Nations. After midnight, when I had already retired to my room, I heard a knock at the door. Klutznick arrived to tell me an almost incredible story. 'Chief Rabbi,' he said to me, 'they have gone mad. My secretary has just cabled from Chicago that Rabbi Miller [chairman of the Presidents' Conference of Major American Jewish Organizations] has given evidence before the US Congress and has argued against the granting of MFN status to Romania. Rabbi Miller alleged that *aliyah* to Israel has been halted. He suggests that the Jackson–Vanick Amendment should be used against Romania.'

This amendment had been primarily enacted against the Soviet Union and was meant to force the Soviet leaders to open the gates for Jewish emigration. I had opposed this amendment from the moment it was conceived. Coming from a Communist country, I wondered how anyone could be so naive as to believe that a great Communist superpower, such as the Soviet Union, would surrender to such an ultimatum and accept such a humiliating smack in the face. What made the passing of the amendment by the US Congress even more extraordinary was that it occurred after the Soviet Union had already opened the gates and allowed between 30,000 and 50,000 Jews to leave annually.

At the same time the campaign in the Jewish press against the Soviet Union continued unabated. It was similar in character to the campaign waged against Romania in 1958, when Romania reopened her gates to emigration. Both campaigns were equally illogical. When I attended a WJC meeting in Jerusalem, I asked, 'Why are you protesting now? What will you do when the gates of the Soviet Union are closed?' Nobody was able to give me an answer.

Rabbi Miller's claim that Romania had stopped Jewish emigration was totally untrue. Thousands of Jews were leaving Romania every year. His claim that there were 100,000 Jews in Romania was also untrue. His allegation that 30,000 Jews had asked for *aliyah* and had been refused was an even greater lie. In fact, at that time – 1975 – there were only 45,000 Jews in Romania and only 800 had asked for emigration papers.

Curiously, there were three sets of statistics about Romania – mine, those of the Government and those of the World Zionist Organization. In 1957, the Romanian Government had carried out a census and stated afterwards that there were 130,000 Jews in the country. My figure was 300,000. During my visit to London, a journalist asked me to explain the discrepancy between our figures and challenged me to say that I rejected the official figures. I explained that in Romania it was against the law to ask a person what his religious affiliations were. A man could say whatever he liked about his religious beliefs. There was also confusion about the precise meaning of citizenship, nationality and religious beliefs. Many people confused citizenship and nationality and nominated both categories as 'Romanian'. Jews wanted to hide their origins and described themselves as 'Romanians' instead of as 'Jews'. I myself had stated that I was a Romanian citizen of Jewish nationality of the Mosaic cult!

In 1975, the Romanian Government stated that there were 25,000 Jews in the country. The Jewish press, including the London *Jewish Chronicle*, claimed that there were 100,000 Jews in Romania. Neither figure was correct. The true figure was the one I gave – 45,000. I

al Allon experiencing the 'Rosen Shock' at the Choral Temple, Bucharest

Visiting the Pope, 1986

ght: With President Bush

ow: With Prime Minister
zhak Shamir and deputy
me Minister Shimon
es at the dinner in
usalem in honour of my
tieth anniversary as Chief
bi, 19 June 1988

Above: Being greete
as Chief Rabbi by Vi
President Emil
Bodnăraş, 1948

Left: With President
Groza

arles Jordan in Bucharest just before going to Prague, where he was murdered, 1967

th Nahum Goldmann, 1970

Amalia, my wife, accompanying Golda Meir in Bucharest, 1972

With Menachem Begin in the Choral Temple, 1977

th Lord Jakobovits, Chief Rabbi of Great Britain, in Bucharest

omo Goren, Chief Rabbi Emeritus of Israel, speaking at the Choral Temple on the occasion of my
tieth anniversary as Chief Rabbi, 1978

Amalia, when I met her for the first time

arrived at this figure, as well as the earlier one of 300,000, through a careful study of the number of Jews who had survived the war, the death- and birth-rates, and the number of those who had gone to Israel.

When Klutznick first heard of Rabbi Miller's statement, he exclaimed, 'I can't believe it.' He asked that the statement be verified, but, alas, it was confirmed. I sent a cable to Rabbi Miller, who had had no first-hand information about events in Romania, and I protested against his allegations.

I was particularly angry that he had made the statement without consulting me. 'We are not silent Jews,' I told him. 'On the contrary, we are perhaps Jews who voice their problems too much. Who gave you the authority to speak on our behalf without first consulting us? Why did you not check if your statement would harm or benefit our community? Your entire speech is incorrect. Your figures are wrong. Please come to Romania next week. You will discover with your own eyes that your data is wrong.'

When I returned to Bucharest, the Foreign Minister said to me, 'Is your conscience clear? Is it not your duty to repudiate publicly the statement made by Rabbi Miller? Please leave for Washington and try to make a statement before the US Congress.'

'No,' I replied, 'I am not going to Washington. I am going to Israel.'

I went to see Yochanan Cohen and asked him to inform Jerusalem that I would be arriving in Israel within a day or two to discuss a vital problem affecting Romanian Jewry. On the following day, which happened to be a Friday, the Ambassador told me that there was no need for me to travel to Israel. Thoroughly roused, I replied, 'Anyone who rebuffs a leader of a community of 45,000 Jews, who says that he has something vital to discuss, will bear a heavy responsibility.'

I had established a close relationship with the American Embassy in Bucharest, and the Ambassador, Harry Barnes Jr, came to see me on the Saturday afternoon; we sat and talked for four hours. The purpose of his visit was itself surprising and significant. He wished to provide me with arguments to convince the Israeli Government not to continue the campaign against the granting of MFN status to Romania! The Ambassador was well aware that Rabbi Miller had taken his line from certain Israeli circles and was anxious to emphasize that this attitude not only harmed Romania, but it also damaged Israel's own interests.

At eight o'clock next morning, on Sunday, the Israeli Ambassador arrived at my house with a new message from Jerusalem: 'Please come today.' On arrival at Ben-Gurion airport, I called a press conference with the help of Leib Cooperstein, then chairman of the local journalists' association, who had become a friend after at first expressing reservations about me. I told the journalists, 'I have come to rectify a dramatic mistake. The Jackson–Vanick Amendment is illogical, dangerous and anti-Jewish. It is illogical because the amendment seeks to punish the countries which are not permitting emigration, yet somebody now wants to use this amendment against Romania. But Romania has had the highest Jewish emigration rate since the war, more than any other country in the world – almost 300,000. This policy is also dangerous because it gives the impression that the 45,000 Jews now in Romania are enemies of the Romanian people, and that is not true. It is anti-Jewish because it will harm Jewish interests, and it is putting us in an impossible position by showing a lack of gratitude to a government that has supported us in everything we have asked for.'

When a certain Israeli official came to see me at my hotel, I said to him, 'Why are you not condemning Hungary which has 100,000 Jews, and a Chief Rabbi who attacks Zionism? There is no *aliyah* from Hungary, but Hungary has been granted MFN status by the Americans. Why don't you protest?'

He gave me an answer which I found totally cynical and illogical. 'In Hungary,' he said, 'there is no Chief Rabbi Rosen to stoke up the fires of *aliyah*!' It was impossible for me to understand the logic of such an answer.

The Minister of Foreign Affairs, Yigal Allon, invited me to his home. I demanded an explanation for the Israeli campaign against Romania. Allon was very conciliatory. We agreed that at the following week's meeting of the WJC, when prominent Jewish personalities would be present, we should reach an agreement on this question.

Before that meeting, to be held in Geneva, I met Joseph Finklestone at the Swiss resort of Grindenwald. He asked me for an interview for the *Jewish Chronicle*, and I agreed. He wanted to know why my figures about Romanian Jews were different from those given by Israeli sources, and I answered frankly. He asked me further questions and the interview became quite explosive, because, in fact, it was a categorical denial of the 'information' given by the Jewish Agency and by the Jewish mass media in Israel and abroad. However, I imposed the condition that I could ask for the interview not to be published. He could go ahead and print the interview the following week if he did not receive any restraining cable from me by the Thursday, when the *Jewish Chronicle* went to press.

On the evening before the WJC meeting I had a meeting with Goldmann, Klutznik, Sapir and the Canadian delegate. At times the discussion became very heated. At one point, Sapir exclaimed, 'I am not afraid of rabbis.' I replied, 'Neither did I fear Stalin's ministers, and I certainly do not fear you.' I told him that I had given the *Jewish Chronicle* a statement with my figures about Romanian Jews and said bluntly, 'If you think my figures are wrong, you can issue a correction. If you want to lie and you want me to support your lie, then you'll have to tell me first what the lie is. I am only a rabbi and not a prophet, so how am I to know what kind of figures are convenient to you. Your figure of 100,000 Jews in Romania is not true. I have given the true one to Joseph Finklestone. Prepare your denial.'

Sapir put his hands on his head and said, 'What is it that you want?' I replied that I wanted to make a statement criticizing those who undertook campaigns without consulting the leaders of the community affected. 'You create an atmosphere of treason,' I said to him. 'Whoever does not agree with you is a traitor. I want you to propose a vote of confidence in me and in my policy of the MFN and Romania.'

Eventually we did come to an agreement: at the morning meeting I would give a report without attacking anyone; Goldmann would then move a vote of confidence in me. After that, I had to ask the *Jewish Chronicle* to cancel the interview. Everything seemed to have been taken care of. But the general meeting later did not turn out as I expected. When it opened, I sensed an air of excitement. The delegates had heard rumours of the clash between me and Sapir on the previous evening. I told the delegates, 'I did not sleep last night; I spent all the time preparing what not to tell you! I am now in the situation of Rabbi Kopel Reich of Budapest, who was once asked how long it took him to prepare a sermon. He answered, "It takes me more to prepare what I shall *not* say, than what I shall say." '

To my surprise, Sapir interrupted me more than once. I had to stop and remind him of the agreement we had reached the previous night. This had no effect. I then said to him that I would tell a story which had relevance to our problem: 'A Jewish merchant could not sleep during the night. His wife asked him why he was not asleep. He answered that he had done his calculations and was certain that in the morning he would be bankrupt, and so would not be able to pay his debts.

' "Tell me, my dear Moshe," asked the wife, "to whom do you have to pay money?"

' "To Shlomo," was the answer.

' "Come with me," replied the wife. She took her husband by the hand and went with him to Shlomo's house. It was three o'clock in the morning. Moshe knocked on the window of his creditor. When Shlomo came to see what he wanted, Moshe told him.

' "Tomorrow morning I will be bankrupt. Up till now, my dear Shlomo, I have been unable to sleep. Now it's your turn not to sleep for the rest of the night." '

Turning to Sapir, I remarked, 'If you keep on interrupting, I will be forced to say something that will keep you awake for many nights. Last night I did not sleep and tonight you will not sleep.'

Sapir stood up and left the hall in a huff. He was not very amused. However, Goldmann then moved a vote of confidence in me, which was unanimously approved. Rabbi Miller withdrew his criticism of Romania and the *Jewish Chronicle* cancelled the publication of my interview. The final result was that the US Government approved the granting of MFN status to Romania.

It is very sad for me that my relationship with Sapir should have ended on this note of disagreement, for I had a high opinion of his ability and his achievements. He was a good Jew and was devoted to the Jewish people and to Israel. Alas, I was never to meet him again. A week after our Geneva meeting, I arrived in Israel and arranged to talk to him on a Thursday morning at the Jewish Agency, of which he had become chairman. On Wednesday, Rafael Bashan, a journalist from *Yediot Achronot,* visited Sapir. At the end of their meeting, Bashan told him that he was going to see me. Sapir said to him, 'Rabbi Rosen is the only man who has defied me by telling me that he does not fear me. Tell him that he has not many such admirers as me!'

The same day, Sapir collapsed and died at a settlement which he was visiting. In his arms was a Sefer Torah. When I arrived at the Jewish Agency on the Thursday morning, I saw his coffin being taken out for the funeral procession. May his memory be blessed.

The problem of MFN status became central to my relationship with the Romanian Government and the Government of Israel. There was always tension in Romania each year around the month of June, when the two Houses of Congress reapproved the granting of MFN status. There was always the possibility that the privilege would be withdrawn if Romania was not deemed to have conformed to the ideal of freedom of emigration as envisaged in the Jackson–Vanick Amendment.

Year after year, from 1975 on, we had the same nerve-racking procedure. The opening shots were attacks on Romania in the United

States and a Romanian response denying the allegations. The Romanians, who feared that the status would be withdrawn and their economy would be hit, turned to me for help. My role became ever more vital. The Israelis did not conduct the campaign against Romania openly. However, the leaders of the pro-Israel lobby in Washington were involved in a sophisticated campaign. They did not ask that MFN status be withheld from Romania, but that the possibility should always be there so that the Romanians should be frightened into agreeing to increase the number of Jews leaving for Israel.

Undoubtedly we had a problem both in regard to the figures of emigrants announced and to the numbers actually leaving for Israel. *Aliyah* to Israel was continuing, but I cannot claim that everybody who wanted to leave could do so immediately. One year, for example, the Romanians issued 1,000 permits for emigration and announced this figure. The Israelis said that this figure was incorrect because only 800 Jews had arrived. It was implied that the Romanian authorities had issued misleading figures, but the truth was that 200 people had delayed their departure because they were receiving medical treatment or wanted their children to finish their studies at colleges and universities.

A very strange situation developed. The US administration was in favour of Romania receiving MFN status and was glad that there was someone like me to put forward Romania's case. Despite the pro-Israel lobby's activities, the status continued to be granted. But the Romanians began to feel bitter.

In 1979, there were indications that Romania was going to lose the vote in Congress. The Romanian authorities implored me to go to Washington and once again plead Romania's case. I approached the Israeli Ambassador in Bucharest, Aba Geffen, and told him to inform Jerusalem of the Romanian request. I pointed out that I was awaiting a visit from Leon Dulczin, head of the World Zionist Organization, and I was very reluctant to leave Bucharest. Could he ask the Israeli Government to do everything possible to help Romania so that my trip would be unnecessary? I was given that assurance.

On the following day, however, a government official arrived with an urgent request from the Romanian leadership that I should leave immediately for Washington. The official took out an exit visa and an aeroplane ticket and handed them to me. When I tried to explain that my trip to Washington was unnecessary, the official remarked solemnly, 'Chief Rabbi, the Government has asked me to find out from you what evil things the Romanian Government has done to you, so evil that you are prepared to take away the bread from the mouths of our children? What have you asked from the President that has not been granted to you? How can you repay us in such a manner?' This remarkable appeal ended with the words, 'Please leave for Washington.'

After such an appeal I had again to find out what the true situation was. I rushed to the Israeli Embassy and saw Geffen. Afterwards I went to the American Embassy, where I was told that both the State Department and the Romanian Embassy in Washington believed Congress would approve the status. I, therefore, remained in Bucharest and welcomed Dulczin. However, this particular crisis gives some idea of the frenetic atmosphere that then prevailed in Bucharest.

The State Department followed up the Congress vote by making an important and, for me, highly significant agreement with the Romanian Government. Every two months I was to provide the Americans with details about Jewish emigration: how many people had asked to leave, how many requests had been approved and how many had actually left the country. The Minister of Cults, Ion Roşianu, and the deputy Minister of External Affairs, Cornel Pacoste, urged me to accept this proposal, which was, indeed, an extraordinary one. The idea behind it was to avoid the clashes with the Israelis and the pro-Israel lobby in Washington. I was determined that I should make my position clear from the beginning. I talked to both Ministers and told them, 'I am a Romanian citizen. I am a member of the Romanian Parliament. I am bound, therefore, by a loyal pledge to this country. However, by accepting this new role I would have the duty to tell the truth and only the truth, even if it was not favourable to Romania. I want to hear from you that you agree with this view.' Both men assured me that they accepted this definition of my role. I then accepted the offer.

After a meeting with Geffen at my house, I decided that I must not keep the arrangement secret. By publicizing it as much as possible, I would oblige the Romanian authorities to keep strictly to the agreement. All synagogues in the country were informed and details were published in our communal newspaper.

Every Jew who wanted to leave for Israel, and asked for a definite answer, could register his request with the community. There were two strict conditions: only Jews could register and only Jews who wished to settle in Israel. I insisted that non-Jews and Jews who wished to leave for other countries were not my concern. Every two months I had to have a meeting at the bureau for passports and had to receive precise information about which requests had been approved and which not, and who was actually leaving. I then had to send the figures to the State Department in Washington and to the Presidents' Conference of Major Jewish Organizations in the USA. This system worked well and Romania regularly obtained the privileged MFN status from Congress and the US administration.

Nevertheless, the pressure that had been exerted by Jewish organizations in the United States and, indirectly, by some Israelis to make it difficult for Romania to obtain this status rankled with the Romanians. They also suspected that this pressure was still continuing, though in a less obvious manner. When Rabbi Schindler, then chairman of the Presidents' Conference, visited Bucharest, he was told by the new Foreign Minister, Stefan Andrei, in my presence, 'What you are doing is an insult to the Jewish population of Romania. Do you consider that Jews are some kind of material to be used as barter? Do you think that if you give us sugar, we will give you Jews? We allowed 300,000 Jews to leave Romania before the MFN system started in 1975. I could have understood your conduct, even if I did not approve of it, had our gates been closed to Jewish emigration, but our gates have long been open to the Jews. What you have been doing is not only wrong but incomprehensible.' It was a bitter statement with which I totally sympathized.

Relieved though the Romanians were to obtain the vital American concessions, there was a less pleasant feeling, too. I heard that some Romanians were saying, 'See how low we have sunk that we have to rely on the Rabbi to get our bread.'

A Romanian variant of the Jew Süss situation was created: the Jew helps the country by bringing in essential foreign currency and food, which is precisely his sin. His very success is seen as humiliating for the country. Frankly, I did not consider the people who felt bitter as anti-Semitic. It was a natural feeling in the circumstances. The actions of some Israelis added to the bitterness. Logic played little part in the matter.

Speaking at the Choral Temple, in the presence of Leon Dulczin, I remarked that of the 45,000 Jews then in Romania, 20,000 were over the age of sixty and they would not be leaving for Israel. Was this because they were not Zionists? No. Forty years earlier they had returned from German concentration camps and had wished to settle in Israel. For one reason or another their applications had been refused. For years they waited and suffered without jobs, many of them almost dying from starvation or malnutrition. I had managed to help some of these good Jews with the aid of the Joint.

So who were those leaving for Israel? I asked rhetorically. Most were, of course, good Jews who wished to live in Israel. But some anti-Zionists had changed their minds after realizing that they had no prospects in Romania and were seeking to emigrate. There were also new converts to Judaism who asked for exit papers. If the campaign against Romania continued and there was a reaction against the Jews, those who would suffer most would be the elderly Jews, the real Zionists, who had tragically failed in their aim, and, therefore, would be remaining in Romania. We were playing with their future, with their destiny. Was it right that these people should be sacrificed for the sake of Christian converts? There was also a moral question. The Romanian Government had allowed the Jews to leave, had granted freedom for Jewish education and had allowed the entry of the Joint. How could we Jews fail to help such a government? How could we return evil for good?

Yet I realized in October and November 1979 that another campaign was being conducted against me in Israel and in the United States. I was sufficiently experienced in such matters to appreciate that this was not the work of one misguided man but of a group working behind the scenes. The message that was being propagated insistently was that I was helping the Romanian Government to stop *aliyah*.

I decided to leave immediately for Israel, where I called a press conference. In front of me sat a hostile group of journalists. I could see it from the anger on their faces and the aggressive questions they asked. Noticing that I was not making any progress, I said to them, 'Perhaps you are right. Perhaps I have made mistakes. But I want you to know that I have done nothing without the approval of the Israeli Government. The statement that Romanian Jews should register with the community for *aliyah* and that I would be responsible for providing the figures was drawn up at my home by the Israeli Ambassador, Abba Geffen, who consulted the Israeli Government at every stage. If you are opposed to the arrangement, you should question the Israeli Government.'

This revelation took the journalists by surprise. That the Chief Rabbi of Romania, who was a Member of the Romanian Parliament, should publicly state that he had consulted the Israeli Embassy before agreeing to an important step involving the Government of Romania was certainly unexpected. The press conference quickly ended after this bombshell, and Avram Ben-Melleh of Israel Radio–TV telephoned Geffen in Bucharest to confirm my claim. Taken by surprise, Geffen replied diplomatically, 'My contacts are with the Ministry for Foreign Affairs and nobody else.' However, his words were seen as neither a denial nor a confirmation of my claim.

I was naturally upset and I warned Yosef Govrin, then director of the Eastern European section at the Israeli Foreign Ministry, that if Geffen did not, within a few days, confirm my remarks, I would publicly challenge him. Geffen tried to get in touch with me when I returned home, but I was out. He came to see me late at night and brought with him a message from Prime Minister Menachem Begin, asking me to turn over a new leaf in my relationship with Geffen. I replied that we needed more than a leaf; we needed a whole new book. Geffen apologized to me and said that he would find a way of confirming my statement. He did so eventually, but not, in my view, in a very convincing fashion.

The worst attacks on me were launched by a writer in *Davar*, the Israeli Labour Party newspaper. When Chana Zemer, the editor, telephoned me and asked for my reactions to the attacks in her paper, I told her that the articles about me were full of lies. Nevertheless, I was prepared to meet the writer of the articles. We met in Chana's presence, in her office, and I said to the man, 'It is vital in your profession to be honest. If somebody gives you damaging information about a certain person, is it not your duty first to ask this person's reaction before publishing the story? You have accused me of being against *aliyah*, but everybody knows that I have devoted all my life to promoting *aliyah*. How can you write such stuff without speaking to me first?'

'Chief Rabbi,' he replied, 'the people who gave me the information about you were of such high standing that I felt bound to believe them.' I learned that journalists were receiving typed material from some Israeli groups, containing all kinds of accusations against me.

I invited the *Davar* writer to visit Romania and to discover for himself what the real situation was. He accepted the offer and joined me on my Chanucah tour of the country. On returning to Israel, he wrote a four-page complimentary article under the clever heading, '*HaRosen shel Romania*' (Rosen of Romania) – Rosen in Hebrew means 'Duke'.

Obscure sources in Israel had for many years tried to undermine my position and to humiliate me. I never discovered the reasons for this totally illogical campaign. When I mentioned the attacks to a long succession of Israeli leaders, such as Yigal Allon, Golda Meir,

President Zalman Shazar and Menachem Begin, they all distanced themselves from them and assured me that I was faithfully carrying out the work requested by the Israeli Government.

I remember a particularly lively exchange with Yigal Allon, after he had become Foreign Minister. I told him that I would not remain in Romania if the attacks continued. He replied in an agitated tone, 'What do you want from me? I have nothing to do with the attacks. We admire you. I cannot understand what these people are doing behind my back.' Looking earnestly at me, he then remarked, 'You are the captain and you are not allowed to leave the ship. In any case, the captain is the last person who leaves a sinking ship.'

'I know this rule,' I replied, 'but I don't know of a rule which says that somebody can order the captain not to leave it and, meanwhile, sends a bomb to blow up his ship!'

In 1982, when I reached the age of seventy, I decided to spend a few days in Braşov with my wife. I was not feeling well again and was very tired, but I had hardly settled myself down at the hotel when a Romanian government official called on me and said in a nervous voice, 'The vote in Washington is going against us. We are losing. We would like to have your advice.'

I realized that what the authorities really wanted was that I should leave for Washington and try to persuade the congressmen and senators to change their minds. This happened in the middle of August and the tremendous heat was affecting my breathing. I really felt unwell and the last thing I wanted to do was to undertake an exhausting trip to Washington. I knew that I would find very few important people there at that time of the year as they would all be on holiday.

As in every crucial moment of my life, I asked my wife her opinion. Though no other person in the world was so concerned about my health and welfare, she immediately said to me, 'You must go to Washington, even if you are one hundred per cent certain of losing. You must show the people and Government of Romania that you are determined to help them.'

I returned to the room where I had left the official and said, 'Please inform the Government that I will leave at once for Washington.'

I first went to New York. As I feared, I could hardly find a single Jewish leader there. However, Dr Israel Singer, of the WJC, quickly understood the importance of my mission and proved very helpful. Edgar Bronfman returned specially from a holiday in Europe and we began to contact all available senators. Jack Spitzer, president of the B'nai B'rith, and other friends joined me in my campaign. We

258

organized receptions in the Senate and House of Representatives. I stressed the tremendous importance of MFN status to Romania and to the Jewish community. I wrote an article in the *New York Times* under the title, 'Don't Make Us Scapegoats'. Somehow we managed to change the outlook of a number of senators and congressmen. Romania once again obtained the valuable privilege.

This time, nobody, either in Israel or elsewhere, dared to criticize my work in defending MFN for Romania. On the contrary, I was congratulated by the Israeli Ambassador and by other personalities.

Nahum Goldmann used to say, 'The difference between me and my opponents is only five years. After five years they hold the same opinion as I do. It is only a matter of time.'

Looking back at the story of MFN, I can conclude that Goldmann was right: the same had happened to me.

42   'The Jews of Silence'

I had not visited the Soviet Union since 1955. My pro-Zionist views had become so well known that I considered it dangerous for me to visit that country again. However, when Chief Rabbi Levin of Moscow was about to celebrate his seventieth birthday and sent me an invitation to take part in the festivities, I was tempted to go. I showed the invitation to Bodnăraş, who remarked, 'Chief Rabbi, I consider you a modest man. But if you knew how prominently you figure in our relations with the Soviet Union, you might consider yourself an important person. However, if you want to visit Russia, we'll grant you an exit visa. You can go to Russia. Whether you are able to return, however, is another matter.' Knowing Bodnăraş well, I concluded that he meant to warn me against such a trip. I apologized to Levin and did not go to Moscow.

The Government of the Soviet Union regularly complained about my support of Zionism and Israel. The Choral Temple in Bucharest was viewed by the Russians as a 'Zionist nest'. Although in the 1950s and 1960s I was a prominent figure at Eastern European ecumenical events, the Soviet authorities did not invite me to any of their gatherings, although they invited all the other heads of cults in Romania. Their snub was deliberate, but I was not too upset. I felt that to visit the Soviet Union under such circumstances would not prove a very pleasant experience.

Then, in 1975, the Central Board of Deputies of Australian Jews invited me and my wife to come to Australia for Holocaust Day and to be the guest-speaker at the official commemoration ceremony. We spent two weeks in Melbourne and Sydney. On our way home we were invited to visit the Far East Jewish communities in Manila, Bangkok, Singapore and Tokyo. Our programme included a visit to China, too. Yet, despite the intervention of a leading travel agent, I was unable to obtain seats for my wife and myself on an aeroplane flying to Peking. Pondering what to do, I remarked to my wife, 'Let's travel back to Bucharest via Moscow!' She agreed.

I thought, 'Let me try. Let me use this occasion to pass through Moscow and see whether I can do something for my brethren there.'

We sent a cable to my hosts in Melbourne informing them of our destination. That, I estimated, was important. I also informed my secretary-general, Emil Schechter, in Bucharest. The more people who knew where I was travelling to the better, I thought. And I sent a cable to Chief Rabbi Fishman in Moscow, informing him that I was planning to visit Moscow for three days, together with my wife, and asking him to reserve a room for us in a hotel. My arrival day had to be on Wednesday 30 April and my departure on Sunday 4 May. I requested that he should send the reply to the Imperial Hotel, Tokyo, where we were staying. We waited in vain. There was no reply. After waiting for eight days, I said to my wife, 'Let us fly to Moscow on our reserved flight. If nobody awaits us at Moscow airport, we'll take the next plane to Bucharest.'

When we arrived at Moscow airport, we found Chief Rabbi Fishman and Moshe Tandednik, president of the Moscow synagogue, awaiting us. They told me that my cable had reached them that very day. They had been summoned to the Foreign Ministry and informed that my wife and I were arriving, and that we should be considered as guests of the Government.

We had landed on 30 April, on the eve of the huge Moscow May Day parade. There was not a single room to be found at any Moscow hotel. Chief Rabbi Fishman had informed the Romanian Ambassador of our arrival, and he immediately offered to accommodate us in an apartment at his residence.

Incidentally, my journey had fuelled strange speculations and created some alarm. The Romanian Ambassador in Peking, Gavrilescu, told me later in Washington, where he was in a new post, 'Chief Rabbi, the Arabs were the first to inform me that you intended to visit Peking. An Arab ambassador asked me to give him details of your trip. I breathed more easily when I learned that you had cancelled your visit to Peking.' The Israeli national newspaper *Ma'ariv* printed a nonsensical story that I was travelling to Peking to recover a fortune in diamonds left by rich Jews, a task supposedly undertaken on behalf of the Israeli Government!

Shortly after receiving the message from the Romanian Ambassador, Chief Rabbi Fishman and Moshe Tandednik were again called to the Foreign Ministry and told that a room had been prepared for me and my wife at the Hotel National. The Foreign Ministry official added that I had stated in my cable that I would be leaving on Sunday, three days later. As the next two days, Thursday and Friday, were 1 and 2 May and public holidays, he asked that I should postpone my departure by one day, so that a meeting with me could be held at the Ministry of Cults on the Sunday.

I naturally accepted the Soviet suggestions for a meeting and the offer of a hotel room, and duly made my excuses to the Romanian Ambassador. However, I noted with some concern that Chief Rabbi Fishman had adopted a very cool attitude towards me. I have to say that he was a man of little learning and even less wisdom. He very reluctantly invited me to address the congregation of his synagogue: I learned that he only asked me to speak from the pulpit on Saturday morning after several members had remonstrated with him. I commented on a quotation from a passage in Jeremiah, as I had done twenty years earlier. After my sermon, I noticed a group of five or six people near the door. A man who told me that he still remembered my sermon of twenty years before, said to me, 'These people are refuseniks. They don't enter the synagogue because they don't feel like doing so. They only use the synagogue as a place to demonstrate.'

After a while, the man added, 'Elie Wiesel writes about "the Jews of Silence" – the Russian Jews. Are these the Jews of silence? No. They are the screaming Jews. We are the Jews of silence, the millions who don't ask for *aliyah* to Israel now. Perhaps we will ask tomorrow or in ten years' time. If not we, then our children. But who speaks out on our behalf? Is it right that a Jew who does not want to go to Israel should not receive any help to maintain his Jewishness? Has such a Jew to disappear as a Jew? All the propaganda is about the Jews of silence, but it is we and not they' – he pointed a finger at the people at the door – 'who are such Jews! It is we who are the "Soviet Jews" and not they, because the moment they register to leave Russia, their interests and all their efforts are no longer directed towards Russian Jewry. We who remain, we are the "Soviet Jews".'

I listened to the man with sympathy as his opinion coincided with mine. Think of most of the refuseniks of the past twenty years, who have become symbols of the movement. Where are they now? In Israel or in some other country, particularly the United States. Where are the Panovs and the others? We all know that they have settled down comfortably in some Western country.

I have been asked if the methods which proved so successful in

Romania could have been applied in the Soviet Union. If my policy had not been adopted, would the vast majority of Romanian Jews be in Israel today? Did not the Romanian authorities use the same arguments and follow the same line as the Soviet authorities and did I not oppose them? I felt that it was a tragic mistake for the Romanians to adopt such an attitude and that we had to convince them that their interests coincided with our interests as Jews. Of course, it is possible to follow the same course in the Soviet Union. The Russians have a good political mind, too.

For many years before the arrival of Mikhail Gorbachev as leader of the Soviet Union, I tried to convince Israeli circles to adopt a new policy towards the USSR, but I failed. I once told my wife, 'I am beginning to think that these people, who follow a hard line against the Soviet Union, don't want the *aliyah* of Soviet Jews to Israel. They are as clever as I am and are good Jews. If a new policy is so obviously logical and if the present policy is so clearly unsuccessful, yet is persevered with, that can only mean that they are against *aliyah*.' I said these harsh words out of a sense of bitterness and hopelessness, with a feeling that I faced a stunning paradox.

After the war, when the Jewish Communists in Romania began their fight against Zionism, they adopted several slogans. One of them was: 'Zionism is the poisonous arm of Anglo–American imperialism and aims to take the Jews out of the Socialist camp and place them in the capitalist camp.' Our answer was: 'This is not true. It is not our concern to take part in the struggle between Socialism and capitalism. We have one aim only – to build a Jewish state of our own.'

World Jewish leaders have adopted a policy of holding demonstrations against the Soviet Union. For what purpose? To take the Jews out of Odessa and send them to Philadelphia, thus substantiating the slogan coined by the Jewish Communists? Such a policy has no relevance to our Jewish national ideal.

How many Russian Jews who leave the country settle in Israel? It used to be fifteen or twenty per cent, now it is less than five per cent. The political status of millions of Jews has been undermined by these policies of confrontation. In order that there should be Jewish emigration from the Soviet Union to Israel, we have to ensure that there are real Jews in the USSR. Nothing has been done, however, to provide a true Jewish religious and cultural life among those who are left in the Soviet Union. There was no physical danger to the lives of Russian Jews; the danger was a spiritual one. Not Jews but Jewishness was, and still is, in danger. Otherwise, the whole problem of Russian

263

Jews does not exist. For me it is immaterial whether a Jew lives in Odessa or Philadelphia.

Consider my own position. I am the leader of a Jewish community in a Communist country. From the start of my leadership, the authorities were against my presence at international gatherings of Jewish organizations. My answer was, 'It is my right to have Zionist ideals and to seek to rebuild our country, Israel. I am part of the Jewish people. You must not take that right away from me.' But today the whole Jewish influence in the world is concentrated on one slogan: 'Let My People Go'. This slogan has, in my view, become an anti-Zionist slogan.

Let me explain another paradox. The slogan comes from the Bible (Exodus), when Moses asks the Egyptian king to 'Let my people go, that they may serve God'. Even Moses, under the circumstances of terrible slavery of the Jews, did not ask for their exit without giving a reason. The entire slogan was not just an appeal for the Jews to be allowed to run out of Egypt, but that they be able to become 'Jews serving God'. This was the purpose of the Exodus.

Today's Zionists are cutting off Moses' appeal. They neglect the very meaning of the slogan and so they no longer speak as a movement of national liberation, but on behalf of a 'travel agency'.

Why should we be upset if an engineer or a doctor chooses to settle in the United States and not in Israel after leaving the USSR, without any elementary knowledge of Judaism, educated as an atheist and anti-Zionist, and with only one slogan: 'Let us go'? What we should be proclaiming is: 'Let My People Build the Jewish State.' After the death of six million Jews in the Holocaust, we cannot abandon millions of Jews solely because they do not want to leave the Soviet Union immediately and promote only the emigration of Jews who want to settle in the State of Israel.

Who are those very few Soviet Jews arriving now in Israel? Who are the refuseniks? They are mostly intellectuals, engineers, scientists and artists. All these people are essential to the Soviet Union, but not to Israel. Louis Pincus remarked to me in 1972, 'I am glad that most of the Russian engineers are not coming here to Israel and are going elsewhere. I would not know what to do with them if they did come here.' The engineers went to the United States to improve their material lot. They had no Jewish knowledge and upbringing, and it would have been foolish, from their point of view, to choose hardship in Israel when they could enjoy comfort in America.

There is another category of Jews in the Soviet Union: men and women, non-intellectuals, workers and artisans, the great mass of whom are not essential to the Soviet economy. Such people will not find success in the United States, but they are vitally necessary for Israel. They are a very positive element. I speak from my experience of Romanian *aliyah*. The Romanian authorities objected to the emigration of specialists, but were glad to see the departure of 100,000 working Jews whose jobs were quickly grabbed. These Romanian Jews have proved a blessing for Israel.

We should make the question of *aliyah* one of understanding and not of confrontation. We will lose our argument with Gorbachev if we try to pressurize him. His emergence is yet another miracle in Jewish life, but we are not making full use of it.

While in Moscow, I received a message from Aharon Vergelis, editor of the Yiddish-language journal *Sovietish Heimland*, that he would like to see me. I knew that Vergelis was an anti-Zionist and a committed Communist. He had no links with the Ministry of Cults, so his approach to me must have been promoted by another government department. That was its significance: identical messages coming to you on two different lines means that the real source of the message is a man who is higher than both sources! It was on the Sabbath and Vergelis offered to come to my hotel. I told him that I would go to the offices of *Sovietish Heimland* on condition that the Sabbath was not desecrated by smoking and similar actions. I wanted to see what that nest of anti-religious and anti-Zionist propaganda looked like. I went to the office with Tandednik. Vergelis and another writer awaited us. During our four-hour conversation, Vergelis argued that he was a Russian and I was a Romanian. As he was talking, I noticed a painting on the wall with the title *Appikores* (*An Atheist*). I said to Vergelis, 'You are an *appikores* and I am a rabbi. What made you invite me here, if not the fact that we are both Jews?' 'We are both fighting for peace,' he replied.

When I asked Vergelis what his feelings were for Israel, he said that the same question had been put to him when he had visited the house of a rich man in Los Angeles. The question had then come from a black woman writer. He asked her in return what she considered herself to be. 'An American,' she replied. But where were her grandparents living? he asked. In Kenya, she said. What feelings did she have for Kenya? 'That Kenya should live in peace,' she responded. 'These are precisely my feelings for Israel,' said Vergelis. 'My great-great-ancestors may have lived once in the area that is Israel today, but I am Russian now and I have nothing in common with the people of Israel.'

Vergelis was a very unpopular figure among world Jewish communities, some of which boycotted him. He was seen as a particularly unpleasant collaborator in the anti-religious campaigns. However, Vergelis did agree that Russian Jews should be able to come closer to European Jewry and that a bridge should be created. I asked him if he would accept an invitation to attend a meeting of the WJC. He replied that he would personally agree, because it was a good idea, but that 'it does not depend on me'.

We agreed that I should invite him to Romania and that a report about our meeting should appear in the *Sovietish Heimland*. The report duly appeared, but Vergelis never turned up in Bucharest. However, from time to time I receive greetings from him.

On the following day I met Titov, vice-president of the Department of Cults. He began by saying, 'You, Chief Rabbi, travel all over the world, but only to Russia you do not come.' I replied, 'This time, too, I came uninvited.' Titov looked at Tandednik and asked him, 'Why haven't you invited him?' I said, 'Don't forget that I, too, come from a Socialist country and, therefore, know very well that he cannot invite me without your blessing.'

He then thanked me for defending the Soviet Union at the meeting of the WJC in Jerusalem. He added, 'If Romania is attacked and our Chief Rabbi is there, he, too, will defend your country.' I responded by saying, 'Why do you need me to defend you? Send your own Chief Rabbi to the Congress.'

Titov thought for a while and then said, 'Yes, we should take this idea into consideration.' He added, 'Chief Rabbi Rosen, we know you very well. You are a Jewish nationalist, but if our Romanian comrades are content to have a nationalist as their Chief Rabbi, that is their business not ours. Let me speak to you now in the language of the nationalists. Let there be no more cold war. Even the USA has stopped the cold war against us. Only the Jewish people is waging a cold war against the Soviet Union. In campaign after campaign, Jews all over the world are attacking the Soviet Union. What do you think will be the outcome of such a policy? Will it not end in a catastrophe for the Jewish people?'

This was clearly a threat and I felt a chill of apprehension. I replied that what he was saying was not true. Jews had not forgotten that the Soviet Union had saved millions of their brethren from the Nazis. What Jews in the rest of the world wanted was for Jews in the Soviet Union to have a minimum of Jewish life. I myself came from a Communist country where the Government had shown that it was possible for a religious Jewish community to exist in a Communist state.

Titov interrupted me by saying, 'We cannot give the Jews more than we give to other cults.' 'I don't ask for more,' I replied, 'but you are giving us less. Give us equality with the other cults.'

When Titov began to insist that there already was equality, I said, 'With respect, this is not true. Mr Tandednik here is described as the president of the Jewish community of Moscow. Not true. No such community exists. There is no organized Jewish community in the whole of the Soviet Union. Rabbi Fishman is called Chief Rabbi of the Soviet Union and Moscow. Not true. He is the rabbi of a single synagogue. There is no Jewish community like the organized Orthodox Church, which has bishops, metropolitans and a patriarch. Remember also the Roman Catholics. Why don't you consider having the same arrangement for the Jews?'

Titov replied, 'The Soviet Jews don't want it. They want every synagogue to remain separate.' 'I believe you,' I said. 'The Jews don't want it. But I do know the ways of a Communist government. Such a government is always interested in having a partner with whom to discuss important matters, a partner who must have a sense of responsibility. The Soviet Government should oblige the Jews to organize themselves.'

Titov looked at an official who sat next to him and smiled. He said to me, 'Oh, hoh! Nobody has answered me like this. Now I understand what kind of man you are.'

We decided that we should make a start at co-operation. The Russians would be invited to Jewish international gatherings and would accept. An effort would be made to publish Jewish newspapers in Russian and not in Yiddish, which young Jews did not understand, in several major Soviet cities. Titov rejected my proposal that Talmud Torahs should be established, saying that such a step would be against the law. I proposed, for the moment, the establishment of a rabbinical school for 500–600 pupils, aged from six to twenty, that might be called a theological seminary, an institution which was within the frame of the law. In reality, it would be a Talmud Torah, from which future clergymen could be selected. Titov agreed with this suggestion.

Moscow did have a small rabbinical school, but it was not an important institution. Six or seven people, between the ages of thirty and fifty, studied there. For a Jewish community of over two and a half million people, this was totally inadequate. Moreover, Soviet Jewry suffered from feeble or non-existent leadership under Chief Rabbi Fishman. He had married a Christian woman when already in office.

It was clear to me that the Russians were interested in improving relations with the Jews. Our meetings happened on their initiative and, therefore, we had an elementary obligation to show goodwill, to follow them through the gates of understanding and concession which they had opened to us.

Returning to Bucharest, I immediately began to try to put into effect my agreement with the Russians. The first step was to invite representatives of Soviet Jewry to international Jewish gatherings. I thought, 'Let us begin with a non-political organization.' The World Organization of Synagogues seemed to me an ideal place for the Russian Jews to make their entry into world Jewish life. When I went to Jerusalem I spoke to the late Maurice Jaffe, the energetic director of the Union of Orthodox Synagogues, a non-Zionist organization, and suggested that he should invite Soviet Jews to a meeting of the Union. The idea delighted him and he said that he would act on it. I left Jerusalem for Bucharest and awaited a letter from Jaffe confirming his invitation. But no letter ever came and no invitation was ever sent. I learned that certain Israeli circles had advised Jaffe not to extend any invitation to Soviet Jews.

I then approached Brit Ivrit Olamit, the World Hebrew Union, also an ideal organization to deal with such a problem. Its head was Professor Aryeh Tartakover and its director, the writer Simcha Raz. They were delighted at my suggestion that they should invite Russian Jews. I waited for several weeks for the invitation to be issued. Again certain Israeli circles intervened and no invitations were sent.

I invited Tandednik and other Eastern European Jewish leaders to attend a celebration marking the twentieth anniversary of my communal newspaper. Tandednik arrived in Bucharest with his wife. Hungarian, Czechoslovakian, East German and Yugoslavian leaders also came. I proposed to them that the WJC should invite a representative of the Russian Jews to attend its meetings. This was unanimously approved. They also unanimously agreed that all Eastern European Jewish communities should become members of the WJC.

When I told Nahum Goldmann about these decisions, he was delighted. I accompanied Goldmann to the next meeting of the European section of the WJC in Geneva. We expected the news to delight all the delegates, too. But what happened there shook us both. It was almost unbelievable. As I was speaking and advocating the sending of an invitation to Soviet Jews, the microphone suddenly went dead. I thought that this was due purely to a technical fault, but imagine my amazement when a technician, who had walked in to see what had happened, exclaimed, after examining the microphone, 'You should feel ashamed! You wanted to interrupt the speech of this gentleman and so you cut the wires.' There were protestations, but no doubt of the opposition to the proposal. Nothing could be achieved in this bitter atmosphere. Therefore, no invitation was extended to Soviet Jews.

Goldmann suggested that we should discuss the matter again at the autumn meeting of the WJC governing board in Madrid. In the ensuing discussion, a number of delegates spoke against the admission of Soviet Jews.

Goldmann then made a dramatic announcement: 'Gentlemen, please accept my resignation. I cannot continue as president of a world Jewish organization which refuses to send an invitation to two and a half million Jews. No matter what kind of representatives will be sent, they have the right to be here.'

This intervention proved effective and the meeting voted in favour of inviting the Russian Jews. It was also decided that Armand Kaplan, political director of the WJC, and I should prepare the invitation, after discussing it with Russian Jews in Moscow. I left immediately for Bucharest to prepare the ground, and Kaplan flew to Paris. The meeting was due to end formally on the following day. We and the majority of delegates, who also left, assumed that nothing important would occur in our absence. But we were all wrong. A violent anti-Russian resolution was submitted and passed, which was published in all the leading newspapers. A few days later, Kaplan met the Soviet Ambassador at the Soviet Embassy in Paris to inform him of the WJC decision to invite Soviet Jews. He asked for a visa to visit Moscow. The Ambassador showed him a newspaper carrying the report of the anti-Soviet resolution and asked him, 'Do you really want to visit Moscow after such a resolution?'

Thus, for the second time, my effort to bring the Russian Jewish community into the world Jewish gathering failed. The Russian Jews are still not members of the WJC. I have been blocked.

In the spring of 1986 we had a WJC conference and a symposium in Jerusalem. The main topic was Russian Jewry. The opposing views were represented by Leon Dulczin and myself. The moderator was Marc Palmer, from the US State Department. Dulczin strongly contradicted my point of view. He said, 'We have one slogan only: repatriation of all Jews from Russia.' I told him, 'There are two and a half million Jews in the Soviet Union. Let us suppose that Gorbachev fulfils your dream and allows 50,000 Jews to leave every year, and (an even greater dream) that they will all, or most, go to Israel. You will still need fifty years to get all the Jews out of the Soviet Union. What is to happen to the Jews who remain in the country during that time? They will be overwhelmed by assimilation and disappear as Jews.'

When Shlomo Lahat, the Mayor of Tel Aviv, accompanied by his deputy Mayors, came to Romania to participate in our Chanucah celebrations, I spoke to him for hours about my views on Russian Jews.

Later, on arrival in Tel Aviv, I was invited by Lahat to his house to speak on Russian Jews at a reception given in my honour. Among those present was Yitzhak Rabin, the former Israeli Chief of Staff and Prime Minister, who was then Defence Minister. Afterwards Rabin said, 'I have wanted for a long time to hear Rabbi Rosen's thesis. He is right.'

I was also invited by Dulczin to speak on this matter to a group of fourteen or fifteen influential people at a dinner in the King David Hotel. I pointed out that the policy of 'Let My People Go' was bankrupt, while my policy had succeeded. Ninety-seven per cent of Romanian Jews were in Israel and rebuilding the country. I proposed that the 'Let My People Go' campaign should cease for six months. During that interval they should try a new approach and create a new climate of opinion. I could not guarantee success, but if I was proved wrong, they would lose nothing: they could start their campaign once again. But nobody responded, nobody tried to show that I was wrong.

I am glad to note that Edgar Bronfman and Israel Singer have started to adopt my thesis. However, they have not gone all the way. The method of the carrot and the stick, which they have been using, can be employed only by a big power and not by a small people. The only effective method is to show the Communist authorities that we have mutual interests.

The best way of co-operating with the Russians is, paradoxically, the religious way. In a Communist state no cultural activity can develop other than under the control of the Agitprop (Agitation and Propaganda) Section of the Communist Party. By merely establishing cultural clubs, we will only help other *Sovietish Heimland* institutions. In contrast, by first establishing traditional religious communities in ten or twenty big cities, we would create a representative body of Soviet Jewry, and establish an internal (and not an external) Jewish basis for building up, step by step, religious and cultural Jewish centres.

Therefore, it is necessary to give the rabbis of the Jewish world the opportunity of getting in touch with the Soviet Government and with

Soviet Jewry, so that the very foundation of a renewed communal structure of *Yiddishkeit* in Russia can be laid.

Clemenceau used to say, 'War is too serious a matter to be left in the hands of the generals.' Let me paraphrase him and say, 'Soviet Jewry is too vital a matter for the Jewish people to be left in the hands of politicians.'

Let us face the real problem of the threat to the identity of over two and a half million Jews. Instead of 'Let My People Go', we should be calling, 'Let My People Live as Jews'; only after that can we deal with the *aliyah* to Israel of a part of them.

If we want *aliyah*, we need Jews. God forbid that we should lose any more of them.

43 *Who Is an Anti-Semite?*

W henever I have been asked, during my travels throughout the world, whether there is anti-Semitism in Romania, I have normally answered, 'There are anti-Semites in Romania, but not anti-Semitism.'

I point out that it is not possible to eradicate hatred. It is a resentment which has been inculcated in the population for many centuries and has influenced the manner of thinking of so many generations, through education at school and in the army. But there is a difference between the situation in Communist Romania and that of earlier periods, when the country was ruled by so-called 'liberal' and 'democratic' governments. While the Communist Government has suppressed any displays of anti-Semitism and punished them by law and justice, the earlier rulers actually encouraged and organized anti-Semitic excesses. I saw with my own eyes how Jewish students had been beaten up in universities. I witnessed anti-Jewish demonstrations in the streets. I suffered from anti-Semitic cruelty as a child, as a student and as a soldier. Daily I read vicious anti-Semitic attacks in the press. And it was a so-called democratic government that organized terrible pogroms against the Jews and killed large numbers of them.

Of course, anti-Semites still exist and they take every opportunity to dismiss Jews from their posts, as Zionists. This, however, is individual and not state anti-Semitism.

Anti-Semitism can break out in the most unexpected places. Thus, in the 1960s, I was informed of an anti-Semitic scandal at the Bucharest Ballet Theatre. The story was hardly credible. One of the theatre's writers, Sică Alexandrescu, had composed a sketch about a pedlar who was selling trinkets. The background of the story had some truth in it: it was based on a poor man, who, when I was a student in Bucharest, used to be a pedlar in the Jewish area of the city. He ran through the streets the whole day shouting, '*Electrica, electrica!*' It was clear to everyone that the pedlar in the sketch was meant to be a Jewish character. The Jew was meant to be reviled, derided and humiliated. The whole part stank of Nazi-type anti-Semitism.

This sketch, in which a leading role was played by a tall and talented actress, Stela Popescu, proved very much to the liking of the audiences. Every evening at the conclusion of the sketch, the audience rose from its seats and applauded for several minutes. The audience's reaction was itself an anti-Semitic demonstration. It was a deliberate provocation.

When a number of people told me about this scandal and begged me to take action, I decided that, before approaching the Government, I must see it with my own eyes. I said to my wife that we must go to the Ballet Theatre. She must have been very surprised. It was the first time in my life that I had shown any interest in such a theatre, but she soon realized what my intention was. Everyone stared at us as we entered the theatre and took our seats. We watched the anti-Semitic sketch in consternation and disbelief. When we saw the audience rise and applaud it enthusiastically, I stood up too and, in a loud voice, said to my wife, 'Let us leave. I don't want to attend this Fascist demonstration any more!' The audience watched us leave.

I immediately wrote a sharp letter of protest to Bodnăraş and Gheorghiu-Dej, pointing out that this outrage had occurred in a Romanian national theatre. I protested not only as the leader of the Jewish population, but on behalf of a community whose sons had enriched the Romanian language and the arts. The greatest philologists of the Romanian language had been a rabbi, Dr Moses Gaster, and two converted Jews, Lazar Şaineanu and A. Tiktin, and in our own generation the most important scientific authority on the Romanian language is another Jew, A. L. Graur. I myself spoke better Romanian than the hooligans at the Ballet Theatre. How could such an insult to the whole Jewish population be tolerated: that was the question I put in my letter to the Government.

Bodnăraş and Gheorghiu-Dej acted quickly. It was an intolerable situation and highly embarrassing to them. Within days the programme at the Ballet Theatre was changed and the offensive anti-Semitic sketch dropped.

Another – and much more complex – scandal concerned the eminent, late-nineteenth-century Romanian poet-laureate Mihail Eminescu. He was one of the greatest poets ever in European literature, worthy to rank with Goethe and Schiller. My wife and I know many of his lyrical poems by heart. But Eminescu, who died at the age of thirty-nine, also used to be a journalist. As a night editor for the newspaper *Timpul*, his articles were full of anti-Semitic poison. It must be emphasized that anti-Semitic expressions appeared only in his journalistic pieces, which were without much literary value. His poetical work, where he was a genius, is devoid of any kind of anti-Semitism.

I would not insult the great poet's memory by implying that he could have been an anti-Semite if he had been alive after Auschwitz. He was too sensible for that. Therefore, my indignation was roused mainly by the way his recent editors had treated his material, without explanatory notes to make the circumstances clear and without taking a critical stand.

In one of Eminescu's children's stories, a Jew is said to drink the blood of a child, whom he has killed, every morning so that he should be able to steal a chicken's golden eggs. Amazingly, this story was included in a book edited by a known author, Tiberiu Utan, and was sent to schools by the Education Ministry.

I protested strongly to Bodnăraş. Shortly afterwards, during a parliamentary meeting, I was asked to go to the office of President Ceauşescu. With him was Bodnăraş. The President told me that the book containing the offensive story had already been distributed to schools and there was, therefore, a problem. However, he had sent a telegram to all schools forbidding the use of the book. President Ceauşescu thanked me for my intervention and Bodnăraş remarked, 'This was pure Fascism. Thank you for informing us.'

But this was not the end of the Eminescu problem. In September 1980, the Romanian Academy, the country's most prestigious scientific and cultural institution, printed the ninth volume of the complete works of Eminescu. Included in this volume were some of his attacks against Jews. In one article he wrote that Jews were afraid to travel to Russia because there their faces were slashed and their beards cut off; he added, 'Happy Russia!' In another piece he wrote that 'Jews were like locusts and had to be crushed under foot'.

I was utterly amazed that such dangerous drivel, which actually called for the killing of Jews, could be published by our national academy. Even the previous Romanian anti-Semitic regimes had not dared to publish such stuff officially. The pretext used by the Academy was that the entire work of Eminescu was being published and that nothing could be left out. This edition of 5,000 copies sold out within a few days.

I wrote a letter to the president of the Academy, Professor Mihoc, protesting vehemently against the publication of the volume and demanding its immediate withdrawal. Mihoc, whom I met in the Parliament building, told me that he did not know how the volume came to be published. He was a good man and so his statement made the publication even more mysterious and disturbing. As we were talking, the vice-president of the Academy, Anton, walked into the hall, saw us and stopped. He said to me, 'I have read your letter. You did not use an academic style.' 'Sir,' I replied angrily, 'the Academy is printing stuff inciting every hooligan to cut off my beard and you tell me that I did not write to you in an academic manner!'

My protest had no effect. The Academy did not confiscate the volume. Moreover, an orchestrated campaign against me began in literary and academic circles. A Professor Marcea accused me of insulting Romania's national poet. The campaign became so intense that I asked to see President Ceauşescu. He told me that it was too late to withdraw the volume, as it had already sold out, but he assured me that anti-Semitism would not be tolerated in Romania.

This volume appeared two weeks after the publication of an editorial in the weekly *Saptamina* (5 September 1980), the official organ of the Bucharest Municipality, which stunned me. When I saw it, I could hardly believe my eyes. The article was written in the style of Goebbels and Streicher. That it could appear in an official Communist Party journal was incredible. The writer was the young poet Corneliu Vadim Tudor, who used a specially insulting anti-Jewish term, '*Tartan*', to describe the people he was attacking. Everyone reading the article would know that '*Tartan*' had been used in the past to refer to Jews as a kind of floating population, without a homeland. It was a term right out of the *Protocols of the Elders of Zion*, the classic Tsarist anti-Semitic forgery. In the first chapter of these memoirs, the hooligan who beat me up because of my *payot* also called me '*Tartan*', so this article reminded me of my first encounter with anti-Semitism.

I wrote a memorandum to the secretary of the Bucharest Communist Party, George Pana, who was the Mayor of Bucharest and a member of the Politburo. He was responsible for *Saptamina*. I protested strongly at the appearance of the article. When I met him, I noticed that he was confused and did not know how to answer me. He had no idea how and why the article came to be published by the party weekly. It was, indeed, very strange that neither Mihoc nor Pana, the 'bosses' of the Academy and of the newspaper, had any idea of how the situation had arisen.

A few days later Vadim telephoned me and said he wanted to meet me. I told him that he could come to my office. I made sure that Theodore Blumenfeld would also be present when he came. Vadim's first words were, 'You know I am a Ceauşescu man and I want to make peace with you.' I replied immediately, 'Please don't make use of the President's name. Sit down and tell me what you want.'

Vadim said that he was not anti-Semitic and was not referring in his article to Jews. He added, 'I have Jewish friends and I have loved a Jewish girl.'

I said to Vadim, 'I don't want to insult you and I will, therefore, not answer you. I want to ask your permission to use a certain word. If you won't give me that permission, I won't tell you my attitude. I don't want to break the rules of hospitality.'

Vadim replied that I could use the word. I then said to him, 'You are a Fascist. I know that for you this is not an insulting term because you are proud of being a Fascist. Your name is Corneliu, the same as the Iron Guard captain, Corneliu Codreanu. The difference between you two is this: he had the courage to proclaim his hatred openly, but you are a coward. You want to tell me stories. I am older than you. All anti-Semites say their best friends are Jews.'

I took a copy of the article and began to analyse it sentence by sentence, bringing out all its anti-Jewish sentiments. Vadim began to plead and said, 'Let's make peace. Let's take a photograph together.'

He had arrived at my office with another man, a Jewish photographer named Rosenthal, who happened to work at Vadim's newspaper. Next day, he came to me to apologize, saying that he had had no idea of what was to happen: Vadim had called him, without giving him any explanation. Vadim turned to Rosenthal and was about to order him to take the photograph when I interrupted, 'No photograph. You have the temerity to ask me to be photographed with you after you have insulted the Jewish community!' I pressed a button and called in my secretary. 'Please show this man out,' I said, pointing at Vadim.

Vadim had either been rebuked by some powerful person or feared that he had gone too far and might face prosecution. This is the only explanation I can give for his visit to me. However, my sharp rebuke did not have a lasting effect on him. On the contrary, he was to be guilty of further outrageous conduct, directed, this time, at me personally.

After receiving the President's solid assurance, I went to New York, where, at a press conference, I defended the Romanian Government and explained its strong opposition to anti-Semitism. From New York

I flew to Israel, and it was in Jerusalem that I first heard of the appearance in Romania of a violently anti-Semitic pamphlet. The pamphlet claimed on its title page that it had been printed in Paris, but this was a lie: it had been printed in Romania.

This pamphlet contained a monstrous personal attack on me. I was said to be part of a world Jewish conspiracy. I was supposed to be a disciple of the twelfth-century Jewish sage, Maimonides, and an 'agent' of the French educational charity, *Alliance Israélite Universelle*.

Maimonides, a famous codifier of Jewish laws and a doctor, was madly accused of having told Jews to kill non-Jews, to confiscate their possessions and to become masters of the world. The pamphlet reprinted insane pieces by Eminescu, taken from the newly published volume, as well as my letter to the Academy, and Professor Pompiliu Marcea's allegation against me. Vadim's article was also included. The author of the article used a fake Jewish name.

When my friends in Jerusalem learned of this outrageous publication, they were thrown into a state of panic and urged me not to return to Bucharest. They argued that the situation had become too dangerous for me in Romania. I, of course, disregarded this advice and returned quickly to Bucharest and wrote a strong letter to the Ministers of the Interior and Security. I demanded to know who had printed and distributed this counter-revolutionary, Fascist pamphlet. Surprisingly and disturbingly, I received no reply.

Deciding that an exceptional response to the appearance of the pamphlet – and the silence of the Ministers – was essential, I called an emergency conference at the cultural centre of the Bucharest community. I invited seventy-two leading members of the community and the top Jewish writers. I spoke with intense feeling against the appearance of the pamphlet in Romania. Strong protests were taken up abroad. Greville Janner protested in the name of the Board of Deputies of British Jews to the Romanian Ambassador in London. The chairman of the Presidents' Conference of Major Jewish Organizations expressed indignation in Washington. Rabbi Schneer, the prominent New York leader, came specially to Bucharest and saw President Ceauşescu. Following these protests, Ceauşescu, speaking at the Congress of Romanian Trade Unions, in June 1981, condemned racism, chauvinism, mysticism and anti-Semitism.

The anti-Semitic campaign stopped for a few months and then broke out again with increased virulence. Dozens of anti-Semitic articles appeared in various publications and under a variety of signatures. I felt that I had to fight back, otherwise we would be swamped. I saw the first Vice-Premier Ion Dincă several times and kept up the protests.

I left for another visit to Israel and while I was there a volume of poems by Vadim, entitled *Saturnale*, appeared in Bucharest. One of the poems was dedicated to me, in an obvious play of letters on my name. The fourteen verses contained fifteen personal insults. There were such lines as: 'You want culture, you that should sell buttons, you liar, you nobody, you and all your Jews. You traitors, you killed our God.' Yet this Nazi book could be obtained for a while in the national libraries of Romania and bought in the shops. On the day before my return to Bucharest, President Ceauşescu intervened personally and ordered the confiscation of Vadim's book.

Nevertheless, I went ahead with the plan to hold a protest meeting at the Choral Temple. The authorities tried to persuade me to cancel the meeting, on the ground that Vadim's book had been banned. I persisted because I felt that important issues were at stake. Thousands of people turned up at the meeting on Friday evening in the Choral Temple, Jews and non-Jews. Leading academicians and writers went up to the rostrum to protest against the insults directed at the Chief Rabbi and the Jewish people. Some of the speakers became so emotional at the outrage that I had to calm them down. Every synagogue in the country issued a protest.

The president of the World Jewish Congress, Edgar Bronfman, the Chief Rabbi of Great Britain, Lord Jakobovits, the Chief Rabbi of France, Sirat, and hundreds of other leading personalities in the world sent cables of protest against the anti-Semitic revival and of solidarity with me and my community.

So strong was the feeling in legal circles that the president and vice-president of the College of Lawyers of Bucharest came to see me and offered to handle a court case against Vadim for defamation and libel. I went to see the Attorney-General and demanded that Vadim be brought to trial, but the request was not accepted. However, President Ceauşescu made it clear, when he received me, that he would not tolerate such excesses and the anti-Semitic campaign died down.

Yet two particularly outrageous incidents were to occur. In 1986, on the forty-fifth anniversary of the Iaşi pogrom, an article appeared in a Communist newspaper contesting the genuineness of the Holocaust. Another Communist newspaper published a poem with the words 'We Want To Hang You Again.' This was a clear reference to the Bucharest pogrom of 1941, when Iron Guard Fascists hung Jews like cattle in the abattoirs and attached notices with the words 'kosher meat' to their bodies.

There was a widespread outcry against the article and the poem. The authorities responded and the writer and poet were barred from appearing in Romanian publications. The Iaşi commemoration was very impressive: 5,000 people attended the service, among whom were the heads of local authorities and the Ambassadors of Israel and the United States. In my speech, I attacked openly and vigorously all the so-called 'journalists' or 'writers' who tried to profane the memory of our martyrs and I asked the Government to punish these people.

How can one explain this recrudescence of cruel, mad anti-Semitism in Romania after so many years of Communist rule? A new generation had arisen, but many young people had learned anti-Semitism at home. There was another factor: Romania had experienced a strong nationalist revival, which was part of its struggle for independence from the Soviet Union. Traditionally, Eastern European nationalism is linked with anti-Semitism.

The anti-Semitic outburst had a most curious sequel. There are in the United States a number of Romanian publications, including one which supports the Iron Guard. It printed a booklet under the title *Mincinosul* (*The Liar*), which was violently anti-Semitic and which contained the Vadim articles and the contents of the fake pamphlet published in Romania. It also attacked me personally.

This publication referred to strange events, which it claimed, had occurred in Romania. Professor Marcea, who had attacked me in a letter, had been found drowned in a lake. It was not known whether he had committed suicide or had died as a result of an accident. One of the anti-Semitic poets, Ion Lotreanu, had been found hanged, and one of the editors of the disputed Eminescu volume, Alexandru Oprea, was discovered dead in his bath. *The Liar* accused me of being a killer or of using black magic to murder them.

I think that no comment is necessary. *The Liar* continues an old tradition which accuses Jews of being child killers and of drinking their blood, and of poisoning the fountains of the Middle Ages and the leaders of Stalin's Politburo.

Let me conclude this tragi-comic chapter on anti-Semitism with the famous answer given by Andrassy, the Hungarian Foreign Minister, to the question 'Who is an anti-Semite?': 'An anti-Semite is somebody who hates the Jews more than necessary.'

44 *Menachem Begin Visits Bucharest*

*T*he visit of Menachem Begin, Israel's new Prime Minister, to Bucharest, in August 1977, proved to be of great importance for the future of Israeli–Egyptian relations. It was to be followed by the sensational visit to Jerusalem of President Anwar Sadat of Egypt. Begin's stay in the Romanian capital also had a number of intriguing aspects.

Begin, the leader of the right-wing Herut Party, a successor to the Zionist Revisionist Party of Zeev Jabotinsky, had won an unexpected victory in the general election, defeating the Labour Party which had ruled the country since the establishment of the state. Labour had been weakened in the eyes of the Israeli population by the shortcomings revealed in the Yom Kippur War, when Egyptian and Syrian forces gained early victories, and by the corruption scandals which hit the party. Begin benefited from the support of the Jews who had made *aliyah* from the Arab countries, many of whom saw themselves as underprivileged in comparison with the European-born Jews, who largely backed Labour. Though Begin had been born in Poland and, in his formal manners, reminded observers of a Polish aristocrat, these Jews saw an affinity with him and his failure to gain power. He had lost every election before 1977.

His critics abroad, especially in Britain, saw Begin as a former terrorist, who, as leader of the Irgun, had killed many British soldiers in the fight for independence and was responsible for blowing up the King David Hotel with the loss of many British, Jewish and Arab lives. Irgun forces were also accused of a massacre of Arab villagers at Deir Yassin during the War of Independence. However, this was not how he was perceived by his supporters in Israel and his admirers in the Jewish world. He was the object of much adulation as a patriot and as a charismatic leader. He was a man of intense feelings, which he was able to transmit through his remarkable oratory. As he showed in his dealings with President Sadat, he could rise from being a politician to being a world statesman with a vision of peace and conciliation.

When Begin revealed his intention of visiting Bucharest, two senior Romanian officers came to see me and asked my advice. Begin had stipulated that he would not use any vehicle between Friday afternoon – the commencement of the Sabbath – and Saturday evening, as he did not want to desecrate the Sabbath. He would want to attend the Sabbath morning service at the Choral Temple, but the official residence for important visitors was many kilometres away. Could the Jewish community accommodate him in the neighbourhood of the Temple? I replied that we had no house suitable to accommodate the Prime Minister and I suggested that they make use of the Hotel Modern, at the corner of Republicii Boulevard and Armeneasca Street, a short distance from the synagogue. It would take Begin only ten minutes to walk from the hotel to the Choral Temple. This suggestion was accepted. For security reasons, the whole hotel was cleared of guests and put at the disposal of Begin's party.

After the Friday night service I accompanied Begin as he walked along the middle of the empty streets of Sfinta Vineri and Calea Mosilor. Fifty to sixty plain-clothes security men swarmed around us. The pavements were guarded by soldiers, who also watched from windows and rooftops. I learned that as many as 2,000 soldiers and security men made sure that Begin was not harmed.

On the following Sabbath morning, I walked with my wife from our flat in Maria Rosetti Street to the Choral Temple. Coming closer, we caught sight of Begin and his entourage, accompanied by a strong escort, also making their way to the Temple.

My wife and I walked slowly as we did not think it right that we should join the Begin procession and we saw him disappear in the direction of the Temple. Suddenly, from another direction, we saw a second procession and another Begin coming towards us! We stared in amazement at the sight and rubbed our eyes in disbelief. This 'Begin' wore the same kind of clothes as the first one. His appearance was very similar, too. His entourage consisted of the same number of people and he was accompanied by the same number of security men.

Later I understood that two Begins had left the hotel, each taking a different route. The Romanian police feared a possible assassination attempt and wanted to confuse the plotters. I don't know whether they succeeded in confusing them; they certainly confused me – for a time. I was not certain which one was the real Begin and which the double.

Was the real Begin sitting next to me in synagogue that Sabbath morning? Yes, I think so, judging from the conversation I had with him. When I told him of the two Begins, he saw the funny side of the ruse and laughed heartily. His tears were also very genuine when he heard our youth choir sing *Jerusalem the Golden* in the original Hebrew. I said to him, 'Your tears are very significant. Like you, Golda Meir wept here in 1972. It seems that one cannot be Prime Minister in Jerusalem without weeping at the Choral Temple in Bucharest.'

Begin was able to make others weep, even a Prime Minister of Romania. Manea Mănescu arranged a dinner party in Begin's honour, which was also attended by the Foreign Minister, George Makovescu. The food was strictly kosher and everything was arranged in accordance with strict Jewish Orthodox requirements and watched over by our ritual supervisor.

Mănescu spoke first, mentioning the problem of conquered territories and the need to return them to the Arabs. He was presenting the official Romanian view of the Arab–Israeli conflict, which called for the establishment of a Palestinian Arab state on the West Bank and Gaza Strip, which had been conquered by Israel in the Six Day War of 1967.

In front of every guest there was the text of the toast that Begin was to propose in honour of his hosts. But as he rose to respond, Begin made two departures from normal usage at such official dinners. First of all, before referring to the host, the Romanian Prime Minister, he addressed me, using the Hebrew expression '*Mori Verabi*' ('My master and teacher') to stress the precedence of a Jewish religious leader. This was in line with his determination to emphasize his pride in Jewish traditions.

Addressing the Prime Minister and the guests, Begin remarked, 'Please forgive me for not using the text of the toast in front of you. Having heard the Prime Minister speak, I must talk to you about other things.

'This is not the first time that I have been to Romania. I was here before the Second World War. I brought with me Jewish immigrants from Poland, who travelled through Romania to the port of Constanţa and from there left by ship for Palestine. I led two groups of Jews to safety, saving their lives from the oncoming Nazi danger. When I brought the third group of Jews to the border of Romania, we were denied entry into the country. The British Ambassador in Bucharest had intervened with the Romanian authorities and the gates were locked.

'After spending several weeks on the border, we had to return to Poland. Of the 2,000 members of this group, only three survived the Holocaust. The others died in gas chambers or were massacred or burnt alive. Does anyone wish us to return to the same situation? Have we built up a homeland only to allow our enemy to destroy it? Should we once more wander from one country to another? Your Danube is wonderful, it is poetic, but it is full of Jewish blood, just like the Rhine and other European rivers. Never, never, never will we allow what happened to us to happen once again!'

Begin's voice shook with emotion. There was total silence in the hall. I looked at my neighbour, Macovescu, and saw tears running down his cheeks. Begin's words also deeply moved the other Romanian personalities present. They spoke of him afterwards with respect and admiration.

Begin's discussions with President Ceauşescu lasted eight hours. They talked in an office and also while walking around a lake. At times the discussions were heated and agitated, but it was during these talks that the idea of President Sadat's epoch-making visit to Jerusalem was confirmed. Ceauşescu's role was crucial. He was trusted by both Begin and Sadat. The Egyptian leader asked Ceauşescu if Begin was honest and strong, as Begin had been accused of being intransigent and even a warmonger. Had Ceauşescu given a negative answer, had he in any way doubted the success of the Egyptian–Israeli talks for peace, Sadat would never have visited the Jewish state and incurred the wrath of the hard-line Arab states.

I later heard Ceauşescu explain his approach. In January 1980, he received Jack Spitzer, then chairman of the Presidents' Conference of Major American Jewish Organizations, and Alfred Moses, vice-president of the American Jewish Committee, an influential group in the USA. They were discussing Ceauşescu's recommendation that Israel should enter into negotiations with the Palestine Liberation Organization. The Jewish visitors asked how negotiations could take place with people who did not even recognize the right of the Israeli state to exist. Ceauşescu answered, 'That is exactly the way President Sadat spoke in this very room. When I advised him to start negotiations with Begin, he argued that the Israeli leader would never return Suez, Sinai or even El-Arish to Egypt. I then said to President Sadat: "Just sit down together and start talking. By doing so you will convince world public opinion of your goodwill. If the talks take an unfavourable turn and Begin refuses to give back occupied Egyptian territories, you need not go on. The whole world will see that the other side does not want peace."

'I say the same thing to you Jews. Just sit down and start negotiations. If Arafat's attitude continues to be negative, if he continues to refuse to recognize Israel, you can stop talking and declare to the whole world that you have tried to achieve peace but that the enemy has rejected any solution other than the liquidation of the State of Israel.'

However, President Ceauşescu's advice was not taken.

Begin told me that during their discussions as they were strolling near the lake, Ceauşescu resorted to the argument that a too rigid Israeli attitude might lead to a revival of anti-Semitism in some parts of the world. Begin waited for the President to finish his remarks and then said to him solemnly, 'Those governments which make use of anti-Semitism will incur only shame.' It was not an argument that Begin would ever accept.

The Romanians were surprised by events involving Begin. On the last day of his visit, the talks were due to end at Snagov, near Bucharest, before noon. But they continued for a considerable time afterwards and our kosher restaurant was requested by telephone to send a meal to Begin. Morsky, the supervisor, left immediately for Snagov, but was not allowed to enter the room where discussions were taking place. He, therefore, gave the meal to an official, who took it into the room.

When Begin saw the meal without the supervisor, he realized that it had not been watched over for a time. It was not, therefore, kosher, according to the strict tenets of the law. Representing the Jewish state, he felt that he had to show total respect for Jewish religious laws. He, therefore, decided not to eat the meat, but, not wanting to create a problem for his Romanian hosts, he ate the vegetables and the dessert.

President Ceauşescu remarked to some of his aides, 'I don't understand why Begin did not eat the meat. It has been blessed by Chief Rabbi Rosen.'

Both on arrival and departure, Begin behaved unusually and must have infringed protocol rules. When he got off the plane, it was raining heavily. Begin walked towards me, past a number of high officials, and hugged and kissed me. His wife greeted my wife in the same manner. It was obviously meant to be a demonstration of Jewish solidarity. I said to Begin, 'You are kissing not just one man but all the 40,000 Jews now living in Romania. I welcome you on their behalf.'

When Begin was about to board the plane for Israel, he again embraced and kissed me. He wanted to show the watching Romanian leaders and officials that he had the welfare of Romanian Jews very much at heart.

Begin made an immense impression on the Romanians. 'A great, inspiring personality,' Mănescu remarked as we were leaving the airport. These words gave me much pleasure.

45 Meeting the Pope – Ecumenical Relations

We Jews have had an unhappy experience in dialogues with the Christian churches. I am afraid this is the main thought that occurs to me whenever someone mentions ecumenicism and how desirable it is. I cannot forget the disputations between Jews and Christians before, during and after the Spanish Inquisition in the fifteenth century and in other countries later on. There was tremendous Jewish suffering. We were always meant to be the 'losers'.

In my view, dialogue with the Christian churches is not necessary. It is not helpful to either side, because the whole of Christian belief is founded on the assumption that if one Jew exists who does not accept 'the true faith' of the Christian redemption, then the Kingdom of God cannot be realized. The Christian conception is that all Jews who have kept to their Judaism and have not accepted Jesus's mission are sinners. This conception is not acknowledged publicly by all Christian speakers, but I am convinced that, in their hearts, Christian leaders hold strongly to this view.

The Christian churches have tried to gain their objective of converting the Jews by using fire and sword, Inquisition and *auto da fé*. They failed. They now try to obtain their objective by a show of friendship. I have known and been friends with a number of very fine bishops, but their attitude to us Jews is still, 'We await you.' For that reason, though we had good relations with the Romanian churches, we never entered into any theological dialogue. Of course, we can have Jewish–Christian co-operation in regard to general human problems – war and peace, social justice, the atomic threat – but nothing more.

Holding such views, I never made any efforts to visit the Vatican and meet the Pope, which other Jewish leaders so eagerly sought. However, just before Rosh Hashanah in 1985, I received a visit from the Catholic Bishop of Bucharest, Bishop Robu, and the Catholic Bishop of Iaşi, Petru Gherghel.

After wishing me a happy new year, they began a general discussion. Suddenly, Bishop Robu asked me if I would be willing to meet Pope John Paul II. I understood immediately that this was, in effect, an invitation to meet the Pope. No such remark could have been made without the knowledge and approval of the Vatican.

I told the Bishop that I would be happy to meet the Pope. I would make use of the invitation when I next visited Western Europe. A month later, I was asked by the Bishop if I had decided when the meeting could take place. I replied that it could be in February 1986. However, this date proved unsuitable and a new one – 31 May – was set. I then received a formal, written invitation from the Vatican for a private audience with the Pope, which is usually only extended to heads of state.

I was keen to meet the Pope for both personal and political reasons. The Pope had been born in Poland and was once the Bishop of Krakow, which included the area of Auschwitz where my brother Elias had been a rabbi. I learned that the Pope had behaved bravely during the Nazi occupation and was even forced by them to do manual labour. He had shown sympathy for the Jewish agony.

My dear friend and colleague, Chief Rabbi Lord Jakobovits of Great Britain, drew the *Jewish Chronicle*'s attention to the story of Moses and Helen Hiller, who, before being deported from Krakow by the Nazis, had handed over their two-year-old son to Josef Jachowicz and his wife in nearby Dabrowa. Neither parent survived. Mrs Jachowicz became very attached to the little boy, whose first name was Shachne. She loved his bright, inquiring eyes and took him regularly to church. Soon he knew all the Sunday hymns by heart.

A devout Catholic, Mrs Jachowicz decided to have Shachne baptized and went to see the young parish priest, Karol Wojtyla. Revealing the secret of the boy's identity, Mrs Jachowicz told the priest of her wish that Shachne should become a devout Catholic like herself.

The priest listened intently to the woman's story. When she had finished, he asked, 'And what was the parents' wish when they entrusted their only child to you and your husband?' Mrs Jachowicz admitted that Helen Hiller's last request had been that the child should be told of his Jewish origins and returned to his people if his parents died. Hearing this, Wojtyla replied that he would not perform the baptismal ceremony. He explained to the disappointed Mrs Jachowicz that to baptize Shachne while there was still hope that, once the war was over, his relatives might claim him would be wrong.

Shachne Hiller survived the war and was eventually reunited with his relatives in the United States. And the priest, Karol Wojtyla, was later to become Pope John Paul II. No wonder I was intrigued to meet such a man and to pay him respects.

I decided to take up with the Pope two important questions: the Vatican's relationship with Israel and the establishment of a Carmelite convent in Auschwitz. Jews and many friends of Israel found it difficult to understand why the Vatican had still not established full diplomatic relations with the Jewish state. The Pope had received Israeli leaders in audience, but had evaded the question of full state recognition. When once asked whether he intended to recognize Israel formally, the Pope had replied that the time was not right to deal with it. Nevertheless, he had added somewhat enigmatically, 'But you have all my sympathy.'

Various explanations have been given for the Vatican's continued refusal to take the initiative and exchange envoys with Israel. It is claimed that the Vatican fears for the safety of Christian communities in Moslem countries if it made such a gesture of friendship to Israel. Other observers believe that the Vatican has theological difficulties in recognizing a Jewish state. I felt that this was a matter which I should discuss with the Pope.

Jews were profoundly shocked when they learned that Carmelite nuns had established a convent within the former Auschwitz death camp. Arguments that the convent was outside the camp were totally invalid. The walls of the convent overlooked the heart of the camp with its gas chambers. The forbidding building of the convent was used as a store for Zyklon B gas, with which millions of Jews had been killed.

The great majority of people who died at Auschwitz were Jews and died as Jews. Many of them had recited the holiest prayer, the *Shema*, as they took their last breath in the gas chambers. How could Christians be so insensitive as to establish a convent in this place of Jewish martyrdom? How could they fail to understand the pain they were inflicting on the survivors? To Jews the convent was a deliberate insult to the millions of Jews who had died at Auschwitz.

A surprise awaited me when I arrived at the Vatican, accompanied by Theodore Blumenfeld, whose presence I had requested. Monsignor Gati, who met me, with politeness and friendship, asked me not to raise the problem of the convent with the Pope because the Pope was already dealing with it personally. The Monsignor added that there were hopes that a solution favourable to the Jews would soon be found. I understood this to mean that the Christian convent would be removed. Monsignor Gati also requested that I should not bring up the question of the lack of formal diplomatic relations between Israel and the Vatican. He assured me that a 'positive solution' to this problem would be found. What, therefore, was there left for me to discuss? I, nevertheless, hoped that I would have an opportunity to make known to the Pope my strongly held views.

We went through many corridors and halls until we were met by the Prefect of the Vatican. He informed me that an audience normally lasted one or two minutes only, but that the Pope had asked that mine should be extended to ten minutes. The Prefect begged me to ensure that this time limit was not in any way exceeded.

Leaving Blumenfeld behind, I entered the papal room. I had expected the Pope to be sitting on his throne, which would have presented a problem for me. As a Jew and Chief Rabbi, I would have found it difficult to greet him in such a position by bending my knees. As if to avoid any possible embarrassment, the Pope found a solution. I was very relieved to discover that he was standing near the door. We shook hands and he invited me to sit next to him on a canopy. From the first moment the atmosphere was very friendly and relaxed.

The Pope remarked, 'We expected you in February.' I responded by saying that I was surprised that in February he even knew of my existence. 'We follow your every activity,' the Pope said, 'and we want to speak to you. You know that I, also, come from a Communist country. The question of the relationship with a Communist government is an old one for me. But your success is very important for us. We want to speak to you on this matter.'

During our discussion I mentioned that my brother had been a rabbi in Auschwitz before the war, a town which the Pope, as a young priest, knew well. The Pope began to give me his impressions of the peacetime Polish town of Oswiecim (Auschwitz), the home of an important Jewish community. I remarked, 'I don't want to raise the problem of the convent, but you can understand how sensitive Jews are about anything connected with Auschwitz.'

The Pope smiled. 'Don't worry,' he said.

After that we began a discussion about President Ceauşescu's policies. The Pope wanted to know my opinion of Hungarian complaints against Romania's treatment of the Hungarian minority in Transylvania. The Hungarians claimed that they were being persecuted by the Romanians. I said to him, 'I was born in Romania and my father was a rabbi in Romania for fifty-one years. I know, therefore, how the Hungarians treated the Romanians when they were masters in Transylvania. I can tell you that there is no comparison. The Romanians have treated the Hungarians far, far better.'

I also stressed that President Ceauşescu had an important role to play in the efforts being made to bring about peace in the Middle East. This was because he had diplomatic relations with both sides and so was able to speak to both Jews and Arabs.

The Pope began to smile again. 'I understand you, I understand you,' he said.

I thanked the Pope for the speech he had given a few weeks before in the synagogue of Rome in which he attacked anti-Semitism. Our discussion then moved on to the holy name of God – the Tetragrammaton – and we exchanged views and thoughts.

Generally, the Pope spoke with admiration for Jewish values. It was not a diplomatic gesture, but one of genuine friendship.

When I noticed that ten minutes had elapsed, I drew the Pope's attention to the fact, but he asked me to remain and continue our discussion. I feared that the Prefect would be annoyed. Five minutes later, the Prefect opened the door and I stood up. However, the Pope said to him, 'Please wait a little.'

We continued talking for a further five minutes and the Pope then said, 'Now I will call the photographer.' He went to the door, opened it and beckoned the photographer to enter. Blumenfeld was also invited into the room.

I presented the Pope with a book about the Jewish Holy Places in Israel. The Pope presented me with a silver image of himself. He said to me, 'As it is *Erev Shabbat* [the Sabbath eve in Hebrew], I know that you are busy. I will send the photographs to you at your hotel before the Sabbath.'

I informed him that I would be going to a rabbinical conference the following week. He responded in Hebrew, '*Shalom, shalom* to your colleagues and relatives.'

As we shook hands, he remarked, 'We shall see each other again soon.'

It would be pleasant for me to say now that my talk with the Pope led to changes. Alas, it didn't. The Vatican has still not established formal relations with Israel and the Carmelite convent still exists in Auschwitz, though a pledge has been given that it will be removed.

Regarding my relationship with other cults, that with the Orthodox

Patriarchs of Romania was friendly, but I sometimes felt that they did not fully understand what the tenets of Judaism meant for us, nor how deeply we Jews felt about the Holy Land.

An amusing example of incomprehension occurred once on the anniversary of Romania's liberation from Fascism. The date, 23 August, fell on a Saturday and I, of course, walked on foot to the hall where the festivities were being held. It was very warm and I struggled somewhat as I was wearing all my synagogal robes.

The Patriarch Justinian, who was indeed a *'Chassid umot haolam'* ('one of the righteous among gentiles') and a close and devoted friend of mine, passed by me in his comfortable, chauffeur-driven car. He asked his driver to stop the car and said to me, 'It is a shame that you should walk in this hot weather. Please join me in my car.'

I thanked him for the offer, but pointed out that it was forbidden for me to travel in a vehicle on the Sabbath.

'But nobody will see you,' the Patriarch exclaimed.

I pointed to the heavens and said, *'He* will see me!' I kept on walking slowly.

The Patriarch saw me later and I noticed he was puzzled. 'I don't understand,' he said. 'You walked all the way in your heavy robes on a hot day, but the Ambassador of Israel arrived in his car, displaying your cross [the Magen David]. Why could you not do the same?'

I occasionally felt that his successor, Patriarch Justin, still harboured certain prejudices. When meeting me, he invariably asked me, 'What's new in Palestine?' I responded by saying, 'Are you not aware that there is now a State of Israel? As long as you keep speaking to me about a non-existent Palestine, I will not answer you.'

I wonder what the Pope and these Patriarchs would have thought if they knew the full facts of a phenomenon very rare in Jewish history – Christians seeking to become Jews. Given the tragic destiny of the Jews and the heavy burden of observing all the tenets of Judaism, certainly for those who do not fully understand them, it is not surprising that few Christians decide voluntarily to adopt Judaism. There is, of course, the celebrated case of the king of the Khazars and 4,000 of his notables, who adopted Judaism in the lower Volga region of the Crimea in eighth-century Russia, but this is indeed a unique occurrence. Moreover, Judaism does not look for converts. Those who want to become Jews have to pass stringent tests to ensure that they have a real love for Judaism and are not motivated by a desire for some material benefits.

The Jewish people have, of course, benefited from wonderful converts. King David himself was a descendant of Ruth, the convert. In ancient times, special praise was given to converts, and they are the object of a special blessing in the *Amidah* prayer in synagogue. Our Torah asks us on no fewer than twenty-six occasions to love and protect the convert in our midst. The great Aramaic translator of the Bible, Onkelos, and the fascinating master and martyr, Rabbi Akiva, were also converts.

But to be fully accepted, respected and honoured, the convert of Judaism has to display a genuine belief in our Torah, to be a *Ger Tzedek*, a righteous proselyte. I had to be on the look out for men and women who wished to adopt Judaism for one reason only: because they wanted to leave Romania for the United States, Germany or Canada, in search of material improvement, but were unable to obtain exit papers. They learned that Jews were able to leave for Israel and so they decided to become Jews, too. They planned to leave the country, get to Israel and then move on elsewhere if they found conditions there not to their liking. It was not religion but greed that motivated them.

I strenuously refused to allow my *Beth Din* to be misused for this purpose, to become a kind of port for journeys to the United States. I could never accept such an arrangement, for both religious and ethical reasons. I considered the misuse of religion by the would-be emigrants as 'Operation Lie', with which I would never be associated.

Some men and women went to amazing lengths to convince me and the *Beth Din* that they were Jews and, therefore, could be given exit papers. One elderly, married woman came with a tale that she had 'sinned' with a Jew in her youth and that, therefore, her son was a Jew! Apart from being an obvious liar, she was unaware that in Jewish law a person takes his Jewishness from the mother and not from the father. She went away disappointed. Another man paid a large sum of money to have his father, who was buried in a Christian cemetery, reburied in a Jewish cemetery so that he could claim that he was a Jew. He, too, failed to convince me. The lie became obvious after a few questions. The *New York Times* published an article about my opposition to the conversion of Christians, claiming that there was a notice on my door, stating, 'We are not conducting *Gerut* [conversions].'

Yet I have to admit to my sorrow that there have been many thousands of Romanian Christians who, desperate to leave the country, managed, in one way or another, to obtain certificates that they had been converted to Judaism and, consequently, obtained exit papers. Many of them – perhaps thousands – are now living in Israel.

When, however, I became convinced that the would-be convert was really sincere, I accepted and protected him. Even if I considered that the man would not gain materially from settling in Israel and would encounter many difficulties, I would still support him because I felt that genuine faith would overcome all problems.

Such was the case of a peasant, who, for five years, begged to be admitted to Judaism. I tested him throughout this time and I felt he was sincere. I converted him, his wife and children. His daughter even divorced her husband because he refused to be converted. Alas, as I feared, conversion to Judaism brought suffering on the peasant and his family. Their fellow villagers perceived the conversion to Judaism as treason to Christianity, while the local Communists saw the conversion as religious propaganda.

I took the family out of the village and brought them to Bucharest. The father became a guardian at the Jewish cemetery and his wife worked in the kitchen of our kosher restaurant. One day I was surprised to receive a parcel from him, consisting of a sweater and woollen socks which he himself had woven. I reprimanded him severely, telling him that he must not in future spend money and time on giving me such presents. He replied, 'Is it not written in the Torah that one should make gifts of the first wool [*Reishit hagez*] of the lamb, to the Cohen, to the priest? Are you not my Cohen? For me it is forbidden to use it. Only you can.'

This peasant, whose name was Traistaru, became the best Jew in our Bucharest community. Eventually, twenty years after his conversion, he asked for exit papers for himself and his family to leave for Israel. He was successful. They now all live in Nahariya. The man has a grandson who is named Moshe Dayan, after the celebrated Israeli general and politician. In his letters to me, Traistaru addresses me as '*Abba*' (father) and my wife as '*Imma*' (mother). He quotes extensively from the Torah and rebukes me for continuing to live among the gentiles and not coming to live in Israel.

Another very sincere and genuine convert was a Romanian called Voiculescu, who changed his name to Levy and went to live in Israel. Levy had a very gifted boy, whom I sent to a rabbinical seminary in France, in Aix-le-Bains. I considered him as a possible future Chief Rabbi. The boy was very religious and made a point of wearing his *tsitsit* (fringes appended to each corner of the *tallith*) prominently. He later served with distinction in the Israeli army. The family have remained strictly Orthodox Jews, but the boy did not eventually become a rabbi. Alas, there were few such ideal converts to Judaism.

I must stress the great difference between the situation nowadays and that prior to the Second World War. The Church was then used as a nest of hatred and agitation against Jews. The Iron Guard had priests in its leadership. The Patriarch Miron Cristea was an open anti-Semite, calling in his messages for the expulsion of the Jews. Hitler's 'ideology' of destroying the Jews did not penetrate Romania under a racial mask, but under a religious one: 'Kill the killers of God.'

The new Government after 1948 had no interest in *'divide et impera'*, in dividing the cults and ethnic minorities in order to dominate them better. On the contrary, they forbade by law all discrimination, whether racial, religious or national. They encouraged us, the heads of cults, to come nearer to one another and to establish brotherhood among us. This was a revolutionary change in our position.

It is true that there have been some cases testifying to a revival of anti-Semitism, but even the Patriarch Justin (who was no friend of ours) had to be cautious and not tolerate such things.

The present Patriarch, Teoctist, is a very fine priest, a servant of love and brotherhood. Our relationship is excellent. Following the tradition established by his predecessors, Justinian and Justin, who came to the Choral Synagogue to congratulate me on the twentieth and thirtieth anniversaries of my Chief Rabbinate, he was our honoured guest in 1988, when I celebrated forty years as Chief Rabbi.

In the archives of the years before and during the Second World War, there can be found details of many people's attempts to abandon Judaism and to convert to Christianity in order to try to escape the Holocaust. Today, the wave of candidacies for conversion is coming from the other side and has other, different purposes.

46 *Establishing a Museum and Sending Holy Scrolls to Israel*

After hundreds of thousands of my congregants had left the country, what happened to their documents, their art treasures and their testimonies of Jewish existence? What happened when thousands of synagogues were closed? What was to be done with their Siphrei Torah, their holy objects and their books?

Only people who have had to face these problems can understand how difficult these questions were, how important it was to find a positive, Jewish, equitable and ethical solution to them.

In 1977, I decided to establish a collection of Romanian–Jewish historical documents and to house them in a museum. An old synagogue in Bucharest, called the Tailors synagogue, or *Achdut Kodesh* – the Holy Unity – which was empty and had not functioned for twenty-five years, was selected to house the museum. Jews had lived in the country for 600 years and it was a holy duty to record their achievements, their tragedies and their joys. The CDE had deliberately hidden most of the famous Jewish historical documents, in furtherance of their policy of minimizing the importance of the Romanian Jewish community. When the famous Schneerson exhibition, the Tomb of the Unknown Jewish Martyr, opened in Paris in 1965, there were exhibits from most Eastern European countries, including the Soviet Union, Czechoslovakia, Hungary, Poland and Yugoslavia, but none from Romania. Schneerson had appealed to Madame Khrushchev for material on the Holocaust available in the Soviet Union and the Russians had responded. Only the Romanian Jewish Communists were adamant in their refusal and managed to stop any Romanian exhibits leaving for Paris.

Following my well-tried method of taking unilateral action first and receiving approval later, I did not seek any permit for establishing the Jewish museum. When all the exhibits were in place, I invited the

Minister of Cults to the opening. He came and did not voice any criticism of the *fait accompli*. I think he realized that the museum was an essential institution. In any case, it was too late for him to display disapproval. To the same 'inauguration' ceremony, I also invited the American and Israeli Ambassadors and Philip Klutznick, president of the WJC. They came and showed their appreciation of a museum which tries to do justice to one of the great Jewish communities of Europe, its religious splendour and cultural achievements. Beginning with Jewish coins from the times of Bar Kochba, we find there the famous *Travels of Beniamin*, written by Rabbi Beniamin from Tudela, in which we have the first testimony of the existence of the Romanian people. Rabbi Beniamin met the 'Valachs' and provides a brief appreciation of them.

Documents and pieces of synagogal art from many centuries, wonderful pictures of old synagogues, old religious books, the first Jewish press items, documents of nineteenth-century *aliyah* to Palestine and works by famous Jewish painters give a fascinating image of the history of Romanian Jewry.

The section on the Holocaust and on the pogroms in Iaşi, Bucharest and other places is overwhelming. The exhibits provoke sighs and tears. We obtained original photographs of the pogroms from German officers who had been taken prisoner. Exhibited, too, are pieces of soap produced by the Nazis out of Jewish bodies. RIF (*Reines Idishes Fetteu* – Pure Jewish Fat) is inscribed on each piece of soap.

Our museum is now a source of pride not only for us, but also for the whole Jewish people. Jews and non-Jews admire here Jewish culture, Jewish art, Jewish heroism and Jewish martyrdom.

The Romanian Siphrei Torah form a unique chapter in Jewish history. Unlike these exhibits, I was determined that they should not all remain in Romania.

Unlike the experience of other great Jewish communities throughout history, who had suffered catastrophes on a huge scale and lost all their treasures and Siphrei Torah, Romanian Jews had many thousands of Siphrei Torah after the Holocaust. These had been used by the 800,000 Jews who lived in the country before the war, of whom 400,000 perished. Most of the remaining 400,000 began to leave for Israel, but the Siphrei Torah stayed behind. Some towns would have only a few Jews, but numerous Siphrei Torah. The result was anarchy. Some people would go into a synagogue, take out a Sepher Torah and disappear with it. There was absolutely no control, only chaos. Yet apart from its holiness, each Sepher Torah was also, it has to be stressed, financially valuable. How valuable can be gauged from the fact that in 1965 two Jewish merchants arrived in Bucharest from the United States and Israel and offered $2 million for 1,000 Siphrei Torah. I rejected the offer, feeling strongly that this was not a matter for commercial transactions.

I first of all insisted that there should be an absolute embargo on any Sepher Torah leaving the country. I then checked how many Siphrei Torah each local community possessed. If, for example, a community of 500 had forty Siphrei Torah – as often happened – I would take away thirty-seven of them, telling the congregants that three Siphrei Torah were sufficient for their needs, as, indeed, they were. By this method I was able to assemble around 4,000 Siphrei Torah in Bucharest. In 1966, I obtained permission from Bodnăraş to send 500 Siphrei Torah to Israel. However, a few days later, I received a letter cancelling the permission. A long struggle ensued, but I was finally able to obtain approval to send no fewer than 3,800 Siphrei Torah to Israel. We did not ask any payment for them, not even to be reimbursed for the cost of sending them, which was considerable. The Romanian Government, too, made a wonderful gesture of friendship to the Jewish community by giving its approval of the operation.

I established a supervisory committee whose members included Dr Warhaftig, the Israeli Minister for Religious Affairs, and Charles Jordan. On arrival in Israel, the Siphrei Torah were taken to the Heichal Shlomo Centre in Jerusalem. When the distribution of the Siphrei Torah began – priority was, of course, given to Romanian communities in Israel – I granted an interview at the Centre to French Television and to a correspondent of the French newspaper, Le Monde, André Scemama. This interview took place in a hall where 3,500 Siphrei Torah were deposited. Scemama asked me to take one of the Siphrei Torah in my arms and to hold it during my interview. I agreed to do so.

What was embroidered on the kutonet (sleeve) of this scroll? The words 'Hevrat Shomrei Zion – Foosani 1882. Od Evneich venivneit.' These last three words are from the Prophet Jeremiah (31: 4) sending his message to Jerusalem. He, the witness of the destruction of the Holy City, is proclaiming, 'I will rebuild you and you will be rebuilt.'

I saw then, all of a sudden, the fascinating image of women sitting in the shtetl of Focsani, a hundred years ago – at a time when Herzl was still unknown and when the 'Lovers of Zion' (Hovevei Zion) had not yet appeared – embroidering the message of Jeremiah, believing that the time of redemption was near. And now God had given me the unique honour of bringing this embroidered message to Jerusalem. It struck me as incredible that of all the thousands of scrolls in the Centre, I should have picked up this particular one, with its inspiring message. If this is not a miracle, then what is?

47 *The Yiddish State Theatre*

*T*he Yiddish Theatre could have been another force for good among the Romanian Jewish people. After all, Romania was the birth-place of the Yiddish theatre. The first Yiddish theatre in the world was established in Iaşi in 1876, by Abraham Goldfaden, to be followed by one in Bucharest. Gifted writers, poets and playwrights worked for the Romanian Yiddish Theatre, outstanding men like Yitzik Manger, Yaacov Gropper, Schlomo Bickel and Yaacov Steinberg, well known all over the world. Romania also welcomed visits of famous Yiddish groups from abroad. The renowned Vilna Yiddish Troupe, with such personalities as Joseph Buloff, Joseph Kamen and Judith Lares, and the great Baratof travelled the length and breadth of Romania, delighting audiences and setting new standards of excellence.

However, the story of the Romanian Yiddish Theatre is one of tragedy and paradox. The Yiddish Theatre, like other theatres in the country, was taken over by the Romanian Government following the consolidation of power by the Communist Party. The Theatre was, therefore, not under the control of the Federation of Jewish Communities and it was subsidized not by us but by the state. Yet with almost 400,000 Jews in the country and with such outstanding actors and actresses as Dina Koenig, her daughter Leah Koenig (who joined the Habimah Theatre of Israel), Isaac Havis and others of similar calibre available, the Yiddish Theatre could have been a magnificent vehicle for promoting Jewish culture. We could have seen great Jewish plays and the Jewish spirit could have been uplifted as Goldfaden envisaged.

Alas, this great opportunity was not merely missed, but it was misused. The culprit, as in so many other matters, was the CDE. I consider that what they did was sheer anti-Semitism, despite the fact that they were Jews. They forced the theatre's management to put on special shows filled with anti-Zionist and anti-religious slurs and accusations. The shows insulted Jewish aspirations and were, at heart, poisonously anti-Jewish.

The tragedy of the Yiddish Theatre was this: when there was a large Yiddish-speaking population in the country and great artists to serve it, the Jews boycotted the theatre. It was ugly and venomous in their eyes. The attacks on Israel and Judaism revolted them. In contrast, when the situation changed in Romania and the theatre was no longer misused, and was presenting plays of quality, there was no longer a sizeable Jewish public to enjoy it and be inspired by it. The gates of the country had opened and the theatre's public had departed for Israel.

At the height of the anti-Zionist campaign the two directors of the Yiddish Theatre were Uri Benador and Bernard Leibli. The latter was of no importance, but Benador was a respected and talented novelist. He had written a number of books with a Zionist bias before the Second World War (his *Ghetto of the Twentieth Century* was a great success), but, on becoming a Communist, he had switched to writing anti-Zionist diatribes. He did so not only during the period of Stalin's reign of terror, when people argued that it was permissible to do such appalling things to save one's skin, but later when no such pressure existed and no other Jew was writing such tracts. He insulted and vilified Zionism – and the Romanian Jewish people, from whom he sprang. I remember reading, while on holiday, one of his so-called novels, *Gablonz*, which had as its background the pogrom in Iaşi where nearly 12,000 Jews had been murdered. But not a single Jew was depicted as a hero or a martyr. On the contrary, all the Jews were seen as villains; even the rabbi was a 'bandit'. It was the killers who were the heroes. As I read this disgusting book I became so enraged that my wife feared for my health. She insisted on taking the book away from me.

In one of his articles, he launched a bitter attack on the notion of the 'Chosen People' in the Bible, claiming that the idea was racist. On a *Sabbath Hagadol* (the Great Sabbath before the festival of Passover), I saw him enter the Malbim synagogue as I was delivering my sermon. I deliberately changed the course of the sermon and pointed out the difference between the notions of the Chosen People and of the German Nazi *'Herrenvolk'*. The Nazis wanted to dominate the world and kill all those who opposed them, or who, like the Jews, they considered inferior or dangerous. The Chosen People, however, wished to serve the Almighty and suffer for others. According to tradition, the Almighty asked all other peoples in the world if they would undertake to fulfil all the obligations laid down in the Torah. All refused. Only the Jews agreed to take on themselves the great burden and to 'pay' for this 'privilege' with their blood.

Uri Benador took one of Sholem Aleichem's comedies, *Nibe Nime Ni Kukariko*, totally changed the amiable, good-natured story and gave it a new title, *The Clever Shoemaker*. He then turned this story into an anti-Zionist and anti-Jewish play, scoffing at *tallithot* and at rabbis. My congregants came to see me and told me in sorrow about what was happening at the Yiddish Theatre. I sent one of my friends to the theatre to take notes, and he confirmed Benador's blasphemy. The directors then added further insults to the Jewish community by announcing that the theatre, which was going on a provincial tour, would perform on Rosh Hashanah and Yom Kippur, the holiest days of the Jewish calendar.

I considered their conduct totally intolerable. I wrote an indignant letter to the Minister of Education and Culture, Constantza Cracium, and asked her if another ethnic state theatre insulted the Christian religion, as the Yiddish Theatre had insulted and vilified the Jewish religion. I requested that she should immediately investigate my accusations.

A few hours after receiving my request, the Minister telephoned to thank me for bringing the matter to her attention. On the following day a commission of twenty powerful people, including representatives of the Central Committee of the Romanian Communist Party, of the Ministry of Education and Culture and of the Mayor of Bucharest, ordered the theatre to give a special performance of the offensive play. The Yiddish text was fully translated into Romanian. The Commission then thoroughly analysed and discussed the play for three days. The verdict was dramatic: the Yiddish Theatre's tour was cancelled, the play was permanently banned and the two directors were dismissed from their posts.

Uri Benador died a sad and tormented man. In his will he asked that he should be buried in a *tallith* and that an old prayer book belonging to his mother should be placed on his head.

I never blamed anyone for submitting to the Stalinist terror. I was not certain how I would have behaved had I been placed in similar circumstances. A person who leads a normal, civilized existence can have no conception of how he would react to torture and hunger. There were Jews who killed other Jews for a piece of bread. But nobody had forced Benador to act the way he did; he was a man of talent but no character.

When the situation changed and the anti-Zionists were defeated, the

Romanian authorities nominated the talented director, Franz Josef Auerbach (now in Israel), to direct the Yiddish Theatre. He produced Anski's famous play *The Dybbuk* and also a play about Anne Frank. He even produced a show devoted to Chaim Nachman Bialik, the Hebrew national poet. But, alas, there were not enough Jews to appreciate his and the theatre's productions. Schwartsman, the musical director, remarked once, 'I can see how many people there are taking their seats in the hall tonight. If it comes to a fight between them and us, we'll be all right. We are more numerous than they.'

48 *Other Jews in Communist Countries*

*I*n January 1988, I received a very friendly letter from the Patriarch of the Russian Orthodox Church inviting me to participate in the festivities marking 1,000 years of Christianity in Russia. This invitation was followed by a visit to my office by an official of the Soviet Embassy in Bucharest, who encouraged me to accept the invitation. My health at the time was not good and I raised a number of difficulties, but it was clear that the official had been told to make every possible effort to persuade me to travel to the Soviet Union for the festivities. When I pointed out that I would need kosher food, he replied that this could be arranged. I said that I would want to take my wife with me and he responded by saying that this would cause no problem. At the end of our conversation, the official asked me what my opinion was of the policies concerning Jewish matters pursued by the Soviet Governments up to the assumption of leadership by Mikhail Gorbachev. I was astonished at such a question but I answered frankly. I said that the pre-Gorbachev Governments had made major mistakes. A few days later the official sent me a message confirming that all the requests I had made had been accepted.

I must repeat that for decades I had been *persona non grata* in Moscow. This was the first time that such an official and friendly invitation had been extended to me.

In April, I attended at Oxford the World Forum for Survival, at which the dangers facing humanity were discussed: 200 personalities from all over the world were present, including heads of churches and parliamentarians – the Archbishop of Canterbury, Cardinal Koenig and the Dalai Lama were among the religious leaders who came to support the forum. I was surprised to be approached by a Russian metropolitan and an official responsible for the Soviet Government's relations with the churches and asked why I had not answered the invitation from the Patriarch. I had assumed that my agreement to travel to the Soviet Union was known. I immediately confirmed my decision and sent messages to Rabbi Shayevits of Moscow and Professor Levine of Leningrad. I had been in touch with Professor Levine, a fine man and a scholar in Jewish studies, and looked forward to meeting him.

When my wife and I arrived in Moscow in May, we were met by a delegation from the Orthodox Church, but there was no one from the Jewish community.

Yet, on my arrival at the synagogue on Friday afternoon, I was met by a number of Jews who told me how much they appreciated receiving our newspaper. One Jew wept, saying that the nationalist and anti-Semitic organization, Pamyat, was threatening the Jewish community and using slogans like 'Death to the Jews'. But others told me that the man, who had suffered greatly during the Holocaust, was exaggerating. There was no panic among the congregants.

However, there was a distinct difference between the atmosphere in the Jewish community and in the general public. The new openness among ordinary Russians, brought about by Gorbachev's new policies of *glasnost* and *perestroika*, was not in evidence among the Jews. There was a revolutionary change among the Russians. Fear seemed to have disappeared. I had an opportunity of discussing the new situation with Russian clergymen and men of science. They all told me that fear, which had so much affected Soviet life, particularly during the rule of Stalin, had been eradicated. To them this was the most important and desirable change brought about by Gorbachev. But in the Moscow synagogue I found the same fear that I had noticed in the past. The eyes of the congregants still gave the same message: 'Don't believe the authorities. Don't take them seriously.' I was invited to give a sermon to the congregation and I used this opportunity to call on their love for Israel and for the Jewish people.

On the Sabbath afternoon, when I went for a walk, I saw a large group of some sixty to seventy people near the synagogue. They had not come to pray there but to meet each other for a chat. This meeting-place was also used by Jewish boys and girls for courting. I understood that marriages were also arranged there. I tried to start a serious conversation about the Jewish future and presence in the country, in view of the changes announced by Gorbachev, but could get no response. Suspicion was still rampant.

In the main synagogue of Archipova Street 8 nothing had changed, because nobody had tried to bring about a change from within. There are thousands of distinguished Jews in the Soviet Union: intellectuals, scientists and writers, who must be persuaded to start rebuilding the communities. The other cults are organized and have a hierarchy: they have bishops, metropolitans and patriarchs. The Jews have nothing. In fact, Rabbi Shayevits is not Chief Rabbi of Moscow because a Moscow Jewish community does not exist. Russian Jews have to take their destiny into their own hands. Of course, they must be helped from abroad, but it is their presence, their efforts and their own *glasnost* that must open new perspectives. Why can the Lithuanians or the Armenians achieve such a major change and not the Jews?

Running to Moscow and obtaining front-page scoops, without any concrete results, does not bring about the redemption of millions of Jews who have reached the climax of their tragedy.

A minimal programme must be produced for the Jews who remain there. Those who want to leave are no longer interested in what happens in the USSR. The millions who stay in the Soviet Union must be organized into communities; they must emancipate themselves from their present 'establishment' and must proclaim the same lack of fear as other citizens of the USSR.

The atmosphere in the small synagogue of the Lubavitch Chassidim was fervently Jewish. I noticed that they had a *mikvah*. Jewish spontaneity was visible there. In the big synagogue where I gave a sermon I found formality. Throughout Moscow there was not a single kosher restaurant. Much publicity had been given to a newly established Jewish restaurant, but the food there was *trefah*.

I read in the newspaper *Moscow News* sharp criticism of people who had misused their powers in harassing churchgoers. If such an attitude has now been adopted towards the Church, it should be possible to extend it to the synagogues. I was constantly astonished by the changed attitude to the Christian Church. The hall of the giant Rossiya Hotel, where I stayed, was decorated with icons, crosses and other religious objects and looked like the inside of a cathedral during the festivities. At the Bolshoi, a choir of priests joined the Ballet Theatre's choir during a performance. They sang religious and patriotic songs. At the last session of the commemoration, Madame Raisa Gorbachev sat on the dais next to the Patriarch at the main table. Near them were leading figures of the country including many scientists. I thought that such a change in the standing of the Jews of Russia could also be brought about.

On a trip outside Moscow I met by chance an elderly Jew, who had been a Communist for fifty years. We began a discussion which lasted for three hours. The elderly Jew showed me his Communist Party card, with the number eighty-nine on it. This meant that he had been the eighty-ninth member of the party. His breast was full of medals and high decorations. He argued that he was a Russian and not a Jew, but eventually he changed his stance as he became more confident. He told me of the tragedy that had befallen Russian Jews. His own father had been murdered by the Germans. Yet anti-Semitism was still prevalent in the Soviet Union. He claimed to be a good Jew, though not religious. He spoke in Yiddish, but admitted that neither his son nor his grandson knew the language. Did he think the Jews would disappear? Yes, he replied, because nothing was being done for them.

Towards the end of our conversation, he made an unexpected request, 'I am not religious, but I must continue to be a Jew. Please send me a Jewish calendar.' I expressed surprise that he should need a calendar if he did not observe the Jewish religious festivals. He replied that he wanted to know when Yom Kippur occurred. He still occasionally went to a synagogue service, but worried in case it was noted by his non-Jewish neighbours. 'We don't know what could happen here,' he explained.

This man symbolized to me the whole tragedy of Russian Jewry. He was the symbol of the historic mistakes made by Zionist and world Jewish leaders. I recalled with sadness the arguments I had had with Jewish and Israeli leaders and the attacks launched against me.

When I first met Golda Meir I knew that my policy of give-and-take was not favoured by certain circles in Israel. They adopted a cynical line: 'Worse is better.' If conditions in the Diaspora deteriorated, more Jews would leave for Israel and thus it would be better for the Jewish state. I considered this formula not only cynical and immoral, but also unsupported by facts. The very idea that Jewish leaders should welcome a worsening of the Jewish situation in the Diaspora filled me with horror. Secondly, a 'worsening' situation in the Diaspora does not mean *aliyah* to Israel. If Jewish life is not encouraged, a Jew will run to Philadelphia and not to Tel Aviv.

My conflict with these negative Israeli circles occurred at a time when I was able to establish Talmud Torahs, with thousands of pupils – a truly miraculous development in a Communist country. Miraculous, too, was the Romanian Government's agreement to allow *aliyah* to Israel, in sharp contrast to the attitude of the authorities in other Communist countries. I was able to bring thousands of high school pupils into the synagogue. Our lectures on Wednesday evenings were so popular that hundreds of students were unable to gain entrance and had to stand in the street, to the bewilderment of the police.

When I discussed the matter with Golda Meir in 1972, I explained my view that, in contrast to those who believed that the existence of Israel was its total justification, I felt that Israel was only a means for maintaining and strengthening the Jewish people. Golda stared at me with fiery eyes and I thought she was going to gobble me up. I, nevertheless, repeated firmly, 'For me the most important consideration is the Jewish people and the most important means for maintaining the Jewish people is the State of Israel.'

Certain Israeli circles did not accept this point of view. Talmud Torahs and Jewish life generally in the Diaspora were not all that important for them. On the contrary, 'worse was better'. However, in Romania conditions became better and these circles did not welcome the change. When Gershon Jacobson wrote an article in the *Algemeine Journal*, of New York, praising my work, he was visited on the following day by a senior Israeli official, who asked him why he wrote so favourably about me. Jacobson replied that he had himself seen the remarkable improvement in Jewish life in Romania, brought about by my policies. 'All this is not important,' the official remarked. I had become reconciled with Golda and she understood my policies, but I felt that certain Israeli circles were stronger than her.

When my conflict with these circles became particularly harsh, I was invited by Bodnăraş to see him. He said to me, 'My people tell me that there is a conflict between you and the Israeli Embassy in Bucharest. I cannot believe it. You are their agent. Don't think I am a fool. Please explain to me exactly what is happening.'

I told him, 'I am a Zionist and they are Zionists. The difference between us is that they are bureaucrats and I am not.'

I gave him the example of the treatment by the Israeli Embassy of Polak, an outstanding editor of our newspaper and a fine Hebrew scholar who wanted to settle in Israel with his wife. As I did not have a suitable person to replace him with, I told him that I was prepared to pay him $1,000 a month so that he could find a home for his wife in Israel while he remained for another year in Romania, during which time we would find a new editor. His wife and his daughter were not Jewish, and I made an exception in converting them. I also agreed on his leaving, although I was usually against the *aliyah* of our Federation co-workers. He was astonished how I had helped him. After that, when he already had the passports and went to the Israeli Embassy to arrange for his wife's departure, he was subjected to intense interrogation by two officials. They insisted that he leave immediately for Israel. His arguments that *Revista*, with its Hebrew page, would disappear, that nobody would be able to arrange the calendar for the next year, and that I had made special arrangements for him, were dismissed with derision. I protested to the Israeli Ambassador about the treatment meted out to Polak. I sent a copy of my letter of protest to Golda, who reprimanded the Ambassador. I said to Bodnăraş, 'Polak's articles can convert hundreds of young people into Zionists, so that they will wish to go to Israel. The Israeli Embassy should, therefore, be encouraging him to stay here. But, no. They want him to leave and destroy a Zionist paper.'

'Now, I understand,' said Bodnăras. 'We have the same kind of people here in the Communist Party. Bureaucrats are always a danger.'

I was able to convince the Romanian officials and intellectuals that Zionism was a positive force. I acknowledge that, in order to save the Jews, it was necessary to adopt the policy of give-and-take. In any open conflict with the authorities we would inevitably have been the losers.

I am reminded of the story of the Belzer Chassid, who was noted for his loud, demanding voice when praying. When he complained that his prayers had not been answered, another Chassid said to him, 'Why don't you first try a kinder approach to the Almighty?' '*Mit Gitten*', 'Take it easy', was our method, and we succeeded.

It was a special tragedy for the remnants of Polish Jewry, reduced from three and a half million to a few thousand by the Holocaust, that the leadership was grabbed by a handful of Jewish Communists. In the mid-1960s, I was invited to attend the unveiling of a monument at the Treblinka concentration camp. The invitation came not from the Jewish Communists but from the Association of Polish Partisans, whose president was rector of Warsaw University, a non-Jew. When I arrived in Warsaw with my wife, we discovered that we were being boycotted by the Jewish Communists. No Jew came to the airport to greet us or visit us at the hotel.

Before leaving Warsaw I telephoned Hirsh Smolier, one of the leaders of the Jewish Communists, who said that he was too busy to come to see me. I replied that I would come to his office. On arrival there, Smolier offered me a seat. I said to him, 'I don't want to sit in your office after your so-called hospitality. I came here to ask one question. Not only am I the president of a Jewish community in a Communist country, but I am the leader of a Jewish community in a country which is a friend and neighbour of Poland. You may not like it that a rabbi is president of the Federation, but the Romanian Communist Government has agreed on that. How is it conceivable that you should provide hospitality for Lord Janner, leader of a Jewish community in a capitalist country, and insult the president of 300,000 Jews in a friendly Socialist country?'

Smolier replied angrily, 'You have made an alliance with traitors in Bucharest, with a government of traitors. Together you are organizing the sending of Jews to Israel. Because of this act of treachery, we are entitled to treat you in any way we like.'

In 1967, during the time of the Six Day War, a crisis occurred because of a speech by Wladyslaw Gomulka, the Polish leader. He suggested that Jews had a dual loyalty – to Poland and to Israel. He even referred to Jews as a fifth column. Smolier and his son went to Israel and today they are fervent Zionists.

Though his language was objectionable, I consider that Gomulka was fundamentally right. He, in effect, told the Jewish Communists of Poland: 'You have to decide if you are Jews or Poles.' I don't believe that Gomulka, who had a Jewish wife, was anti-Semitic. Ironically, Gomulka performed a greater service to Zionism than any Zionist organization. Without him, Smolier and many Jews like him would still be in Poland. For instance, David Sefard, who wrote the infamous article 'Criminals in White Smocks' during the so-called 'doctors' plot' in Moscow, is now in Sweden because of Gomulka. Some Jewish Communists in Poland, like the Minister Roman Zambrowski, taught the Poles how to be good Communists and how to vilify fellow Jews. They taught that Jews who asked to leave for Israel were traitors. The revenge that Jews enjoyed was to see these opponents of Zionism and Israel having themselves to settle in Israel. Minister Dogaru who, for seventeen years, was witness to my life and death struggle with the CDE, told me when mass emigration occurred, 'All the enemies of Zion are already in Israel. It is only you, Chief Rabbi, the defender of Zion, who remains here.'

I must be frank and say openly that I understand the reasoning behind the decision of the Romanian, Polish and Russian authorities to dismiss Jewish Communists from leading state posts when they announce their desire to settle abroad. How could the authorities agree to persons holding key state posts in a Communist regime if they have lost faith in the system and want to live in another country? Some of those who wanted to leave had once led campaigns for Communism and had become specially unpopular with the public. Now they are also viewed as hypocrites.

Of course, I am not justifying the dismissal of Jews from jobs because they are Jews. This I consider racism and a crime. I have always protested strongly against such measures, as I have already said. But I have a different view about the fate of Jewish Communists, who actually fomented anti-Semitism by their harsh actions.

All these points have a relevance to the situation today in the Soviet Union. If we do not learn the lessons of Russian and Romanian Jewry, if we do not make use of the opportunities that have suddenly arisen, we shall mourn the loss of millions of Russian Jews. This is our last chance. *Glasnost* is already providing concessions with the agreement to establish Jewish cultural centres in the Soviet Union. Jewish leaders must seize the chance to rebuild Jewish life in that big country. Millions of Jews can be brought back to Judaism. Having lost six million Jews in the Holocaust, we must not leave out a single Jew in the Soviet Union. The chance of accomplishing good deeds for Judaism is greater in the Soviet Union today than it was ever in Romania.

49 *Ending and Beginning*

*H*ow dramatic the changes in the Soviet attitude to the Jewish question have been were fully revealed to me when I paid a further visit to the country in April 1989 – this time at the head of an international rabbinical delegation.

This visit originated from a meeting I had had with the Soviet Ambassador in Romania at an American Embassy Fourth of July reception in Bucharest in 1988. The Ambassador asked for my impressions of my trip to the Soviet Union. We later agreed that the time had arrived for a radical change in Jewish–Soviet relations. I suggested that a delegation of influential world Jewish rabbis, such as the Chief Rabbis of Britain and France, the president of the Yeshiva University of New York, Rabbi Lamm, the president of the Appeal for Conscience Foundation, Rabbi Schneer, and myself should undertake the trip.

Despite the fact that we agreed to continue our discussions after my return from a visit to Israel, the Ambassador sent a message to me there through Blumenfeld, the president of the Bucharest Jewish community, to the effect that the Soviet Government agreed to invite the rabbinic delegation to the USSR. Such an initiative was itself indicative of the changed climate in the Soviet Union.

I went to see the Israeli Prime Minister, Yitzhak Shamir, and gave him a full account of my discussions with the Russians. He was pleased with my efforts and invited the Cabinet Secretary, Mr Rubinstein, and other officials to join in discussions with me. They suggested that the delegation should also include three Israeli rabbis. I told them that I felt it was too early to make such a demand. Nevertheless, I transmitted this request to the Russians, who, to my surprise, quickly accepted it. The rabbis chosen were Rabbi Israel Lau, Chief Rabbi of Tel Aviv; Rabbi Shear Yashuv Cohen, Chief Rabbi of Haifa; and

Rabbi Simcha Hacohen Kook, Chief Rabbi of Rehovot. Unfortunately, Chief Rabbi Lord Jakobovits of Britain became ill and Rabbi Lamm was also unable to travel.

We arrived in Moscow on 28 April, immediately after Passover. With the aid of Professor Levine of Leningrad, we arranged a Holocaust Day commemoration at the Leningrad Jewish cemetery. Thousands of Jews took part. I told them frankly, 'Up to now you have not suffered from a bad conscience because the Soviet Government did not permit you to be fully practising Jews. From now on, everything depends on you and on you alone. The Soviet Government has given strong and clear assurances that it does not oppose a revival of Jewish life. Hitler was not able to complete his work because of the heroism of the Russian, American and other Allied armies. If you, the three million Jews of the Soviet Union, don't make use of this unexpected, miraculous opportunity, then you will be helping to complete the Holocaust, helping Hitler and committing national suicide.'

We rabbis were guests of the Soviet Government. We were received by Vladimir Petrovsky, deputy Minister of Foreign Affairs; T. N. Menteshahvili, secretary of the Supreme Soviet; and Ivolgin, vice-chairman of the Council of Ministers' Committee of Religious Affairs. We also met the vice-president of the Academy of Science, Yevgeny Velikhov, and the president of the religious affairs council of the Ukraine.

All these meetings left me with the conviction that there had been a 180-degree change in the attitude of the Soviet Government to the Jewish problem. Encouraged, we demanded that the Soviet Government should permit the legal establishment of an organization of Jewish communities. We pointed out that other religious groups already possessed such organizations; only the Jews were without one. This was an elementary first step which had to be taken. We suggested that up to twenty towns which had Jewish populations of over 50,000 should form committees which would establish a Federation to lead and represent Soviet Jewry. Internal Jewish forces had to be mobilized; Russian Jewry should not have to rely on activities abroad.

The Russian reply was, 'Go ahead. We will not oppose the establishment of such a Jewish body.'

Speaking as leader of the delegation, I said to the Soviet Ministers, 'To convince the Jews to move on this matter, you must do something constructive. You must first of all remove their fear. You have proclaimed *glasnost*. Now you must announce Jewish *glasnost*.

'Secondly, Talmud Torahs must be established.

'Thirdly, foreign rabbis, lecturers and teachers must be allowed to enter the Soviet Union to help Soviet Jewry in its first measures to revive Jewish life.

'Fourthly, a rabbinic school must be established in the Soviet Union.

'Fifthly, a weekly Jewish communal magazine should be published and made available throughout the Soviet Union.

'Sixthly, a kosher restaurant organization should be established with the aid of the American Joint Distribution Committee and other world Jewish philanthropic groups.

'Seventhly, more synagogues should be built. According to official figures, Russian Jews have between 100 and 120 synagogues. There are towns where many thousands of Jews live and yet there is no synagogue or, at most, one synagogue.'

When I mentioned the Talmud Torahs, there was an immediate response from our Soviet hosts. We were told that a new law would be promulgated to make possible the establishment of ethnic schools. 'Everything depends on you,' was the encouraging message.

We all felt that the new positive attitude of our Soviet hosts was not the result of diplomatic tactics. The whole situation is such, the deep and radical revolution is so genuine, that we have strong reasons for believing that the benefits will be extended to the Jewish community there.

I left the Soviet Union with a dramatic feeling that now, when the miracle has happened, when the way for salvation for three million Soviet Jews is open, we must make a supreme effort. In the words of our sage Hillel, if not now, when?

From Moscow we travelled directly to New York. American Jewry has for years been faced with an immense dilemma. Russian Jews obtain their exit papers because they have Israeli visas, but when they arrive in Vienna or Rome, more than ninety per cent of them refuse to travel to and settle in Israel. They are prepared to wait for months for American visas to take them to the 'new world'. All this waiting and travelling is done at the expense of the Jewish people.

However, we cannot feel upset with our brethren in the Soviet Union, because we have done nothing in the past fifty years to maintain and strengthen their Judaism, nothing to light the spark in their Jewish souls. Of course, some American Jews have not forgotten that their parents or grandparents escaped the pogroms of Tsarist Russia and found hospitality in the United States. 'How', they ask, 'can we refuse to help the present-day refugees from Russia?'

Nevertheless, the plight of their grandparents cannot be compared with the situation of the Soviet Jews of today: Soviet Jews do not face any physical dangers, as their grandparents did; the danger today is of assimilation, of disappearance as Jews.

How can their Jewishness be strengthened by going to the United States? In the Soviet Union they have identity cards which state that they are Jewish. In the United States there is no such identification. The last vestige of their Jewishness disappears.

More important is the different situation facing Jews today. When the Jews left Tsarist Russia or the Bolshevik Soviet Union, there was hardly a country that would open the door to them. Only the United States, in a wonderful gesture of friendship and hospitality allowed them to enter, create new lives and prosper. Today there exists, thanks to the Almighty, a Jewish country which has made many financial and political sacrifices to welcome and absorb them. Naturally, the poor misguided Soviet Jews, abandoned for so long by the Jewish leaders and hearing so much about the wonders of the United States and the privations that would face them in Israel, choose to go to America. But by doing so, they are destroying the Zionist idea.

We have reached the high point of a crisis. What should be done now? The Russian Government is opening the gates. The Government is offering the chance for the revival of Judaism in the country. At the same time, 19,000 Soviet Jews are at Ladispol, near Rome, waiting for American visas. Thousands of other Jews in the Soviet Union are watching to see what will happen to them. The American Joint Distribution Committee, the United Jewish Appeal and other charitable organizations have hundreds of millions of dollars at their disposal.

Should some of this money be invested in the Soviet Union to create a network of Jewish schools, to establish new synagogues and to find the right people to bring about an historic change in the situation of the Soviet Jewish people and to prevent the disappearance of millions of Jews? Or should we continue to invest money in an unequivocal act of anti-Zionism to enable the 19,000 Jews in Ladispol to avoid having to leave for Israel and settle in the United States? This would be a signal to the waiting Jews in the Soviet Union that they need not go to Israel because the gates of the United States would be open for them.

Should we continue to give financial support to the thousands of Jews who are now living in the United States and forget the millions of Jews who still remain in the Soviet Union? Should we continue to use slogans whose real meaning is that we will help those who leave but

313

ignore those who remain? This is the true meaning of 'Let My People Go.' Is it not our holy duty to save the millions of our brethren for the Jewish people and thus save the Jewish future?

I am reminded of a remark made by the famous diplomat Talleyrand. When Napoleon killed the Duc d'Enghien, he said, 'It is more than a crime, it is foolish. . . .' Now is a time for courage and frankness. We should tell our brethren in the Soviet Union, 'You are divided into three categories. The first consists of millions of Jews who are not leaving. We are with you and we will help you to return to Judaism. The second consists of hundreds of people who are really anxious to leave for Israel. We are with you, too, and will help you. The third consists of thousands of people who do not wish to leave for Israel but have in mind other countries. We say good luck to them! This is their private affair and has nothing to do with the vital interests of the Jewish people.'

When I think about the future of our Romanian Jewish community, I am bound to feel deep concern. The great mass of Romanian Jews now live and work in the Jewish state. We are now, in 1989, no more than 22,000 strong in Romania, half of that number in Bucharest. With only myself and another rabbi in the whole country, religious life must inevitably suffer. We are fortunate in Bucharest in that we still have Jewish choirs and Talmud Torahs. Sixty communities have synagogues, some youth choirs and Talmud Torahs, but there are many communities in which people are not even able to pronounce prayers at funerals. Through enormous efforts, we have ensured that *kashrut* is observed in all the communities. *Shochetim* travel from Sunday to Friday to every community to carry out *shechita*.

I am sure that the Romanian Jewish community will grow smaller and smaller. Help will be given by the Romanian Government and by the Joint. The truth is, however, that many of our young people are half-Jews or even quarter-Jews. We no longer have the situation which existed in the 1960s and 1970s, when there was a tremendous Zionist surge. All those, with the exception of the elderly, who wanted to leave for Israel have done so. I am happy that we still have Talmud Torahs with 700 children and we have prayers in our synagogues, but I can foresee the time when we will have no Talmud Torahs, no newspaper and no Jewish writers; only pensioners will remain. Even if they were not Zionists, our youngsters would wish to leave for Israel.

I see my task as completed. I have been both a rabbi and a leader. The idea that a rabbi should be merely a spiritual figure is not a Jewish concept. Moses, our first and greatest rabbi, was a leader who dealt with every aspect of life. I was forced to become a political leader so that we could save our Jews. Many times my wife and and I were near to death as we struggled against powerful forces. We were able to go on because we had vowed to ourselves that no threat of death would prevent us from carrying out our work. Our belief in God the Almighty comforted us and sustained us.

For many years I have begged world Jewish leaders to find a successor for my post, but no one seems to care, alas. During the long years of my Chief Rabbinate I have tried to groom a number of possible successors, but one by one they have disappointed me. Now I have less and less satisfaction in fulfilling my task. In my eyes, it has lost its importance. I dream of having time for study and writing in Israel.

Yes, I could have led a much more comfortable life. I could have been a rabbi in Switzerland or led Israeli institutions like *Beit Hatefutzot*. I could have experienced the joys of living in Israel and joining my people in building up the Jewish state. Yet I do not for one moment regret my decision to live in constant danger in Bucharest. To me fell the unique opportunity to save the souls of hundreds of thousands of Jews, to imbue them with the glorious spirit of Judaism and to ensure that they went to Israel as proud and dedicated Jews. Whereas the great majority of Russian Jews who leave the country are *mehagrim* (migrants) trying to escape from Communism, the Romanian Jews were *olim* motivated for *aliyah* because our education enriched them nationally and spiritually.

I do not consider myself a hero. But even if I may seem to lack modesty, I must affirm that I have been, and remain, a man of conscience. I felt the greatest joy in my work when I was able to save lives, to remove people from slavery to human dignity, to educate children in the Jewish way of life. I refused to participate in activities directed against Israel, against *aliyah* and against our holy Torah. I did not consider this resistance as an act of heroism. It was simply impossible for me to do such evil work. My wife and I preferred to face death. Who knows how we would have behaved had we had children of our own and had to worry what would happen to them?

No, it was not any personal power or any special intelligence which brought about the success of my mission. We could so easily have disappeared, 'liquidated' in the last months of the Stalin–Beria terror. Had Stalin lived a few more weeks, our liquidation would have been accomplished. Only the Almighty, with his goodness, saved us at the last moment.

Therefore, I do not look back on my life with any complacency or pride. I am filled instead with gratitude to the Almighty for choosing me for such an historic mission, for guarding and protecting me all these years and for giving me courage and wisdom to accomplish, in President Herzog's words, the 'mission impossible'.

For the Jewish people, the problem of the State of Israel is the foremost one that they have to face. The second problem must be the future of the Jews in Communist countries. Whether we like it or not, we have to acknowledge that, with the great changes that have taken place recently, a new type of society is being built there, especially in the Soviet Union. Millions of Jews live there. The question has to be asked: is there a possibility for Jewish religious life and Jewish culture to exist there and for the various Jewish communities to continue? Or are they condemned to disappear? This book about my life story and about the lives of Romanian Jews in the past sixty years gives the answer: yes, it is possible to resist assimilation, it is possible to continue the golden chain of the Jewish generations, it is possible to grant these Jews the possibility of *aliyah*, of fulfilling the dream of going to Zion and Jerusalem.

I was never a 'Kremlinologist', or a specialist – a man who knows everything about one single subject and nothing more. I felt in my bones that I had to find a way to safeguard Judaism in this new society and, at all cost, to avoid a clash with the authorities, because in such a clash we would inevitably have been the losers. I sought accommodation, but would not agree to make concessions on matters of principle. I looked for moves that would benefit both us and the authorities. I tried to find out what was essential and what was of secondary importance. I tried to combine courage with logic. I have always been a fighter and I will continue to fight for my people.

King Solomon perfectly outlined the situation when he said that there was a time for everything (*Kohelet* III). There is a time to write and a time to read. I have to stop recalling other stories in my dramatic existence. Mine was a life of dedication and work. Despite so many problems, so many dangers, so many threats, so many seemingly impassable obstacles, my mission has been completed.

Yet have I come to my final chapter? No, not at all. Despite my age I have not retired: my work goes on, day by day, hour by hour. *Siyum*, the Jewish way of marking the end of the study of a book, is by starting it anew. We never consider the book as having been 'finished'. After reading or learning the last words, we proclaim, '*Hadran*,' we will return to you, dear book, we will return.

My heart is filled with the same feelings as I contemplate the new beginnings in Jewish life, the opening of new vistas for Jewish life in the Soviet Union and in other parts of Eastern Europe. Is not this the Jewish approach to reality, the *Siyum* marking a new '*Bereshit*', a new beginning? A new chapter in the great Jewish book of life is opening.

Epilogue
by Joseph Finklestone

When I learned that the World Jewish Congress, the American Joint Distribution Committee and *Beit Hatefutzot* were to commemorate the forty years of Chief Rabbi Rosen's Chief Rabbinate and that the dinner would be attended by the Israeli Prime Minister, Yitzhak Shamir, and the then Foreign Minister and deputy Prime Minister, Shimon Peres, I was intrigued.

I recalled the attacks that had been launched on Chief Rabbi Rosen from Jerusalem, the sharp barbs shot by Golda Meir. How would the leaders of Israel's two main parties now evaluate the Romanian Chief Rabbi? How would they explain his triumphs? Would they be generous enough to acknowledge that his policies, evolved in pain and stress, were the right ones and that his critics were wrong?

I determined to be present and see for myself. It was a right decision. The Plaza Hotel in Jerusalem was packed with the leaders of Israel's political, religious, scientific and economic life. I must confess candidly that having come to know and admire Chief Rabbi Rosen I was moved by the words that I heard. Shamir and Peres spoke with an eloquence and warmth which astonished me as they did Chief Rabbi Rosen.

It is right that their words should be noted as should those of other leaders, such as President Herzog of Israel, ex-President of America, Ronald Reagan, and WJC president, Edgar Bronfman. I found myself nodding in agreement at the words of Emeritus Chief Rabbi of Israel, Shlomo Goren: 'When I see Rabbi Rosen, I raise many prayers exalting God. One of them is the prayer one recites when one sees a living miracle. He embodies the miracle of the Jewish Diaspora in Communist countries, he symbolizes self-devotion, self-sacrifice. His life is a great enigma: how was he able to overcome the great dangers threatening him when he started on his way? That is why, when I see him before me, I have the feeling that what I actually see is the destiny of the Jewish people in the Diaspora.

'His wisdom and courage have guided him. In my eyes, he represents the true rabbi. All the others strive to increase their community, but he has concentrated his whole strength, his entire talent on leading his community where all Jews should be, namely in Israel.'

In his speech Prime Minister Yitzhak Shamir said: 'Rabbi Rosen stands as a unique figure in the contemporary history of the Jewish people. He is the only Chief Rabbi in a Communist country who proudly guides his community towards the land of Israel, who gives a Jewish, religious and national education to the believers belonging to his communities, especially to the younger generations. . . .

'Chief Rabbi Dr Moses Rosen has a gift of wisdom and clear-sightedness, and this fact has enabled him, by combining courage and devotion, to succeed in defending his people's dignity against any attempt – no matter how isolated – to make anti-Semitism spring up again.

'His superior intellectual qualities have helped him achieve all this by means of his co-operation and good relations with the Government of the country in which he and his community live. In his personality, we see a wonderful synthesis which reminds us of certain Jewish leaders in the past – *Reish-Galuta* – who, at various times, led our people with genius and magnificence.

'Anyone who has ever visited Romania, who has entered Chief Rabbi Rosen's office in Bucharest and the synagogue in which he officiates, has met his followers and felt their inexpressible longing for Zion, their boundless devotion to the Jewish people, has listened to the songs of Zion performed by the children and the young people – boys and girls – of the Jewish community in Romania, has heard the Chief Rabbi's words imbued with love of Zion and of Eretz Israel, will never forget all this. That was one of the great events in my life and in that of any Israeli Jew.'

Shimon Peres observed that, 'In Rabbi Rosen's case, the saying, "You must create a rabbi" is no longer valid; it should be replaced by "You must create a community." Yes, indeed. Usually, a community creates a rabbi. Here we have before us a rabbi who created a community under the most difficult circumstances.

'Indeed, Chief Rabbi Rosen was elected during a difficult, extremely dangerous period. "Half a miracle" had happened. Half of the Jews, 400,000, had been exterminated in the Holocaust. The other 400,000, who had been saved, remained a problem.

'I have been to Hungary, where the figures seem to be quite different: 600,000 Jews were exterminated and only 100,000 remained there. Between 100,000 and 150,000 reached Israel. Those who remained in Hungary have not led a Jewish life like that of the Jews in Romania. To my great regret, I must tell you that most of them have become assimilated and have left the Jewish community as if it had never existed. A Jewish spark may still be gleaming somewhere, just as we hope that Judaism in the Soviet Union is not quite extinct.

'How was one to cope with the dramatic conditions under which Rabbi Rosen took over? He proved to be immensely wise and extremely courageous. He had to accustom himself to being suspected by both sides and, at the same time, to relying on the trust of both [the regime on the one hand, the community on the other]; he got used to going to the very limit, but not beyond it, to always finding that border, to always saying the right word, to always being the one who gives courage, but also the one who contradicts, the one who incites and the one who pacifies, the one who speaks and the one who is silent, a Jew on his own self and, at the same time, a Jew in a Communist world, a rabbi and a member in the Parliament of a regime of a unique kind.'

In Bucharest, on 5 July 1988, thousands of Jews belonging to the Bucharest community, representatives of all the Jewish communities throughout the country, numerous leaders of the great international Jewish organizations, representatives of institutions in Israel and many Diaspora countries gathered at the Choral Temple to celebrate the five decades of Rabbi Rosen's rabbinical activity and four decades as Chief Rabbi.

President Herzog sent a warm message: 'I am very sorry to be unable to attend the celebration which expresses the profound appreciation of so many organizations and personalities, of your blessed work during the past forty years as Chief Rabbi of the Jewish communities in Romania.

'The "Joint", the World Jewish Congress and we in Israel know very well that you have achieved what is almost impossible to achieve.

'Out of ruins you have raised a Jewish community that had been shattered and gravely mutilated at the time of the Second World War. Under extremely difficult conditions, you have succeeded in maintaining its sacred flame; you have also taken care of its spiritual and physical life and you have managed to strengthen its link with Israel.'

The then President of the United States, Ronald Reagan, joined in: 'Dear Rabbi Rosen I am delighted at the opportunity to extend my most sincere congratulations to you on the celebration of your fifty years as a rabbi and the fortieth anniversary of your election as Chief Rabbi of Romania.

'During these last forty years, you have guided your people with wisdom and courage and have won admiration both within your own country and abroad. In the United States, we have especially appreciated your contributions to better understanding between our two peoples.

'*Mazel tov*, and I offer my best wishes for your health and happiness and hope that you will continue your work for many years to come.'

Edgar Bronfman, who participated in a meeting of dignitaries in Bucharest, remarked, 'Jewish communities all over the world admire Chief Rabbi Rosen and are grateful for his unique vision and achievements. The Jews of Romania had the great good luck of having at the decisive time of its destiny a devoted, skilful and self-sacrificing leader.'

Acknowledgements

I owe a word of gratitude to my good friends, the lawyer Emil Schechter, secretary-general of the Federation of Jewish Communities in Romania and Theodore Blumenfeld, the president of the Jewish community in Bucharest. This book is tribute to their indefatigable work, day and night, their indomitable faith in Judaism, their charity, devotion to the community and attachment to the message of the Torah.

To those mentioned above, and to hundreds of community leaders and the heads of all the sixty-seven Jewish communities in Romania, to the rabbis and officials, to the teachers of the Talmud Torah courses, to the activists in old-age homes and social programmes, to all those who have stood by me in cultural activities, promoting Judaism, to authors, scientists, journalists, to the editorial staff of *Revista Cultului Mozaic*, our magazine, to its editor, Haim Riemer, to all I again extend my gratitude.

A word of praise and my blessings to my friend, the novelist Aurel Dragoş Munteanu, who used all his talent and competence, with true Jewish ardour, and worked very hard to help me conclude this book.

My gratitude and thanks also go to Linda Osband for her inspired and dedicated editing of this book.

Achron, achron haviv – last but not least: my dear Joseph Finklestone. *Veni, Vidi, Vici*: *veni*, he followed me to Tel Aviv and I talked to him for more than fifty hours; *vidi*, he came to Romania and saw with his own eyes what is so obvious in the Jewish life of this country; and *vici*, he identified himself with the saga of Romanian Judaism and assumed its life as if his own. He was instrumental in writing this English version as a true co-author. Step by step, he accompanied me in narrating the grievous story of my life. With his soft words, with his fine psychological sense, Joseph went deep into my soul. My homage, gratitude, admiration and Torah blessings from my heart go to him.

Index

323